WINGS
OF THE NAVY
Second Edition
Flying Allied Carrier Aircraft of World War Two

Captain Eric Brown
CBE, DSC, AFC, RN

Edited by William Green and Gordon Swanborough.

*Illustrated with cutaway and cockpit interior drawings by John Weal
and Aviagraphica.
General arrangement drawings by Dennis Punnett.*

Naval Institute Press
Annapolis, Maryland

Copyright © Pilot Press Limited, 1980 & 1987.

Published and distributed in the United States of America and Canada
by the Naval Institute Press, Annapolis, Maryland 21402.

This second edition first published in 1987 in England
by Airlife Publishing Ltd.

First edition published 1980 by
Jane's Publishing Company.

Library of Congress Catalog Card No. 86-62670.

ISBN 0-87021-995-2

Printed in England.

Contents

Foreword

Carrier-based naval aircraft have always been a very special breed of animal as have also the pilots flying them. Their environment is the immense expanse of sea and ocean that covers so much of our planet; the vast areas of water within a few feet of the surface of which they are catapulted over plunging bow of mother ship and, given good fortune, return to face what is, in my view, the most inherently punishing treatment meted out to an aircraft and the most exacting flying task facing an aviator as a matter of routine — an arrested landing on a heaving deck! Such certainly calls for something exceptional from machine and man alike.

In so far as machine is concerned — and it is the shipboard warplane that provides the subject matter of the pages that follow — few more daunting propositions can have been placed before combat aircraft designers of the late 'thirties and early 'forties than that involving creation of a satisfactory deck-landing warplane. All combat aircraft design embodies a measure of compromise, but none so large a measure as the carrier-based aeroplane, whose designer must strike a counterpoise between demands of combat and dictates of venue in which it will spend its working life; conflicting factors which not many designers were to prove entirely successful in coalescing.

Carrier operations provide a harsh and unforgiving school; one in which shortcomings in an aircraft quickly surfaced. The nautical environment was a daunting one to cater for and to be adjudged *really* successful, a shipboard aircraft had to transcend the good. In truth, and eulogies of the publicists apart, most aircraft to be found on Allied carrier decks during the Second World War infrequently transcended the indifferent. Most had some praiseworthy attributes, but as often as not these were outweighed by shortcomings, their operational successes owing more to valour of crews than intrinsic qualities of aircraft.

The *real* characters of the aeroplanes that, during the conflict, flew from carriers, large and small, in all weathers and under widely varying operational conditions, have become distorted over the years and inherent defects forgotten. Bathed in the roseate glow that so often accompanies time's passage, their rough edges have been smoothed over and their fundamental deficiencies go unrecalled. Thus, a risk arises that history will not do full justice to the competence of the crews that flew them — and flying *some* of them in combat called for a lot of *bravery* as well as competence. The primary purpose of this book, therefore, is to place on record the flying characteristics, good, bad and indifferent, of the principal combat aircraft flown from Allied carriers in the only conflict in which seagoing aviation has played a truly major rôle.

I have attempted to set the scene for these evaluations, presented in chronological sequence of prototype début, by outlining the development histories and subsequent wartime careers of the aircraft concerned. The evaluations themselves are necessarily subjective, but as a former test pilot trained to be objective, I do not believe these to have been markedly influenced by emotion such as pilots tend to feel for a particular aeroplane type which they partnered in the struggle for survival.

While serving for just over 30 years in the Fleet Air Arm, I enjoyed the privilege of flying virtually every type of British aircraft operated by the Royal Navy, from the Fairey Seal of the early 'thirties to the Buccaneer, which, the last of the service's fixed-wing combat aircraft flown from a conventional carrier, today flies with RAF Strike Command and RAF Germany. At the same time, I was given the opportunity to fly a large cross-section of American naval aircraft — not only those that entered the ranks of the Royal Navy but many that remained exclusively US Navy equipment. These fortunate circumstances arose from my years as a test pilot, both at the Royal Aircraft Establishment, Farnborough, and, later, at the US Naval Air Test Center at Patuxent River.

The following chapters have, for the most part, been published as individual features in AIR INTERNATIONAL, and their publication collectively in book form is intended to provide as a permanent record an assessment of the characters of Allied shipboard aircraft of the Second World War. Their true nature risks being irreparably blurred by the mythographers whose closest personal association with those most difficult of ladies, the carrier-borne aeroplanes of the last world conflict, is the air museums in which most of the survivors of those stirring years now reside. I sincerely hope that the contents of this book will arouse a few nostalgic memories in my fellow naval aviators who flew these aircraft and loved or hated their fickle ways.

Eric Brown
Copthorne
Sussex
January 1980

Fairey Swordfish

HAD I BEEN UNAWARE, in 1940, that the Fairey Swordfish shipboard torpedo-bomber was still very much a part of the Royal Navy's first-line aircraft inventory, I feel sure my reaction on first encountering this unlovely example of aeronautical archaism early in that year would have been one of sheer disbelief that the Fleet Air Arm could have actually been endeavouring to fight a *war* with so anachronistic a piece of hardware! I do recall some surprise of the use affectionately rather than derogatorily of the universally-employed and quite unofficial appellation of *Stringbag* — a nickname whose origins were already lost but had perhaps been prompted by the Swordfish's profusion of bracing wires, though more likely deriving from some chance reference to it being as innocuous or as inelegant as a string bag!

Archaic *in concept* the Swordfish assuredly was, but it was not antiquated *in fact*; could this apparently ancient aeroplane have been created to the requirements of a specification issued a mere *seven* years earlier or have seen less than four years of service? Its creators had certainly wasted no effort in endowing it with aesthetic appeal. For a start, its engine appeared to have been applied to the forward fuselage much as an afterthought; massive girder-like struts angled out from the fuselage to support the lower wing centre section, or *vice-versa*; the profligacy of both wing and tail bracing must surely have been a rigger's nightmare, and beneath this conglomeration hung a most substantial-looking undercarriage and a hefty tailwheel. As if this calculated affront to the basic laws of aerodynamics was not enough, there were the open cockpits protected by mere gestures for windscreens, with the cavernous two-seat aft cockpit endowing the aircraft with the appearance of having been badly shot up!

Maybe the Swordfish was the amiable, viceless lady that

her pilots claimed, but by no stretch of the imagination was it a beauty and, having been selected as a fighter pilot, I heaved a hearty sigh of relief that I was unlikely to make closer acquaintance with this ugly duck, however swanlike its reactions might be once airborne; a supposition that was to prove ill-founded before the year's end.

Late in 1940, I was posted to a Martlet (alias Wildcat) squadron, No 802, at Donibristle, in the shadow of the Forth Bridge. This station was also a naval aircraft repair yard and received Swordfish straight from the manufacturer for minor modification before issue to squadrons. Since no regular ferry pilots were available, I found myself on the station roster for this duty and, from time to time, despatched to the new production plant at Sherburn-in-Elmet, between Leeds and Selby, where Blackburn Aircraft had begun to assemble Swordfish, to ferry new aircraft back to Donibristle.

I immediately discovered that claims for the Swordfish's handling qualities had, if anything, been understated; it was unbelievably easy to fly, there being virtually only a 20 knot (37 km/h) speed range to cover climb, cruise and landing. A pair of hamfists were no serious disadvantage in flying the Swordfish, for no aircraft could have been more tractable or forgiving, but its pilot *did* need two qualities: patience and the physical attributes of a brass monkey! The Swordfish ambled along lazily at about 85 knots (157 km/h) if the wind was favourable and staggered along valiantly at barely more than 70 knots (130 km/h) if it was not — it could be somewhat disconcerting at times to be travelling in the same direction as an express train. The cockpit was just as comfortable as an exposed hilltop in a Force 10 gale — the elongated aft cockpit was even worse as it provided the perfect wind scoop — with its occupant freezing in consequence.

Of course, the mundane task of ferrying Swordfish be-

Fairey Swordfish II Cutaway Drawing Key

1 Rudder structure
2 Rudder upper hinge
3 Diagonal brace
4 External bracing wires
5 Rudder hinge
6 Elevator control horn
7 Tail navigation light
8 Elevator structure
9 Fixed tab
10 Elevator balance
11 Elevator hinge
12 Starboard tailplane
13 Tailplane struts
14 Lashing down shackle
15 Trestling foot
16 Rear wedge
17 Rudder lower hinge
18 Tailplane adjustment screw jack
19 Elevator control cable
20 External bracing wires
21 Elevator fixed tab
22 Tailfin structure
23 Bracing wire attachment
24 Aerial stub
25 Bracing wires

26 Port elevator
27 Port tailplane
28 Tailplane support struts
29 Dinghy external release cord
30 Tailwheel oleo shock absorber
31 Non-retractable Dunlop tailwheel
32 Fuselage framework
33 Arrester hook housing
34 Control cable fairleads
35 Dorsal decking
36 Rod aerial
37 Lewis gun stowage trough
38 Aerial
39 Flexible 0·303-in (7,7-mm) Lewis machine gun
40 Fairey high-speed flexible gun mounting
41 Type O-3 compass mounting points
42 Aft cockpit coaming
43 Aft cockpit
44 Lewis drum magazine stowage
45 Radio installation
46 Ballast weights
47 Arrester hook pivot
48 Fuselage lower longeron
49 Arrester hook (part extended)
50 Aileron hinge
51 Fixed tab
52 Starboard upper aileron
53 Rear spar
54 Wing ribs
55 Starboard formation light
56 Starboard navigation light
57 Aileron connect strut
58 Interplane struts
59 Bracing wires
60 Starboard lower aileron
61 Aileron hinge
62 Aileron balance
63 Rear spar
64 Wing ribs
65 Aileron outer hinge
66 Deck-handling/lashing grips
67 Front spar
68 Interplane strut attachments
69 Wing internal diagonal bracing wires
70 Flying wires
71 Wing skinning
72 Additional support wire (fitted when underwing stores carried)
73 Wing fold hinge
74 Inboard interplane struts
75 Stub plane end rib
76 Wing locking handle

77 Stub plane structure
78 Intake slot
79 Side window
80 Catapult spool
81 Drag struts
82 Cockpit sloping floor
83 Fixed 0·303-in (7,7-mm) Vickers gun (deleted from some aircraft)
84 Case ejection chute
85 Access panel

86 Camera mounting bracket
87 Sliding bomb-aiming hatch
88 Zip inspection flap
89 Fuselage upper longeron
90 Centre cockpit
91 Inter-cockpit fairing
92 Upper wing aerial mast
93 Pilot's headrest
94 Pilot's seat and harness
95 Bulkhead
96 Vickers gun fairing

97 Fuel gravity tank (12·5 Imp gal/57 l capacity)
98 Windscreen
99 Handholds
100 Flap control handwheel and rocking head assembly
101 Wing centre section

102 Dinghy release cord handle
103 Identification light
104 Centre section pyramid strut attachment
105 Diagonal strengtheners
106 Dinghy inflation cylinder

tween Sherburn-in-Elmet and Donibristle hardly provided the basis for a valid assessment of any finer operational points of this sedate, good-natured dowager of an aeroplane, which I could not help but feel to be astonishingly out of place in a dramatically competitive conflict between technologically advanced nations such as was taking place at the time. But finer points it assuredly appeared to possess, or else how, on the evening of 11 November 1940, could Swordfish of Nos 815 and 819 squadrons from HMS *Illustrious,* and Nos 813 and 824 squadrons from HMS *Eagle,* all flying from the former carrier, have enjoyed almost unbelievable success in

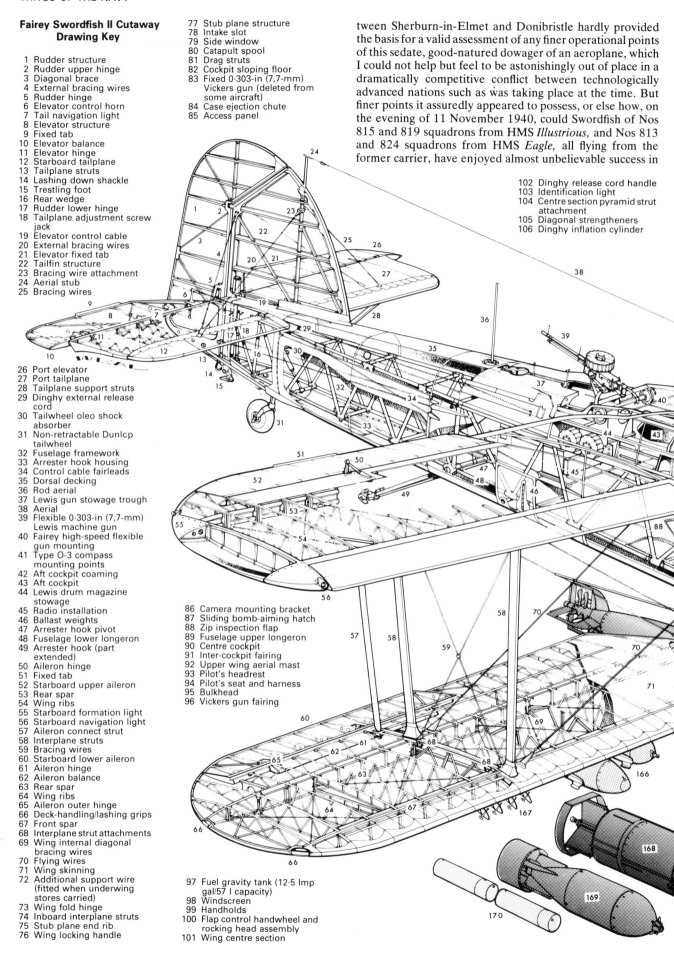

attacking the Italian fleet lying at anchor in Taranto Harbour?

Fortuitously, during the course of 1941, I was to be enabled to fill something of the gap in my knowledge of the Swordfish's operational capabilities, and by that time, the archaic "Stringbag" had received acclaim for yet another exploit — its participation in the destruction of *Bismarck*. The Swordfish certainly seemed, in the public eye at least if not necessarily in that of its crews, to be charismatic; the first chapters had been written in what was to become the Swordfish legend. Yet, Fairey's torpedo-bomber was obsolete by any standard; its concept had been *passé* before it had even put wheel to carrier deck. Before examining the service career and flying characteristics of the Swordfish, it is therefore perhaps necessary to set the scene by delving a little into

the development history of this contradiction of an aeroplane.

The conception of the Swordfish dated back to the beginning of the 'thirties and the drawing board of one Marcel Lobelle, Fairey Aviation's Belgian chief designer who was perhaps more noteworthy for his competence with the orthodox rather than outstanding talent for innovation. Lobelle was working simultaneously on two aircraft, both shipboard biplanes of classic formula, one being intended to meet the requirements of specification S.9/30, which called for a fleet spotter-reconnaissance aircraft, and the other being a private venture intended for the dual two-seat

107 Type C dinghy stowage well
108 Aileron control linkage
109 Trailing edge rib sections
110 Rear spar
111 Wing rib stations
112 Aileron connect strut
113 Port upper aileron
114 Fixed tab
115 Aileron hinge
116 Port formation light
117 Wing skinning

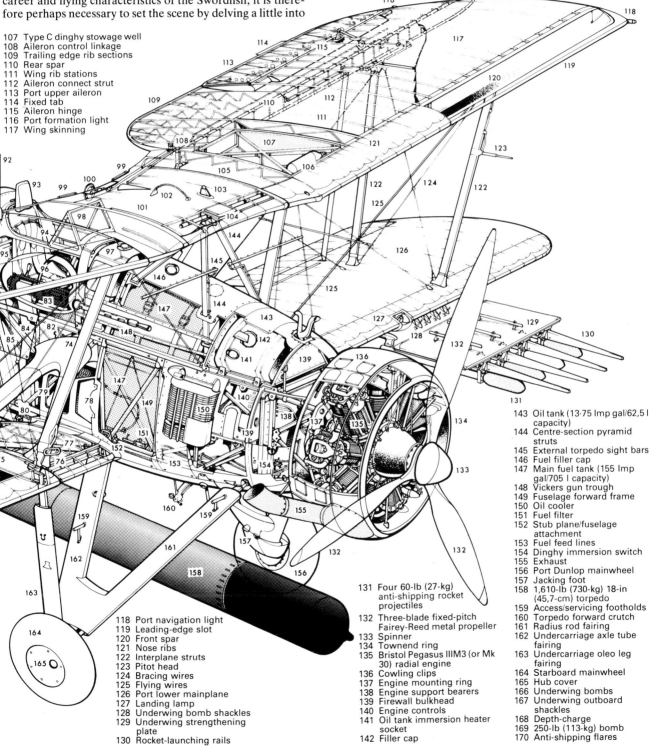

118 Port navigation light
119 Leading-edge slot
120 Front spar
121 Nose ribs
122 Interplane struts
123 Pitot head
124 Bracing wires
125 Flying wires
126 Port lower mainplane
127 Landing lamp
128 Underwing bomb shackles
129 Underwing strengthening plate
130 Rocket-launching rails

131 Four 60-lb (27-kg) anti-shipping rocket projectiles
132 Three-blade fixed-pitch Fairey-Reed metal propeller
133 Spinner
134 Townend ring
135 Bristol Pegasus IIIM3 (or Mk 30) radial engine
136 Cowling clips
137 Engine mounting ring
138 Engine support bearers
139 Firewall bulkhead
140 Engine controls
141 Oil tank immersion heater socket
142 Filler cap

143 Oil tank (13·75 Imp gal/62,5 l capacity)
144 Centre-section pyramid struts
145 External torpedo sight bars
146 Fuel filler cap
147 Main fuel tank (155 Imp gal/705 l capacity)
148 Vickers gun trough
149 Fuselage forward frame
150 Oil cooler
151 Fuel filter
152 Stub plane/fuselage attachment
153 Fuel feed lines
154 Dinghy immersion switch
155 Exhaust
156 Port Dunlop mainwheel
157 Jacking foot
158 1,610-lb (730-kg) 18-in (45,7-cm) torpedo
159 Access/servicing footholds
160 Torpedo forward crutch
161 Radius rod fairing
162 Undercarriage axle tube fairing
163 Undercarriage oleo leg fairing
164 Starboard mainwheel
165 Hub cover
166 Underwing bombs
167 Underwing outboard shackles
168 Depth-charge
169 250-lb (113-kg) bomb
170 Anti-shipping flares

torpedo-bomber and three-seat spotter-reconnaissance rôle. Both were thoroughly conventional in concept, with simple, fabric-covered stainless-steel strip-and-tube structures.

The PV aeroplane, known at the time as the "Greek machine" — the Hellenic Navy presenting the best sales prospect — was flown from Harmondsworth airfield by Chris Staniland on 21 March 1933, its Panther VI engine subsequently giving place to a Pegasus IIM and by which time the aircraft was being viewed by its parent company as a potential contender for S.15/33, which, calling for a somewhat more versatile aircraft than the earlier specification, had been issued shortly after the "Greek machine" had begun its test programme. On 11 September 1933, however, Staniland found himself unable to extricate the aircraft from a flat spin and bailed out.

Although this loss of the PV machine was something of a blow, Lobelle and his team — which included H E Chaplin who was later to become chief designer — completed retailoring the basic design to meet more fully the requirements of specification S.15/33, and within seven months, the test programme had been resumed with a second aircraft, which, flown on 17 April 1934, was designated TSR II, the designation TSR I being retrospectively applied to the first machine. Apart from the insertion of an additional fuselage bay and the application of four degrees of sweep on the upper wing to restore the CG, the TSR II differed from its predecessor in detail only.

Trials with the TSR II at the A&AEE, Martlesham Heath, produced generally satisfactory results, although a measure of longitudinal instability was reported when diving with the CG well aft, spin recovery was considered lethargic and there was some criticism of stalling behaviour. Something of the order of a hundred minor changes and modifications had

been introduced by the time specification S.38/34 had been written around the TSR II and, on 23 April 1935, Fairey Aviation was awarded a production contract for 86 machines, the Ministry augmenting this as an afterthought in the following month with a contract for an additional three machines specifically for development purposes.

Intended to combine the rôles of both Blackburn Baffin and Fairey Seal aboard Royal Navy carriers and offering only a marginal performance improvement over either, the production version of the TSR II, on which the name Swordfish had by now been bestowed, may be considered in retrospect as an overly conservative approach to the future torpedo-bomber-reconnaissance needs of the Fleet Air Arm. Its adoption suggested a lack of imagination on the part of the Admiralty and a reluctance to depart in any way from the tried and tested. Yet anomalously, in the same month that the thoroughly traditional Swordfish was ordered into production, prototypes of the Blackburn Skua were also ordered and this was a radical enough naval aeroplane by British and, indeed, world standards of the time. Perhaps the built-in obsolescence of the Swordfish can best be seen in the context of shipboard torpedo-bomber development taking place contemporaneously elsewhere.

Barely more than a week prior to the issue of the first Swordfish production contract, in the USA the Douglas company had flown the XTBD-1, a cantilever monoplane three-seat shipboard torpedo-bomber of light-alloy stressed-skin semi-monocoque construction, embellished with fully-enclosed cockpits and retractable main undercarriage members. On the other side of the world, Katsuji Nakamura of the Japanese Nakajima concern had reached quite an advanced stage in the design of a torpedo-bomber of essentially similar configurational and structural concept to an Imperial Navy 10-*Shi* specification. These were both significant developments, sounding the death knell of the bi-plane torpedo-bomber, yet another two-and-a-half years were to elapse before, on 9 November 1937, a British specification (S.24/37) calling for a shipboard *monoplane* capable of delivering a torpedo was to be issued!

Production of the Swordfish was facilitated by its simple, unsophisticated structure and deliveries to the Fleet Air Arm began in the early summer of 1936, successive contracts following, and by early 1940, when Fairey Aviation was to

(Above left and below) The true progenitor of the Swordfish, the TSR II (K4190), in its initial form. The specification to which the Swordfish was to be built was written around the TSR II after numerous minor changes and modifications had been introduced

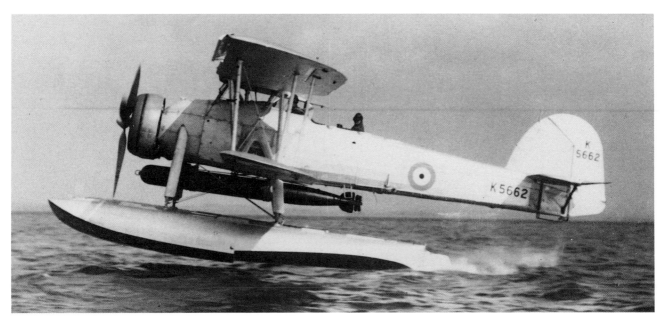

(Below right) The first pre-production Swordfish (K5660), which was flown initially on 31 December 1935, and (above) the third pre-production aircraft (K5662) which was assembled as a floatplane and sent to the Marine Aircraft Experimental Establishment

transfer to Blackburn Aircraft responsibility for continued Swordfish manufacture, the parent company was to have delivered 692 aircraft. The first unit to take on the Swordfish was No 825 Squadron, which exchanged its Fairey Seals during the course of July 1936, Nos 811 and 812 squadrons replacing their Baffins and No 823 Squadron its Seals before the end of the year.

As production at the Hayes factory gained momentum, further squadrons were commissioned: No 813 forming on Swordfish in January 1937, the Blackburn Shark being ousted during the course of 1938, when Nos 810, 820 and 821 squadrons received Swordfish which thus became the *only* Royal Navy torpedo-bomber, Nos 822 and 824 squadrons also receiving Swordfish to replace their Seals and No 814 Squadron being formed on the Swordfish late in the year. Two more squadrons, Nos 816 and 818, had been formed with Swordfish by the time the FAA went to war in September 1939, giving the service a total of 13 Swordfish-equipped squadrons. Of these, a dozen were embarked aboard five carriers as follows Nos 810, 814, 820 and 821 squadrons aboard *Ark Royal,* Nos 811 and 822 squadrons aboard *Courageous,* Nos 813 and 824 squadrons aboard *Eagle,* Nos 823 and 825 squadrons aboard *Glorious,* and Nos 816 and 818 squadrons aboard *Furious.* No 812 Squadron was shore based and in addition, two catapult flights, Nos 701 and 702 with float-equipped Swordfish, were serving with battleships and cruisers.

Two more squadrons, Nos 815 and 819, were to be formed on Swordfish before, in the spring of 1940, this anachronic but amiable dowager of an aeroplane began to reveal amazonian proclivities. For the first months of the war, the Swordfish had been confined to routine convoy escort and fleet protection duties, and, apart from an abortive attack on the U-30 on 14 September 1939, had had little opportunity to demonstrate the more pugnacious side of its nature. On 11 April 1940, however, Swordfish of Nos 816 and 818 squadrons from HMS *Furious* mounted the first co-ordinated torpedo attack — albeit abortive — to be made from a carrier in the annals of warfare. The two German cruisers reportedly lying at anchor at Trondheim proved to be destroyers and the torpedoes launched by the Swordfish grounded in shallow water.

Two days later, however, the Swordfish more than compensated for this failure when a floatplane catapulted from

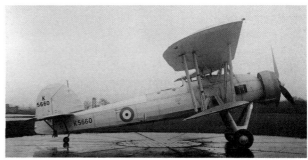

HMS *Warspite* did such an extraordinary job of spotting for the guns of its mother vessel that it was to be considered directly responsible for the destruction of no fewer than *seven* destroyers in Ofot Fjord, rounding off this outstanding operation by dive bombing and sinking U-64 at anchor in Bjervik Fjord, the first U-boat to be destroyed by the FAA in WW II.

The Swordfish had been blooded and from here on it was to see, for better or worse, almost continuous action throughout the remainder of the war, from both carriers and shore bases. No 812 Squadron, operating under RAF Coastal Command control, pioneered what was subsequently to become a major Swordfish activity, mounting diurnal and nocturnal minelaying sorties from various shore bases from May 1940. No 825 Squadron also came under Coastal Command's aegis at this time and, operating from Detling, flew a series of valorous daylight sorties against the *Wehrmacht* as British forces fell back on Dunkirk — the losses suffered in this type of action may well be imagined.

It was, of course, the action at Taranto that really launched the Swordfish legend, but prior to that memorable operation of 11 November 1940, during the course of June, No 830 Squadron had been formed on Malta and, under RAF control, had initiated an epic series of sorties from Hal Far, which, by the end of the year, was to account for 9,000 tons of Axis shipping*, while Nos 810, 818 and 820 squadrons, embarked on HMS *Ark Royal*, had participated in the distasteful action against the French Fleet at Oran and Mers-

*Between May and November 1941, No 830 Squadron was to account for a further 110,000 tons of enemy shipping, apart from damaging another 130,000 tons, this being a record never to be equalled, and in concert with the Albacores of No 828 Squadron, the Swordfish of No 830 were to sink a further 400,000 tons of shipping by the end of 1942.

(Above) A Swordfish (L9781) of No 810 Squadron flying over HMS Ark Royal in 1939, this unit having converted to the Swordfish from the Blackburn Shark during the course of the previous year. (Below left) The eighth series production Swordfish (K5933) photographed during manufacturer's trials prior to delivery to the Royal Navy

el-Kebir. At Taranto, the Swordfish from HMS *Illustrious* sunk the battleship *Conte de Cavour,* heavily damaged the battleships *Littorio* and *Caio Duilio,* together with a *Trento-* and a *Bolzano-*class cruiser and two destroyers, and also sent two auxiliaries to the bottom, yet, although the shore batteries alone had fired more than 13,000 rounds, only two Swordfish had been lost.

Action followed action. Swordfish of No 815 Squadron participated in March 1941 in the Battle of Cape Matapan and, in May, were involved in the destruction of the *Bismarck,* No 825 Squadron from HMS *Victorious* and Nos 810 and 818 squadrons from HMS *Ark Royal* taking part in this engagement, while the ubiquity of the Swordfish had been demonstrated by No 814 Squadron, which had assisted the RAF in operations during a revolt in Iraq, and by No 815 Squadron, which had flown strikes from Cyprus against French shipping and shore targets in Syria. Thus, when I renewed acquaintance with the Swordfish in the autumn of 1941, I tended to be a little more charitable in my attitude towards its operational potential than I had been when ferrying *Stringbags* from Sherburn-in-Elmet to Donibristle at the beginning of the year.

In September 1941, my fighter squadron was sent, for some unaccountable reason, to an airfield in the Orkneys possessing the rather unlikely name of Twatt, a fact affording an irresistible subject for badinage and ribaldry for the squadron wags. It transpired that we were to practice attacks on Swordfish simulating torpedo and mine-laying sorties, and as it was inconceivable that the experience gained would be of much use to Wildcat pilots, the enemy having nothing in his inventory in the category of the Swordfish, our task was obviously to aid in clueing up the *Stringbag* boys in evasive tactics.

As squadron armament officer, I was assigned the task of assessing the ability of the Swordfish to evade fighter attack. I was already familiar with the amiability and tractability of the Swordfish, and I soon discovered that it possessed quite remarkable manoeuvring qualities which completely belied its appearance of unwieldiness. It could be stood on its wing-tips and almost turned around in its own length! I even braved the gale-force winds in the rear cockpit to assess the field of fire of the observer's single rifle-calibre Lewis gun and found that, puny as defensive armament though this machine gun undoubtedly was, it possessed an excellent field of fire upward and to the rear and, with one in every three bullets a tracer, was likely to prove decidedly off-putting to any fighter pilot successful in coaxing his mount down to the sort of speeds at which the Swordfish trundled along.

All in all, the usually ladylike Swordfish, with its unsuspected ability to demonstrate quite unladylike antics, was not quite the soft touch for fighters that I had previously supposed, but once its pilot had committed the aircraft to that straight-and-level torpedo-aiming run, then the fighter pilot was presented with a sitting duck. Any enemy fighter pilot incapable of making mincemeat of a Swordfish or anti-aircraft gunner unable to hit it during that final slow run-in for the drop *had to be a tyro*!

The suicidal aspect of Swordfish operations under conditions of enemy fighter superiority was to be demonstrated shortly afterwards, on 12 February 1942, when the battle-cruisers *Scharnhorst* and *Gneisenau* and the heavy cruiser *Prinz Eugen* broke out of Brest in bad weather and made the passage through the English Channel, catching the British with pants at half mast. Six Swordfish of the re-forming No 825 Squadron took-off from RAF Manston led by Lt-Cdr Eugene "Winkle" Esmonde and, despite a low cloud base, poor visibility and the fact that the few Spitfires that could be mustered at short notice as top cover had been engaged by the *Luftwaffe* well away from the main action, performed an heroic attack on the German vessels through an intensive barrage of anti-aircraft fire followed by attacks from fighters flying with flaps and undercarriages down. None of the Swordfish survived and no torpedo found its target, and it was thus that the Swordfish ended its career as a torpedo-bomber, thereafter being confined primarily to the anti-submarine rôle.

At the time of the previously mentioned channel dash, I was with a Sea Hurricane squadron and as our designated carrier was fitted with a catapult, we had used a Swordfish at Gosport for catapult launching experience. Each pilot that had not previously flown a Swordfish was given a quick general briefing and an equally hurried circuit in the aircraft before it was loaded onto Gosport's catapult. He was then given two launches with a fellow pilot in the rear cockpit; they changed places and the process was repeated. Later in 1942, I became a deck landing instructor aboard HMS *Argus*; the Swordfish was included in our aircraft stable and was the ideal vehicle with which to impart the rudiments of this difficult art. It was an absurdly simple aeroplane to fly and it was so easy to deck land that it was difficult to imagine even first-timers having problems with the Swordfish and they seldom did. The view that its cockpit offered for deck landing

A Swordfish floatplane (L2742) of No 701 Catapult Flight flying near Gibraltar during 1938. From January 1940, all the Catapult Flights were pooled under No 700 Squadron. A Swordfish floatplane catapulted from HMS Warspite claimed the first FAA U-boat 'kill' of World War II

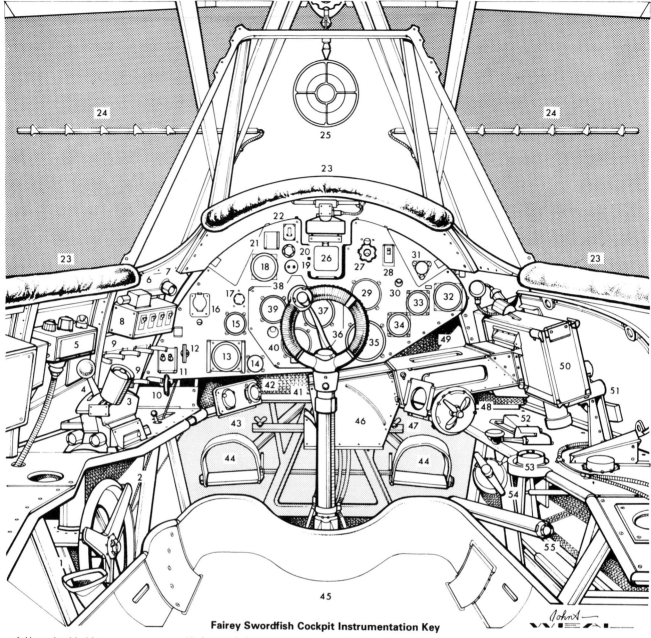

Fairey Swordfish Cockpit Instrumentation Key

1 Very pistol holder
2 Elevator trim handwheel
3 Throttle lever (with press-to-transmit button)
4 Mixture control lever
5 Radio control switchbox
6 VHF radio controller
7 Cockpit light dimmer switch
8 Lighting switch-panel (front to rear: recognition/navigation lights/landing lamp/pitot head)
9 Very pistol cartridge holding clips (8)
10 Inertia starter clutch control ring
11 Inertia starting switch
12 Automatic boost control cutout
13 Boost pressure gauge
14 Priming pump
15 Air pressure gauge
16 Bomb jettison switch
17 Landing lamp deflection control
18 ASI
19 Compass lamp two-pin socket
20 Compass lamp dimmer switch
21 Compass correction card holder
22 Fuel gauge control switch
23 Cockpit coaming padding
24 Torpedo sight bars (with illuminated spacers)
25 Ring gunsight
26 Compass
27 Torpedo sight control switch
28 Starter switch
29 Engine speed indicator
30 Fuel pressure warning light
31 Torpedo sight dimmer switch
32 Clock
33 Oil pressure gauge
34 Oil temperature gauge
35 Turn-and-bank indicator
36 Brake control lever
37 Artificial horizon
38 Gun-firing button (on control grip)
39 Direction indicator
40 Altimeter (partially obscured by control grip)
41 Control column
42 Air intake shutter control
43 Oil by-pass valve control
44 Rudder pedals
45 Pilot's seat
46 Ammunition box/feed section
47 Stopwatch holder
48 Fuel control cock
49 Ammunition feed
50 Fixed machine gun (delated from some aircraft)
51 Gun aft mounting bracket and side fairing
52 Downward identification morse key
53 Rudder bias control
54 Air operated gun cocking control
55 Rudder bias control rod

was by no means perfect, but the Swordfish had such perfect manners that one could hardly go wrong.

The Swordfish carried 155 Imp gal (·7051) of fuel in its main tank and 12·5 Imp gal (571) in a gravity tank, both located behind the Pegasus III engine. For starting, the fuel cock was set to MAIN ONLY, the throttle was opened a half-inch and the oil cooler bypass control was set IN. A couple of matelots then energised the inertia starter by cranking the

starting handle, one standing on the starboard wheel facing aft and the other on the starboard wing facing forward. They cranked away until peak speed was attained and then one of the red-faced and perspiring ground crew would signal the pilot to engage the clutch. As soon as the ground crew called "contact", the pilot switched on the ignition and the hand starter magneto. If he was lucky, the immense propeller began flailing and as soon as the hideously noisy Pegasus was running smoothly he switched off the hand starter magneto. The throttle was opened slowly to 1,000 rpm and the engine allowed to warm up until the oil temperature reached 15°C. Power checks were then performed with one of the matelots lying across the tailplane. The rpm and oil pressure were checked at cruising boost but with the mixture control at ALTITUDE, and then, with mixture control in override position, the throttle was opened fully and take-off boost, static rpm and oil pressure checked.

Taxying was the essence of simplicity, although the Swordfish had a tendency to weathercock in high winds and in such conditions it was advisable to have a couple of matelots on the wingtips. For take-off, the elevator was trimmed three degrees nose up, half full port bias was applied to the rudder, the mixture control was set RICH (override), the flaps were raised fully and the oil bypass control was set IN. The throttle was opened slowly to full power of +2 lb boost and 2,200 rpm, the take-off run was short, any swinging tendency being easily counteracted by the rudder, and climb could be initiated at 70 knots (130 km/h). When stabilised in the climb boost was reduced to +½ lb. The climb was a long drawn out affair in which, theoretically, you could reach a cruise altitude of 5,000 ft (1,525 m) in about 10 minutes with a take-off weight of the order of 6,750 lb (3,062 kg).

In cruising flight at 85 knots (158 km/h) the Swordfish was very stable about all axes and was very easy to fly on instruments, but harmony of control was somewhat spoiled by over sensitivity of rudder, although this cancelled itself out in aiding the slightly heavy ailerons in endowing this ungainly-looking aircraft with agility totally out of keeping with its appearance and its rate of turn was phenomenal. It has been alleged that the Swordfish was easier to fly than a Tiger Moth and although this is perhaps an exaggeration in some respects, it was undeniably viceless and liberties could be taken with the Swordfish that would have guaranteed any other aircraft stalling and spinning long before. Indeed, this total lack of vice proved the undoing of the occasional pilot, for the Swordfish would forgive most things, but even so ladylike an aeroplane expected its pilot to demonstrate some rudiments of gentlemanliness in handling; no aeroplane may be taken totally for granted.

It was hardly necessary to trim the Swordfish into a dive and 200 knots (371 km/h) could be clocked if the necessary considerable altitude was available, the control forces chang-

(Above) A Royal Navy Swordfish landing aboard the USS Wasp in the Mediterranean during Malta re-supply operations

(Above) The undercarriage of a Swordfish (V4387) snagging an arrester wire immediately prior to nosing over on HMS Attacker during convoy escort duty between Curacao and the UK in 1942, and (below) another Swordfish after its pilot had made a heavy dead stick landing aboard the same vessel

Female auxiliary personnel 'womanhandling' torpedoes for shore-based Swordfish operating in the torpedo-strike role under RAF Coastal Command control in 1940. At this time, the Swordfish was also serving from shore bases in the diurnal and nocturnal mine-laying roles

(Above Swordfish Mk II (LS268), this Blackburn-built model having a strengthened lower mainplane which, with metal underside skinning, was stressed for eight 25-lb (11,3-kg) solid-head armour-piercing or 60-lb rocket projectiles, and was powered by the improved Pegasus 30 engine. (Below left) A Swordfish Mk I (L2840/G) flying early in 1943 as a test aircraft for rocket projectiles

ing little under these conditions, and dives at torpedo-carrying weight to the maximum permitted engine rpm of 2,860 did not produce undue vibration or flutter. The Swordfish remained stable in all axes, manoeuvring precisely in the vertical plane, and it was popularly supposed—although I admit that I never personally confirmed the supposition—that the ideal method of dive bombing was to fly almost immediately above the target and then turn the Swordfish over to the near-vertical, diving until the target could be seen above the upper wing. With a forward CG no real muscle had to be applied in recovery, gentle pressure pulling the Swordfish positively and reasonably rapidly out of the dive, but with the CG aft the elevator called for some muscle and response was sluggish. Violent use of the elevator was certainly to be avoided.

There was no warning of a stall other than a gentle sink which occurred at about 52 knots (96 km/h) and the Swordfish regained flying speed immediately without the least tendency to spin. The rudder bias was somewhat inadequate in a power-off glide, but a normal landing was ridiculously easy. With mixture set RICH, carburettor air intake set COLD and brakes checked OFF, the Swordfish would virtually land itself. This was normally effected without flap at 70 knots (130 km/h) on an airfield and at 60 knots (111 km/h) on

a carrier. Flap—which was just an eight-degree symmetrical drooping of the ailerons by rotation of a knurled wheel set in the trailing edge of the upper mainplane above the pilot's head—was only used for catapulting, its use for a carrier landing not normally being advocated as it encouraged the aircraft to float over the arrester wires.

The ill-fated attack by Swordfish of No 825 Squadron on the German naval force in the English Channel in February 1942, saw, as previously stated, the demise of the *Stringbag* in the torpedo-dropping rôle, but it certainly did not signal the end of this old-stager's operational career. Quite the contrary. The Swordfish was already immersed in adaptation for new weapons and new rôles. Production, which had become the sole responsibility of Blackburn Aircraft at Sherburn-in-Elmet from 1940, resulting in the unofficial use of the appellation of *Blackfish* in some quarters, had declined during the course of 1942, in which year only 271 examples were to be delivered as compared with 415 in the previous year, but was on the upswing again. Output was destined to be more than doubled during 1943, in which year 592 *Blackfish* were to be delivered, although this boost in production was a tribute more to the tractability of the Swordfish than to outstanding efficacy in the ever more varied tasks to which it was assigned.

In September 1942, I joined the Service Trials Unit at Arbroath, where the test programme listed for the Swordfish reflected the fact that, having been replaced aboard the fleet carriers by the Albacore and the Avenger in the classic torpedo-bombing rôle, it had taken on a new lease of life in the anti-submarine warfare rôle. Most of the consequent work involved performance and handling trials with a clutter of external stores and was related to the decision to operate the Swordfish from the new escort carriers that were being commissioned and the MAC-ships, or Merchant Aircraft Carriers, which were planned. Incredibly, it did not seem to matter what one slung under a Swordfish, for external loads made little or no difference to handling or performance. The heaviest load that I ever lifted beneath a Swordfish comprised a Leigh Light and its battery pack, an 18-in torpedo and eight 100-lb (45,35 kg) anti-submarine bombs! There was really no logical reason why it should ever have flown at all with this mass of stores, but fly it did, albeit that the 20 knot speed range covering climb, cruise and landing that I mentioned earlier had diminished to a mere 10 knots (18·5 km/h). Of course, this was not the ideal load to be carrying around in mid-Atlantic at dead of night, but it was what was being contemplated at the time. The real problem was to get this dead weight off the minideck of the MAC-ship from which the Swordfish was to operate.

The advent of ASV radar and rocket projectiles for anti-submarine warfare were, of course, of very considerable importance to the Swordfish, the use of both of which devices was pioneered by this now-primitive biplane. An ASV-equipped Swordfish of No 812 Squadron flying from Gibraltar had been responsible for the first nocturnal sinking by aircraft of a submarine on 21 December 1941, and air tests with a Swordfish of rocket projectiles took place at Thorney Island 10 months later, on 12 October 1942, and the combination of these two developments was to have a dramatic effect on anti-submarine operations.

The problem of getting heavily laden Swordfish off small carrier decks was inevitably given to RAE Farnborough to solve, and the Establishment came up with the answer in the form of RATOG (Rocket Assisted Take-Off Gear) which comprised a pack of two solid fuel rockets fitted to either side of the fuselage and slanted inwards so that the thrust line was as near as possible through the aircraft's CG, the rockets exhausting beneath and just beyond the trailing edge of the lower mainplane. The *modus operandi* was to raise the tail as early as possible during the take-off run, depress the firing button on the control column at the predetermined point in the run and then bring the tail down to almost the three-point attitude just before reaching the end of the deck. There was no change of trim when the rockets fired.

By the time I was posted to the RAE in January 1944, the Swordfish had already been proofed in its RATOG trials, but one of the first tasks I was allocated at Farnborough was proofing the RATOG installation on the minimally-modified Swordfish Mk II, this merely having strengthened lower mainplanes with metal underside skinning and stressed for toting and launching eight 60-lb (27 kg) rocket projectiles, or, alternatively, 25-lb (11,34-kg) solid-head armour-piercing projectiles, which, fired at a range of 600 yards (549 m), easily pierced the plating of a U-boat's pressure hull. The 690 hp Pegasus IIIM3 engine, which had been retained for the initial batch of Mk IIs, had given place to the improved Pegasus 30 which had a similar rating at 4,750 ft (1 450 m), and at a take-off weight of 9,000 lb (4 082 kg) with a 12 knot

(Above and immediately below) One of the last Blackburn-built Swordfish Mk Is (V4689/G) photographed at Boscombe Down while undergoing trials with ASV Mk X radar. Note Leigh Light under starboard lower mainplane

An idea of the considerable load-lifting capability of the Swordfish is provided by this photograph (above) of a Mk III with stores under fuselage and lower mainplane

(Above right and below) A Swordfish Mk III seen in July 1944 with an ASV Mk X radome between the undercarriage legs, antennae on forward outboard interplane struts and, beneath the lower mainplane, rocket launching rails inboard and flare racks outboard

A number of Swordfish Mk IIs, including HS553 (illustrated above) were fitted with cockpit canopies to render them more suited for training tasks in Canada. Aircraft so modified were sometimes erroneously referred to as Swordfish Mk IVs

Fairey Swordfish Specification

Power Plant: One Bristol Pegasus IIIM3 nine-cylinder radial air-cooled supercharged engine rated at 775 hp at 2,200 rpm at sea level and 690 hp at 3,500 ft (1 065 m) at 2,200 rpm, with five-minute combat rating of 750 hp at 2,525 rpm at 4,750 ft (1 450 m), driving three-bladed fixed-pitch Fairey-Reed metal propeller. Fuel capacity: 155 Imp gal (705 l) in fuselage main tank and 12·5 Imp gal (57 l) in gravity tank, with provision for 60 Imp gal (273 l) capacity auxiliary tank in mid-cockpit position or one 69 Imp gal (314 l) auxiliary tank slung from torpedo crutches.

Performance: (Mk I at 8,700 lb/3 946 kg) Max speed, 139 mph (224 km/h) at 4,750 ft (1 450 m), 132 mph (212 km/h) at sea level; max cruise, 128 mph (206 km/h) at 5,000 ft (1 525 m) at max weak mixture power; econ cruise, 104 mph (167 km/h) at 5 000 ft (1 525 m); range at econ cruise (with 1,500-lb/680-kg bomb load), 546 mls (878 km), (with max standard internal fuel and no external stores), 770 mls (1 240 km), (with 69 Imp gal/3141 external auxiliary tank), 1,030 mls (1 657 km); take-off distance at max loaded weight (9 250 lb/4 196 kg) to clear 50 ft (15,24 m), 725 yds (663 m); deck run at max loaded weight into 20 knot (37 km/h) wind, 180 yds (164,5 m), into 30 knot (55 km/h) wind, 115 yds (105 m), into 40 knot (74 km/h) wind, 62 yds (57 m); time to 5,000 ft (1,525 m) at max weight, 10 min; service ceiling at max weight, 10,700 ft (3 260 m) at 8,700 lb (3 946 kg), 12 400 ft (3 780 m); landing distance over 50 ft (15,24 m) at 8,100 lb (3,674 kg), 550 yds (503 m).

Weights: (Late production Mk I) Empty, 4,700 lb (2,132 kg); empty equipped, 5,200 lb (2,359 kg); loaded, 8,100 lb (3,674 kg); max loaded, 8,700 lb (3 946 kg); max overload, 9,250 lb (4 196 kg).

Dimensions: Span, 45 ft 6 in (13,87 m), lower mainplane, 43 ft 9 in (13,34 m); width (mainplanes folded), 17 ft 3 in (5,26 m); length (tail down), 36 ft 1 in (11,00 m); flying attitude, 36 ft 4in (11,07 m); height (tail down), 12 ft 10½ in (3,92 m), flying attitude), 13 ft 5¾ in (4,11 m); gross wing area, 607 sq ft (56,39 m²).

Armament: One fixed forward-firing 0·303-in (7,7-mm) Vickers machine gun in starboard fuselage decking (deleted from some aircraft) and one 0·303-in (7,7-mm) Lewis machine gun with 600 rounds on Fairey high-speed flexible mounting in rear cockpit. One 1,610-lb (730-kg) 18-in (45,7-cm) torpedo, one 1,500-lb (680-kg) sea mine, or 1,500-lb (680-kg) bomb load (ie, two 500-lb/226,8-kg bombs beneath fuselage and two 250-lb/113,4-kg bombs beneath the wings, or one 500-lb/226,8-kg bomb beneath fuselage and similar bomb under each wing).

(22 km/h) wind, the aircraft demanded 650 ft (198 m) of deck for a normal unassisted take-off, but with RATOG the Swordfish literally leapt of within 270 ft (82 m) with firing initiated after 100 ft (30 m) of free run.

By the beginning of 1944 — in which year 420 Swordfish were to roll off Blackburn's assembly line — the amiable old *Stringbag* was still proving remarkably impervious to the wartime practice of modification. Apart from some changes in instrumentation and the previously-mentioned metal skinning of the lower mainplane underside, plus, in the case of the Mk III, a rather undignified protuberance between the lady's legs accommodating air-to-surface (ASV) Mk X radar, a Swordfish leaving Blackburn's Sherburn-in-Elmet line in 1944 was extraordinarily similar to one that had rolled off the parent company's Hayes line eight years earlier. This was despite a radical change in operational rôle, for this ageing yet still sprightly creation of the early 'thirties was, in the mid 'forties, performing yeoman service in combating the U-boat menace from escort carriers and MAC-ships. A dozen or so squadrons were operating from — or were to operate from during the course of the year — the escort carriers *Activity, Archer, Avenger, Battler, Biter, Campania, Chaser, Dasher, Hunter, Rapana, Stalker, Striker, Tracker* and *Vindex,* and Swordfish pooled from Nos 836, 840 and 860 (Netherlands) squadrons were aboard some 18 MAC-ships. The *Stringbags* frequently operated under the most appalling conditions, particularly while on escort duty with convoys to the Soviet Union, and there can be little doubt that their success was due to a combination of sturdiness and *lack* of sophistication. The exploits of the Swordfish operating from escort carriers and MAC-ships were so numerous that it would be fruitless to attempt to do justice to the subject here, but it is worthwhile recalling that while escorting one convoy to the Soviet Union, Swordfish from *Vindex* and *Striker* amassed more than a thousand hours of anti-submarine patrols within 10 days, while, in September 1944, Swordfish from the former carrier sank four U-boats in a single voyage.

The last operational Swordfish squadron was No 836, which had served as a pool for MAC-ship aircraft crews and was disbanded on 21 May 1945, and it was an aircraft from this squadron operating from the MAC-ship *Empire Macandrew* that recorded the last contact between a Swordfish and a U-boat on 20 April 1945. Thus ended the fighting career of one of the most remarkable aircraft in the annals of aerial warfare, albeit one that never impressed me as a fighting machine in a war that saw the dawn of the jet age, but I should stress that I never flew the Swordfish operationally and am therefore not emotive about its qualities. However, its record stands proud as a monument to undeniable operational success and one must examine this remarkable contradiction to put the Swordfish in historical perspective.

Its survival throughout WW II despite obsolescence places the *Stringbag* in somewhat the same category as the Junkers Ju 87, although the former was not subjected to the same progressive development as the latter. Both were operated primarily in an environment in which enemy fighters were conspicuous by their absence or where air superiority could be guaranteed. In the case of the Swordfish, this environment was out in the ocean beyond the range of enemy fighters or under cover of darkness before night fighting became an art. When fighters were around the Swordfish still had a measure of protection in its remarkable manoeuvrability, but when the chips were down as in the aiming run of a torpedo attack it was totally vulnerable. I would not detract from the great actions in which the Swordfish participated, nor especially from the gallant aircrew who fought these actions, but the hard fact is that these aircrew should never have been exposed to such danger in equipment so ancient in concept and I cannot believe that a more technologically advanced aircraft could not have done as well or even better. □

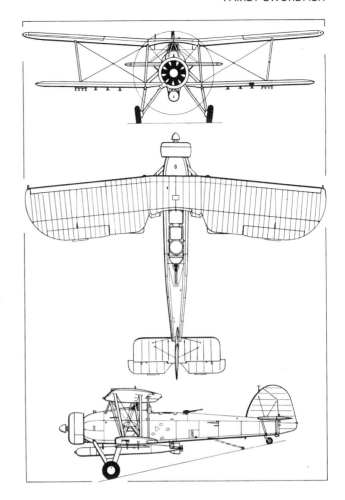

The general arrangement drawing (above right) depicts the standard production Swordfish Mk I. Illustrated below is a Swordfish Mk II (LS326), which, at the time of writing, remains in airworthy condition at RNAS Yeovilton. This is the sole surviving airworthy example of this aircraft type

Vought Chesapeake

WITH THE DEFEAT OF FRANCE, the RAF and the Royal Navy found themselves legatees to outstanding portions of contracts placed with US aircraft manufacturers by the French government; ungrateful recipients of varying quantities of a variety of aircraft of dubious potential value and for which no clear idea existed as to possible use. Included in this legacy was the Vought-Sikorsky V-156-B1, an export version of the US Navy's prematurely ageing and undeniably obsolescent SB2U scout-bomber, which began to arrive in the UK in the early summer of 1941, and to which, in its inimitably imaginative fashion, the Admiralty assigned the inspiring appellation of Chesapeake.

It was not that the Chesapeake was a *bad* aircraft; it was simply outmoded, and its performance and handling characteristics, never vivacious from the earliest days of its US Navy predecessors, had been brought much closer to the vapid by British insistence on heavier armament, a measure of armour protection, more fuel and other weight-imparting changes introduced into the contract after its transfer from the French to the British government in October 1940 — changes imposed on an already marginally underpowered aeroplane without any commensurate increases in power.

The Chesapeake had begun life as the V-156-F, a version of the US Navy's SB2U-2 for France's *Aéronavale*. The original prototype of the Vought scout-bomber — and in US Navy parlance, the "bomber" portion of the category implied *dive* bomber — which sported the tongue-twisting and memory-taxing designation of XSB2U-1, had flown on 4 January 1936, and, although somewhat innovatory of concept in so far as shipboard aircraft of the day were concerned in being a cantilever monoplane with folding wings and fully-retractable main undercarriage members, had suffered the misfortune of being committed to production at a time

when its fabric-covered steel-tube structure had already been rendered *passé* by standardisation on the light-metal stressed-skin monocoque. Such would undoubtedly have been utilised by Rex Beisel and his team had they initiated work a mere 12 months later. Thus, a configurational pace-setter though it may have been, it had been overtaken by developments in structures before it saw a carrier deck; it synthesized years of Corsair *biplane* structural experience and, as such, had marked the end of an era.

The US Navy's Bureau of Aeronautics had been impressed enough with the performance of the XSB2U-1, however, to have ordered 54 production SB2U-1s on 26 October 1936, these going to VB-2 aboard *Lexington* and VB-3 aboard *Saratoga,* following this up, on 27 January 1938, with a contract for a further 58 aircraft, which, with minor internal changes, were to be delivered as SB2U-2s. Meanwhile, French interest in procurement of the Vought scout-bomber as a means of accelerating modernisation of the *Aéronavale* prompted display of a company demonstrator, the V-156, at the *Salon de l'Aéronautique International* in Paris in October 1938, and four months later, on 22 February 1939, an initial contract was signed in France for 20 V-156-Fs for the *Aéronavale,* a follow-on contract for a similar batch being signed on 16 May.

The first V-156-F was flown at Orly after reassembly on 6 August 1939, and a squadron, AB 1, was formed on this type at Lanvéoc-Poulmic during the course of the autumn, with a second squadron, AB 3, forming in December. The V-156-F, while essentially similar to the US Navy's SB2U-2, differed from its American counterpart in respect of equipment. The single 0·3-in (7,62-mm) machine gun in the starboard wing centre section of the SB2U-2 gave place on the V-156-F to a pair of 7,5-mm Darne guns mounted one on each side of the fuselage; the fence-type dive brakes previously rejected by the US Navy were introduced in the upper and lower surfaces of the outboard wing panels, and the swinging bomb displacement crutch, which ensured clearance of the propeller arc and the export of which was, for some inexplicable reason, denied by the US Navy, was omitted.

Although AB 1 completed carrier trials aboard *Béarn*, the V-156-F's brief participation in the Battle of France was to be purely land-based and it was to be flown with rather more valour than effect — the entire aircraft complement of AB 3 was to be eliminated when, on the morning of 10 May 1940, a *Luftwaffe* bomb destroyed the hangar in which, *Drôle de Guerre* style, the V-156-Fs had been placed overnight, while the activities of AB 1 were to be somewhat inhibited by the fact that the French R/T with which its V-156-Fs had been equipped proved useless and the Darne machine guns invariably seized after the first few rounds!

Six weeks prior to the V-156-F being committed to battle, the French government had placed an order with Vought-Sikorsky for a further 50 V-156-Fs and it was these aircraft that were to find their way into the Royal Navy's inventory as Chesapeakes. On 28 March 1940, when the contract was signed, Vought-Sikorsky was engaged in fulfilling another contract calling for 57 aircraft that had been ordered on 25 September 1939 for the US Marine Corps as SB2U-3s. The SB2U-3 was a *long-range* scout-bomber and, in consequence, had provision for very much more internal fuel than either SB2U-1 or -2, this being housed in a trio of unprotected integral tanks in the torsionally stiff box nose section of the wing. The effect on the handling characteristics of almost trebling the internal fuel capacity is best left to the imagination.

When the V-156-F contract passed to the British government in October 1940 — at which time the first airframe built against this contract was already in final assembly — one of the changes stipulated was the provision of the 125 US gal (473 l) wing centre section integral tank similar to that of the SB2U-3, turning what was now referred to as the V-156-B1 into something of an hybrid. This and other changes demanded under the amended contract imposed quite a load on Vought-Sikorsky's drawing office for the remainder of the year.

Some vague idea that the aircraft might be used in the defensive rôle from Royal Navy escort carriers — though such maritime raiders as the Condor would surely have shown the underpowered Vought a clean pair of heels under most circumstances — presumably prompted the decision to increase forward firepower substantially, and four 0·30-in (7,62-mm) calibre machine guns with 500 rpg were mounted in pairs in the wings, outboard of the propeller disc. Armour protection, too, was increased, the pilot being provided with head-and-shoulders and seat armour, the rotating seat of the second crew member being armoured, armour plate being bolted to the rear portion of the floor and the aft bulkhead of the second cockpit, and the underside and back of the main fuel tank also being protected by armour plate. The specified maximum bomb load was three 500-pounders, the swinging bomb displacement crutch on the fuselage centreline being reinstated, but the fence-type air brakes favoured by the *Aéronavale* were discarded.

The first production V-156-B1 Chesapeake was flown on 26 February 1941, and was accepted at the factory a month later, on 26 March, the aircraft being shipped to Liverpool and assembled at the nearby Burtonwood Aircraft Repair Depot. Two of the first of these (AL908 and AL911) were at the A&AEE, Boscombe Down, in June, but most of the Chesapeakes were assigned to Lee-on-Solent, where, on 14 July, No 811 Squadron had 14 of them. One or two were

(Above) The first production V-156-F photographed on 18 May 1939, at Stratford, Connecticut, prior to French acceptance, and (below) V-156-F No 3 shortly after its delivery to France

(Head of opposite page) SB2U-1 (BuAer 0740) of US Navy Sqn VB-3 "High Hats" operating from the USS Saratoga in 1939, and (below) the XSB2U-1 photographed early in its flight test programme in 1936. For its day, the XSB2U-1 possessed exceptionally clean lines. After more than seven months of testing this prototype crashed in the Norfolk (Virginia) area on 20 August 1936 and was totally destroyed.

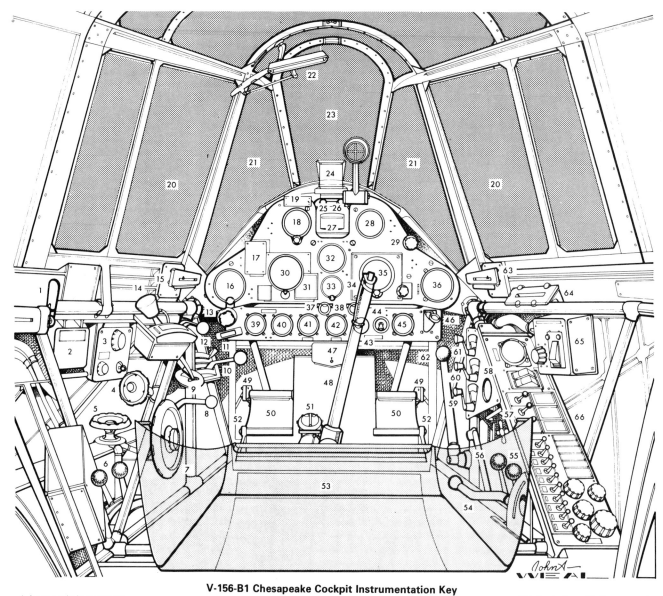

V-156-B1 Chesapeake Cockpit Instrumentation Key

1 Inter-cockpit message carrier
2 Radio installation station box
3 Switch box
4 Aileron tab control handwheel
5 Rudder tab control handwheel
6 Port wing guns charging levers
7 Elevator tab control handwheel
8 Wobble pump control
9 Fuel valve control
10 Bomb release lever
11 Propeller governor control
12 Mixture control lever
13 Carburettor heat control
14 Throttle
15 Port mainwheel mechanical position indicator
16 Accelerometer

17 Altimeter conversion card holder
18 Altimeter
19 Correction card holder
20 Sliding canopy
21 Fixed quarterlights
22 Adjustable rear-view mirror
23 Windscreen
24 Gunsight installation: illuminated sight (centre) and auxiliary ring sight (right)
25 Undercarriage warning light (green)
26 Undercarriage warning light (red)
27 Compass
28 Turn-and-bank indicator
29 Fuel gauge pump
30 Directional gyro
31 Card holder
32 Airspeed indicator

33 Clock
34 Control grip-mounted trigger button
35 Artificial horizon
36 Fuel contents gauge
37 Fire extinguisher
38 Cowl flap control
39 Tachometer
40 Manifold pressure gauge
41 Engine gauge unit
42 Ignition switch
43 Carburettor air temperature gauge (partially obscured by control grip)
44 4-way switch
45 Cylinder temperature gauge
46 Priming pump
47 Map case
48 Control column
49 Brake pedal adjustment
50 Rudder pedals

51 Cockpit ventilation control
52 Rudder pedal adjustment
53 Pilot's seat
54 Seat adjustment lever
55 Starboard wing guns charging levers
56 Undercarriage emergency release control
57 Emergency release valve
58 Hydraulic system pressure gauge
59 Tailwheel lock/release lever
60 Undercarriage control lever
61 Flaps control lever
62 Hydraulic hand pump
63 Starboard main wheel mechanical position indicator
64 Flap position indicator
65 Switch box
66 Pilot's main electrical distribution panel

taken on strength by No 786 Squadron and, of course, others found their way to the Service Trials Unit (No 778 Sqdn) at RNAS Arbroath were I was to encounter the venerable Vought.

The Chesapeake was a clean enough aeroplane, if somewhat unexciting , with a tail end that seemed to belong to the era of the biplane and a front end that appeared to be struggling into the age of the monoplane. Its fuselage was a chrome-molybdenum steel tubular welded structure, the

forward portion of which was covered by mostly removable light metal panels and the rear portion was covered by fabric. The wing was of single-spar type, with the metal ribs and metal skinning forming a torque box forward of the spar, aft of which the centre section had metal skinning and the outboard panels were fabric covered. It was built in three sections: the centre section, which incorporated a trailing-edge split-type hydraulically-actuated flap, and the outer panels, which, attached by three hinges and manually-folded upward, carried fabric-covered metal-framed ailerons which could be hydraulically-drooped as auxiliary flaps in concert with the centre-section flap. The undercarriage consisted of two single-strut, oleo-pneumatic shock-absorber, semi-cantilever legs, which retracted hydraulically and swivelled through 90 deg to lie flat in wells immediately aft of the centre-section mainspar, and a non-retractable castoring tailwheel.

The 14-cylinder two-row Pratt & Whitney R-1535-SB4-G engine, driving an Hamilton Standard variable-pitch constant-speed two-bladed metal propeller, was carried by a tubular steel mount so designed that the entire power plant forward of and including the firewall could be removed as a unit from the airframe. It offered a take-off rating of 825 hp at 2,625 rpm, which was available for one-and-a-half minutes, and an equivalent five-minute emergency rating at 7,500 ft (2 285 m), the normal maximum rating being 750 hp at 2 550 rpm from sea level to 9,500 ft (2 895 m), this having a 30-minute limit.

It was not until July 1942 that I was to find an opportunity to fly the Chesapeake. By this time, of course, the comparatively long take-off run demanded by the Vought and its various other shortcomings, some of which, let it be said, stemmed directly from British efforts to render it a "fully operational" aeroplane, had made proposals to use it from escort carriers patently impracticable, and the Chesapeake had been relegated to training tasks, as had also its counterpart in the US Navy. Unbeknown to me at the time, however, was the fact that the US Marine Corps SB2U-3s, which had been assigned the somewhat more emotive name of Vindicator, had flown their first and last combat missions during the previous month, in that most vital naval duel of WW II, the Battle of Midway. Had I been aware of this fact, I would certainly have experienced some compassion on that July morning, when I first hoisted myself into the cockpit of AL915, for those Marine Corps pilots that had faced Zero-Sen fighters and the anti-aircraft defences of Vice-Admiral Chuichi Nagumo's carrier task force in this sitting duck of an aeroplane.

Although the Chesapeake was no longer considered as a potentially operational aircraft, the Service Trials Unit at Arbroath still had two examples of the type, AL910 and AL915, with which we were performing dive-bombing and deck landing assessments. The cockpit was situated almost level with the wing leading edge and proved roomy in the usual American style, although I can believe that a tall pilot would have experienced some discomfort for even with the adjustable seat in its lowest position, a six-footer must have found the sloping sides of the aft-sliding canopy pressing on his ears. View from the cockpit was comparatively good although the framing of the small clear-vision panel irritatingly detracted from forward view. The instruments were quite neatly arranged, but the layout of the panels would have been considered somewhat illogical in later years, and the control column was awkwardly far forward, causing me to reach uncomfortably.

The starting procedure was simple, the propeller being turned two or three times by hand, the fuel cock being set to RESERVE, the throttle being opened one-third and the mixture control set to RICH. The propeller control was pulled out fully for coarse pitch, the carburettor air intake set to COLD, the cowling gills opened, and the generator and battery switched on. A starter cartridge was then inserted into the breech in the upper right corner of the lower instrument panel and the fuel pressure was built up to 5 lb/sq in, the priming pump being screwed home and the ignition switched on. The starter switch was then operated and, as the engine turned over, the hand fuel pump was worked until the Twin Wasp Junior engine was purring sweetly.

Two of the batch of V-156-B1 Chesapeakes that reached the Royal Navy, AL909 (above) and AL934 (below), both photographed in the summer of 1941

The V-156-B1 Chesapeake (AL943 being seen flying over the Solent in June 1942) embodied features of both the SB2U-2 and SB2U-3 of the US Navy and US Marine Corps, and lacked the fence-type dive brakes utilised by the French V-156-F. The obsolescence of the Chesapeake rendered its operational use impractical

As the Chesapeake had no parking brake, it was necessary to hold the toes on the brake pedals while starting and running up, and after a few minutes, the propeller control was depressed fully to fine the pitch, the throttle was eased open to provide maximum cruise boost and the magnetos were checked. Then the throttle was pushed to the gate and the boost and revs checked. At full throttle the engine purr became a very healthy growl indeed, though, as I was soon to discover, the enthusiasm of the growl did not betoken a sufficiency of power to pull the Chesapeake off the ground in much less than 1,000 ft (305 m) even at the comparatively light weight of 7,500 lb (3 400 kg) at which I was taking-off — with full armour and the maximum 1,500-lb (680-kg) bomb load almost 1,700 ft (520 m) of airfield was called for!

For take-off, the throttle was pushed to the gate, but as

Vought-Sikorsky V-156-B1 Chesapeake Cutaway Drawing Key

1 Propeller hub
2 Hamilton Standard variable-pitch constant-speed propeller
3 Propeller shaft housing
4 Propeller governor constant speed unit
5 Oil strainer unit
6 Carburettor cold air intake grille

7 Carburettor
8 Cowling forward ring
9 Pratt & Whitney R-1535-SB4G Twin Wasp Junior twin-row radial engine
10 Exhaust collector ring
11 Exhaust outlet
12 Fire extinguisher installation
13 Engine lower bearers
14 Oil tank (9·2 Imp gal/41,8 l capacity)
15 Cowling gills
16 Starter motor
17 Aerial mast
18 Oil cooler assembly
19 Generator
20 Oil cooler intake duct
21 Oil cooler intake
22 Leading-edge skinning
23 Wing front spar
24 Starboard navigation light
25 Starboard formation light
26 Starboard aileron
27 Aileron hinge fairing
28 Flotation bag inflated (design provision but not fitted on British aircraft)
29 Wing gun access panels
30 Windscreen
31 Telescope sight (replaced by ST1A sight on British aircraft)
32 Instrument panel
33 Control column
34 Pilot's flare pistol
35 Rudder pedal assembly
36 Fuselage bottom frame
37 Flare cartridge clip
38 Seat support frame
39 Elevator tab handwheel
40 Angled coaming frame
41 Pilot's seat
42 Downward-view quarterlights
43 Rear-view mirror
44 Cockpit sliding canopy
45 Pilot's back armour
46 Pilot's headrest
47 Wing fold position

48 Aerial
49 Hydraulic filler neck
50 Hydraulic system tank
51 Life raft and emergency (rations/signals) equipment
52 Turnover frame
53 Canopy track
54 Fuel filler cap fairing

55 Flotation bag CO_2 cylinder (not installed in British aircraft)
56 Fuselage main fuel tank (98·2 Imp gal/446,4 l capacity)
57 Under-tank armour support frame
58 Compressed air cylinder
59 Observer's emergency rudder pedal (and control column assembly
60 Radio equipment (Bendix TA-12C and RA-10DB)
61 Aerial lead-in
62 Chart desk

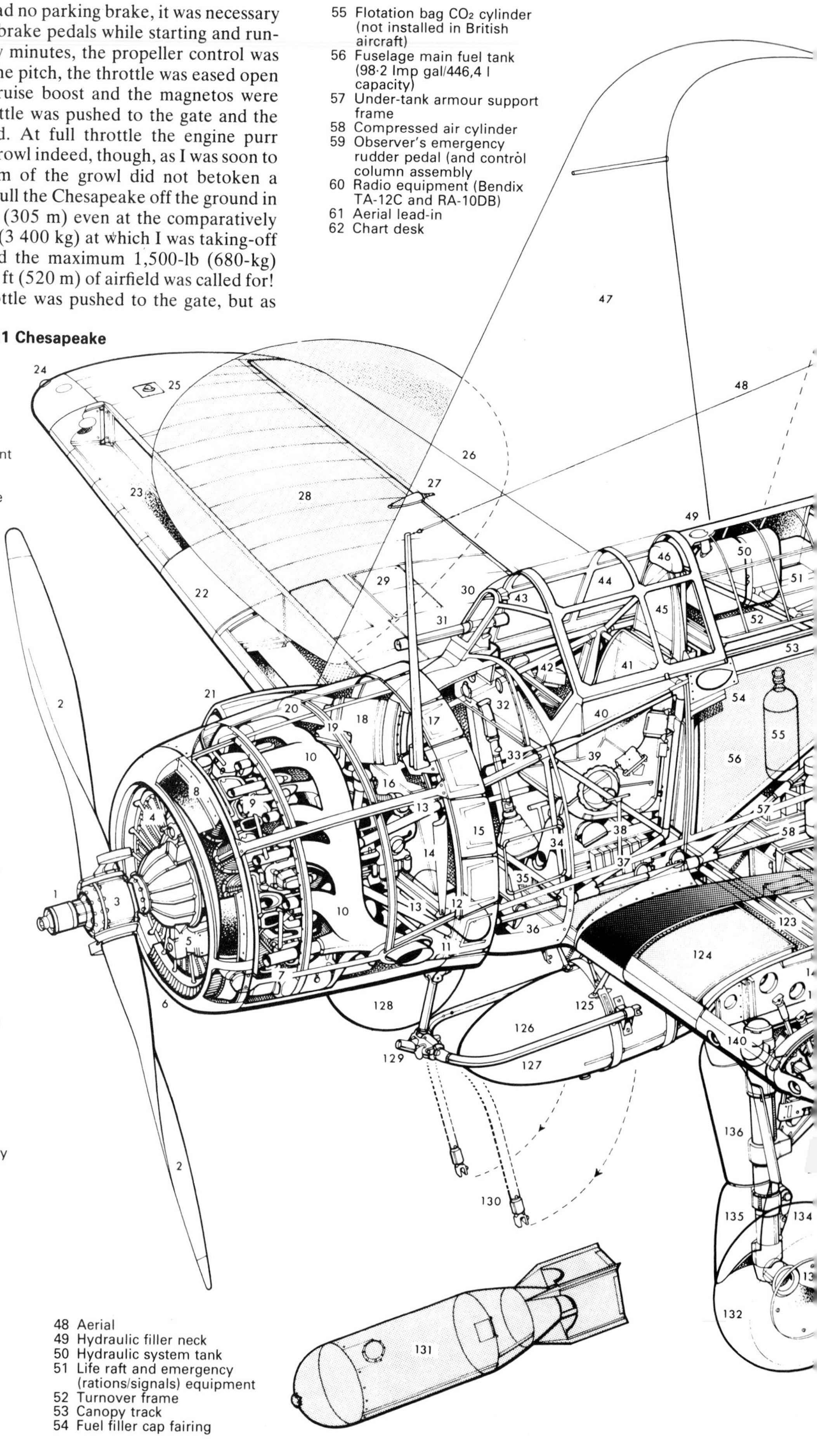

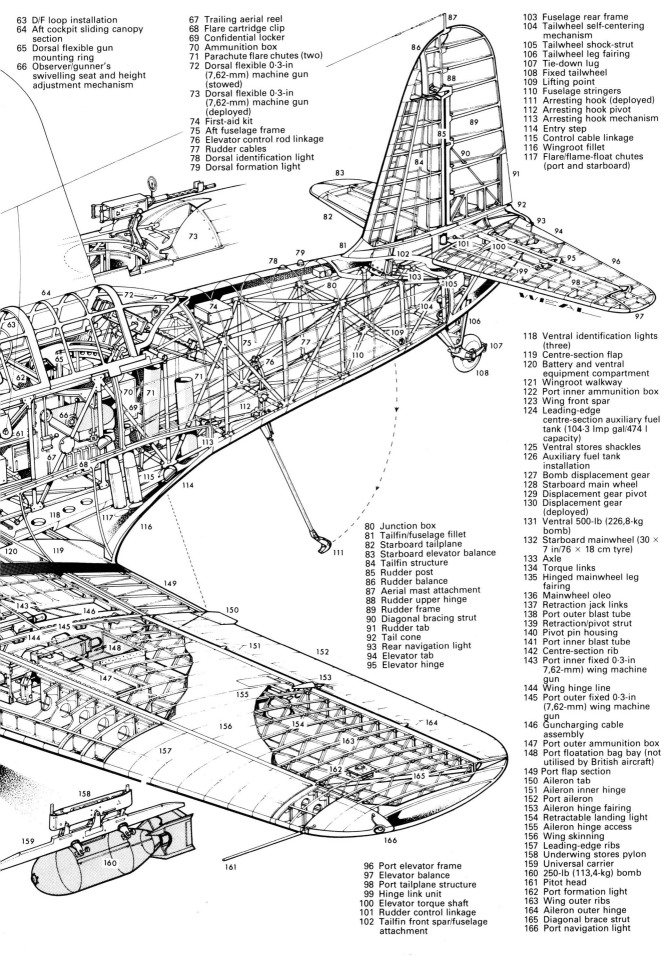

63 D/F loop installation
64 Aft cockpit sliding canopy section
65 Dorsal flexible gun mounting ring
66 Observer/gunner's swivelling seat and height adjustment mechanism
67 Trailing aerial reel
68 Flare cartridge clip
69 Confidential locker
70 Ammunition box
71 Parachute flare chutes (two)
72 Dorsal flexible 0·3-in (7,62-mm) machine gun (stowed)
73 Dorsal flexible 0·3-in (7,62-mm) machine gun (deployed)
74 First-aid kit
75 Aft fuselage frame
76 Elevator control rod linkage
77 Rudder cables
78 Dorsal identification light
79 Dorsal formation light

80 Junction box
81 Tailfin/fuselage fillet
82 Starboard tailplane
83 Starboard elevator balance
84 Tailfin structure
85 Rudder post
86 Rudder balance
87 Aerial mast attachment
88 Rudder upper hinge
89 Rudder frame
90 Diagonal bracing strut
91 Rudder tab
92 Tail cone
93 Rear navigation light
94 Elevator tab
95 Elevator hinge

96 Port elevator frame
97 Elevator balance
98 Port tailplane structure
99 Hinge link unit
100 Elevator torque shaft
101 Rudder control linkage
102 Tailfin front spar/fuselage attachment

103 Fuselage rear frame
104 Tailwheel self-centering mechanism
105 Tailwheel shock-strut
106 Tailwheel leg fairing
107 Tie-down lug
108 Fixed tailwheel
109 Lifting point
110 Fuselage stringers
111 Arresting hook (deployed)
112 Arresting hook pivot
113 Arresting hook mechanism
114 Entry step
115 Control cable linkage
116 Wingroot fillet
117 Flare/flame-float chutes (port and starboard)

118 Ventral identification lights (three)
119 Centre-section flap
120 Battery and ventral equipment compartment
121 Wingroot walkway
122 Port inner ammunition box
123 Wing front spar
124 Leading-edge centre-section auxiliary fuel tank (104·3 Imp gal/474 l capacity)
125 Ventral stores shackles
126 Auxiliary fuel tank installation
127 Bomb displacement gear
128 Starboard main wheel
129 Displacement gear pivot
130 Displacement gear (deployed)
131 Ventral 500-lb (226,8-kg) bomb
132 Starboard mainwheel (30 × 7 in/76 × 18 cm tyre)
133 Axle
134 Torque links
135 Hinged mainwheel leg fairing
136 Mainwheel oleo
137 Retraction jack links
138 Port outer blast tube
139 Retraction/pivot strut
140 Pivot pin housing
141 Port inner blast tube
142 Centre-section rib
143 Port inner fixed 0·3-in 7,62-mm) wing machine gun
144 Wing hinge line
145 Port outer fixed 0·3-in (7,62-mm) wing machine gun
146 Guncharging cable assembly
147 Port outer ammunition box
148 Port floatation bag bay (not utilised by British aircraft)
149 Port flap section
150 Aileron tab
151 Aileron inner hinge
152 Port aileron
153 Aileron hinge fairing
154 Retractable landing light
155 Aileron hinge access
156 Wing skinning
157 Leading-edge ribs
158 Underwing stores pylon
159 Universal carrier
160 250-lb (113,4-kg) bomb
161 Pitot head
162 Port formation light
163 Wing outer ribs
164 Aileron outer hinge
165 Diagonal brace strut
166 Port navigation light

there was no automatic boost control, care had to be exercised not to exceed the maximum permissible boost. The undercarriage was raised as soon as 110 knots (204 km/h) IAS was attained, the flap being raised first, and the speed for best climb was 115 knots (213 km/h) IAS, but climb proved something short of exhilarating and at around 1,100 ft/min (5,60 m/sec) was even less than that of the Skua, which was scarcely the most sprightly of the Navy's aircraft. Prior to commencing the climb, the fuel cock control was moved to AUXILIARY (integral centre section tank), all fuel for take-off having been drawn from below the main tank standpipe, and there was a marked nose-up trim change when the undercarriage came up. An altitude of 10,000 ft (3 050 m) was reached in about 10 min, by which time climb rate had fallen to some 900 ft/min (4,57 m/sec), and above this altitude speed was reduced by two knots (3,7 km/h) per 1,000 ft (305 m), with 15,000 ft (4 570 m) being attained in 17 min.

The Chesapeake proved to be stable about all axes but was sensitive to loading and, for example, if the contents of the wing centre section tank were exhausted and full ammunition happened to be carried for the aft-firing gun, it became markedly unstable longitudinally, while with full fuel and ammunition but without bombs, it was necessary to remove the aft floor and bulkhead armour, the arrester hook and the landing flares in order to keep the CG within the aft limit. Its performance in the cruise may best be described as sedate, 120 knots (222 km/h) IAS being recommended for range, but at 70 per cent power, 187 knots (346 km/h) was clocked at 11,000 ft (3 350 m). Visibility was good in all directions except downwards, which is precisely where it is needed most if an aircraft is intended to fulfil the dive bombing rôle, and manoeuvrability was poor, the ailerons being heavy and ineffective. It shuddered unimpressively in a tight turn and if pulled into a g stall a sharp wing drop invariably occurred. Stall recovery called for a considerable increase in speed as, once stalled, the wing remained stalled and an additional 15 or 20 knots (28 or 37 km/h) had little or no effect. With weight down to about 7,000 lb (3 175 kg), the Chesapeake stalled at 66 knots (122 km/h) all up, at 70 knots (130 km/h) with undercarriage down and at 62 knots (115 km/h) with undercarriage and flaps down, and the ailerons drooped.

Although spinning and aerobatics were not officially permitted, the aircraft could be spun provided that the weight was not in excess of 8,000 lb (3 629 kg) and the CG was not further aft than 27 per cent MAC, standard recovery methods being used, and it could be looped and slow-rolled, but the lack of control crispness rendered such anything but enervating. One of our primary interests at Arbroath, however, was the diving characteristics of the Chesapeake.

The manufacturer and the US Navy had tinkered with various means of providing a decelerating mode for this aerodynamically clean aeroplane to prevent speed building up excessively and necessitating a premature pull-out or an inaccurately shallow dive. Hamilton Standard had proposed

(Above left) SB2U-1s of VB-3 "High Hats", which, in December 1937, became the first US Navy squadron to equip with this type, and (below) the first series SB2U-1 (BuAer 0726) photographed during flight trials in August 1937. Fifty-four of the -1 version of the SB2U were ordered.

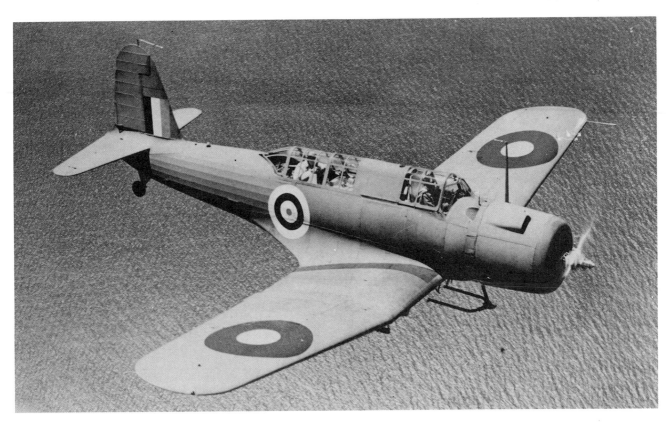

(Above and below left) The first production V-156-B1 photographed while undergoing flight testing from the manufacturer's Stratford, Connecticut facility early in 1941. The general arrangement drawing (below right) illustrates the V-156-B1 Chesapeake as supplied to the Royal Navy

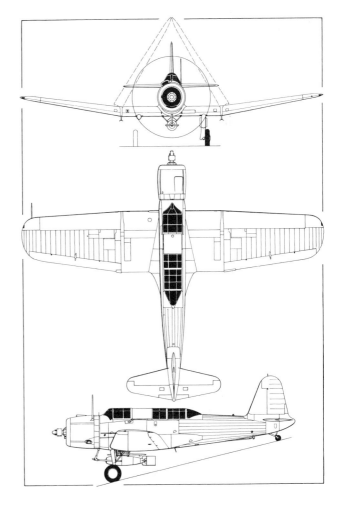

a braking propeller, the idea being to reduce the pitch to virtually zero upon entering the dive, but this dictated an extremely low dive entry speed in order to fine the blade pitch and both hydraulic and pneumatic pitch changing systems failed to produce entirely satisfactory results. Attention had then turned to more orthodox fence-type air brakes which were extended from the outer wing panels, but at the diving speed required by the US Navy, these brakes produced excessive buffeting and were pronounced unacceptable (although later adopted by the *Aéronavale*). Finally, in November 1939, Admiral Towers, chief of the Bureau of Aeronautics, agreed to dispense with the requirement for dive brakes and use the undercarriage in lieu, an idea that carried over to the Chesapeake and one that I readily admit that I did not like as the landing gear had not been designed for such a function.

I had already discovered that in shallow dives with the undercarriage up the Chesapeake tended to become somewhat tail heavy. With the undercarriage down, the reverse was obviously the case and nose heaviness became accentuated as speed built up, necessitating retrimming. The *modus operandi* was to avoid lowering the flap or drooping the ailerons when extending the undercarriage. The propeller pitch control was pulled to its limit, the mixture control set to RICH, the throttle was set at about one-third open, the cowling gills were closed and the canopy was opened. The Chesapeake was steady enough in the dive, but even with the

Vought-Sikorsky V-156-B1 Chesapeake specification

Power Plant: One Pratt & Whitney R-1535-SB4-G Twin Wasp Junior 14-cylinder two-row radial air-cooled engine rated at 825 hp at 2,625 rpm (for one-and-a-half min) for take-off and 750 hp at 2,550 rpm from sea level to 9,500 ft (2 895 m). Two-bladed Hamilton Standard constant-speed metal propeller of 11 ft (3,35 m) diameter. Internal fuel capacity, 202·5 Imp gal (920 l) divided between 98·2 Imp gal (446 l) main tank and 104·3 Imp gal (474 l) wing centre section integral tank.

Performance: (Main tank only and no armour) Max speed, 227 mph (356 km/h) at sea level, 250 mph (402 km/h) at critical altitude; cruise at 70% power, 220 mph (354 km/h) at 11,000 ft (3 350 m); range, 650 mls (1 046 km) at 220 mph (354 km/h); initial climb, 1 370 ft/min (6,96 m/sec); time to 15,000 ft (4 570 m), 13·4 min; service ceiling, 26,500 ft (8,075 m); (full internal fuel and full armour) Max speed, 225 mph (362 km/h) at sea level, 247 mph (397 km/h) at critical altitude; cruise at 70% power, 215 mph (346 km/h) at 11,000 ft (3 350 m); range, 1,340 mls (2 156 km) at 215 mph (346 km/h); initial climb, 1 050 ft/min (5,33 m/sec); time to 15,000 ft (4 570 m), 18 min; service ceiling, 22,700 ft (6,920 m); (full internal fuel, full armour and 1,500-lb/680-kg bomb load) Max speed, 198 mph (319 km/h) at sea level, 215 mph (346 km/h) at critical altitude; cruise at 70% power, 181 mph (291 km/h) at 11,000 ft (3,350 m); range, 1,170 mls (1,882 km) at 181 mph (291 km/h); initial climb, 600 ft/min (3,04 m/sec); time to 15,000 ft (4 570 m), 41 min; service ceiling, 16,400 ft (5 000 m); take-off distance, zero wind (at 6,953 lb/3 155 kg), 760 ft (232 m), (at 8,128 lb/3 687 kg), 1,100 ft (335 m), (at 9,763 lb/4 428 kg), 1,690 ft (515 m); landing speed with half fuel (at 6,599 lb/2 993 kg), 69 mph (111 km/h), (at 7,398 lb/3 356 kg), 73 mph (117 km/h, (at 7,533 lb/3 417 kg), 74 mph (119 km/h).

Weights: Loaded (no armour and fuel in main tank only), 6,953 lb (3,155 kg); (full armour and max internal fuel), 8,128 lb (3 687 kg), (plus max bomb load), 9,763 lb (4 428 kg).

Dimensions: Span, 41 ft 10⅞ in (12,77 m), (folded), 16 ft 0 in (4,88 m); length, 33 ft 11¾ in (10,36 m); height (propeller vertical, tail down), 14 ft 3 in (4,34 m), (propeller horizontal), 12 ft 1 in (3,68 m), (folded), 16 ft 4 in (4,98 m); wing area, 274·1 sq ft (25,46 m²), including centre section beneath fuselage), 305·3 sq ft (28,36 m²).

Armament: Four fixed forward-firing 0·3-in (7,62-mm) Browning machine guns in wings with 500 rpg and one 0·3-in (7,62-mm) gun on flexible mounting in rear cockpit, plus three 250-lb (113,4-kg) or 500-lb (226,8-kg) bombs.

undercarriage extended, the dive angle had to be limited to about 60 deg. Another limiting factor was, of course, the poor aileron control which greatly affected bombing accuracy as aileron turns on to the target are the only means of correcting misalignment once commited in the dive. In short, as a dive bomber the Chesapeake could be considered as one of the also-rans.

Another assessment of the Chesapeake that we had to make at the Service Trials Unit was that of deck-landing capability. The normal approach speed was 75 knots (139 km/h) and the Chesapeake was beautifully stable, but it was necessary to open the engine cowling gills fully and these immediately obscured the view of the deck, also resulting in slight tail buffet and loss of elevator response. The options were to make the final approach with the aircraft crabbed to starboard or ignore the book and approach with the gills only partly open. Although engine temperature usually remained within limits during an approach with partly-opened gills, there was a rapid temperature rise in the event of a baulked landing and the gills had to be opened very smartly indeed to avoid overheating. Even with the gills almost closed this aircraft was difficult to three-point.

The foregoing will have made the Chesapeake seem a rather dreary aeroplane, as, indeed, it was, but it did have some good features. First and foremost was its superbly reliable Twin Wasp Junior engine and, secondly, it offered quite a respectable range with full fuel, both highly desirable attributes in any naval aircraft. But in all fairness, by the time we were evaluating the Vought scout-bomber at Arbroath it was hardly in the first flush of its youth. Its advent in service with the US Navy in 1938 *had* signified a noteworthy advance in shipboard aeroplane development, yet it had been overtaken so rapidly by events that youth had translated directly to senility. Perhaps the test reports that we eventually submitted at the Service Trials Unit were to be regarded as more of the nature of a requiem than valediction, for as a first-line service aeroplane the Vought scout-bomber was already dead. □

An SB2U-3 Vindicator of the US Marine Corps' Scouting Squadron (VMS 1) operating from MCAS Quantico. This unit was redesignated VMSB-131 on 1 July 1941, and was to convert to TBF-1 Avengers before seeing combat in the Pacific conflict

Blackburn Skua and Roc

Too, BIG, too slow ... *too late!* This uncomplimentary epitaph had already been coined by the Fleet Air Arm for the Skua and its turreted offspring, the Roc, by September 1940, when I was posted to No 759 FAA Fighter School at the newly-opened Royal Naval Air Station at Yeovilton, Somerset. The inadequacies of their performance and their tardiness in reaching the service were matters on which, at that time, I could do no more than speculate, but I could certainly attest to their very considerable size. Fresh from Netheravon and the Battle Trainer, which itself, was no minimus by contemporary single-engined aircraft standards, I was expecting something daintier than these monsters perched loftily above my head on tall and apparently fragile undercarriages, either one representing a great deal of ironmongery to be hoisted into the air by one small Perseus engine.

I was already aware that these Blackburn progeny were by no means the most favoured of aircraft in the inventory of the FAA of the day, but let it be said from the outset that the more unsavoury aspects of their reputations, if not *entirely* illdeserved, owed much to hearsay and exaggeration. Conceived barely five years earlier and already adjudged obsolescent in their intended rôles, they had now been assigned to advanced training tasks and we fledgling naval fighter pilots who had been expecting to get into the "hot rod" league forthwith could not but help wonder if we had been sent to the right stable.

Considering the radical nature of their design by British standards at the time of their conception, the Skua and the Roc were competent enough, maintaining Blackburn's name for rugged naval aircraft and adequately fulfilling the demands of the specifications that had given them birth, but as combat aircraft they were failures. It was perhaps their specifications that were ill-conceived, owing too much to contemporary tactical misconceptions and making insufficient allowance for developments in the potential opposition; shortcomings that were to be compounded in the aircraft in which they resulted by belated deliveries and then with an engine that fell somewhat short of the ideal.

The specification to which the Skua had been designed (O.27/34) had been framed by the Air Ministry in 1934, and was advanced enough for its day, but the tempo of combat aircraft development was just about to accelerate unprecedentedly; the advanced in design of the mid 'thirties was to be *passé* before the birth of the 'forties unless the subject of a continuing genealogical process keeping it in the forefront of its class. Sadly, the Skua had been subjected to no such process, and in that autumn of 1940, it was hard to believe that, only a few short years earlier, this decidedly substantial and certainly underpowered aeroplane was forseen as much as a two-seat fleet fighter as dive bomber!

Created by G E Petty, then Blackburn's assistant designer, and flown for the first time at Brough by Flt Lt A M "Dasher" Blake on 9 February 1937 — within a few months of the anticipated *service entry* of the aeroplane at the time its

The second prototype Skua (K5179) which differed from the first prototype primarily in having a lengthened nose. It was later fitted with turned-up wingtips. (Head of page) A Skua (L2928) of No 801 Sqdn at Donibristle, summer 1939

requirement had been formulated and eight months after no fewer than 190 examples had been ordered "off the drawing board" — the Skua had broken new ground from more than one aspect. Not only had it been the first British shipboard aircraft to be built to the modern all-metal cantilever mono-plane formula; it was the first British aircraft to have been designed with a view to the dive bombing mission being the first among equals in its repertoire. Years later*, the designer was to record Blackburn's regret at not being allowed to proceed with a simplified version of the Skua with a fixed undercarriage for the RAF as an answer to the 'Stuka', but as the use of such aircraft presupposed a measure of aerial superiority, I recall wondering at the time just *where* the RAF could have used these aircraft had it possessed them.

Of course, there is no gainsaying that the structure of the Skua was advanced in its day — had it been less so the

---

*The 5th Sir George Cayley Memorial Lecture given by G E Petty in 1958.

drawing board-to-prototype process might not have taken such an unconscionably long time — comprising a flush-riveted Alclad fuselage incorporating watertight buoyancy compartments beneath the pilot's floor and aft of the gunner's cockpit; a three-piece two-spar wing with a heavy-duty centre section bolted under the fuselage so that its upper surface formed the bottom of the forward watertight compartment and with sealed watertight bays between the main spars of the outer panels, and a metal cantilever tail assembly with fabric-covered movable surfaces.

To cater for its dive bombing rôle, the Skua's wing carried a flap of modified Zap type, which, housed in a recess between aileron and root, fulfilled the functions of both normal flap and dive brake. It was operated by an hydraulic jack between the inner flap runners in the mainplane, a flow control valve in the system forming an hydraulic lock for any flap position and relieving the main system of the considerable pressure set up by the deployment of the flap at speed. An unusual feature of the tail assembly was the placing of the entire elevator surface aft of the rudder trailing edge, endowing the aft end of the Skua with a distinctly odd appearance and intended to prevent blanketing and aid spin recovery.

The wing outer panels were manually folded aft about an inclined hinge, twisting to rest parallel with the fuselage, the leading edge being uppermost, and to meet stowage requirements a somewhat abbreviated centre section was dictated. As the mainwheel oleo-pneumatic shock-absorber struts were attached to the extremities of this centre section, the relatively narrow wheel track of 9 ft 7 in (2,92 m) resulted. The mainwheels retracted outwards and upwards into the outer wing panels under the action of an engine-driven hydraulic pump, and the fixed tailwheel had a self-centering shock-absorber strut with castoring fork.

Whereas the two prototypes had been fitted with the perfectly satisfactory, if insufficiently powerful, poppet-valve Mercury engine, force of circumstances — all Mercuries being earmarked for the expanding Blenheim programme — dictated the use of the less-than-satisfactory and no more powerful sleeve-valve Perseus in the production Skua. This drove a three-bladed two-position (10 deg pitch range) de Havilland propeller of 11 ft 6 in (3,50 m) diameter and offered 830 hp st 2,650 rpm for take-off and 745 hp at 2,400 rpm at 6,500 ft (1 980 m). There were two main tanks between the cockpits, these each being of 62 Imp gal (282 l) capacity, and these could be supplemented by a 39 Imp gal (177 l) reserve tank in the forward watertight compartment.

The first aircraft of the final production batch of Skuas (L3007) sporting a yellow finish with black diagonal bands on all surfaces for the target-towing role. This aircraft was originally delivered to No 20 Maintenance Unit at Aston Down in August 1939 and was built for the target-towing role from the outset

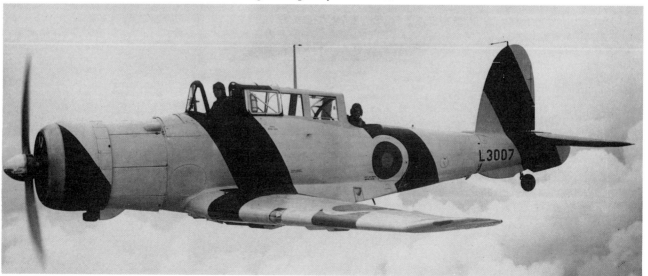

Armament included provision for a quartet of 0·303-in (7,7-mm) Browning Mk II machine guns widely spaced in the outer wing panels and a Lewis Mk IIIE of similar calibre on a Fairey pillar-type mounting in the rear cockpit. For dive bombing, a single 500-lb (226,8-kg) SAP bomb was carried on retractable ejector arms in a recess in the underside of the centre fuselage, these arms swinging the bomb clear of the propeller arc in a diving attack. Alternatively, two Light Series carriers mounted one under each mainplane could each carry four 30-lb (13,6-kg) practice bombs.

The Skua's turret fighter counterpart, the Roc, was likewise ordered "off the drawing board" and was to prove to have been singularly appropriately named, for the situation with which it was intended to contend was to prove just about as mythical as the legendary eastern bird from which it had acquired its appellation. The subject of a production contract (28 April 1937) only nine months after that let for the Skua, the Roc differed essentially in having a marginally wider fuselage amidships to accommodate a Boulton Paul A Mk II power-driven turret mounting four 0·303-in (7,7-mm) Brownings provided with 600 rpg. In short, the Roc was envisaged as a naval equivalent of the RAF's Boulton Paul Defiant, but at least in the day rôle it was visualised that the land-based fighter would operate in concert with Hurricanes, whereas the FAA had nothing to operate the shipboard Roc in concert with other than the Sea Gladiator! Of course, the fighter-versus-fighter mêlée was conveniently considered to be outside the two-seat shipboard fighter scenario. Even so, with the sort of performance of which the Roc was capable, I cannot to this day envisage quarry, other than the occasional maritime patrol flying boat or floatplane, incapable of transforming this cumbersome bird into prey. Fortunately for the FAA, the service was never to be called upon to take the Roc into combat and, to the best of my knowledge, it was never deck-landed.

Apart from the turret, the Roc differed from the Skua in a number of more minor respects. For example, the mainplane was rigged with two degrees of dihedral outboard of the centre section which obviated the need for the upturned wingtips featured by the Skua; the wing-mounted armament was deleted, the view being that, apart from weight considerations, its retention would afford the pilot temptation to use it offensively and he would be less likely to think in terms of manoeuvring his aircraft so that the turreted armament could be used to best advantage; the internal fuel capacity was reduced but provision was made for the mounting of a flush

The seventeenth production Skua (L2883) seen with Zap flaps fully deployed. This aircraft, delivered to Worthy Down on 10 January 1939, was the first to feature a modified tail oleo to overcome tailwheel judder and the first to leave Brough with arrester hook fitted

fitting 70 Imp gal (318 l) overload fuel tank beneath the centre section, and a 12-ft (3,66-m) diameter propeller had been fitted. The end product had seen yet further decline in an already inadequate power-to-weight ratio, which, coupled with an erroneous tactical concept, had rendered the Roc nothing less than a disaster.

By the time of my introduction to this ill-fated duo, all thought of using the Roc operationally had been discarded, of course, and the Skua itself had but a few more months of operational service remaining to it.

Once in the cockpit I felt as though I was seated in a greenhouse, an effect produced by the near-vertical flat-panelled windscreen, intended to afford good vision in wet weather, and the deep, aft-sliding hood. I adjusted my seat — which had a very wide adjustment range — so that my shoulders were way above the cockpit sill and religiously ran

A flight of Skuas of No 800 Squadron, that nearest the camera being L2934, the sixty-eighth production aircraft delivered to the unit mid-April 1939. No 800 Squadron's Skuas participated in the attack on Oran when the French Navy refused to surrender, participating in the bombardment of Genoa and the Battle of the Tyrrhenian Sea

through the preliminaries: (1) Activate main switch and undercarriage indicator switch when green lights should indicate that the undercarriage is locked; (2) Check that the undercarriage emergency actuating knob is not in the operative position and that the safety clip is in place; (3) Open cowling gills; (4) Check movement of flying controls; (5) Turn propeller pitch knob to fine position; (6) Check the

hydraulic hand pump by lowering and raising the flaps, and ensure that the control lever returns to neutral; (7) Set carburettor air intake to COLD; (8) Lock the canopy in the fully-open position.

After completing this check, the master fuel cock was turned on, the primer selector cock was turned to CARBURETTOR and the pump operated until 2 lb/sq in (0,14 kg/cm²) was

Blackburn Skua Cockpit Instrumentation Key:

1 Headphones socket
2 Speaking tube
3 Undercarriage control lever safety lock
4 Undercarriage control lever
5 Flap control lever
6 Rudder trim tab handwheel
7 Elevator trim tab handwheel
8 Telephone and microphone socket
9 Terminal blocks
10 Landing lamp dipping control lever
11 Engine controls friction adjuster
12 Engine throttle lever
13 Undercarriage and flaps instruction plate
14 Arrester hook indicator lamp
15 Safety harness release control
16 Arrester hook instruction plate
17 Arrester hook release control knob
18 Landing lamps switch and instruction plate
19 Mixture control lever
20 Terminal block
21 Rudder trim tab position indicator

22 Brake triple pressure gauge
23 Elevator trim tab position indicator
24 Flap position indicator
25 Coffman multi-breech engine starter loading handle
26 Hydraulic system pressure gauge
27 Propeller pitch control (green)
28 Air intake control (white)
29 Cockpit heating control (yellow)
30 Starboard cockpit lamp dimmer switch
31 Port cockpit lamp dimmer switch
32 Carburettor cut-out control
33 Engine starting push-button
34 Magneto switches
35 Control locking strut (port)
36 Clock
37 Undercarriage position indicator
38 Engine starter main switch
39 Watch holder
30 Port cockpit lamp
41 Reflector gunsight

42 Gunsight mounting
43 Speed restriction plate
44 ASI
45 Artificial horizon
46 Rate-of-climb indicator
47 Altimeter
48 Direction indicator
49 Turning indicator
50 Fuel cock panel (left to right: forward reserve tank, port main tank, starboard main tank and master)
51 Gun fire push-button
52 Brake lever
53 Control grip
54 Compass
55 Control column
56 Rudder pedals
57 Rev counter
58 Starboard cockpit lamp
59 Boost pressure gauge
60 Oil temperature gauge
61 Oil pressure gauge
62 Compass card holder
63 Engine temperature gauge
64 Control locking strut (starboard)
65 Cowling gill control handle

66 Oxygen regulator/contents gauges
67 Fuel contents gauge (forward reserve tank)
68 Fuel contents gauge (port main tank)
69 Fuel contents gauge (starboard main tank)
70 Fuel priming selector cock
71 Fuel priming pump
72 Identification lamp switchbox
73 Navigation lamp switch
74 Headlamp switch
75 Wireless morsing key
76 Hydraulic handpump handle
77 Fuel system diagram plate
78 Seat adjustment lever
79 Engine data plate (partially obscured by seat)
80 Pilot's seat
81 Signal pistol
82 Map box
83 Bomb fusing switches
84 Pitot head heating switch
85 Spin chute release control
86 Spin chute jettison control
87 Bomb jettison switchbox
88 Bomb selector switchboxes
89 Undercarriage emergency selector valve
90 Selector value safety clip

(Above and below) A Skua (L2928) of No 801 Squadron (also illustrated on page 29). No 801 was temporarily shore-based at Detling, Kent, during the Dunkirk evacuation in June 1940, operating over the beaches as a fighter unit of RAF Coastal Command

registered on the fuel pressure gauge. The engine was then turned over twice by hand and with the mixture control lever at NORMAL and eight or nine strokes of the primer pump, the magneto switches were activated. A cartridge was now inserted in the breach of the Coffman starter mounted on the portside of the cockpit, the starter was switched ON and the starter button pressed until the engine was firing evenly. At this stage, I recall most clearly an odd whispering sound emitted by the sleeve-valve Perseus which was warmed up at a fast tick-over for five minutes. A little throttle was applied until the oil pressure settled and the inlet oil temperature rose above 5°C (41°F). The air intake heat control was set to COLD and as soon as the oil temperature reached 15°C (59°F) the engine could be opened up for taxying.

After reaching take-off position, the elevator and rudder tabs were set to neutral and 7 deg port respectively, the mixture control and propeller pitch checked for NORMAL and FINE, and the cowling gills fully opened. Unless ample runway was available, some 25 deg of flap was applied for take-off, although this had an adverse effect on an already poor initial climb rate. It was necessary to get the tail well up at the start of the run and the Skua had to be held at a constant tail-up attitude until it left the runway of its own volition, the unstick distance being about 475 yards (434 m) with 25 deg of flap. It was vital not to pull the aircraft off the ground prematurely.

As soon as the aircraft was clear of the ground the undercarriage was raised, but if speed was below 100 knots (185 km/h) ASI, a red warning light came on and a warning horn sounded. The flaps were raised at about 120 knots (222 km/h) and at around 500 ft (150 m) to complete the somewhat lumbering take-off process, and with the aircraft cleaned up, the gills fully open and the propeller in coarse pitch, the sea level climb rate was about 740 ft/min (3,76 m/sec) for a fully laden aircraft, increasing to a maximum of about 930 ft/min (4,72 m/sec) at around 6,000 ft (1 830 m), after which it fell off fairly rapidly — the Skua was credited with an initial climb in excess of 1,500 ft/min (7,6 m/sec) but I can only say that if such *was* achieved then the aircraft must have been lightly laden indeed. The service ceiling, I was told, was about 19,000 ft (5 790 m), but I took my instructor's word for that as I didn't want to grow old proving it!

Aerobatics were prohibited below 5,000 ft (1 525 m) and deliberate spinning was prohibited under any circumstances, although I was never entirely sure why. It was rumoured that the Skua was something of a killer in a spin, tightening up disastrously after a few turns, and this had resulted in the provision of an anti-spin chute in the rear fuselage, a ring in the cockpit connecting with a long wire attached externally to the fuselage which tripped a spring-loaded hatch just behind the rudder. My instructor told me that recovery in the event of an accidental spin was effected in the normal manner (ie, application of full opposite rudder followed by forward pressure on the stick), the tail chute being used only in the event of control action failing to check the gyrations. I was also told that, if the aircraft was still spinning at 3,000 ft (915 m) I should get out immediately.

In a flat-out level run at full throttle, with two-and-a-half pounds of boost and the Perseus turning at 2,750 rpm — which it was not permissible to maintain for more than five minutes — the Skua could turn in a stately 195 knots (362 km/h) at 6,700 ft (2 040 m), and if the cowling gills were opened this was promptly knocked back to about 176 knots (326 km/h), but normally an even more sedate pace was set, the max continuous cruise with mixture control set to NORMAL, no more than one-and-a-quarter pounds of boost and 2,400 rpm, being of the order of 160 knots (296 km/h). The

Skua was no hot rod by any stretch of the imagination. It could not be sideslipped, and the stalling characteristics left something to be desired. On a straight glide with flaps and undercarriage extended, the stall occurred at around 66 knots (122 km/h) ASI, a wing dropping sharply and usually without warning, several hundred feet sometimes being required for recovery. With the aircraft cleaned up, the stall occurred at around 72 knots (133 km/h), and a high speed stall could result at almost any speed if the stick was pulled back coarsely and the stalling incidence reached, hence the aerobatic height limitation.

It was while diving that the Skua really came into its own.

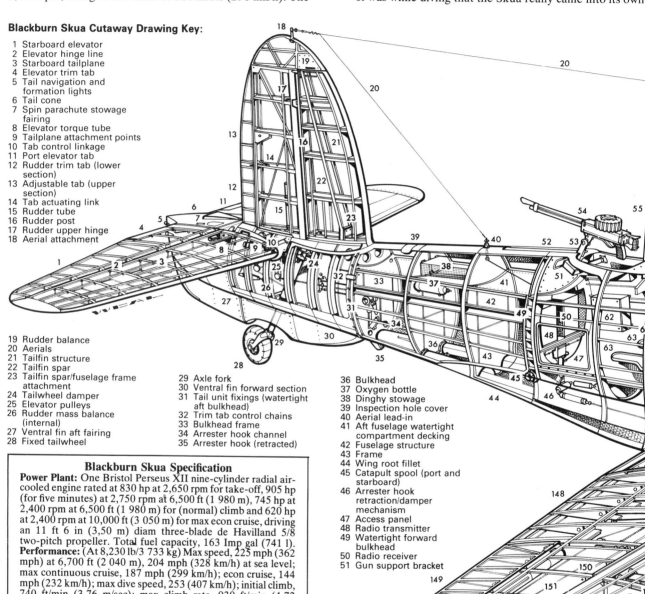

Blackburn Skua Cutaway Drawing Key:

1 Starboard elevator
2 Elevator hinge line
3 Starboard tailplane
4 Elevator trim tab
5 Tail navigation and formation lights
6 Tail cone
7 Spin parachute stowage fairing
8 Elevator torque tube
9 Tailplane attachment points
10 Tab control linkage
11 Port elevator tab
12 Rudder trim tab (lower section)
13 Adjustable tab (upper section)
14 Tab actuating link
15 Rudder tube
16 Rudder post
17 Rudder upper hinge
18 Aerial attachment

19 Rudder balance
20 Aerials
21 Tailfin structure
22 Tailfin spar
23 Tailfin spar/fuselage frame attachment
24 Tailwheel damper
25 Elevator pulleys
26 Rudder mass balance (internal)
27 Ventral fin aft fairing
28 Fixed tailwheel

29 Axle fork
30 Ventral fin forward section
31 Tail unit fixings (watertight aft bulkhead)
32 Trim tab control chains
33 Bulkhead frame
34 Arrester hook channel
35 Arrester hook (retracted)

36 Bulkhead
37 Oxygen bottle
38 Dinghy stowage
39 Inspection hole cover
40 Aerial lead-in
41 Aft fuselage watertight compartment decking
42 Fuselage structure
43 Frame
44 Wing root fillet
45 Catapult spool (port and starboard)
46 Arrester hook retraction/damper mechanism
47 Access panel
48 Radio transmitter
49 Watertight forward bulkhead
50 Radio receiver
51 Gun support bracket

Blackburn Skua Specification

Power Plant: One Bristol Perseus XII nine-cylinder radial air-cooled engine rated at 830 hp at 2,650 rpm for take-off, 905 hp (for five minutes) at 2,750 rpm at 6,500 ft (1 980 m), 745 hp at 2,400 rpm at 6,500 ft (1 980 m) for (normal) climb and 620 hp at 2,400 rpm at 10,000 ft (3 050 m) for max econ cruise, driving an 11 ft 6 in (3,50 m) diam three-blade de Havilland 5/8 two-pitch propeller. Total fuel capacity, 163 Imp gal (741 l).
Performance: (At 8,230 lb/3 733 kg) Max speed, 225 mph (362 mph) at 6,700 ft (2 040 m), 204 mph (328 km/h) at sea level; max continuous cruise, 187 mph (299 km/h); econ cruise, 144 mph (232 km/h); max dive speed, 253 (407 km/h); initial climb, 740 ft/min (3,76 m/sec); max climb rate, 930 ft/min (4,72 m/sec) at 6,000 ft (1 830 m); service ceiling, 19,100 ft (5 820 m); absolute ceiling, 20,500 ft (6 250 m); time to service ceiling, 43 min; landing speed, 75 mph (121 km/h); take-off distance (25 deg flap), 475 yds (432 m); landing distance, 450 yds (411 m).
Weights: Empty equipped, 5,496 lb (2 493 kg); take-off, 8,230 lb (3 733 kg).
Dimensions: Span, 46 ft 2 in (14,07 m); length, 35 ft 7 in (10,84 m); height (over radio mast), 14 ft 2 in (4,32 m); wing area, 312 sq ft (28,98 m²); width folded, 16 ft 2 in (4,93 m); wheel track, 9 ft 7 in (2,97 m).
Armament: Four 0·303-in (7,7-mm) Browning Mk II machine guns in wing outer panels, one 0·303-in (7,7-mm) Lewis Mk IIIE machine gun in rear cockpit of Fairey pillar-type mount, and one 500-lb (226·8-kg) SAP bomb.

52 Dorsal armament stowage slot
53 Fairey pillar-type gun swivel mounting
54 Lewis Mk IIIE machine gun
55 Gunner's aft canopy section (raised)
56 Cockpit canopy frame
57 Aerial mast
58 Sliding window sections
59 Wind deflector panel
60 Ammunition stowage
61 Gunner's seat cushion
62 First aid/stores
63 Gunner's foot rests
64 Bulkhead
65 Trailing aerial reel
66 Aft cockpit floor level
67 Bulkhead frame
68 Bomb recess aft fairing
69 Bomb pylon
70 Starboard mid-fuselage fuel tank (62 Imp gal/282 l capacity)
71 Oxygen cylinder

72 Fuel filler cap
73 Port mid-fuselage fuel tank (62 Imp gal/282 l capacity)
74 Spin chute external release cable
75 Support struts
76 Canopy fixed centre section
77 Dorsal identification light
78 Pilot's sliding canopy
79 Crash turnover pylon
80 Cockpit coaming
81 Seat harness
82 Pilot's seat
83 Adjustment lever
84 Cockpit floor level
85 Control linkage
86 Forward underfloor watertight compartment
87 Flare chute
88 Mid-section diagonal half frames
89 Forward reserve fuel tank (39 Imp gal/177 l capacity)
90 Filler neck
91 Oil tank (10 Imp gal/45,5 l capacity)
92 Filler cap
93 Control column grip
94 Reflector sight
95 Windscreen
96 Oil filler cap
97 Port aileron
98 Port wingtip formation light
99 Dihedral wingtip
100 Deck-handling hold
101 Port navigation light

102 Port wing watertight compartment
103 Anti-freeze spray pipe
104 Airscoop outlets
105 Ducting
106 Oil radiator cooler
107 Alcohol tank
108 De-icing hose
109 Compressed air reservoir
110 Starter housing
111 Engine support frame
112 Adjustable cooling gills
113 Bristol Perseus XII nine-cylinder sleeve-valve engine
114 Oil cooler ducts
115 Oil cooler intakes
116 Three-blade propeller
117 Spinner
118 Generator housing
119 Cowling fastening clips
120 Exhaust collector ring
121 Controllable air intake
122 Exhaust outlet
123 Mainwheel hinged fairing
124 Port Dunlop mainwheel
125 Bomb ejector release arms (extended)
126 Semi-armour-piercing (SAP) 500-lb (226,8-kg) bomb
127 Starboard mainwheel hinged fairing
128 Starboard Dunlop mainwheel
129 Radius arm
130 Mainwheel oleo leg
131 Oleo leg fairing

132 Telescopic strut
133 Undercarriage pivot point
134 Wing/fuselage forward attachment
135 Undercarriage hydraulic jack
136 Bomb recess forward fairing
137 Wing/fuselage aft attachment
138 Smoke float (port and starboard wing roots)
139 Smoke float bay doors
140 Mainwheel well
141 Forward spar
142 Wing machine gun ports
143 Blast tube
144 Two fixed Browning Mk II machine guns (port and starboard)
145 Ammunition magazines
146 Flap hydraulic jack
147 Wing fold hinge line
148 Starboard flap section
149 Starboard aileron frame
150 Wing ribs
151 Aileron tie-rods
152 Aileron push-pull/pulley link
153 Aileron bell-crank
154 Starboard wing watertight compartment

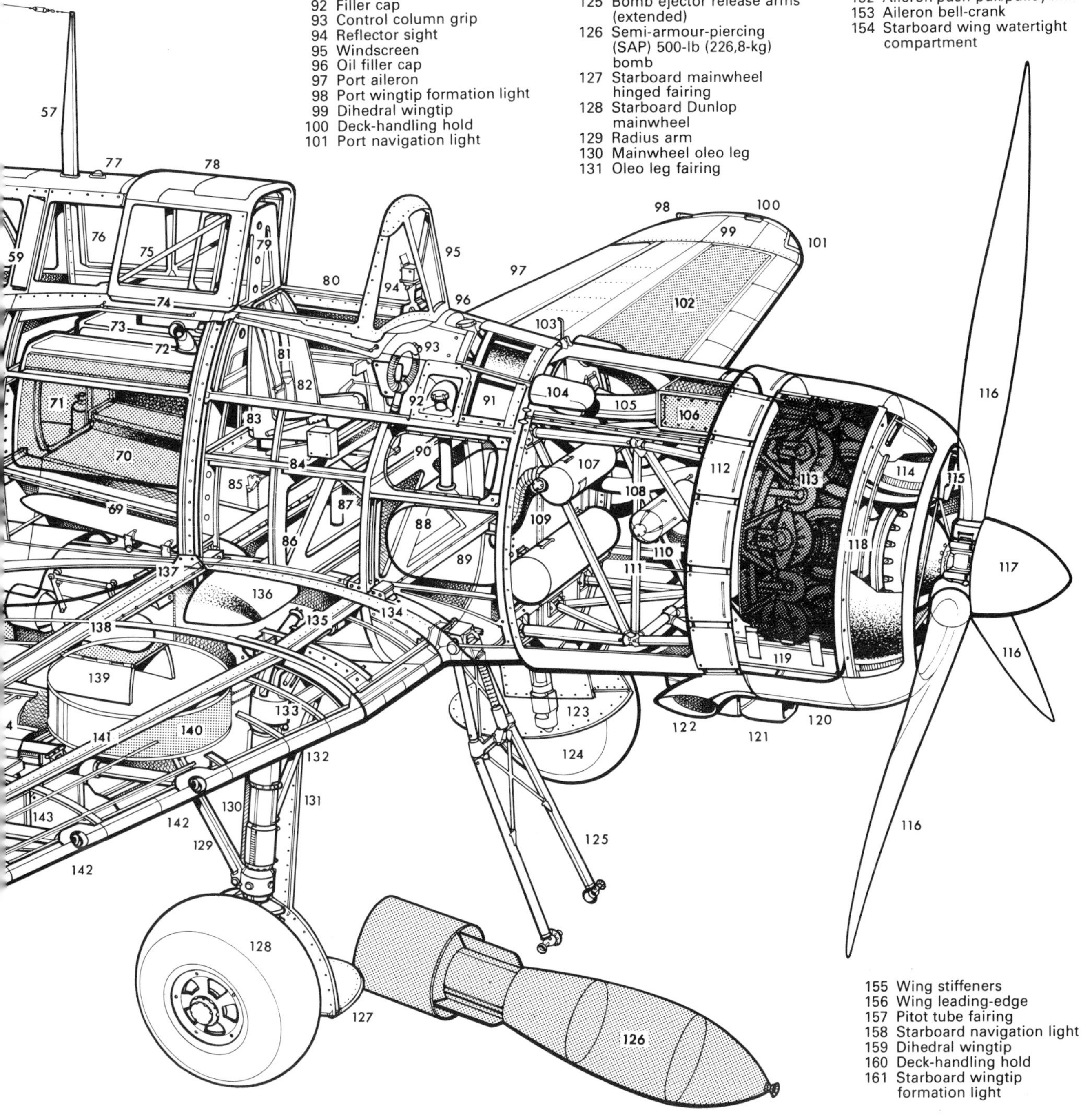

155 Wing stiffeners
156 Wing leading-edge
157 Pitot tube fairing
158 Starboard navigation light
159 Dihedral wingtip
160 Deck-handling hold
161 Starboard wingtip formation light

The technique that we were taught was to approach target at about 8,000 ft (2 440 m) at right angles, keeping it in sight until it disappeared under the leading edge of the wingtip, pulling up until it reappeared at the trailing edge and then winging over into a 70 deg dive, extending the Zap flaps fully and keeping the target at the top of the engine cowling. Release height was 3,000 ft (915 m) and pull-out was commenced, simultaneously retracting the flaps, being completed at around 1,500 ft (460 m) to avoid the bomb blast and any light flak. The elevator force required to pull out was heavy.

Subsequently, I was to fly quite a number of US and German dive bombers and the Skua matched up well with the best of these as regards its diving characteristics, but it had only a two-position propeller and this tended to overspeed in the dive before terminal velocity was reached. However, a nicely screaming propeller was always to be considered a psychologically aggressive asset in any dive bomber.

The Skua accumulated a pretty poor landing record on both carriers and land, much of this being conveniently attributed to the naval pilot's general lack of familiarity with monoplanes, but in truth it did not *have* very good landing characteristics. The approach was normally made with some engine to flatten the gliding angle and the recommended circuit speed was 120 knots (22 km/h), turning into wind for a straight approach at not less than 500 ft (152 m) maintaining a speed of not less than 80 knots (148 km/h) and completing flattening out before closing the throttle. The view from the cockpit was not ideal and the long-stroke Vickers oleo-pneumatic shock-absorber legs were of the bouncy type, which, combined with the fact that the Skua was nose heavy,

meant that on cutting the engine one tended to land on the main wheels rather than make a three-pointer. On a carrier deck the arrester hook was prone to missing the arrester wires with the inevitable result of a barrier crash. The Dunlop pneumatic brakes had to be applied with the utmost care and then only in an emergency, for harsh braking during taxying or the landing run would tip the Skua over on its nose as certainly as God made little apples. The landing distance was about 450 yards (410 m).

My introduction to the Roc was anything but auspicious. I well remember clambering onto the wing and over the cockpit sill of this "turreted Skua" for the first time that autumn, 40 years ago, and the somewhat timorous feeling that it evoked. Yeovilton was still no more than three semi-completed runways — from which labourers had to be cleared every time we wanted to fly — and a sea of mud. Somehow the omens did not seem propitious for my initial essay with this unprepossessing-looking aeroplane, and, indeed, on take-off during my first Roc solo, one undercarriage leg hit a pile of rubble hastily dumped by workmen crossing the active runway without permission. Although I certainly felt the thump, everything seemed to work until I came in to land. Then the leg that had hit the rubble refused to extend. Eventually, I was instructed to belly land in the mud, so reducing the Navy's Roc strength by one aircraft — for which no tears were shed.

In so far as the Roc was concerned, it had one thing over the Skua and that was that its four-gun Boulton Paul turret did serve to keep the tail down and, in consequence, it suffered fewer ground accidents, but the impression of being underpowered was even more marked than with the Skua. The handling characteristics did not differ markedly from those of the Skua, but performance was certainly impaired by the weight and drag of the turret, and climb in particular suffered. At 7,800 lb (3 538 kg), this was 710 ft/min (3,6 m/sec) increasing to 830 ft/min (4,2 m/sec) at 5,700 ft (1 735 m), and in seeking an improvement, tests were conducted with the smaller-diameter Skua propeller. With this the sea level climb rate deteriorated even further, to 670 ft/min (3,4 m/sec), but increased to 1,000 ft/min (5,1 m/sec) at 5,900 ft (1 800 m) and 1,900 ft (580 m) were added to the opera-

(Above left) The majority of production Rocs, such as L3084 illustrated, were delivered direct from the factory to maintenance units for distribution to second-line squadrons. This particular aircraft went to No 27 MU Shawbury at the end of August 1939 and was converted for target towing. (Below) The prototype Roc (L3057) was, in fact, the first production aircraft and, together with the next two aircraft, was utilised for contractor's trials

(Above and below) Rocs operating from RNAS Donibristle in November 1939. The aircraft in the foreground (L3118) and the furthermost aircraft (L3114) in the upper photograph have rear fairing sections lowered to permit turret rotation. The Roc's first-line service spanned only a few months and although intended for shipboard operation it never made a deck landing. A few Rocs survived in the target-towing role until mid-1943 when spares were finally exhausted

tional ceiling. In the event, the Roc was never to equip a squadron, although four had joined the eight Skuas of No 806 Sqdn at Eastleigh in February 1940, and six others joined the six Skuas on the strength of No 801 Sqdn in the following June. As for the rest, these were delivered direct to RAF maintenance units for distribution to second-line FAA units, such as our No 759 Fighter School at Yeovilton.

Whatever its shortcomings as a combat aircraft may have been, the Skua had at least seen its brief hour of glory. Nos 800 and 803 squadrons had been the first recipients of this then-new *fighter*-cum-dive bomber when, late in 1938, the initial Skuas to be accepted by the FAA had been ferried to Worthy Down to supplant the Nimrod and Osprey biplanes of these units aboard the equally new carrier *Ark Royal*. No 801 Squadron had followed suit aboard *Furious* and, when war came, some had been with No 806 Squadron at Eastleigh. The *Ark Royal* had taken its complement of Skua squadrons to Freetown, Sierra Leone, for South Atlantic convoy protection patrols, but not before, on 25 September 1939, a Skua of No 803 Squadron had gained the FAA's first "kill" of WW II by bringing down a Do 18 flying boat while escorting the battleships *Nelson* and *Rodney* off Heligoland.

Nos 800 and 803 squadrons were to be disembarked at Hatston, near Kirkwall in the Orkneys, in January 1940, and it was from here that the aforementioned hour of glory was to be achieved. On 10 April 1940, seven of No 800's Skuas accompanied by nine from No 803 had made a 330-mile (530-km) night flight from Hatston to arrive — at the very limits of their radius — at dawn over Bergen Harbour, sinking the cruiser *Konigsberg* alongside the Skoltegrund Mole as the result of a classic dive bombing attack, all but one of the Skuas regaining their base. Re-embarked aboard *Ark Royal* 11 days later to cover the ill-fated Narvik operation, they enjoyed less luck, virtually all being lost, some failing to find the carrier and ditching at sea, others being shot down, two

landing on Swedish soil and being interned, and others being abandoned in Norway.

Shore-based at Detling in Kent, No 801 Squadron had flown missions over the Dunkirk beaches in June 1940, one of these Skuas having provided a graphic example of this Blackburn aircraft's innate sturdiness when it wallowed back to Detling riddled with holes — there were allegedly nine holes in one propeller blade alone and the top cylinder of its Perseus engine had been shot away, as had also the pilot's windscreen and canopy — and with the gunner dead and the pilot dying at the controls. Meanwhile, the losses suffered by the Skua squadrons of the *Ark Royal* had been made good and in May the carrier had proceeded to the Mediterranean, participating in the attack on Oran when the French Navy refused to surrender. The Skuas of No 800 Squadron subsequently escorted numerous convoys from Gibraltar to Cape Bon, provided air cover at Dakar and participated in the bombardment of Genoa and the Battle the Tyrrhenian Sea. In November 1940, I had found myself, together with two other fledgelings from my course at Yeovilton, flying replacement Skuas to Nos 801 and 803 squadrons at Hatston from Blackburn's factory at Brough. We were attached to the squadrons for a short period until their own replacement pilots arrived.

At the time, they were engaged in missions against targets on the Norwegian coast; hairy sorties that stretched the range capabilities of the Skua to the limit, the long and arduous outward flights across the North Sea being enlivened with knowledge of the ever-present possibility of a committee of Messerschmitt Bf 109Es being on hand to greet their Norwegian landfall. The Bf 109E versus Skua could hardly be considered a fair match, so the pilots of the latter had to employ tactical cunning in order to survive such encounters, this usually involving withdrawal from the target area by diving to sea level and hugging the steep fjord walls. If, in

Three Rocs were mounted on floats, the type having been intended from the outset to include the role of float fighter in its repertoire, and the second of these, L3057, is illustrated below. Flown on 23 December 1938, it had an enlarged underfin fitted to improve stability, but performance proved disappointing and the aircraft was relegated to the role of instructional airframe. L3057 was originally the very first Roc

A close-up of Roc L3118 flying from RNAS Donibristle in November 1939 where it was operated briefly by No 769 Squadron which flew a miscellaneous fleet of aircraft. The general arrangement drawing (below right) depicts the standard production Skua, the lower side profile illustrating the Roc fighter derivative

spite of this hair-raising tactic, a Messerschmitt pilot persisted in his pursuit, the Skua's observer would open up with his Lewis at the limit of the weapon's range, which was just outside the effective firing range of the German fighter's armament. If this didn't dissuade the pursuer, then, at a word from the observer, the Skua's pilot would dump his flaps with a dramatic effect on closing speed and the Messerschmitt pilot now found himself so busy attempting to avoid collision that he had no time to get the Skua in his gunsight. Nevertheless, despite this and other artifices employed by their crews, the losses in Skuas on operations of this type were high as they were highly vulnerable during the approach to the target area, and it was clearly apparent that the operational days of these aircraft were strictly numbered.

No 800 Squadron embarked at Gibralter with its Skuas in March 1941 aboard *Furious,* and upon the carrier's return, the Skuas gave place to Fulmars at Lee-on-Solent and *finis* was written to the operational career of this Blackburn aeroplane, although the Skua *nearly* soldiered on a little longer. I was stationed at Donibristle in the summer of 1941, when a TOP SECRET signal arrived, ordering all former Skua operational pilots to pick up aircraft from various nominated centres and report with them forthwith to the Royal Naval Air Station St Meryn, near Padstow in Cornwall. There it was revealed that a plan had been prepared to fly the Skuas from Exeter in a strike against the *Scharnhorst* and the *Gneisenau* at Brest! Brest must surely have been just about the most heavily defended of any target at that stage in the conflict, and the designated strike leader, while stating his willingness to lead this "death or glory" attack, presented the powers-that-were most forcibly with his view that many if not all the valuable crews that would participate in the attack would be lost in a futile attempt to destroy these targets as the Skuas had no more chance of penetrating the highly concentrated flak under which the vessels would shelter, let alone the intensive fighter cover that would undoubtedly be mounted, than would an iceberg of survival in hell. Commonsense won the day, the plan was abandoned and the Skuas were returned to their more mundane tasks of advanced training and target towing. *Sic transit gloria!* □

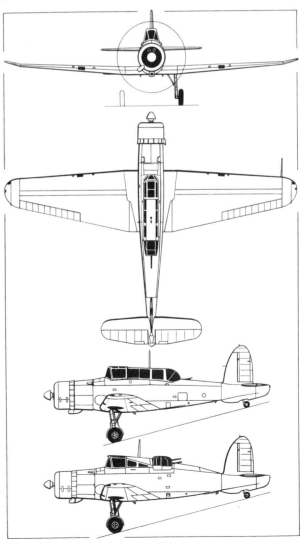

Grumman Wildcat

THE DESIGN of any combat aircraft involves a measure of compromise and that of the shipboard single-seat fighter perhaps more than most as its success depends particularly heavily on the right balance being struck between the demands of combat and the dictates of the venue in which it is to spend its working life; it is essentially an amalgam of conflicting elements. A masterpiece in coalescence of the contradictory factors called for in a fighter suited to the naval environment was, in my view, the corpulent but rugged and pugnacious little warplane, which, created by Leroy Grumman and his associates Leon A Swirbul and William T Schwendler in the late 'thirties, was to establish Grumman's famed genus *Felis*.

A venomous-looking little bumble-bee of a fighter, the Wildcat — destined to be the progenitor of a dynasty of "Cats" — made up for its lack of aesthetic appeal in purposefulness of appearance, but pulchritude was never to be a characteristic of carrier-based single-seat fighters until the début, some years later, of the ballerina-like Seafire, and elegance was certainly no criterion by which a naval fighter was adjudged in late 1940, when the Wildcat began to appear

(Head of page) F4F-3s of VF-3 flown by Cdr J S Thach (foreground) and Lt Edward H O'Hare, and (below) the XF4F-2 in its original configuration with Cyclone engine, short-span wings and rounded tail surfaces. This prototype was to be reworked as the XF4F-3 with a larger wing and a two-stage supercharged Twin Wasp engine.

in the inventory of the Fleet Air Arm. Not that we knew the portly little Grumman by that gloriously emotive appellation in those days, for their Lordships of the Admiralty had, in their wisdom, seen fit to bestow the singularly uninspiring name of Martlet on this first American recruit to the ranks of Britain's seagoing naval air component.

At the time I had joined the Fleet Air Arm at the outbreak of WW II, the service's fighter armoury had been far from impressive, comprising as it did the Gloster Sea Gladiator and the Blackburn Roc, with the Fairey Fulmar in prospect. The single-seat Gladiator biplane was a beautiful flying machine, but, by 1940, a complete anachronism; the two-seat Roc, with its powered four-gun turret tucked in behind the pilot, was more like the mythical bird that it was named after than a serious military aeroplane, and, in any case, was destined never to be operated from a carrier, while the elegant Fulmar, when it arrived, had been conceived to a misguided specification. Suddenly, into this stable of mediocrities was led what was to us a *real* warhorse; an aircraft that bid fair to re-establish the Fleet Air Arm in the fighter business in earnest. I was overjoyed when I learned that I had been posted to No 802 Squadron at Donibristle to participate in the formation there of the second FAA squadron to be mounted on this new Grumman fighter.

I shall never forget that November day in 1940 when I had my first sight of the Martlet, which, incidently, had still to be dubbed officially Wildcat by the US Navy. I was sitting in the crew room with other pilots awaiting the arrival of our first squadron aircraft which the CO had gone to collect from Abbotsinch where the Martlets were being assembled after shipment to the Clyde. An air of excited expectancy understandably pervaded the crew room as we discussed the prospect of getting to grips with what we had been told was quite a "hot number", but all conversation ended abruptly as a low whine overhead brought us to our feet. As we scurried to the windows they were almost shattered by the thunderclap of noise as the Martlet nearly lifted the roof off. As I pressed my face against the glass, I saw this tiny, barrel-like aeroplane shooting vertically skyward, gyrating in a breathtaking series of vertical rolls. The anticipation of getting into its cockpit was almost too much to bear.

The fighter cavorting with such abandon over Donibristle on that winter's day had, in fact, been flown as a prototype more than three years earlier, on 2 September 1937, yet as we took delivery it had still to enter service with the US Navy for which it had been created! Unbeknown to us, the Grumman fighter's start had fallen somewhat short of the auspicious; its first prototype, the XF4F-2, had been dogged by misfortune. Its R-1830-66 Twin Wasp engine had proffered a crop of crankshaft bearing failures which had kept the aircraft on the ground for considerable periods; a fire in the aft fuselage had followed and then, during a simulated deck landing at Anacostia, the engine had cut and heavy damage had resulted. This sequence of events had hardly commended the new fighter to its intended user service and, not surprisingly, the production contract had been awarded to the competitive Brewster XF2A-1.

Disappointed at having lost the battle but convinced that there was still a war to be won, Grumman had persisted with reworking the basic aircraft and mating the airframe with a new Twin Wasp engine with a two-speed two-stage supercharger. The prototype, by now redesignated XF4F-3 (alias G-36), had resumed flight testing on 12 February 1939. By this time, a larger wing had been fitted to keep the loading within acceptable limits despite the weight growth that had resulted from the new engine's supercharger with its intercooler and associated ducting, and the angular wing and tail surface tips that were to become almost a Grumman trademark had made their appearance. A stream of changes and modifications had followed, many associated with what was for some time to prove an elusive search for satisfactory engine and turbo-supercharger cooling.

Finally, in August 1939, Grumman had received a production order for 54 F4F-3s and, with the commencement of World War II in Europe, the company began to solicit orders for the new fighter from both France and the UK. A French order had been placed before the end of 1939, calling for 81 aircraft with which it was intended to equip squadrons aboard the *Béarn,* and the carriers *Joffre* and *Painlevé* then under construction. Since the Twin Wasp with the two-stage two-speed supercharger specified for the US Navy's F4F-3s was not available for export, the French elected to power their fighters with the R-1820-G205A version of the Wright Cyclone, whereas the British, who placed a contract for 100

fighters for the FAA, selected the Pratt & Whitney S3C4-G version of the Twin Wasp, both these engines having single-stage two-speed superchargers. The two export models had been designated G-36A and G-36B by the parent company, and both were fixed-wing carrier fighters, but when the Royal Navy learned of the forthcoming availability of a folding-wing version of the aircraft, it was concluded that this desirable feature warranted a small delay in delivery.

The first export aeroplane, a G-36A for France's *Marine Nationale,* had flown at Bethpage on 11 May 1940, the day after the *Wehrmacht* began the assault that was to lead to France's defeat. As a consequence of the débâcle on the continent of Europe, the entire batch of Grumman fighters ordered by France had been transferred to Britain and it was these aircraft that had begun to reach Britain in the previous August, had been issued to No 804 Squadron at Hatston in the Orkneys and were now arriving at Donibristle for our squadron. Designated Martlet Mk Is, the first half-dozen of the ex-French contract fighters had been assembled by Scottish Aviation and, apart from one for Boscombe Down trials, had been delivered to No 804 Squadron which had attained full strength by November when deliveries switched to us.

No 804 had experienced a few difficulties with the Martlet's narrow-track, "squashy" undercarriage and a number of minor accidents had led to the formation of a "Wingtip Club", and Boscombe Down trials, while pronouncing the Grumman fighter to be reasonably pleasant to fly and free of vices, found some grounds for criticism. Carbon monoxide contamination of the cockpit was noted and faults included a violent draught whenever the canopy was opened in flight, other than at low rpm, and the lack of auto-boost meant that the pilot had to give his attention to manual adjustment of boost throughout the flight. The omission of provision for jettisoning the canopy and the somewhat confusing arrangement of some of the controls were also criticised. Faults the Grumman fighter may well have had, but for me, in November 1940, it was a case of love at first sight; the Martlet

(Above right) An F4F-3A of US Marine Corps Squadron VMF-121 at Quantico. The F4F-3A had a single-stage two-speed supercharger and relatively few (95) of this model were built. (Below) An F4F-4 of US Navy Squadron VF-41 (the original VF-4) aboard the USS Ranger, this being one of the first US Navy units to operate the Wildcat

(Above and below left) The first export Grumman G-36A for France's Aéronavale, this eventually being diverted to the UK as a Martlet Mk I (AX753). This aircraft, the first of 81 ordered by France, was first flown at Bethpage on 11 May 1940

was one of those few aircraft that I have encountered over the years with which I have instinctively felt rapport.

After the CO had completed his impromptu exposition of the Martlet's *joie de vivre* and had landed, I walked around the aircraft, taking in every detail of its sturdy fuselage, stubby mid wing, squat undercarriage, powerful radial engine and wide-chord propeller blades. Among its features were two not previously seen as equipment on British-operated aircraft — its 0·5-in (12,7-mm) Colt-Browning machine guns and its sting-type arrester hook.

The cockpit held its quota of surprises. It was unexpectedly roomy and all the instruments were calibrated in metric units, although all other traces of its originally-intended Gallic recipient had been removed. Its unique features included gun cocking handles, tailwheel lock and toe brakes on the rudder pedals. Sitting on the parachute pack, I realised that the control column was much farther forward than in British fighters, and even with the rudder pedals adjusted fully rearward, I was at full stretch with one pedal pushed fully forward, and I certainly could not press the foot brake with my toes. This was to trouble me later, until I developed a technique to overcome the problem. Coordinated rudder/brake control was vital during take-off and landing in the Martlet, the wide fuselage of which blanked the rudder when the aircraft was in the tail down position, seriously reducing rudder effectiveness to control swing on take-off due to slipstream effect and engine torque, or on landing in a crosswind.

Perhaps the Grumman fighter was as ugly as sin to the aeronautical aesthete, but to me the Martlet was a little beauty and I savoured every second of my flight initiation. The starting procedure was simple: fuel pressure was first raised by the hand-operated wobble pump, and a plunger-type pump was then operated to prime the Wright Cyclone engine, which, turned over by an inertia starter, emitted a deep throaty roar as it came to life. That Cyclone absolutely oozed power by comparison with the engines to which I had become accustomed. Taxying, on the other hand, required

circumspection, especially in a crosswind which could get under a wing and bring the opposite tip very close to the ground — hence No 804 Squadron's "Wingtip Club". A similar situation could result from taxying too fast around corners, and as the aircraft rolled on its remarkably soft, narrow-track undercarriage, we pilots were soon to learn caution.

Before taking-off, the tailwheel had to be locked, but even with this precaution a vicious take-off swing could develop to the left if not countered smoothly by brake and rudder operation right from the start. My technique was to have my toes on the upper part of the rudder pedals and to use touches of brake and slow throttle opening to keep straight during the initial part of the run, and then, as the speed increased, I slid my toes on to the lower portions of the rudder pedals and depended on strong rudder movement for directional control. There is no doubt that take-off was a hazardous operation until, a few months after the Martlet came into FAA service, the small, solid rubber-tyred tailwheel was replaced by a much larger pneumatic type which raised the tail about nine inches (23 cm) and unblanked just enough of the rudder from the fuselage in the ground attitude to ease the directional control problem. Care had to be taken not to exceed the maximum boost of 45½ in manifold pressure as no automatic boost control was fitted on these early Martlets. The Hamilton hydromatic propeller in fine pitch gave 2,500 rpm and pulled the aircraft into the air in a remarkably short distance.

After unstick the pilot had some moments of high workload as he wound the undercarriage up by cranking a hand lever on the starboard cockpit wall. This operation took about 29 turns and was usually initiated after a speed of 130 knots (210 km/h) was reached, when the engine was throttled back to 37½ in boost. After the undercarriage was fully tucked away, the vernier adjustment on the pitch control was used to reduce rpm to 2,300 and the climb established at 134 knots (250 km/h). At this stage also, the canopy was pulled shut, this always being left fully open during take-off, no draught or buffet being experienced at the lower end of the speed range.

The manual undercarriage retraction system inevitably led to a "roller-coaster" climb-out on many occasions; it also led to one of the first Martlet accidents in the UK when the R/T lead attached to the right earpiece of the pilot's headset became entangled in the undercarriage handle on take-off and the pilot wound his head down into the cockpit and crashed, receiving serious head injuries. Incidentally, the radio fitted to the Martlet was very much superior to any British R/T in service in 1940.

The initial climb rate was one of the most sensational

aspects of the performance of this little fighter. At 3,300 ft/min (16,8 m/sec), there was nothing around to touch it, and it was no slouch in level flight. Although we were to find that level speed was lower than that claimed, with top speed of 265 knots (491 km/h) at 15,000 ft (4,570 m) and about 248 knots (459 km/h) at sea level, it was as good as the Hurricane Mk I and, in so far as we were aware at the time, the fastest fighter available for embarked operations. It was also a man-oeuvrable aeroplane with a good rate of roll, but it needed plenty of stick handling on the part of the pilot to get the best out of it. By comparison with its British counterparts it was more stable to fly and therefore heavier to manoeuvre.

I was to engage in many mock combats with RAF Hurricanes and Spitfires and was soon convinced that the Martlet was a formidable fighting aircraft, capable of holding its own in every phase except that it was slower than its RAF opponents in the dive. However, this shortcoming was more than compensated for by its steep climb, excellent turning circle and completely innocuous stalling characteristics. The pilot had a better all-round view from the Martlet and, of course, there were those 'fifty calibre machine guns which were to prove to be possibly the best fighter weapons of the war, although, admittedly, somewhat less reliable than the British 0·303-in (7,7-mm) gun in that they were more prone to seizing in low temperatures. Nevertheless, for the first time, the fighter pilots of the Fleet Air Arm could feel themselves to be in the same league as their RAF contemporaries, and we of No 802 Squadron were certainly exhilarated by the news that, on 25 December 1940, the Martlet had drawn blood and had thus gained for itself the distinction of being the first US fighter in British service to destroy an enemy aircraft in WW II. This notable event had taken place when two Martlets of No 804 Squadron patrolling Scapa Flow had intercepted and forced down a Junkers Ju 88.

Of course, while we were familiarising ourselves with the idiosyncracies of this Grumman fighter at Donibristle, development had been proceeding apace at its parent company's Bethpage plant, where the first of our Martlet Mk IIs had, in fact, flown during the previous October, albeit still with *fixed* wings. Grumman had devised an ingenious hydraulically-operated wing folding mechanism in which the mainplanes pivoted about the mainspar as they folded back to lie against the fuselage sides, and, as previously related, the British Admiralty had opted to await the availability of the folding-wing variant, which, with the two-row Pratt & Whitney S3C4-G Twin Wasp as opposed to the single-row Wright R-1820-G205A Cyclone powering the French-contract fighters with which we had been issued, had been assigned the

(Above) A Royal Navy Martlet Mk II undergoing manufacturer's trials with national insignia temporarily and crudely overpainted, and an NX series experimental registration applied, and (below) a Martlet MK III in North Africa mid-1941 serving with the Royal Navy Fighter Unit. This was one of 30 F4F-3As assigned to Greece and then diverted to the UK.

(Above right and below) Early production F4F-4s photographed during manufacturer's trials prior to delivery to the US Navy. The F4F-4 was the first Wildcat to feature wing folding and the British Navy's Martlet Mk IV was essentially similar apart from the engine which was an R-1820-40B Cyclone, a single-stage two-speed unit.

Grumman Wildcat Mk II Cockpit Instrumentation Key

1 Cylinder temperature gauge
2 Fuel cock
3 Elevator trimming tab control
4 Throttle lever friction nut
5 Mixture control lever
6 Throttle lever
7 Rudder trimming tab control
8 Port aileron trimming tab control
9 Arrester hook control
10 Engine speed indicator
11 Flap selector lever
12 Undercarriage warning lamp
13 Propeller speed control
14 Tailwheel locking control
15 Carburettor heat control
16 Windscreen de-icing control
17 Supercharger control
18 Propeller selector switch
19 Propeller safety switch
20 Reflector sight lamp dimmer switch
21 Ignition switch
22 Fuel handpump
23 Cockpit lamp
24 Reflector sight
25 Reflector sight mounting
26 Directional gyro
27 Artificial horizon
28 ASI
29 Altimeter
30 Turn-and-bank indicator
31 Rate-of-climb/descent indicator
32 Boost gauge
33 Oil temperature/oil pressure/fuel pressure triple gauge
34 Inertia starter switch
35 Fuel contents gauge
36 Fire extinguisher control
37 Cylinder priming pump
38 Cowling gills control
39 Carburettor temperature gauge
40 Temperature gauge
41 Volt/ammeter
42 Generator/battery/gun master switches
43 Gun selector switches (6)
44 Cockpit lighting rheostats
45 Canopy locking control
46 AVR-20 receiver
47 R.3003 push-buttons (2) and switch
48 AVT-15 transmitter
49 Undercarriage ratchet release
50 Undercarriage control
51 Undercarriage mechanical indicator
52 Torque tube
53 Electric boost pump switch
54 Rudder pedals
55 Pilot's seat
56 Control column (shaded)

designation Martlet Mk II. Translating an ingenious wing-folding design into functioning hardware proved to be somewhat more time consuming than had been anticipated, however, and it had been decided, therefore, to accept the first 10 British-contract aircraft *without* wing folding; the first *genuine* Mk II was not to arrive until August 1941.

The initial US Navy version, the F4F-3, also lacked wing folding and was being built in parallel with the export aeroplanes. The first F4F-3 had been delivered to US Navy squadron VF-4 on 5 December 1940, this unit having taken

its new equipment to sea aboard the USS *Ranger,* together with the similarly-equipped VF-7 aboard USS *Wasp*, early in 1941, on a shakedown cruise to Guantanamo. This cruise had thrown up a number of problems. The windscreen of the F4F-3 had revealed a tendency to collapse and had demanded strengthening in consequence; some carburation problems at altitude demonstrated a need for fuel tank pressurization, and after several unpleasant incidents, including at least one fatality, resulting from a tendency on the part of the specified wing flotation bags to inflate of their own accord in flight, it had been decided to delete this item of equipment.

These early service snags were progressively ironed out and additional squadrons began working up on the F4F-3 throughout 1941, including VF-42 aboard USS *Yorktown*, VF-5 aboard USS *Ranger* (joining VF-4 which was to be redesignated VF-41), VF-71 aboard the USS *Wasp* (VF-7 aboard the same carrier becoming VF-72), VF-3 aboard the USS *Saratoga* and VF-8 aboard the USS *Hornet*. As a result of delay in production of the two-stage two-speed super-charged R-1830-76 engine, a production batch of fighters was completed with the single-stage R-1830-90 Twin Wasp and these, known as F4F-3As, were assigned in May 1941 to VF-6, which later took them aboard the USS *Enterprise,* and to US Marine Corps squadron VMF-111 at Quantico, the similarly-based VMF-121 receiving standard F4F-3s, as did also VMF-211 at Ewa.

With the arrival of folding-wing Martlet Mk IIs to replace our fixed-wing Mk Is during the summer of 1941, No 802 Squadron began preparations to embark aboard the tiny escort carrier HMS *Audacity,* a converted German merchant vessel of 5,600 tons. The Martlet Mk II had been tested at Boscombe Down where it had been found to weigh about 1,000 lb (454 kg) more than the Mk I, but then, apart from the somewhat heavier Twin Wasp engine, it had wing-folding, with the inevitable weight penalty that such imposed, and toted an extra pair of 0·5-in Colt-Browning M-2s. Understandably, this extra weight had some affect on per-formance and Boscombe Down testing revealed a maximum speed in MS gear of 254 knots (471 km/h) TAS as 5,400 ft (1 647 m) and the same speed in FS gear at 13,000 ft (3 965 m), a range of 773 nm (1 432 km) being achieved at 15,000 ft (4 575 m) cruising at 143 knots (265 km/h) IAS at full throttle in weak mixture and MS gear.

The first thing that I noticed with the Martlet Mk II was the improvement in forward view resulting from the smaller-diameter, more tapered cowling of the Twin Wasp engine. Prior to starting, the fuel cock was set to MAIN, the throttle was opened a half-inch, the mixture control was set to idle cut-off, the propeller master switch ON, the propeller selector switch to AUTO, the propeller speed control was pushed fully in, M ratio supercharger was pushed in, the carburettor heat control was set to COLD and the cowling gills were opened. The propeller was turned by hand two or three times, the engine was primed, the booster pump switched on, the ignit-ion switch was turned to BOTH ON and the starter energised for

20 seconds. As soon as the Twin Wasp began to fire regularly, the mixture control was moved slowly to AUTO RICH, and with the engine running steadily it was noticeable how much quieter a combination was the Twin Wasp and Curtiss elec-tric propeller than had been the Cyclone and Hamilton Stan-dard propeller of the Martlet Mk I.

The engine was run as slowly as possible for half-a-minute and then warmed up at a fast tick-over, the priming pump being screwed down and the booster pump switched off. After the usual checks, the tailwheel was unlocked and taxy-ing commenced, but care had to be exercised not to overheat the less-than-efficient brakes, particularly in a high wind. The elevator trim tab was set one division forward, the rudder tab three divisions starboard and the aileron tab to neutral; the flaps were set DOWN and the supercharger in M ratio. The tailwheel was locked and it was advisable to taxi a short distance to ensure that it had centralised and locked. It was also advisable to avoid taking-off out of wind owing to the wing-dropping proclivity resulting from the narrow-track undercarriage.

The Martlet Mk II had a strong tendency to veer to port during take-off, this being accentuated by the use of the flaps, and its was necessary to hold the aircraft down until 140 knots (259 km/h) IAS had been reached, and to throttle back before selecting undercarriage UP and commencing cranking the handle. Maximum rate of climb was 140 knots (259 km/h) up to 12,000 ft (3 660 m) — changing to 'S' gear at 10,000 ft (3 050 m) — and thereafter was reduced by three knots for each additional 2,000 ft (610 m). The controls were effective and well harmonised and the stalling characteristics were good, the clean stall coming at 85 knots (157 km/h) and at 79 knots (146 km/h) with flaps and undercarriage down. Before entering a dive the cowl gills were closed and the

Two of the ex-French contract Grumman G-36As (BJ556 above right and BJ513 below) after delivery to the Royal Navy as Martlet Mk Is. Delivery of these fighters to the UK began on 27 July 1940, and the first Royal Navy unit to receive them was No 804 Squadron at Hatston

Grumman F4F-4 Wildcat Cutaway Drawing Key

1 Starboard navigation light
2 Wingtip
3 Starboard formation light
4 Rear spar
5 Aileron construction
6 Fixed aileron tab
7 All riveted wing construction
8 Lateral stiffeners
9 Forward canted main spar
10 'Crimped' leading edge ribs
11 Solid web forward ribs
12 Starboard outer gun blast tube
13 Carburettor air duct
14 Intake
15 Curtiss three-blade constant-speed propeller
16 Propeller cuffs
17 Propeller hub
18 Engine front face
19 Pressure baffle
20 Forward cowling ring
21 Cooler intake
22 Cooler air duct
23 Pratt & Whitney R-1830-86 radial engine
24 Rear cowling ring/flap support

25 Controllable cowling flaps
26 Downdraft ram air duct
27 Engine mounting ring
28 Anti-detonant regulator unit
29 Cartridge starter
30 Generator
31 Interdooler
32 Engine accessories
33 Bearer assembly welded cluster joint
34 Main beam
35 Lower cowl flap
36 Exhaust stub
37 Starboard mainwheel
38 Undercarriage fairing
39 Lower drag link

40 Hydraulic brake
41 Port mainwheel
42 Detachable hub cover
43 Low-pressure tyre
44 Axle forging
45 Upper drag link
46 Oleo shock strut
47 Ventral fairing
48 Wheel well
49 Pivot point
50 Landing light
51 Main forging
52 Compression link
53 Gun camera port
54 Counter balance
55 Anti-detonant tank
56 Retraction sprocket
57 Gear box
58 Stainless steel firewall
59 Engine bearers
60 Actuation chain (undercarriage)
61 Engine oil tank
62 Oil filler
63 Hoisting sling installation
64 Bullet resistant windscreen
65 Reflector gunsight
66 Panoramic rear-view mirror

67 Wing fold position
68 Adjustable headrest
69 Shoulder harness
70 Canopy track sill
71 Pilot's adjustable seat
72 Instrument panel shroud
73 Undercarriage manual crank

74 Control column
75 Rudder pedals
76 Fuselage/front spar attachment
77 Main fuel filler cap
78 Seat harness attachment
79 Back armour
80 Oxygen cylinder
81 Reserve fuel filler cap
82 Alternative transmitter/receiver (ABA or IFF) installation
83 Battery
84 IFF and ABA dynamotor units
85 Wing flap vacuum tank
86 Handhold
87 Turnover bar
88 Rearward-sliding Plexiglas canopy
89 Streamlined aerial mast
90 Mast support

91 One-man Mk IA life-raft stowage
92 Upper longeron
93 Toolkit
94 Aerial lead-in
95 Elevator and rudder control runs
96 'L'-section fuselage frames
97 IFF aerial
98 Dorsal lights
99 Whip aerial
100 Wing-fold jury strut
101 Fin fairing
102 Access panel
103 Tailwheel strut extension arm

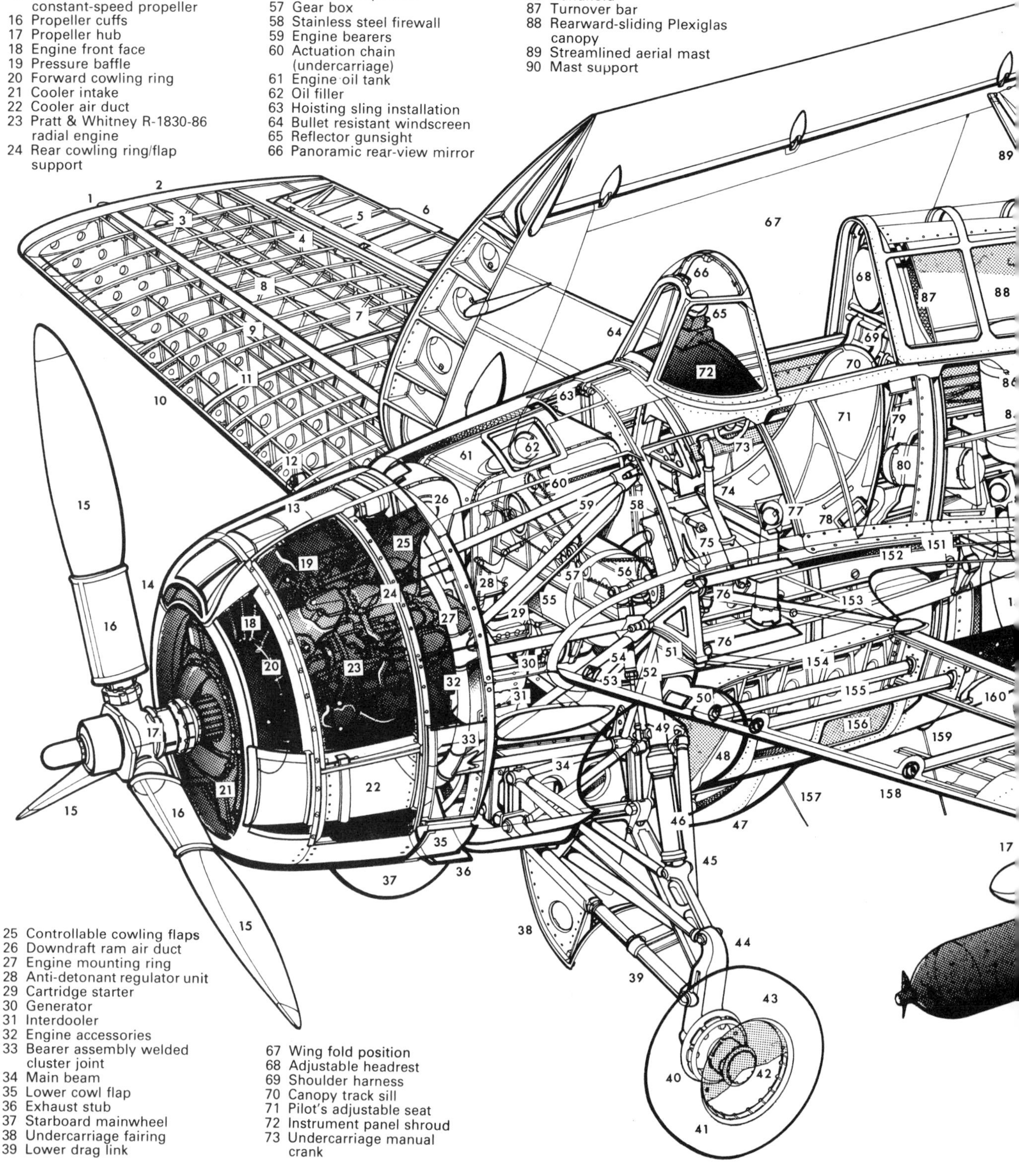

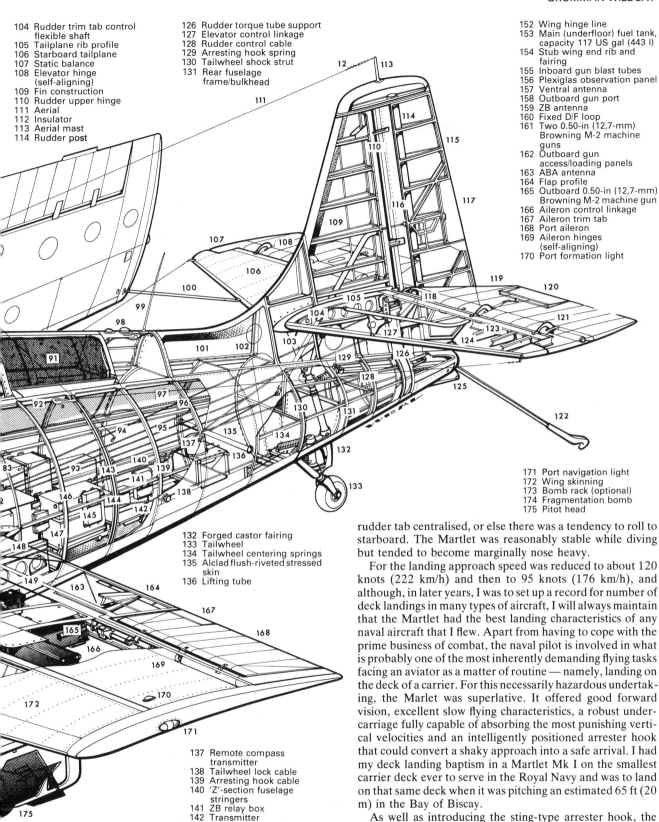

104 Rudder trim tab control flexible shaft
105 Tailplane rib profile
106 Starboard tailplane
107 Static balance
108 Elevator hinge (self-aligning)
109 Fin construction
110 Rudder upper hinge
111 Aerial
112 Insulator
113 Aerial mast
114 Rudder post

126 Rudder torque tube support
127 Elevator control linkage
128 Rudder control cable
129 Arresting hook spring
130 Tailwheel shock strut
131 Rear fuselage frame/bulkhead

152 Wing hinge line
153 Main (underfloor) fuel tank, capacity 117 US gal (443 l)
154 Stub wing end rib and fairing
155 Inboard gun blast tubes
156 Plexiglas observation panel
157 Ventral antenna
158 Outboard gun port
159 ZB antenna
160 Fixed D/F loop
161 Two 0.50-in (12,7-mm) Browning M-2 machine guns
162 Outboard gun access/loading panels
163 ABA antenna
164 Flap profile
165 Outboard 0.50-in (12,7-mm) Browning M-2 machine gun
166 Aileron control linkage
167 Aileron trim tab
168 Port aileron
169 Aileron hinges (self-aligning)
170 Port formation light

171 Port navigation light
172 Wing skinning
173 Bomb rack (optional)
174 Fragmentation bomb
175 Pitot head

132 Forged castor fairing
133 Tailwheel
134 Tailwheel centering springs
135 Alclad flush-riveted stressed skin
136 Lifting tube

137 Remote compass transmitter
138 Tailwheel lock cable
139 Arresting hook cable
140 'Z'-section fuselage stringers
141 ZB relay box
142 Transmitter
143 Elevator and rudder tab controls
144 Antenna relay unit
145 Radio junction box
146 Receiver unit and adapter
147 Inertia switch
148 Radio equipment support rack
149 Entry foothold
150 Reserve fuel tank, capacity 27 US gal (102 l)
151 Fuselage/rear spar attachment

115 Rudder construction
116 Aluminium alloy leading-edge
117 Rudder trim tab
118 Elevator torque tube
119 Port elevator
120 Elevator trim tab
121 Elevator hinge (self-aligning)
122 Arresting hook (extended)
123 Tailplane spar
124 Rear navigation light
125 Towing lug

rudder tab centralised, or else there was a tendency to roll to starboard. The Martlet was reasonably stable while diving but tended to become marginally nose heavy.

For the landing approach speed was reduced to about 120 knots (222 km/h) and then to 95 knots (176 km/h), and although, in later years, I was to set up a record for number of deck landings in many types of aircraft, I will always maintain that the Martlet had the best landing characteristics of any naval aircraft that I flew. Apart from having to cope with the prime business of combat, the naval pilot is involved in what is probably one of the most inherently demanding flying tasks facing an aviator as a matter of routine — namely, landing on the deck of a carrier. For this necessarily hazardous undertaking, the Marlet was superlative. It offered good forward vision, excellent slow flying characteristics, a robust undercarriage fully capable of absorbing the most punishing vertical velocities and an intelligently positioned arrester hook that could convert a shaky approach into a safe arrival. I had my deck landing baptism in a Martlet Mk I on the smallest carrier deck ever to serve in the Royal Navy and was to land on that same deck when it was pitching an estimated 65 ft (20 m) in the Bay of Biscay.

As well as introducing the sting-type arrester hook, the Martlet brought with it another innovation to British carrier aviation, this being tail-down catapult launching. All previous FAA aircraft had been catapulted from a cradle arrangement, which involved a tedious loading process when ugly, heavy steel spools sticking out of the aircraft at four points were fitted into the claws of the four-legged cradle. The Martlet, on the other hand, had only a single small steel hook under its belly to which one end of a wire strop was attached while the other end went around a shuttle fitted

Among the many Grumman fighters supplied to the UK through Lend-Lease were a batch of Cyclone-engined F4F-4Bs designated Martlet Mk IVs by the Royal Navy, one of these (FN202) being seen above on test with British Mk I rocket launchers under the wings. (Immediately below left) Another example of the Lend-Lease Martlet Mk IV (FN106) photographed in September 1942

almost flush into the catapult slot in the forward end of the carrier's deck. This innovation brought simplicity in catapult design, a weight and drag saving on the aircraft, and the further important advantage that the aircraft got airborne at an angle of attack giving it maximum lift without the pilot having to rotate it immediately after launch.

In September 1941, No 802 Squadron finally set sail aboard HMS *Audacity* to escort a convoy to Gibralter. We comprised eight pilots with six Martlet Mk IIs parked at the aft end of *Audacity's* tiny flight deck measuring a mere 420 ft (128 m) by 60 ft (18 m). Since there was no hangar, the Martlets were permanently on deck and the foremost had only 300 ft (91 m) in which to take-off. The maximum speed of *Audacity* was only 14·5 knots (27 km/h) and so it was all very tight. This applied particularly to the landing as, with only two arrester wires, a barrier and its associated safety trip wire, the test of pilot skill in a rough sea was just about the ultimate. Quite apart from the risk involved, there was the hard fact that any accident to one of our Martlets depleted the convoy's operational air cover by one-sixth.

(Immediately above left) One of the fixed-wing Martlet Mk IIs (AM958), 10 of these being accepted by the Royal Navy to avoid undue delivery delays, and (below) a standard folding-wing Martlet Mk II (AM980), deliveries of which commenced in August 1941 and being deployed in the following month by No 802 Squadron aboard HMS Audacity engaged in escorting a convoy to Gibraltar

We soon ran into U-boat trouble, and on 20 September, after a night attack which cost us three ships, our rescue vessel, prominently displaying red crosses, was detached to pick up survivors. This proved too much of a temptation for an Fw 200C Condor of KG 40 that had apparently been shadowing the convoy, for it made a low-level bombing run, leaving the defenceless vessel a mass of flame. The marauder had barely time to close its bomb-bay doors, however, when it was bounced by two of our Martlets, flown by Sub-Lts N H Patterson and G R P Fletcher, which despatched the Condor in a single concerted quarter attack, the entire tail end of the fuselage breaking off.

The next close encounter between our Martlets and the Condors of KG 40 took place during the second voyage of *Audacity* in November 1941. Again two Martlets made quarter attacks but one was shot down during the first firing pass, succeeding only in setting one of the Condor's engines afire, although the second Martlet finally finished off the Focke-Wulf. This combat served to further a belief that I had been forming that a head-on attack was the most likely to succeed

with impunity to the attacker, and my chance soon came — twice in succession — to put my belief into practice.

It proved more difficult than I had imagined to position my Martlet for a head-on attack and, indeed, my first such was largely fortuitous — a chance confrontation after losing my quarry in cloud. Once committed, the head-on attack is a hair-raising affair. I was fully occupied in sighting, firing and breaking away over my target, but I can imagine that the Condor pilot must have been going through hell, sitting behind his controls, flying straight and level and praying that his gunners would swat this portly little wasp spitting venom directly at him. One such pass was enough, and my lasting impressions were of the Condor's widscreen crumbling under the weight of lead from my sextet of 'fifties and of the very violent evasive action necessary to prevent collision with the monster.

The results of my second encounter with a Condor were similar, but by no means all our attacks on these marauders ended in success, for KG 40's pilots were adept in the art of using cloud cover and masters of the technique of gently

The Martlet Mk V alias Wildcat Mk V was an Eastern Motors-built FM-1 with a Twin Wasp engine and only four wing guns, JV330 being illustrated above and JV377 below. The latter is seen preparing to take-off from HMS Searcher, an escort carrier from which No 882 Squadron flew 167 sorties with this version of the Grumman fighter over the landing beaches during the invasion of Southern France in August 1944

Grumman F4F-4 Wildcat Specification

Power Plant: One Pratt & Whitney R-1830-86 Twin Wasp 14-cylinder two-row radial air-cooled engine with two-speed two-stage supercharger rated at 1,200 hp at 2,900 rpm for take-off, military ratings of 1,200 hp at 2,700 rpm from sea level to 1,800 ft (550 m) and 1,135 hp at 2,700 rpm at 3,400 ft (1 035 m), and normal ratings of 1,100 hp at 2,550 rpm at sea level to 3,300 ft (1 005 m) and 1,090 hp at 2,550 rpm at 11,300 ft (3 445 m). Three-blade constant-speed Curtiss Electric propeller of 9 ft 9 in (2,97 m) diam. Internal fuel capacity of 144 US gal (545 l) with provision for one 58 US gal (220 l) drop tank beneath each wing.
Performance: (Clean aircraft at 7,975 lb/3 621 kg) Max speed, 274 mph (441 km/h) at sea level, 320 mph (515 km/h) at 18,800 ft (5 735 m); max range cruise, 161 mph (259 km/h) at 5,000 ft (1 525 m); initial climb, 1,950 ft/min (9,9 m/sec); time to 10,000 ft (3 050 m), 5·6 min, to 20,000 ft (6 100 m), 12·4 min; service ceiling, 34,000 ft (10 370 m); max range, 830 mls (1 335 km), with two 58 US gal (220 l) drop tanks, 1,275 mls (2 051 km); take-off distance (in calm), 213 yds (195 m), (15-knot/28 km/h wind), 137 yds (125 m).
Weights: Empty, 5,895 lb (2 676 kg); normal loaded, 7,975 lb (3 621 kg); max take-off (two drop tanks), 8,762 lb (3 978 kg).
Dimensions: Span, 38 ft 0 in (11,59 m); span folded, 14 ft 4 in (4,35 m); length, 29 ft 0 in (8,85 m); height (tail down and propeller vertical), 11 ft 4 in (3,44 m); wing area, 260 sq ft (24,15 m²).
Armament: Six 0·5-in Colt-Browning M-2 machine guns with 240 rpg or (FM-1) four 0·5-in guns with 430 rpg.

manoeuvring to bring maximum firepower to bear against the attacker. Indeed, our only other success — the fourth Condor "kill" of that voyage — resulted from another head-on attack which actually ended in a collision in which the sturdy Martlet survived and the Condor did not!

Subsequent to No 802 Squadron's successful début in combat over the Atlantic and with the passage of the Lend-Lease Act resulting in momentum of Martlet deliveries accelerating, the Grumman fighter steadily gathered importance in the FAA's inventory, as it was doing simultaneously in the ranks of the US Navy and Marine Corps by whom it had been officially known as the Wildcat from 1 October 1941. But its combat initiation in the Pacific was to be rather less auspicious than it had been over the Atlantic, although the circumstances were, of course very different. When, on 7 December 1941, Japanese forces attacked Pearl Harbor, only one of the three carriers attached to the US Pacific Fleet, the USS *Enterprise,* possessed a fully-equipped squadron of the Grumman fighters, this being VF-6 with F4F-3As. VF-3 was still working up aboard the USS *Saratoga* in San Diego, and the third carrier, the USS *Lexington,* carried the Brewster F1A-equipped VF-2, VMF-211 had just re-equipped with F4F-3s at Ewa in south-west Oahu, and on the day of the Japanese attack, *Enterprise* was transferring half of this unit — USMC fighter squadrons had an establishment of 24 aircraft — to Wake Island.

Nine of VMF-211's F4Fs were destroyed on the ground at Ewa in the first wave of Japanese attacks, and the detachment of the squadron on Wake Island lost seven out of eight F4Fs caught on the ground on the next day. Those few that survived on Wake put up a fierce defence, but all resistance on the island came to an end before the New Year began, and its was being tacitly admitted by the US Navy that, in fighter-versus-fighter combat, the F4F was outclassed by the A6M2 Zero-Sen. The Japanese fighter was superior in speed and climb at all altitudes above 1,000 ft (305 m), and was the better of the two in both service ceiling and range. In a dive, the American and Japanese fighters were virtually equal, but the turning circle of the Zero-Sen was very much smaller than that of the F4F by reason of its lower wing loading and, in consequence, lower stalling speed. However, by concentrating on the two-plane fighter element and evolving such tactics as the "Thach Weave", in which two F4Fs criss-crossed back and fourth, each thus covering the other's tail, the US Navy and USMC pilots gradually gained the measure of their more

nimble opponents, taking full advantage of the Grumman fighter's virtues, such as its superior firepower and structural integrity. Dogfighting with the Zero-Sen was assiduously avoided.

Unlike the Martlet Mk II, which had been built against a British contract, subsequent fighters of the basic type delivered to the FAA from 1942 were supplied under Lend-Lease arrangements and conformed more closely to the models that were being delivered simultaneously to the US Navy. The Martlet Mk IV, for example, was similar to the American service's F4F-4 except in respect of the engine which was the Wright R-1820-40B Cyclone, a single-stage two-speed unit and similar to the R-1820-G205A of the Martlet Mk I. The parallel F4F-4 was the first model with wing folding to attain US Navy service, and although the prototype had featured hydraulically-actuated folding mechanism, the heavy and complicated system that such demanded had been dispensed with for the production model, the wings of which were folded manually by flight deck crews. The F4F-4 was to be the first version of the Grumman fighter to be built in *really* large numbers — contracts were to total 1,169 of which the first five were delivered at the end of 1941 and the remainder during 1942 — and by August 1942, when Operation *Watchtower* for the invasion of Guadalcanal and Tulagi was mounted, F4F-4s formed the sole fighter equipment aboard the three participating carriers.

As previously stated, the Martlet Mk II had taken on a fair amount of weight by comparison with the Mk I, and although the F4F-3 and -4 shared the same engine, which was not so with the two Martlets, the weight of the later model had peaked at 7,964 lb (3 616 kg), or some 13 per cent more than the F4F-3. The adverse effect of this weight escalation had occasioned no little concern, the deterioration in take-off distance and landing speed being viewed as particularly unfortunate, since the greatest future value of the Grumman

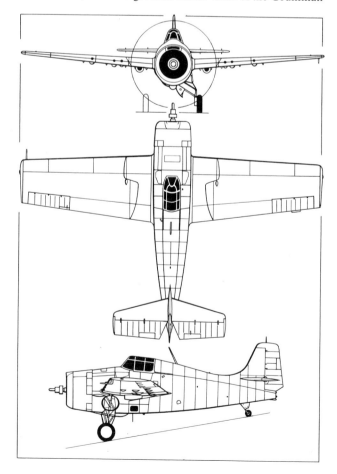

The general arrangement drawing on the opposite page represents the F4F-4 and FM-1 (Wildcat Mk V) and the photographs above and below right illustrate the final production model of the Wildcat, the Eastern Motors-built FM-2. This was designated Wildcat Mk VI in Royal Navy service, the example illustrated bottom right being JV642. Note the 58 US gal (219,5 1) drop tanks.

fighter was seen as its potential service aboard escort carriers with their regrettably short flight decks. As a consequence, in 1942, Grumman made a concerted effort to evolve a lighter version of the F4F-4 tailored for the smaller carriers. This weight paring process centred on the use of the newly-available R-1820-56 Cyclone which could provide 1,350 hp at 2,700 rpm as compared with the 1,200 hp at 2,900 rpm of the F4F-4's R-1830-86 engine.

Some 500 lb (227 kg) lighter than the F4F-4, the production of this new version was entrusted to the Linden, New Jersey, factory of Eastern Motors, which, under a contract awarded in April 1942, had been building the F4F-4 as the FM-1, the Eastern-built model differing from that built by Grumman primarily in having the outboard pair of 0·5-in (12,7-mm) guns deleted with an increase in the number of rounds from 1,440 to 1,720. The FM-1s assigned to the FAA were known as Martlet Mk Vs, but the lightened model, which was assigned the designation FM-2 and of which deliveries began during 1943, was to sport the FAA designation Martlet Mk VI only briefly for, in January 1944, their Lordships of the Admiralty concluded that, in the interests of uniformity, the name Martlet would henceforth be dropped and the US appellation standardised.

The FM-2 alias Wildcat Mk VI was, from some aspects, the most satisfactory of all versions of the little Grumman fighter to fly, some of the early faults that had persisted having been finally rectified. For example, this model could be spun with impunity whereas the spinning of its predecessors was not permitted and in the event of an inadvertent spin a great deal of muscle power had to be exerted to get the control column forward, the recovery characteristics being somewhat short of pleasant. The Wildcat Mks IV, V and VI operated primarily from the Royal Navy's escort carriers, in which it became normal FAA practice to embark a single squadron equipped with four-six of the fighters, plus up to a dozen anti-submarine aircraft.

From 1943, the portly little Grumman fighter was eclipsed by its creators' second 'Cat', the F6F Hellcat, perhaps the greatest of all WW II carrier-based fighters, rapid production of which allowing it to become established as the standard fighter on all US Navy fast carriers by August 1943, but the FM-1 succeeded, in turn, by the FM-2 was the most numerous fighter serving aboard the US Navy's escort carriers until the end of the war, seeing extensive service in both the Pacific and the Atlantic.

Leaving aside my emotional affection for the first of the

Grumman shipboard fighter monoplanes, I would still assess the Wildcat as the outstanding naval fighter of the early years of WW II. Its ruggedness meant that it had a much lower attrition rate on carrier operations than, say, the Sea Hurricane or the Seafire, and although it had neither the performance nor the aesthetic appeal of the latter, it was the perfect compromise solution designed specifically for the naval environment, to such a degree indeed that it was easier to take-off or land on an aircraft carrier than on a runway, where it was inclined to be fickle about the direction it took up. With its excellent patrol range — I actually flew one sortie of four-and-a-half hours in this fighter — and fine ditching characteristics, for which I can vouch as a matter of personal experience, this Grumman fighter was, for my money, one of the finest shipboard aeroplanes ever created.☐

Douglas Dauntless

THE BARGE, THE CLUNK: epithets bestowed on the Douglas Dauntless by its crews were legion and for the most part derogatory yet possessing an element of affection withal. Mundane by contemporary performance standards, the Dauntless was underpowered, painfully slow, short on range, woefully vulnerable to fighters, and uncomfortable and fatiguing to fly for any length of time, being inherently noisy and draughty. But it did possess certain invaluable assets that mitigated these shortcomings. Its handling characteristics were, for the most part, innocuous and it was responsive; it was dependable and extremely sturdy, capable of absorbing considerable battle damage and remaining airborne, and, most important, it was an *accurate* dive bomber.

Throughout the Pacific War, it remained the principal shipboard dive bomber available to the US Navy; it was the *only* US aircraft to participate in all five naval engagements fought exclusively between carriers, and deficiencies notwithstanding, it emerged with an almost legendary reputation as the most successful shipboard dive bomber of all time — albeit success that perhaps owed more to the crews that flew it in truly *dauntless* fashion than to the intrinsic qualities of the aeroplane itself.

By the time I first flew the Dauntless, in early October 1944, its place in the annals of naval aviation was already thoroughly established, a fact undoubtedly colouring my attitude towards this trim but unimposing and relatively small aeroplane on first acquaintance. I found it hard to believe that *this* was the legendary scourge of the Japanese Navy; the principal US weapon employed in those climactic carrier battles of the Pacific. As I hoisted myself over the cockpit sill of JS997 Dauntless DB Mk I, the first of nine SBD-5 Dauntlesses supplied for evaluation by both the Royal Navy and the RAF, I recall wondering if this stocky but not displeasing aeroplane would reveal in flight some hidden quality not rendered evident by external appraisal.

The genesis of the Dauntless had been complex; its gestation had been protracted. My introduction to it came at a time when its service career had long passed its apex and its obsolescence, already tacitly admitted by the US Navy when first committing this warplane to combat, had degenerated to the obsolete. Its progenitors had been the Alpha, Beta and Gamma mailplanes of the late 'twenties and early 'thirties, and its true sire had been the Northrop XBT-1, which, embodying many of the structural techniques of the commercial models, had been created by Edward A Heinemann under the aegis of John K Northrop. First flown on 19 August 1935, the XBT-1 evinced sufficient promise to warrant a contract a year later, on 18 September 1936, for 54 production BT-1s, and these were to serve primarily with VB-5 aboard USS *Yorktown* and VB-6 aboard USS *Enterprise*.

The BT-1 revealed few endearing characteristics; some aspects of its handling were reputedly little short of vicious, particularly at low airspeeds when lateral stability was exceptionally poor and the rudder ineffective, a torque roll as likely as not accompanying any application of power during a deck approach and several fatal crashes ensuing. On the surface, the BT-1 provided a poor basis for further development. Indeed, it is likely that evolution of the basic design would have ended with delivery of the last of the production aeroplanes but for an early amendment to the original contract authorising completion of one BT-1 as the XBT-2 with an inward-folding fully-retractable undercarriage in place of the aft-folding semi-retractable and faired arrangement. This change, in itself hardly likely to translate sow's ear into silk purse, was fortuitously, to set in train an incremental modification programme destined to recast the XBT-2 as the true forerunner of the Dauntless.

Flight testing of the XBT-2 was initiated on 22 April 1938, revealing no significant advance over the BT-1, and had barely got under way when this prototype suffered quite extensive damage as a result of a wheels-up landing. Ed Heinemann seized the opportunity presented by the return of the aircraft to the factory for repair to eradicate one of the more serious shortcomings of the XBT-2, its inadequate power, seeking and obtaining authority, on 21 June 1938, to replace the Twin Wasp Junior engine and two-blade controllable-pitch propeller with a more powerful. Cyclone and a three-blade constant-speed propeller. This change produced a noteworthy improvement in speed performance but exacerbated some of the least desirable handling characteristics of the aircraft.

Fixed slots were introduced on the wing to maintain aileron control at low speeds; a dozen different sets of ailerons were tested and no fewer than 21 different tail surface combinations were evaluated. The end product was an aeroplane possessing eminently more satisfactory handling characteristics; a high standard of manoeuvrability throughout the speed range, light control responses and a docile attitude towards carrier operation. In short, the prototype of the Dauntless.

The Northrop Corporation, which had been formed in January 1932 with the Douglas Aircraft Company holding 51 per cent of the stock, had meanwhile been dissolved and had become Douglas's El Segundo Division, and when a production contract for the reworked dive bomber was placed on 8 April 1939, this change and the adoption of the all-embracing classification of scout-bomber were reflected by the assignment of the designation SBD, indicating Scout Bomber Douglas.

The first production Dauntless, an SBD-1, was flown on 1 May 1940 and delivered to the US Navy on 6 September. This was almost identical to the definitive XBT-2, apart from the introduction of two 15 US gal (56,81) centre section auxiliary tanks boosting total capacity to 210 US gal (795 l) and the installation of a production series Wright Cyclone engine, the R-1820-32 affording 1,000 hp at 2,350 rpm for take-off and having a normal maximum rating of 950 hp at 2,300 rpm from sea level to 5,000 ft (1 525 m).

The SBD-1 undeniably offered a capability advance over the equipment that it succeeded, but such had been the tempo of combat aircraft development during its gestation that it no longer met US Navy requirements; the service was by now relying on the Curtiss SB2C for the quantum advance that it sought. Not that the Douglas *née* Northrop fell short of its guaranteed performance, but the Curtiss, ordered a year earlier, on 15 May 1939, bid fair to provide 50 knots (93 km/h) more speed and tote twice the bomb load over substantially greater ranges. Thus, *before* its introduction to the

carriers, the Dauntless was seen as being underpowered, with performance and load-carrying capabilities well below those foreseen to be demanded by the Pacific conflict now considered inevitable in most US Navy circles. It was already obsolescent!

The structure of the Dauntless was extremely strong but also rather heavy, and with the chosen engine its power-to-weight ratio inevitably resulted in a rather sluggish performance, especially with a worthwhile external load. The wing, which employed the "multi-cellular" system of construction originated by John Northrop, was a duralumin structure consisting of several false spars and plate ribs with "top hat" section stringers supporting the flush-riveted dural sheet stressed skinning. The centre section was rectangular with

(Above) Progenitor of the Dauntless, the Northrop BT-1, the example illustrated belonging to US Navy Squadron VB-6 aboard the USS Enterprise and which re-equipped with the SBD-2 Dauntless during 1941

(Above right) The second production SBD-1 Dauntless (BuNo 1597) assigned to the commanding officer of US Marine Corps Squadron VMB-2, and (below) the eighth SBD-1 (BuNo 1603) prior to delivery to VMB-1 at Quantico NAS. (Head of opposite page) An SBD-5 of US Navy Squadron VB-10 from the USS Enterprise (in the background) in March 1944

The initial USAAF version of the Dauntless, the A-24, seen with perforated dive flaps lowered. The A-24 was essentially similar to the Navy's SBD-3 apart from instrumentation and radio equipment

the outer sections tapered in chord and thickness, but an odd feature of the wing for a shipboard aeroplane of the era of the SBD-1, was the lack of any provision for folding, the outer panels being rigidly affixed to the centre section by attaching angles and double plates, with characteristic fairing bulges covering the joints.

Fixed "letter-box" slots were inserted in the wings ahead of the metal-framed fabric-skinned ailerons, and the remainder of the wing trailing edges were occupied by combined spoilers and flaps, both upper and lower halves of these split surfaces being hinged. These were hydraulically operated, and the lower halves, which continued across the centre section, served in orthodox fashion for take-off and landing, the upper and lower halves being opened in unison to brake terminal velocity in a dive. These spoiler-flaps were exten-

sively perforated with 1·75-in (4,45-cm) holes — an NACA innovation — to inhibit tail buffeting.

The oval-section duralumin semi-monocoque fuselage was built up of channel-section transverse frames with extruded stringers and dural skinning. For ease of manufacture, the fuselage was split longitudinally, the upper half in one piece and the lower in three, plus a tail cone, the forward lower section including the built-in centre section. Aft of the rear cockpit, sheet metal bulkheads divided the rear fuselage into a series of watertight compartments. The tail fin was built integral with the fuselage and, like the tailplane, was of metal stressed-skin construction, the rudder and elevators being metal framed and fabric skinned.

The main oleo shock-absorber legs were cantilever units with stay struts mounted on knuckle forgings which rotated on retraction, the legs hinging at the extremities of the centre section and being raised hydraulically inwards, the wheels lying flat in wells forward of the main spar. The Cyclone engine was carried by a tubular steel mount and enclosed by an NACA cowling with controllable exit louvres on top of the cowling. A Hamilton Standard Hydromatic fully-feathering propeller was fitted, and all fuel was accommodated by unprotected centre section tanks and the previously-mentioned auxiliary tanks.

The pilot sat fairly high in the fuselage beneath a sliding section of a continuous "greenhouse" canopy and was provided with a pair of 0·5-in (12,7-mm) Browning machine guns, the breeches of which protruded into the cockpit where they could be cleared and cocked in the event of a stoppage. Each gun was provided with 360 rounds stowed in containers behind the fireproof bulkhead carrying the engine mount. The observer-gunner had a single drum-fed 0·3-in (7,62-mm) weapon with 600 rounds and which, when stowed, was accommodated by a compartment in the top of the fuselage which was closed flush by folding doors. The pilot was provided with a three-power telescopic sight which was intended for use both in aerial gunnery and dive bombing, and a duplicate set of controls was included in the rear cockpit for emergency use. A cradle beneath the fuselage could carry a single 500-lb (226,8-kg), 1,000-lb (453,59-kg) or 1,600-lb (725,7-kg) bomb and swung forward and downward to ensure that its load cleared the propeller disc. A fixed rack for one 100-lb (45,36-kg) bomb was located under each outer wing section.

The US Navy did not deem it advisable to deploy SBD-1s

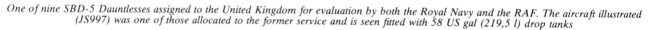

One of nine SBD-5 Dauntlesses assigned to the United Kingdom for evaluation by both the Royal Navy and the RAF. The aircraft illustrated (JS997) was one of those allocated to the former service and is seen fitted with 58 US gal (219,5 l) drop tanks

aboard its carriers, primarily because of their inadequate range, work already being in hand at El Segundo that was to increase internal fuel capacity by almost 50 per cent and a series of contractual changes allowing for the revised fuel system to be introduced with the 58th production aeroplane: the first SBD-2. The bulk of the initial 57 production Dauntlesses were therefore assigned to the US Marine Corps' Air Group One at Quantico, Virginia, VMB-2 commencing working up on the SBD-1 from late 1940, with VMB-1 following suit in 1941 (towards the end of which year these units being redesignated VMSB-232 and -132 respectively).

Whereas the SBD-1 carried all fuel in welded centre-section tanks comprising two 90 US gal (341 l) main tanks and two 15 eliminated the auxiliary tanks and supplemented the two centre section main tanks with two 65 US gal (246 l) tanks in the outer wing panels to raise maximum internal capacity to 310 US gal (1 173 l). However, it was only practical to use all the additional capacity for ferrying, the maximum ferry range being raised from 1,060 nm (1 964 km) at 123 knots (229 km/h) to 1,468 nm (2 721 km) at 128 knots (237 km/h). For operational missions, internal fuel was effectively limited to 260 US gal (984 l) with which range with, for example, a single 500-lb (226,8-kg) bomb was increased by 338 nm (626 km) to 1,172 nm (2 172 km).

This quite considerable boost in range capability was not, of course, achieved without exacting penalties on take-off distance, climb rate, service ceiling and stalling speed, and, furthermore, CG reasons dictated removal of one of the 0·5-in (12,7-mm) cowl guns. The SBD-2 did introduce an automatic pilot, however. If unusual in so small an aeroplane, this piece of equipment was very desirable in view of the reconnaissance ranges of which the Dauntless was now capable.

Like the SBD-1, the SBD-2 as initially delivered to the US Navy was hardly to be considered combat worthy in that it lacked a bullet-proof windscreen, any form of armour protection or self-sealing fuel tanks — in the event, some SBD-2s were later to be fitted with aluminium alloy fuel tanks with self-sealing liners reducing total internal capacity to 260 US gal (984 l). By the time that the Japanese struck at Pearl Harbor, three US Navy squadrons, VS-6 and VB-6 aboard *Enterprise* and VB-2 aboard *Lexington,* were mounted on SBD-2 Dauntlesses, combat worthy or no, and deliveries of what can be considered the first fully combat worthy Dauntless, the SBD-3, had, in fact, begun nine months before hostilities started in the Pacific.

It was the SBD-3 that was to become the US Navy's true workhorse of the Pacific War and to carry much of the burden of that service's offensive operations until 1943, when the marginally more efficacious SBD-5 was to become available. Indeed, but for the availability of the SBD-3, the conflict in the Pacific might well have pursued a very different course during its first critical year. The SBD-3 was dubbed somewhat sardonically the "Speedy Three", a caustically humorous allusion to the fact that it was anything *but* speedy, having taken on weight without any commensurate increase in power and all aspects of its performance suffering in consequence, although, in truth, only nominally so.

Alclad was used in lieu of dural in the SBD-3, an R-1820-52 engine replaced the -32, although ratings remained unchanged, and the self-sealing fuel tanks comprised two of 75 US gal (284 l) capacity in the centre section and two of 55

The SBD-4 Helldiver JS997 (illustrated above right and below) was flown by the author at the RAE Farnborough for comparison purposes with the Curtiss Helldiver and the Vultee Vengeance and was considered one of the most effective aeroplanes designed for dive bombing

Douglas SBD-3 Dauntless Cutaway Key

1 Aerial stub
2 Rudder balance
3 Rudder upper hinge
4 Rudder frame
5 Rudder tab
6 Rudder lower hinge
7 Tailfin structure
8 Port elevator
9 Port tailplane
10 Tailfin root fillet
11 Frame
12 Fuselage frame/tailfin pickup
13 Tailplane spar attachment
14 Tailplane structure
15 Elevator torque tube
16 Tail navigation light
17 Elevator tab hinge fairing
18 Elevator hinge
19 Elevator tab
20 Elevator frame
21 Elevator outer hinge
22 Tailplane forward spar
23 Fixed tailwheel (pneumatic or solid)
24 Arresting hook uplock
25 Fuselage frame
26 Lift point

47 Canopy aft sliding section (closed)
48 Ammunition box
49 Oxygen cylinder
50 Oxygen rebreather

69 Catapult headrest
70 Canopy forward sliding section
71 Compass
72 Perforated dive flap
73 Aerial mast
74 Aileron tab
75 Port aileron

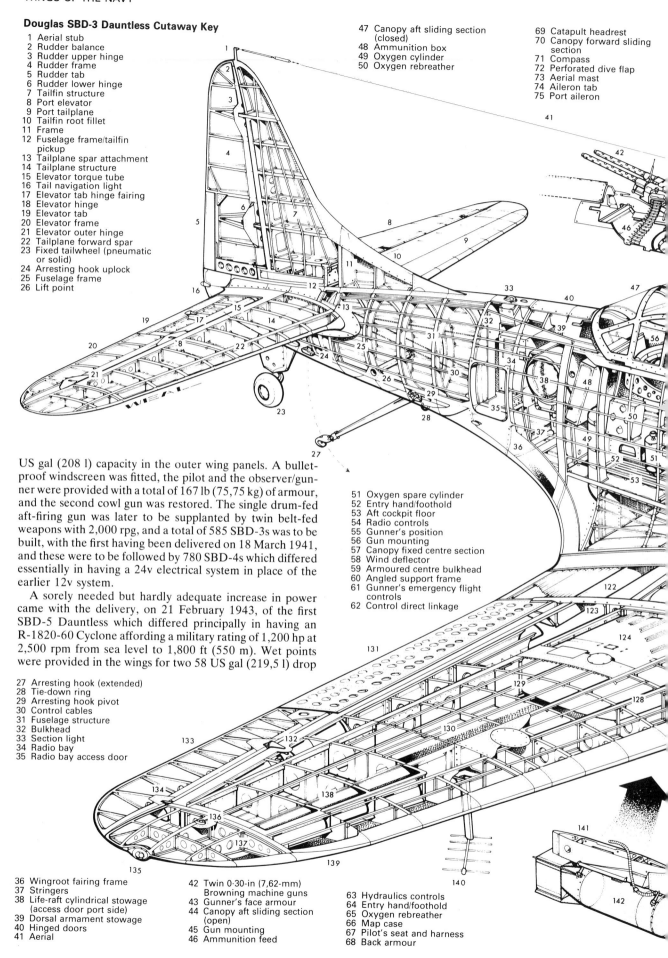

US gal (208 l) capacity in the outer wing panels. A bullet-proof windscreen was fitted, the pilot and the observer/gunner were provided with a total of 167 lb (75,75 kg) of armour, and the second cowl gun was restored. The single drum-fed aft-firing gun was later to be supplanted by twin belt-fed weapons with 2,000 rpg, and a total of 585 SBD-3s was to be built, with the first having been delivered on 18 March 1941, and these were to be followed by 780 SBD-4s which differed essentially in having a 24v electrical system in place of the earlier 12v system.

A sorely needed but hardly adequate increase in power came with the delivery, on 21 February 1943, of the first SBD-5 Dauntless which differed principally in having an R-1820-60 Cyclone affording a military rating of 1,200 hp at 2,500 rpm from sea level to 1,800 ft (550 m). Wet points were provided in the wings for two 58 US gal (219,5 l) drop

51 Oxygen spare cylinder
52 Entry hand/foothold
53 Aft cockpit floor
54 Radio controls
55 Gunner's position
56 Gun mounting
57 Canopy fixed centre section
58 Wind deflector
59 Armoured centre bulkhead
60 Angled support frame
61 Gunner's emergency flight controls
62 Control direct linkage

27 Arresting hook (extended)
28 Tie-down ring
29 Arresting hook pivot
30 Control cables
31 Fuselage structure
32 Bulkhead
33 Section light
34 Radio bay
35 Radio bay access door

36 Wingroot fairing frame
37 Stringers
38 Life-raft cylindrical stowage (access door port side)
39 Dorsal armament stowage
40 Hinged doors
41 Aerial

42 Twin 0·30-in (7,62-mm) Browning machine guns
43 Gunner's face armour
44 Canopy aft sliding section (open)
45 Gun mounting
46 Ammunition feed

63 Hydraulics controls
64 Entry hand/foothold
65 Oxygen rebreather
66 Map case
67 Pilot's seat and harness
68 Back armour

76 Aileron tab control linkage
77 Port formation light
78 Port navigation light
79 Pitot head
80 Fixed wing slots
81 Wing skinning
82 Underwing radar antenna (retrofit)
83 Port outer wing fuel tank (55 US gal/208 l capacity)
84 Aileron control rod
85 Telescopic sight
86 Windscreen

87 Armoured inner panel
88 Instrument panel shroud
89 Two 0·50-in (12,7-mm) machine guns
90 Control column
91 Switch panel
92 Instrument panel
93 Case ejection chute
94 Ammunition box
95 Engine bearer upper attachment
96 Armoured deflection plate
97 Machine gun barrel shrouds
98 Engine bearers
99 Oil tank
100 Exhaust slot
101 Oil cooler

114 Engine bearers
115 Bomb displacement crutch (in-flight position)
116 Hydraulics vent
117 Case ejection chute outlet slot
118 Engine bearer lower attachment
119 Starboard mainwheel well
120 Wingroot walkway
121 Starboard/inner wing fuel tank (75 US gal/284 l capacity)

127 Wing nose ribs
128 Multi-spar wing structure
129 Wing ribs
130 Stiffeners
131 Perforated dive flaps
132 Aileron inner hinge
133 Starboard aileron frame
134 Aileron outer hinge
135 Starboard navigation light
136 Starboard formation light
137 Wingtip structure
138 Fixed wing slots
139 Wing leading-edge

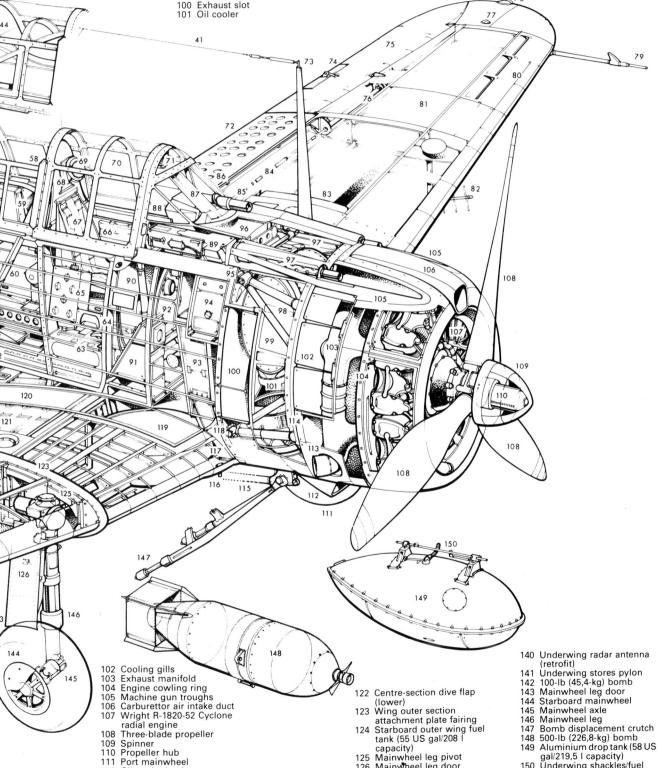

102 Cooling gills
103 Exhaust manifold
104 Engine cowling ring
105 Machine gun troughs
106 Carburettor air intake duct
107 Wright R-1820-52 Cyclone radial engine
108 Three-blade propeller
109 Spinner
110 Propeller hub
111 Port mainwheel
112 Oil cooler intake
113 Exhaust outlet

122 Centre-section dive flap (lower)
123 Wing outer section attachment plate fairing
124 Starboard outer wing fuel tank (55 US gal/208 l capacity)
125 Mainwheel leg pivot
126 Mainwheel leg door actuation

140 Underwing radar antenna (retrofit)
141 Underwing stores pylon
142 100-lb (45,4-kg) bomb
143 Mainwheel leg door
144 Starboard mainwheel
145 Mainwheel axle
146 Mainwheel leg
147 Bomb displacement crutch
148 500-lb (226,8-kg) bomb
149 Aluminium drop tank (58 US gal/219,5 l capacity)
150 Underwing shackles/fuel line

Although the Dauntless saw no operational service with either the Royal Navy or the RAF, it was flown in combat by No 25 Squadron of the Royal New Zealand Air Force, one of whose aircraft (NZ5049) is seen above. (Below left) The A-24 version of the Dauntless was found to be too slow, too short on range and too vulnerable by the USAAF. The general arrangement drawing on the opposite page illustrates the SBD-5

tanks and with these the maximum range in the reconnaissance rôle was raised to 1,340 nm (2 483 km). No fewer than 2,964 examples of the SBD-5 were to be turned out at El Segundo, and it was this near-definitive Dauntless that was to be sent to the UK for evaluation.

To me, the SBD-5 Dauntless looked exactly what it was: a decidedly *pre-war* aeroplane of obsolescent design and certainly overdue for replacement. Its primary purpose at the RAE Farnborough was for comparison with the Curtiss SBW-1B Helldiver and the Vultee Vengeance IV as a dive bomber, and of the nine supplied to the UK, four had been assigned to the Royal Navy and the remainder to the RAF for trials purposes. The combination of Wright Cyclone engine and Hamilton Standard Hydromatic propeller that I had come to appreciate so much in the Grumman Wildcat influenced me favourably but during my first take-off in this ageing dive bomber, my impression was that it needed every single one of the twelve hundred horses that its R-1820-60 Cyclone could muster, and with the lower-powered Cyclones of earlier models, carrier take-offs with any substantial external loads could well have bordered on the hairy!

The cockpit was commodious and offered relatively good view for take-off, which, in clean condition in calm from grass

required some 1,200 ft (366 m). Once airborne, the Dauntless laboured upwards at a maximum initial rate of 1,430 ft/min (7,26 m/sec), which, with a 1,000-lb (453,59-kg) bomb, was reduced to 1,190 ft/min (6,04 m/sec). During the climb, the cockpit was extremely noisy and draughty, and there were signs of lateral instability. It took about eight minutes to reach 10,000 ft (3,050 m) and about another five to attain its Vmax critical altitude of 14,000 ft (4,270 m) at which the clean aeroplane could just about touch 221 knots (410 km/h). I could not help but feel that, with so sluggish a performance, the Dauntless must have been an easy "kill" for the pilot of any determined Zero-Sen fighter, yet I was later to learn that its loss rate in the Pacific had been lower than that experienced with any other US Navy shipboard aeroplane — a tribute to its innate robustness and ability to survive quite heavy battle damage.

The practical combat radius of the SBD-5, based on 20 min warm-up and idling, 10 min rendezvous at 60 per cent normal sea level power and auto-lean, climbing to 15,000 ft (4 570 m) and allowing for five min combat with full military power at 1,500 ft (460 m), plus 10 min at max normal power, return at 1,500 ft (460m) and 60 min for a rendezvous, reserve and landing, was 285 nm (528 km) with a single 500-lb (226,8-kg) bomb, this being increased to 450 nm (834 km) with a pair of drop tanks, and these radii were certainly not *too* great for Pacific-type operations. But although cockpit noise must have been taxing on protracted flights at the 120 knot (222 km/h) cruise of the Dauntless, the controls were light and the pilot had the advantage of an auto-pilot — indeed, this was the first auto-pilot that I had ever flown.

If the performance of the Dauntless was "sedate", particularly with external load, at least it had few vices. It was a pleasant aircraft to fly and its controls were light and responsive unless it was heavily laden, and its stall, which, power off, ranged from about 68 knots (126 km/h) at 10,000 lb (4 536 kg) to some 62 knots at about 8,500 lb (3 856 kg), was totally innocuous. But it did have one bad habit and that was a vicious *g* stall, particularly off a tight left-hand turn, reminiscent of that of the Fw 190. It would snap inverted without warning, the nose falling through the horizontal and a spin ensuing if corrective action was not taken immediately.

My primary interest in the Dauntless lay in its dive bombing characteristics and so I staggered up to 15,000 ft (4 570 m), retarded the throttle, pulled up the nose slightly above the horizon on reaching the target and pulled the diamond-shaped handle marked "D" on my right which deployed both spoilers and flaps in unison. These were very slow to operate and it was therefore necessary to activate them before half-rolling into the dive and not on actually initiating the dive. Ideally, one flew slightly to one side of the target and once abreast began the dive, rotating onto the target with aileron. Acceleration was slow so that an angle between 70 and 75 deg was not as frightening as it could be in some of the Dauntless's contemporaries, and I only picked up a speed of 240 knots (445 km/h) in the 35-40 seconds that it took me to get down to the bomb release height of 1,500 ft (457 m).

Using the Mk VIII reflector sight, which, in the SBD-5, had supplanted the telescopic sight of earlier models and which had had a tendency to fog over in a dive owing to the sudden temperature changes, and making line corrections easily with the pleasantly light ailerons, I could sense that the Dauntless was a very accurate dive bomber. I say "sense" advisedly, as I had neglected to activate the windscreen heater, which, too, had been introduced with the -5 sub-type, and the windscreen fogged over at around the halfway point of the dive. Needless to say, I did not neglect to use the heater in subsequent dives.

The bomb release was a red button marked "B" on the top of the stick, electrical arming and release circuits having replaced manual release partway through SBD-3 production, and there was a selector for individual bombs or salvo. The spoiler-flaps had to be retracted before commencing the pullout owing to their slow operation and their high drag which would have slowed the aircraft too much for tactical getaway if retraction had been left until after the pullout. In truth, the Dauntless could not easily maintain level flight with the upper spoilers extended. Recovery was positive, pulling about 5 g, and while frankly, I did not consider the Dauntless to be as *good* a dive bomber as the Ju 87, I was left with the

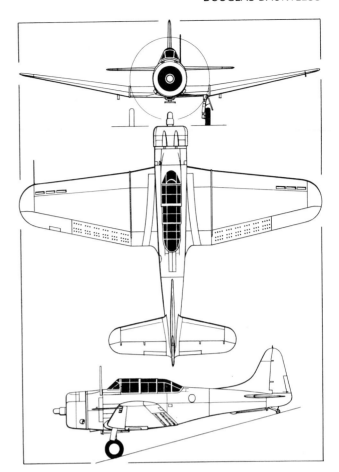

opinion that it was certainly one of the most effective aeroplanes designed to fulfil that rôle.

Among the best features of the Dauntless were its landing characteristics which were very easy. View for deck landing was good, and the controls crisp and effective, the flaps giving adequate drag to require a reasonable increment of engine power, which, when cut, gave a very definite deceleration, although the undercarriage was a little on the bouncy side.

The SBD-5 was not quite the end of Dauntless evolution as, somewhat belatedly, a still more powerful version of the Cyclone was applied, the R-1820-66 offering 1,350 hp at 2,700 rpm for take-off and military ratings of 1,300 hp at 2,600 rpm from sea level to 4,000 ft (1 220 m) and 1,000 hp from 11,300 to 17,500 ft (3 445 to 5 335 m). This power plant was installed in the final Dauntless production model, the SBD-6, but the heyday of the veteran dive bomber had long since passed and, as a result of contractual cutbacks, only 450 production SBD-6s were completed, these, with non-metallic self-sealing tanks of 284 US gal (1 075 l) total capacity and ASV radar, were delivered between March and July 1944 to bring Dauntless production to an end.

The Dauntless remained until late 1944 the primary US Navy shipboard dive bomber and equipped no fewer than 20 US Marine Corps squadrons, but it faded from service rapidly with the end of hostilities. It had established an enviable record for reliability and toughness and its career in the Pacific had certainly been illustrious. Yet, from the performance standpoint it had been a very mediocre aeroplane and having operated for much of the time in a non air superiority environment, one is left with a deep respect for its crews. I personally did not find the hidden quality in the Dauntless that I had sought on the strength of its remarkable operational reputation. I could only conclude that it was to be numbered among that handful of aeroplanes that have achieved outstanding success against all odds. □

Douglas SBD-5 Dauntless Specification

Power Plant: One Wright R-1820-60 Cyclone nine-cylinder radial air-cooled engine rated (military) at 1,200 hp at 2,500 rpm from sea level to 1,800 ft (550 m) and 1,000 hp at 2,500 rpm from 8,100 ft (2 470 m) to 13,800 ft (4 205 m), or (normal) 1,000 hp at 2,300 rpm from sea level to 5,700 ft (1 735 m) and 900 hp at 2,300 rpm from 9,300 ft (2 835 m) to 15,800 ft (4 815 m). Three-blade Hamilton Standard Hydromatic constant-speed propeller of 10 ft 10 in (3,30 m) diam. Total internal fuel capacity of 260 US gal (984 l) divided between two (centre section) 75 US gal (284 l) tanks and two (outer panel) 55 US gal (208 l) tanks. Provision for two jettisonable 58 US gal (219,5 l) underwing tanks.
Performance: (Clean aeroplane with max internal fuel at 9,530 lb/4 322 kg) Max speed 229 mph (368 km/h) at sea level, 253 mph (407 km/h) at 16,600 ft (5 060 m); range cruise, 144 mph (232 km/h) at 5,000 ft (1 525 m); max range, 1,295 mls (2 084 km); initial climb, 1,300 ft/min (6,6 m/sec); time to 10,000 ft (3 050 m), 8·0 min, to 20,000 ft (6 095 m), 18·3 min; service ceiling, 26,500 ft (8 075 m); stalling speed (power off), 76 mph (122 km/h; take-off distance (calm) 833 ft (254 m) (15 knot/28 km/h wind), 510 ft (155 m). (With 1,000 lb/453,6-kg bomb) Max speed, 221 mph (356 km/h) at sea level, 245 mph (394 km/h) at 15,800 ft (4 815 m); range cruise, 144 mph (232 km/h) at 5,000 ft (1 525 m); max range, 1,100 mls (1 770 km); initial climb (military power), 1,620 ft/min (8,23 m/sec), (Normal power), 1,190 ft/min (6,04 m/sec); time to 10,000 ft (3 050 m), 9·4 min, to 20,000 ft (6 095 m), 24·3 min.
Weights: Empty, 6,675 lb (3 028 kg); loaded (max internal fuel), 9,530 lb (4 322 kg); max take-off (one 500-lb/226,8-kg bomb and two drop tanks), 10,855 lb (4 924 kg).
Dimensions: Span, 41 ft 6⅜ in (12,66 m); length, 32 ft 6 in (9,91 m), height, 12 ft 11 in (3,94 m); wing area, 325 sq ft (30,19 m²).
Armament: Two 0·5-in (12,7-mm) Browning machine guns with 360 rpg in upper nose cowling and two 0·3-in (7,62-mm) Browning guns on flexible mount with 2,000 rpg in rear cockpit. One 500-lb (226,8-kg), 1,000-lb (453,6-kg) or 1,600-lb (725,76-kg) bomb, or 650-lb (294,84-kg) or 325-lb (147,42-kg) depth charge beneath fuselage, and provision for two 100-lb (45,36-kg) bombs or two 325-lb (147,42-kg) depth charges beneath wings.

Fairey Albacore

A MIABILITY, RELIABILITY AND STURDINESS! These were, by general consensus of its pilots, the primary virtues of Fairey's Albacore three-seat shipboard dive-and-torpedo-bomber-reconnaissance biplane; valuable attributes indeed but hardly sufficient in themselves to result in an outstanding combat aeroplane. In retrospect, the Albacore epitomised the ascendancy of the conventionalists over the visionaries; the least adventurous approach that could possibly have been made to solving the problem of replacing the venerable and patently obsolescent Swordfish. That the authorities should have opted to perpetuate the biplane configuration at a time when the imminence of its final demise in all operational rôles was surely obvious to all is difficult to comprehend today, forty years on; particularly so when it is recalled that, at the time the definitive specification was being framed that was to give the Albacore birth, the US Navy was already preparing to introduce into service its first shipboard *monoplane* torpedo-bombers.

Not that Fairey had failed to proffer a monoplane proposal intended to fulfil the Navy's requirement, but in their wisdom, the authorities decided that, for the tasks required of the new aircraft, the monoplane was still very much an unknown quantity. Thus, Fairey had gone about what can only be considered as the over-development of an anachronistic formula. Admittedly, the design team made as many concessions to modernity as could usefully be incorporated in an aircraft whose basic configuration was already *passé* while still on the drawing board. There is no denying that the Albacore *did* offer some advances over the aircraft that it was intended to succeed — notably in terms of crew comfort — but the result was inevitably an unspectacu-

lar aeroplane and one lacking some of the qualities responsible for the success of its predecessor. Indeed, the inferior manoeuvrability of the Albacore and its less responsive controls, coupled with substantially larger dimensions affording the opposition an easier target, were to result in the Swordfish outliving its intended successor whose career from inception to demise was to prove most noteworthy for its brevity.

Intended to fulfil the requirements of specification S.41/36, the Albacore had been effectively ordered "off the drawing board", the two prototypes. L7074 and L7075, being the first aircraft in a contract for 100 placed with Fairey' Hayes factory in May 1937. If its biplane configuration can be ignored, it may be said to have offered numerous features, which, in so far as the British Fleet Air Arm of the day was concerned, were quite innovatory. For example, it had an all-metal monocoque fuselage, a sleeve-valve engine driving a variable-pitch propeller, automatic leading-edge slats on the upper mainplanes and hydraulically-operated flaps on the lower intended primarily for use as dive brakes; its cockpits were fully enclosed and offered such welcome aids to comfort as heating circuits. Further refinements included a windscreen wiper for the pilot and even a device that automatically launched the dinghy in the event of ditching. Small wonder that the Albacore was promptly pronounced a "Stringbag" for gentlemen by the first pilots to convert from the Swordfish. They were not to evince such enthusiasm, however, over the performance of their new mount which they adjudged decidely sedate, while lack of control responsiveness also gave reason for misgivings.

The arrival of the Albacore in the squadrons had been

notably belated. Its 14-cylinder two-row sleeve-valve Taurus engine was reputedly an outstanding power plant, smooth running and incredibly quiet after the Pegasus of the Swordfish — the low noise level being a characteristic of the sleeve-valve design which was to earn for the Hercules-powered Beaufighter the grim soubriquet of "Whispering Death" from the Japanese some years later. Unfortunately, the Taurus had suffered its development problems and, as a consequence, the first prototype Albacore had not flown until 12 December 1938, some nine months later than scheduled.

Delay had piled on delay, with the result that the first service deliveries had not been effected until mid-March 1940, at least a year later than anticipated at the time the first contract had been placed. By May 1942, when I was to make my first acquaintance with the Albacore at the Deck Landing Training Unit in which I was serving at Arbroath, Fairey's Hayes factory was — so I was told at the time — full of Albacores when it should have been full of Fireflies, and this last British operational biplane had barely more than 18 months of operational service left to it.

In the summer of 1942, however, the Albacore was still at the pinnacle of its operational career, with about 14 FAA squadrons mounted on the type, both ashore and afloat. Whatever other qualities it had revealed, the Albacore had proved painfully slow and very vulnerable. Its operations had, for the most part, been of note more for the valour of the Albacore crews than for achievements, particularly heavy casualties having been sustained during the previous July, when Albacores launched from *Furious* and *Victorious* had attacked Petsamo and Kirkenes. Albacore pilots mourned the loss of manoeuvrability that had been available to them with the Swordfish — you could more or less wrap a "Stringbag" around its own length — and if the controls of the earlier biplane had not been exactly crisp, those of the Albacore were sluggish by comparison.

My first impression of the Albacore was one of size. It seemed so much larger than its predecessor and those thick wings and that massive undercarriage, let alone the wealth of struts and bracing wires, were eloquent of the sort of performance that one might expect. Of course, its beautifully-cowled Taurus offered a lot more power than the Pegasus of the old "Stringbag" but I wondered how much of this was absorbed in compensating for the built-in drag.

A single-bay all-metal biplane, the Albacore was essentially simple in concept. Its equi-span fabric-covered wings

(Head of the opposite page and above left top) Albacores of No 826 Squadron which flew nocturnal operations against Rommel's Afrika Korps and resupply missions for forward 8th Army units, operating at times from Dekeila, Haifa, Benghazi, Blida and Hal Far. (Immediately above left and below) The first prototype Albacore (L7074) which first flew on 12 December 1938

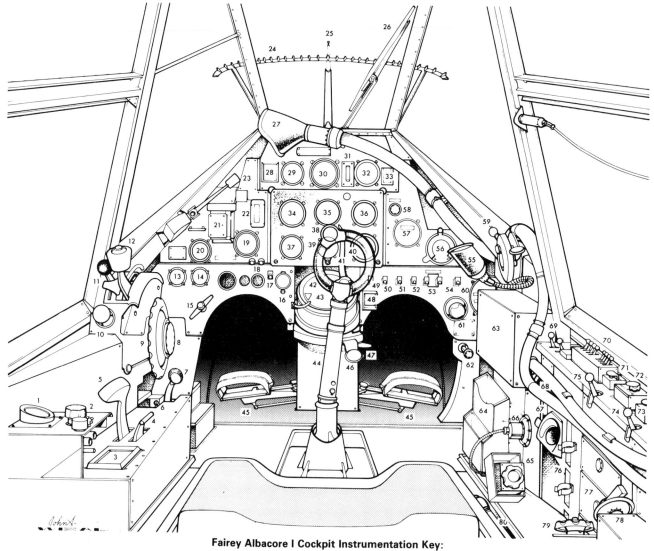

Fairey Albacore I Cockpit Instrumentation Key:

1 Brake system accumulator pressure gauge
2 Hydraulic hand pump connections
3 Ground-to-air signals card holder
4 Arrester hook release lever
5 Flap control lever
6 Landing lamp switch
7 Landing lamp dipping lever
8 Rudder trimming tab control (inner handwheel)
9 Elevator trimming tab control (outer handwheel)
10 Throttle lever friction adjuster
11 Mixture control lever
12 Throttle control lever (with bomb release switch)
13 Carburettor air intake heat control
14 Carburettor cut-out control
15 Fuel cock control
16 Arrester hook indicator lamp
17 Arrester hook switch
18 Ignition switches
19 Clock
20 Hydraulic pressure gauge
21 Fire extinguisher switch

22 Fuel pressure gauge
23 Propeller speed control lever
24 External torpedo sight
25 External bead gunsight
26 Windscreen wiper
27 Speaking tube mouthpiece
28 ASI correction card holder
29 Oil temperature gauge
30 Cylinder temperature gauge
31 Oil pressure gauge
32 Boost pressure gauge
33 Compass deviation card holder
34 ASI
35 Artificial horizon
36 Rate-of-climb/descent indicator
37 Altimeter
38 Browning gun and gun camera firing button (on control grip)
39 Direction indicator and setting knob (partially obscured by control grip)
40 Turning indicator (partially obscured by control grip)
41 Brake operating lever (on control grip)

42 Control grip
43 P.4 compass
44 Control column
45 Rudder pedals
46 Oil cooler flap control
47 Cockpit heating control
48 Cartridge starter firing switch
49 Cartridge starter master switch
50 Windscreen wiper switch
51 Pitot head heater switch
52 Formation lights switch
53 Navigation lights switches (port and starboard)
54 Downward recognition light selector switch
55 Cockpit lamp
56 Fuel contents gauge
57 Engine-speed indicator
58 Torpedo sight dimmer switch
59 Identification light switchbox
60 Navigation lights dimmer switch (partially obscured by bomb distributor)
61 Engine priming pump
62 Cartridge starter re-loading control
63 Automatic bomb distributor

64 Maps/computer card stowage bins
65 Torpedo sight control switch (OR camera exposure-indicator lamp for PR duty)
66 Torpedo sight control switch plug
67 Signal pistol housing
68 Speaking tubes
69 Bomb fusing switches
70 Bomb selector switches
71 Bomb container jettison switch
72 Bomb jettison switch
73 Bomb master switch
74 Headrest release control
75 Safety harness release control
76 Signal pistol cartridge stowage clips (2)
77 Signal pistol cartridge stowage bins (2)
78 Fuel jettison control
79 Fuel jettison control air supply stop valve
80 Seat operating handle and locking plunger

carried ailerons on both top and bottom planes and hydraulically-operated flaps on the inboard portion of each lower mainplane. Automatic slats had originally been incorporated in the leading edges of the outboard portions of the upper mainplanes, but their unsatisfactory characteristics had led to their deletion. The light alloy monocoque fuselage incorporated steel-tube engine mounting, centre section and tail bay, the centre section being bolted to the monocoque

decking between the cockpits. The fixed tail surfaces were of stressed-skin construction and all movable control surfaces were fabric covered.

After clambering into the Albacore's cockpit, which was a long way off the ground, I found no major departure from the essentially simple theme that characterised the entire aircraft, the layout being very neat and clinical. Both the pilot's cockpit forward of the mainplanes and the crew's cockpit aft of the mainplanes — the two being divided by a very substantial 193 Imp Gal (877 1) fuel tank — were enclosed by a wealth of transparent panelling, and view from the lofty pilot's perch was most impressive, being very good forward, above and below. The Albacore had certainly been designed with an eye to ease of deck landing, and I could certainly understand the Swordfish boys' initial delight at exchanging their draughty cockpits for all this luxury.

The starting procedure for the Taurus sleeve-valve engine was quite straightforward, as, indeed, was everything about the Albacore. The propeller was turned slowly a couple of times by hand as a safeguard against oil causing an hydraulic lock of the pistons or sleeves, the induction system primed and the ignition switched on. The Coffman starter charger knob on the lower righthand side of the panel was pulled out slowly, the starter was switched on and the priming pump handle pulled. One stroke of the pump was given as the starter button was pushed, and the engine usually firing readily, being warmed up at a fast tick-over until cylinder temperature reached about 100°C (212°F) and oil temperature 15°C (59°F). After a few minutes warm-up, the Taurus was opened up to maximum boost for weak mixture cruise, propeller operation checked, the magnetos tested for drop with rich mixture and then full throttle (3,000-3,100 rpm), and boost and oil pressure checks.

Final checks on tabs, mixture, propeller pitch, etc. and the Albacore was ready to go, and once again I was struck by the very good view offered by the cockpit and the sewing machine-like qualities of the Taurus engine, which, after the raucous bellowing of the Pegasus of the "Stringbag", reminded me of the purr of a contented cat. The Albacore revealed no vices during the take-off run and, at 11,185 lb (5 074 kg), was pulled off at about 60 knots (111 km/h) IAS with 3,100 rpm and four-and-three-quarter pounds of boost, the climb out starting at about 85 knots (157 km/h) IAS, and the recommended climbing speed being some 96 knots (178 km/h) IAS at 2,800 rpm with three-and-a-half pounds of boost up to 6,000 ft (1 830 m). This altitude was reached in about eight minutes, or some three-and-a-half minutes less than was required by the Swordfish. Above 6,000 ft (1 830 m) it was recommended that the climbing speed be reduced by a knot (1,85 km) per 1,000 ft (305 m).

The Albacore was certainly a well-behaved and likeable aircraft. It was somewhat unstable longitudinally and a

(Above) Albacore N4259 photographed during service trials with an 18-in torpedo prior to allocation to a squadron, and (below) an unusual view of Albacore X9058, illustrating the excellent view offered the pilot and the extensive rear cockpit glazing

The tenth Albacore (L7083), illustrated below, left the parent company's Hayes factory late in 1939 and was delivered to the Royal Navy in the spring of 1940. Despite being patently obsolescent at the time of its debut, it was to be followed by a further 790 aircraft

Fairey Albacore I Cutaway Drawing Key:

1 Spinner
2 De Havilland three-blade variable-pitch propeller
3 Propeller gear casing
4 Exhaust ring securing struts
5 Annular exhaust nose ring
6 Bristol Taurus II 14-cylinder radial engine
7 Cowling joint cover plate
8 Cowling securing straps
9 Cable shackle fairings
10 Engine support ring
11 Engine lower bearer strut
12 Fuel pump
13 Engine accessories
14 Throttle/mixture levers
15 Carburettor
16 Oil heater
17 Oil tank (16 Imp gal/73 l capacity)
18 Intake fairing
19 Carburettor air intake
20 Gunsight bead (fixed forward-firing 0.303-in/7,7-mm machine gun in starboard lower mainplane root)
21 Starboard lower mainplane skinning
22 Starboard lower aileron
23 Stainless steel interplane bracing wires
24 Bracing wire attachment fairings
25 Lower mainplane internal bracing
26 Starboard aft interplane strut
27 Interplane strut bracing
28 Rear spar
29 Starboard lower mainplane ribs
30 Front spar
31 Starboard navigation light
32 Starboard lower handholds
33 Starboard forward interplane strut
34 Leading-edge automatic slat
35 Starboard upper handhold
36 Starboard upper mainplane tip
37 Aileron outer hinge
38 Starboard upper mainplane ribs
39 Front spar
40 Rear spar
41 Starboard upper aileron
42 Aileron control lever
43 Strengthened rib
44 Aileron centre hinge
45 Intemediate rib
46 Aileron inner hinge
47 Upper mainplane root end fitting
48 Aerial mast
49 Armour plate
50 Pilot's headrest
51 Sliding cockpit canopy hood
52 Gunsight ring
53 Windscreen wiper

54 External torpedo sight
55 Pilot's seat
56 Control grip/fixed 0.303-in/7,7-mm Browning gun firing button
57 Instrument panel
58 Rudder pedal assembly
59 Floor support cross beam
60 Oil cooler tunnel
61 Oil cooler assembly
62 Overload oil drain cock
63 Handhold/foot step
64 Overload oil tank
65 Underfloor control linkage
66 Elevator control horns
67 Inboard jury strut
68 Upper longeron
69 Hydraulic brake accumulator
70 Fuselage fuel tank (193 Imp gal/877 l capacity)

71 Diagonal jury brace
72 Solid centre-section
73 Fixed canopy section
74 Wing fold pivot
75 Starboard window (aft cockpit)
76 Navigator's compass
77 Navigator's folding swivel seat
78 Bomb-aimer's position
79 Ventral bomb-aiming window
80 Accumulators
81 Entry door (aft cockpit)
82 Cockpit floor support
83 Forward catapult spool
84 Radio receiver

85 Gunner's raised fire step
86 Float chute
87 Smoke float stowage bins (flame floats on starboard side)
88 Radio transmitter
89 Gunner's folding seat
90 Electrical panel
91 Wind deflector panel
92 Aerial lead-in
93 Gunner's hinged canopy section (raised)
94 Aerial
95 Reflector gunsight
96 Single (or twin) 0.303-in/7,7-mm Vickers 'K'-gun
97 Gun stowage trough
98 Gun mounting arm

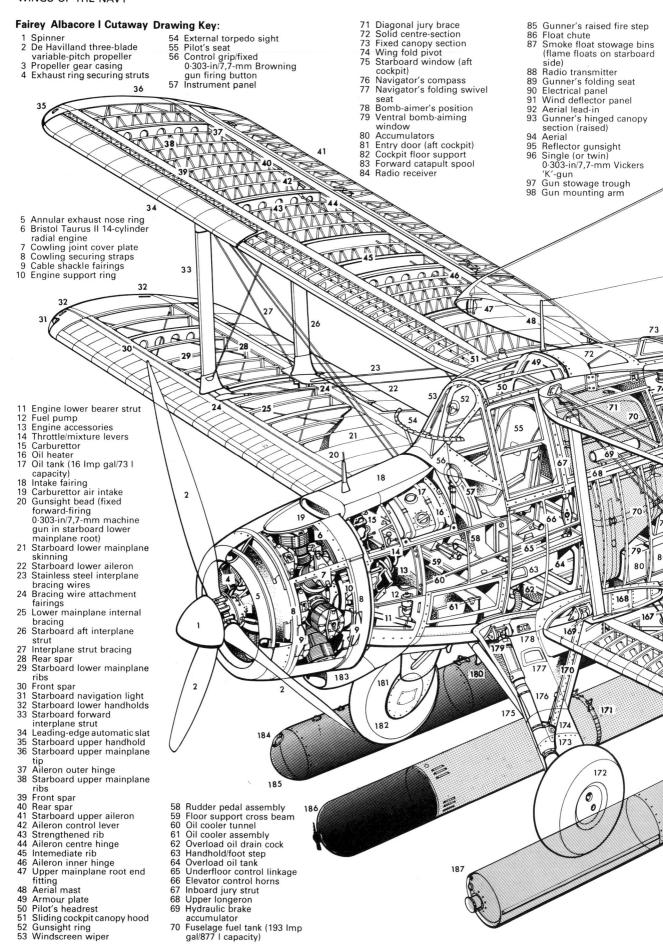

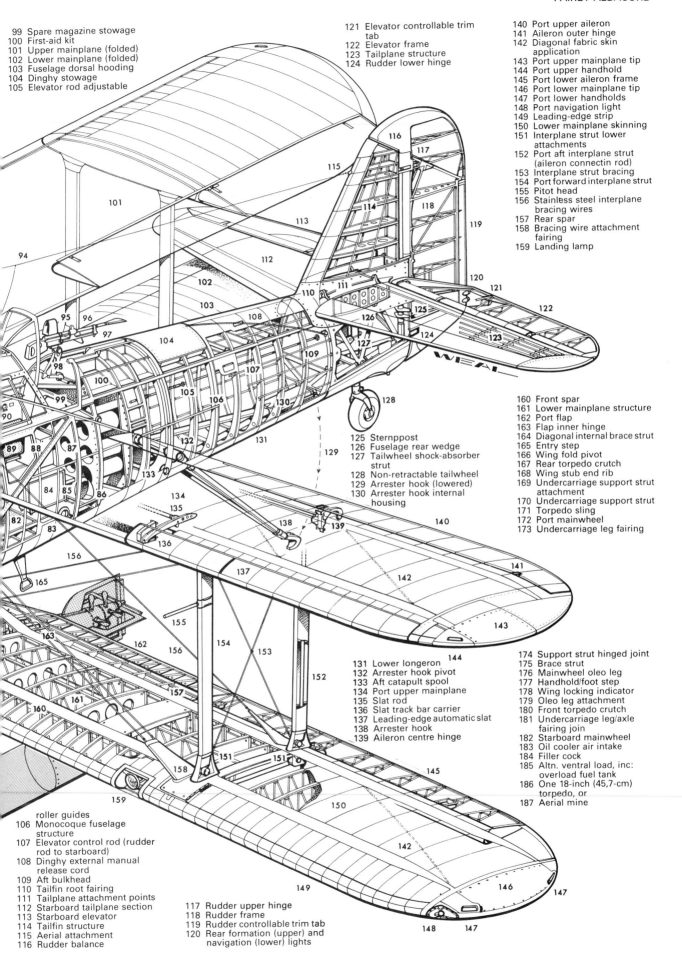

99 Spare magazine stowage
100 First-aid kit
101 Upper mainplane (folded)
102 Lower mainplane (folded)
103 Fuselage dorsal hooding
104 Dinghy stowage
105 Elevator rod adjustable

121 Elevator controllable trim
     tab
122 Elevator frame
123 Tailplane structure
124 Rudder lower hinge

140 Port upper aileron
141 Aileron outer hinge
142 Diagonal fabric skin
     application
143 Port upper mainplane tip
144 Port upper handhold
145 Port lower aileron frame
146 Port lower mainplane tip
147 Port lower handholds
148 Port navigation light
149 Leading-edge strip
150 Lower mainplane skinning
151 Interplane strut lower
     attachments
152 Port aft interplane strut
     (aileron connectin rod)
153 Interplane strut bracing
154 Port forward interplane strut
155 Pitot head
156 Stainless steel interplane
     bracing wires
157 Rear spar
158 Bracing wire attachment
     fairing
159 Landing lamp

125 Sternppost
126 Fuselage rear wedge
127 Tailwheel shock-absorber
     strut
128 Non-retractable tailwheel
129 Arrester hook (lowered)
130 Arrester hook internal
     housing

160 Front spar
161 Lower mainplane structure
162 Port flap
163 Flap inner hinge
164 Diagonal internal brace strut
165 Entry step
166 Wing fold pivot
167 Rear torpedo crutch
168 Wing stub end rib
169 Undercarriage support strut
     attachment
170 Undercarriage support strut
171 Torpedo sling
172 Port mainwheel
173 Undercarriage leg fairing

131 Lower longeron
132 Arrester hook pivot
133 Aft catapult spool
134 Port upper mainplane
135 Slat rod
136 Slat track bar carrier
137 Leading-edge automatic slat
138 Arrester hook
139 Aileron centre hinge

174 Support strut hinged joint
175 Brace strut
176 Mainwheel oleo leg
177 Handhold/foot step
178 Wing locking indicator
179 Oleo leg attachment
180 Front torpedo crutch
181 Undercarriage leg/axle
     fairing join
182 Starboard mainwheel
183 Oil cooler air intake
184 Filler cock
185 Altn. ventral load, inc:
     overload fuel tank
186 One 18-inch (45,7-cm)
     torpedo, or
187 Aerial mine

     roller guides
106 Monocoque fuselage
     structure
107 Elevator control rod (rudder
     rod to starboard)
108 Dinghy external manual
     release cord
109 Aft bulkhead
110 Tailfin root fairing
111 Tailplane attachment points
112 Starboard tailplane section
113 Starboard elevator
114 Tailfin structure
115 Aerial attachment
116 Rudder balance

117 Rudder upper hinge
118 Rudder frame
119 Rudder controllable trim tab
120 Rear formation (upper) and
     navigation (lower) lights

(Above) The second Albacore (L7075) photographed in 1939 while on test from the Great West aerodrome. Note externally-mounted dinghy pack on top of rear fuselage. (Below left) A standard production Albacore (X9058), this view showing graphically the very considerable wing span of this torpedo-bomber biplane

degree of concentration had to be exercised when climbing through cloud, the ailerons proved to be on the heavy side, while the elevator was fairly sensitive, but it was a safe aeroplane for instrument flying. When it came to manoeuvrability, however, I could not help feel some concern for Albacore crews that came up against fighter opposition or met up with heavy groundfire. I should perhaps make it clear at this juncture that my operational career was as a fighter pilot and so my attitude to manoeuvrability was inevitably biased. I do know that the majority of the Albacore pilots well liked the flying characteristics of this decidedly sedate biplane while decrying its lack of agility in operational situations. Its cruise performance was better than that of the Swordfish, although only nominally so, being about 9 knots (17 km/h) faster in weak mixture cruise at 2,500 rpm, and I was told that this advantage increased to some 17 knots (31

km/h) with rich mixture at 2,800 rpm. I was prepared to believe this, but never had the patience to work the Albacore up to full gallop. Of course, it was not in level speed that the Albacore scored over the Swordfish but in range and service ceiling, both of which were almost doubled.

The Albacore was designed for diving at speeds up to 215 knots (400 km/h) IAS with flaps either up or down, and it was certainly steady in a dive, recovery being easy and smooth, but some care had to be taken not to use the elevator too sharply. The Albacore could not, of course, be spun and aerobatics were definitely not permitted. The stall was a fairly innocuous affair, taking place at about 68 knots (126 km/h) with flaps up in normal loaded condition and at some 66 knots (122 km/h) with flaps down. The final approach was made at 75 knots (139 km/h) and throughout this gentle beast behaved impeccably, leaving one with an impression of quiet reliability and efficiency but the inescapable conclusion that here was a truly unspectacular aeroplane.

I have two very distinct recollections of the Albacore and the first of these sharply remembered incidents involved bouncing one off the North Sea in the region of St Andrews when carrying out anti-fighter attack tactics when serving in a Service Trials Unit at Crail. The theory was that straight and level flight at nought feet over the sea would effectively counter any fighter attack, which, in fact, it did, but in my enthusiasm to get really low I misjudged the distance beneath my feet that the damned big undercarriage extended — until the Albacore made skimming contact with the water! Comments from the rear cockpit were voluble in telling me that the wheels were wet and spinning! The Albacore certainly was a *forgiving* aeroplane. The second incident took place while I was stationed with the Service Trials Unit at Arbroath in 1942, and resulted from a crazy wager that I would fly every aircraft type that we had under the Tay Bridge! This was easy enough under the centre spans, but when the wager progressed to the much smaller spans nearer the bank . . . .! The Albacore proved to be the tightest fit in this silly escapade and it says much for the tolerance of the citizens of Dundee that they never once complained about these performances, bless their hearts.

The FAA specially formed No 826 Squadron to take the Albacore and this unit received a dozen aircraft at RNAS Ford, Sussex, on 15 March 1940. Ten weeks later, on 31 May, three weeks after the *Wehrmacht* invasion of the Low

Another view of the second Albacore (see opposite page) during manufacturer's trials in 1939. Development and production of this type suffered numerous delays, the initial flight test programme commencing some nine months later than scheduled and service deliveries being initiated more than a year late

Countries, No 826 took its Albacores into action, attacking E-boats off Zeebrugge and bombing road and rail communications at Westende, between Ostende and Nieuwpoort, on the Belgian coast, fortunately without encountering much opposition. Over the next six months, before embarking aboard *Formidable*. No 826 flew operations under Coastal Command's direction, the majority from Bircham Newton, Norfolk, but on occasions from Detling and Jersey, escorting a total of 92 convoys, laying 214 mines in enemy waters and dropping 56 tons of bombs, and during the course of these — mostly nocturnal — operations, it was to claim five enemy aircraft destoyed or damaged at a cost of four Albacores.

On 26 November 1940, No 826 finally took its Albacores aboard a carrier for the first time, joining *Formidable*, together with the similarly-equipped No 829 Squadron which had been formed at Lee-on-Solent in June, to escort a convoy to Cape Town. These two *Formidable*-based squadrons were destined to be the first Albacore-equipped units to participate in a naval operation of any importance, the carrier's complement of a dozen Albacores mounting three strikes against an Italian naval force south-west of Crete on 29 March 1941. Using torpedoes for the first time, the Albacores, in concert with a smaller number of Swordfish, pressed home their attacks through exceedingly heavy anti-aircraft fire, recording at least one hit on the Italian Navy's flagship, the battleship *Vittorio Veneto*. Two months later, on 25 May, four Albacores from *Formidable* dive-bombed the enemy-occupied airfield at Scarpanto, Crete, but such was the damage suffered by the carrier as a result of *Luftwaffe* attack that she was forced to withdraw for repairs and her complement of aircraft could thus play no further rôle in the Cretan campaign.

Many other FAA squadrons had meanwhile equipped with the Albacore, the first of these, following close on those embarked aboard *Formidable*, having been Nos 828 and 827 formed at Ford and Yeovilton in September and October 1940 respectively. Sadly, the success achieved by the Albacore in its first action during the Battle of Cape Matapan was not to be maintained, for the next major operation in which it participated, an attack on the harbours of Petsamo and Kirkenes in July 1941 mounted by Nos 817, 822, 827 and 828 squadrons flying from *Victorious* and *Furious*, was to produce only limited results and heavy casualties. Even less successful was the attack launched from *Victorious* in the following

March by the Albacores of No 817 Squadron against the battleship *Tirpitz*. But if further major successes were to elude it, the Albacore was to enjoy a number of more minor successes during the relatively brief operational career left to it.

After returning to the Mediterranean in July 1941, *Formidable* disembarked No 826 Squadron in North Africa and, initially operating from the satellite airfield of Ma'aten Bagush, this unit's Albacores patrolled the coastline and operated in conjunction with the cruisers of the Alexandria-based 7th Squadron. Subsequently, this squadron flew nocturnal bombing attacks against Rommel's *Afrika Korps* and resupply missions for forward 8th Army units. In the meantime, No 828 Squadron had arrived in Malta with Albacores, and had commenced sorties from Hal Far against targets in Italy, Sicily and North Africa, mounting far-ranging torpedo strikes over the Mediterranean, but one of the most extraordinary operational missions flown by the Albacore took place

Albacores of No 828 Squadron, shore-based at Hal Far, Malta, are seen below flying over the island's shoreline prior to an anti-shipping strike

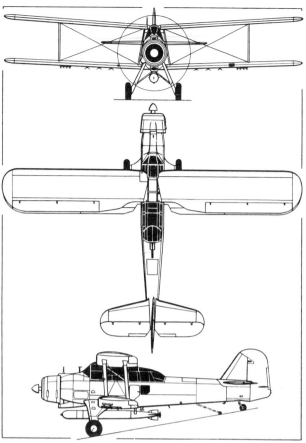

(Below) A formation of Albacores from the Royal Naval Air Torpedo School carrying practice torpedoes en route to an attack on a target vessel. The Albacore's first-line service career was relatively brief and this type had left the Fleet Air Arm's operational strength by the end of 1943

on 9 July 1942. On this occasion, nine aircraft of No 826 Squadron were refuelled by Bombays on an airstrip some 250 miles (400 km) behind the enemy lines in order to deliver a night attack on a convoy near Tobruk.

Albacores were to play a significant rôle during Operation *Torch,* the Allied invasion of North Africa, four squadrons, Nos 817, 820, 822 and 832, participating and flying anti-submarine and anti-surface vessel patrols, and attacking airfields and strongpoints resisting the invasion forces. By this time, November 1942, the Albacore was serving with or had seen service with 14 FAA squadrons and, incidentally, two RAF squadrons, but its days of widespread service usage were by now strictly numbered, and within a year, all but two squadrons had re-equipped, these being No 820, which was to be the last to fly Albacores from a carrier, having taken part in the invasion of Sicily and the Salerno landing while operating from *Formidable,* and No 841, which, since its inception in July 1942, had been exclusively shore-based in the UK and had operated under the aegis of RAF Fighter Command at Manston.

Both of these squadrons were disbanded during the course of November 1943, but the Albacore still lingered on. No 841 Squadron handed its Albacores to No 415 Squadron RCAF, which equipped its 'A' Flight with these aircraft for (primarily nocturnal) coastal operations. Thus, although no longer included on FAA operational strength, the Albacore continued to play a rôle, highlights of its career with the Canadian squadron including the sinking of the torpedo boat *Greif,* on 24 May 1944, and the suppression of enemy E-boats attempting to interfere with Allied shipping following the invasion of Normandy. As a result of its service with No 415 Squadron, the Albacore gained two distinctions: it was the last operational biplane to be used by the RCAF and the only one ever to see action.

The Albacore's operational life (excluding its service with the RCAF) had spanned only three war years, a total of 800, including prototypes, having been built by the time the last had been rolled off the assembly line in 1943. It had served from the Arctic to the Equator and for all its limitations and deficiencies, which, for the most part, stemmed from the unimaginative specification that had begotten it, was a like-able aeroplane, gentle with the ham-fisted and possessing no vices. It could absorb quite a lot of punishment and remain airborne, it was reliable, and if fighters could be kept off its back, it was efficient. Many more famed aircraft of World War II were far less deserving of such an epitaph. □

Fairey Albacore Specification

Power Plant: One Bristol Taurus XII 14-cylinder sleeve-valve two-row radial air-cooled engine rated at 1,085 hp at 3,100 rpm for take-off and having a max rating (five minutes) of 1,130 hp at 3,100 rpm at 3,500 ft (1 065 m). Three-bladed de Havilland variable-pitch propeller. Internal fuel capacity: 193 Imp gal (877 l) in fuselage tank.
Performance: Max speed (torpedo-bomber at 11,186 lb/5 074 kg), 159 mph (256 km/h) at 4,000 ft (1 220 m); econ cruise, 114 mph (183 km/h) at 6,000 ft (1 830 m); range (with 1,610-lb/730-kg torpedo), 930 mls (1 497 km), (with four 500-lb/226,8-kg bombs), 710 mls (1 143 km); time to 6,000 ft (1 830 m), 8·0 min; service ceiling (at 11,186 lb/5 074 kg), 20,700 ft (6 310 m), (at 12,300 lb/5 579 kg), 15,000 ft (4 570 m).
Weights: Empty equipped, 7,250 lb (3 292 kg); normal loaded, 11,186 lb (5 074 kg); max loaded, 12,500 lb (5,670 kg).
Dimensions: Span, 49 ft 11¾ in (15,23 m); length, 39 ft 11¾ in (12,18 m); height (tail down) 12 ft 6 in (3,81 m); wing area, 607 sq ft (56,39 m²); wheel track, 8 ft 3¾ in (2,53 m).
Armament: One 0·303-in (7,7-mm) Browning machine gun in starboard lower mainplane and one 0·303-in (7,7-mm) Vickers 'K' machine gun on flexible mount in rear cockpit. External loads of six 100-lb (45,36-kg) AS and four 20-lb (9,0-kg) bombs, six 250-lb (113,4-kg) GP or SAP and four 20-lb (9,0-kg) bombs, three 500-lb (226,8-kg) GP or SAP bombs, or one 1,610-lb (730-kg) 18-in (45,70-cm) torpedo.

Fairey Fulmar

THE DELIVERY to RNAS Worthy Down in June 1940 of the first production Fulmar fleet fighters to await the arrival of No 806 Squadron was certainly accompanied by some heartfelt sighs of relief within the hallowed halls of the Admiralty. The Royal Navy at last had a shipboard fighter packing healthy firepower and coupling this most desirable of attributes with a performance which could at least be considered respectable. It was to be said of the handsome Fairey monoplane that it lacked the fighter's first essential — speed. There is no gainsaying that it *was* slow by then contemporary land-based single-seat fighter standards, but it was not short of other qualities and, if incapable of taking on a Messerschmitt Bf 109 on anything like equal terms, its advent was, in so far as the Fleet Air Arm was concerned, very welcome indeed.

The Fulmar was not a lightly-loaded short-range interceptor in the category of the Spitfire and any performance comparison with such was therefore unfair; it was a sizeable and fairly weighty two-seat shipboard fighter for the defence of the Fleet, possessing plenty of endurance and offering the reconnaissance capability so vital to naval forces. It was indeed fortunate that barely six months after what may be referred to as the first *true* prototype of the Fulmar had flown, with Fairey's test pilot Duncan Menzies at the controls, No 806 Squadron, with a full complement of Fulmars, should be embarked aboard *Illustrious* and heading for the Mediterranean. It was also quite fortuitous.

Much of my early training had been undertaken on the Fairey Battle, a gentle and amiable beast but not really of the stuff that breeds fighter pilots. I was immediately reminded of this ponderous day bomber-cum-advanced trainer upon being introduced to the Fulmar for the first time, but although only marginally smaller, the new fighter presented nothing of the massive clumsiness that I associated with the Battle. Its relationship appeared closer to that smaller, cleaned-up and generally-improved intended successor to the Battle, the exceptionally sleek-looking P.4/34, of which I had seen many illustrations in the aviation magazines of the day. The fine lines were still there but the Fulmar imparted an impression of purposeful sturdiness rather than one of

ballerina-like grace that had seemed to characterise its forerunner; the more prominent nose radiator of the fighter endowed it with a somewhat pugnacious appearance.

Unbeknown to me at the time was the fact that the Fulmar *was,* to all intents and purposes, the P.4/34. It was fortuitous that when specification O.8/38 calling for a two-seat naval fighter was issued, Fairey had been flight testing its P.4/34 contender and that this should have provided a sound basis for an aircraft meeting the new requirement, otherwise No 806 Squadron would have in all probability still been

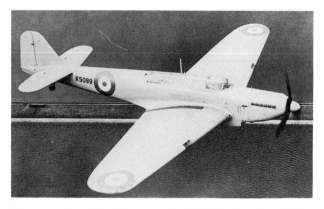

The progenitor of the Fulmar was the P.4/34 day bomber, the first example of which (K5099) is illustrated above and the second (K7555) below. A production Fulmar Mk II is illustrated at the head of the page

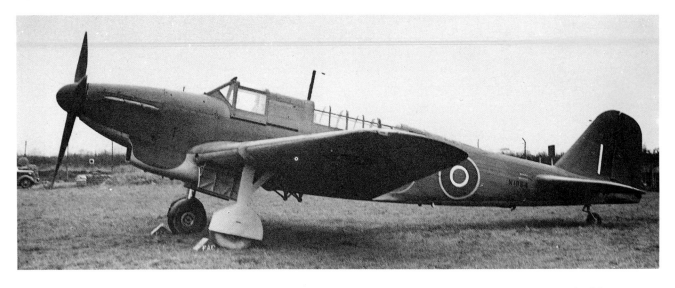

(Above and immediately below left) The first production Fulmar (N1854), which flew on 4 January 1940 at Ringway, was utilised for prototype trials, being retained by the manufacturer for development purposes and eventually being modified to Mk II standards

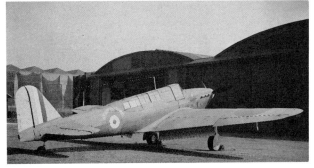

mounted on Skuas when it set sail aboard *Illustrious* in July 1940, for the design development of an entirely new fighter from scratch would certainly have added a couple of years to the time scale. Marcel Lobelle's design to the P.4/34 requirement had been stressed for dive bombing and it was thus sufficiently robust without basic structural redesign to absorb the punishment that would be meted out to it during the course of shipboard operation, and it had proved possible to modify in essential respects the second prototype of the light bomber, which had flown a year earlier, on 19 April 1937, as a flying mock-up of the proposed fleet fighter. It was thanks to the availability of this aircraft that there had been no need for a prototype of the Fulmar as such, and what was to be referred to as the prototype (N1854), which first flew at Ringway on 4 January 1940, was in fact, the first production aircraft.

The first genuine Fulmar had flown only 20 months after, on 5 May 1938, instructions to proceed had been issued — an extraordinary achievement by any standard — and the principal changes by comparison with the original bomber prototype were the provision of wing folding, catapult points and deck-arrester gear, a later, uprated mark of Rolls-Royce Merlin engine and, of course, a battery of eight wing-mounted 0·303-in (7,7 mm) Browning machine guns. It was

(Immediately above left) The second Fulmar (N1855), which, together with N1858 (below), went to the A & AEE for trials, the latter eventually being used by Fairey for tests with a number of devices, including Youngman and double-split flaps

hardly to be expected that speed and climb performance would compare favourably with the smaller and lighter RAF fighters powered by the same engine. At this point in time, navigational aids which could be operated by a pilot had reached an insufficient stage in development to guarantee that a single-seat fighter would be capable of regaining its carrier in inclement weather, rendering, in the British view, provision of a second seat for a navigator *de rigueur,* and coupled with the fuel load necessary for the desired endurance of some four hours, a pretty substantial aeroplane would have been inevitable even had it not been based on an existing bomber design.

The second Fulmar (N1855) had flown on 6 April 1940, joining the first aircraft at the A&AEE at Boscombe Down on 3 May, spinning trials being completed a week later. The first Production Trials Aircraft (N1856) had come off test on 7 May and had been delivered to the Service Trials Unit at Lee-on-Solent within three days; another (N1858) had arrived at the A&AEE for armament trials on 21 May, and within four weeks a further 10 Fulmars had been delivered and, partly mounted on the new fighter, No 806 Squadron had embarked on *Illustrious* for a work up. By the beginning of September 1940 — a mere eight months after the first example had flown and its existence still a closely guarded secret — the Fulmar was flying combat missions over the Mediterranean in defence of the Malta cnvoys!

The fact that so short a time elapsed between initial production deliveries and first combat missions spoke volumes for the basic rightness of the Fulmar. It was a comfortable aeroplane in every sense of the word — it looked right, it felt right when one sat in the cockpit and it was certainly easy to fly. It possessed a pleasant, forgiving nature and if its combat performance could be criticised — and such criticisms should in truth be levelled at the specification which had brought about its existence — there was little with which the most fastidious of pilots could find fault in its handling characteristics. In short, everybody liked it.

The Fulmar was of flush-riveted stressed-skin construction with fabric-covered control surfaces and a sturdy, wide-track, inward-retracting undercarriage. Its cockpit had a clinical look about it for it was big enough to have afforded the designers scope to keep its layout neat and tidy, which is more than can be said for most naval aircraft of the day. It was the first naval fighter to feature the classic "T" arrangement of the blind flying panel, and the view from the the pilot's seat was good despite the longish nose. the pilot sat directly over the wing leading edge and thus had a particularly good downward view for reconnaissance.

Taxying the Fulmar was easy as both ground stability and brakes were good, and it had a tendency towards tail heaviness. Although it was inclined to crab a little to port, take-off was generally straightforward and short, with the medium-supercharged Merlin VIII, which was rated at 1,080 hp at 3,000 rpm and with 4 lb boost for take-off, giving the smooth power surge so beloved by all who flew behind that remarkable Rolls-Royce engine. Under standard day conditions at sea level with zero wind and at 9,800 lb (4 445 kg), it lifted off from a grass field within 320 yards (293 m), clearing 50 ft

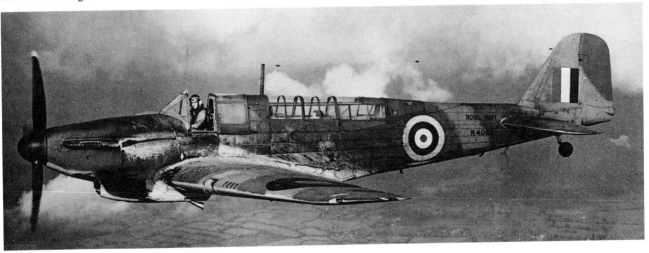

(Above) A production Fulmar Mk I (N4062) delivered to the Royal Navy in late 1940 and (below) the seventh Fulmar Mk I (N1860) with the Royal Navy's Fulmar Flight in the Western Desert in 1941, this performing convoy patrols along the coast

Fairey Fulmar I Specification

Power Plant: One Rolls-Royce Merlin VIII 12-cylinder 60 deg vee liquid-cooled engine rated at 1,080 hp at 3,000 rpm for take-off and 1,035 hp at 3,000 rpm at 7,750 ft (2 370 m) driving three-bladed constant-speed fully-feathering propeller of 11 ft 6 in (3,50 m). Fuel capacity, 155 Imp gal (705 l) in fuselage and provision for 60-gal (273 l) flush-fitting ventral tank.

Performance: (At 9,800 lb/4 445 kg with 100 octane fuel and 9·5 lb boost) Max speed, 246 mph (396 km/h) at sea level, 256 mph (412 km/h) at 2,400 ft (730 m), 246 mph (396 km/h) at 9,000 ft (2 745 m), 220 mph (354 km/h) at 20,000 ft (6 095 m), (with 87 octane fuel and 4·0 lb boost), 213 mph (343 km/h) at sea level, 246 mph (396 km/h) at 9,000 ft (2 745 m); initial climb, 1,105 ft/min (5,61 m/sec), at 7,000 ft (2 135 m), 1,210 ft/min (6,15 m/sec); service ceiling, 22,400 ft (6 827 m); time to 7,000 ft (2 135 m), 6·0 min, to 20,000 ft (6 095 m), 26·5 min; max range, 830 mls (1 336 km) at 10,000 ft (3 050 m) at 150 mph (241 km/h).

Weights: Empty, 6,915 lb (3 137 kg); empty equipped, 7,384 lb (3 349 kg); normal loaded, 9,672 lb (4 387 lb); max take-off, 9,800 lb (4 445 kg).

Dimensions: Span, 46 ft 4½ in (14,14 m); length, 40 ft 3 in (12,27 m); height (tail down), 10 ft 8 in (3,25 m); folded width, 17 ft 10 in (5,44 m); wing area, 342 sq ft (31,77 m²); wheel track, 15 ft 8½ in (4,79 m).

Armament: Eight 0·303-in (7,7-mm) Browning machine guns with 500 rpg (plus single 0·303-in/7,7-mm Vickers 'K' gun on flexible mounting in rear cockpit of a few aircraft), and two 250-lb (113,4-kg) SAP or GP bombs, or two 250-lb (113,4-kg) B or 100-lb (45,36-kg) AS bombs.

(15,25 m) within a total distance of 510 yards (466 m). Climb was rather mediocre at 1,105 ft/min (5,60 m/sec) at sea level, increasing steadily to reach at around 7,000 ft (2 135 m) about 1,200 ft/min (6,10 m/sec), but at least this latter rate did not fall off too rapidly up to 15,000 ft (4 570 m), although by the time 20,000 ft (6 095 m) was attained the gain in altitude had dropped to a barely perceptible 270 ft/min (1,37 m/sec). Directional trim was sensitive and, for an aircraft of the size and weight of the Fulmar, the controls were relatively light and responsive, although they were too heavy and the aircraft too stable to permit the Fulmar to "mix it" with the extremely nimble but woefully under-armed Italian single-seaters that were to be among its first opponents.

Of course, the Fulmar pilot only needed to get a short bead on an Italian fighter to be pretty certain that his octet of Brownings would produce a "kill", but if he didn't get his opponent with that first burst, he rarely got a second chance. The Italian fighters of the day could not be classed as hot-rods in the international speed stakes, but a normally loaded Fulmar using 100 octane fuel and at 3,000 rpm plus 9·5 lb boost could barely touch 222 knots (412 km/h) at 2,400 ft (730 m) as its maximum level speed. It was extremely steady in a dive — during one test it was taken to 360 knots (668 km/h) and about 4 g was pulled during recovery, although some distortion of gun panels and cowlings resulted — but it

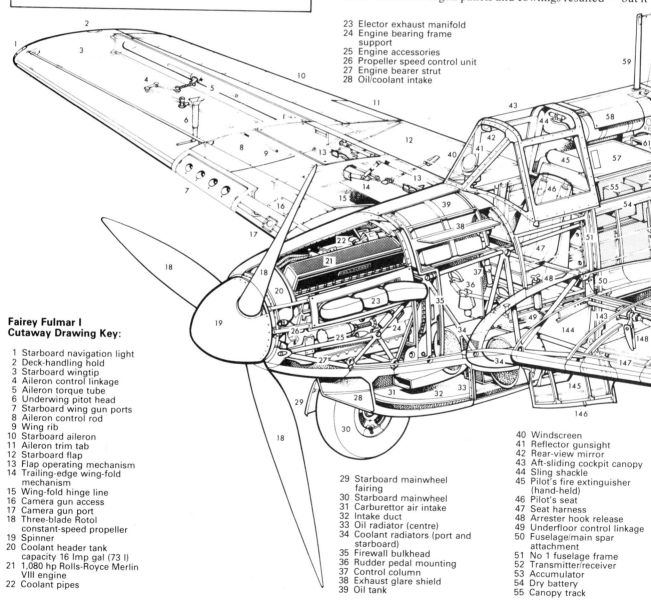

Fairey Fulmar I Cutaway Drawing Key:

1 Starboard navigation light
2 Deck-handling hold
3 Starboard wingtip
4 Aileron control linkage
5 Aileron torque tube
6 Underwing pitot head
7 Starboard wing gun ports
8 Aileron control rod
9 Wing rib
10 Starboard aileron
11 Aileron trim tab
12 Starboard flap
13 Flap operating mechanism
14 Trailing-edge wing-fold mechanism
15 Wing-fold hinge line
16 Camera gun access
17 Camera gun port
18 Three-blade Rotol constant-speed propeller
19 Spinner
20 Coolant header tank capacity 16 Imp gal (73 l)
21 1,080 hp Rolls-Royce Merlin VIII engine
22 Coolant pipes
23 Elector exhaust manifold
24 Engine bearing frame support
25 Engine accessories
26 Propeller speed control unit
27 Engine bearer strut
28 Oil/coolant intake
29 Starboard mainwheel fairing
30 Starboard mainwheel
31 Carburettor air intake
32 Intake duct
33 Oil radiator (centre)
34 Coolant radiators (port and starboard)
35 Firewall bulkhead
36 Rudder pedal mounting
37 Control column
38 Exhaust glare shield
39 Oil tank
40 Windscreen
41 Reflector gunsight
42 Rear-view mirror
43 Aft-sliding cockpit canopy
44 Sling shackle
45 Pilot's fire extinguisher (hand-held)
46 Pilot's seat
47 Seat harness
48 Arrester hook release
49 Underfloor control linkage
50 Fuselage/main spar attachment
51 No 1 fuselage frame
52 Transmitter/receiver
53 Accumulator
54 Dry battery
55 Canopy track

lost quite a lot of height during a recovery from a spin. Stalling speed with flaps and undercarriage up was some 66 knots (122 km/h) — although Boscombe Down tests had shown that this could be reduced by about 3·5 knots (6,5 km/h) if the gun ports were faired over — and with flaps and undercarriage down was 56 knots (105 km/h), landing run at 9,800 lb (4 445 kg) being about 310 yards (283 m) after touching down at 55 knots (103 km/h). One of the principal demands of the O.8/38 specification had been, of course endurance, and the Fulmar more than met this requirement with 4·75 hours at 10,000 ft (3 050 m), speed being 130 knots (241 km/h). This speed, as well as being that for max specific range at this altitude, was assessed on control grounds as the minimum speed for comfortable continuous cruising.

In so far as deck-landing characteristics were concerned,

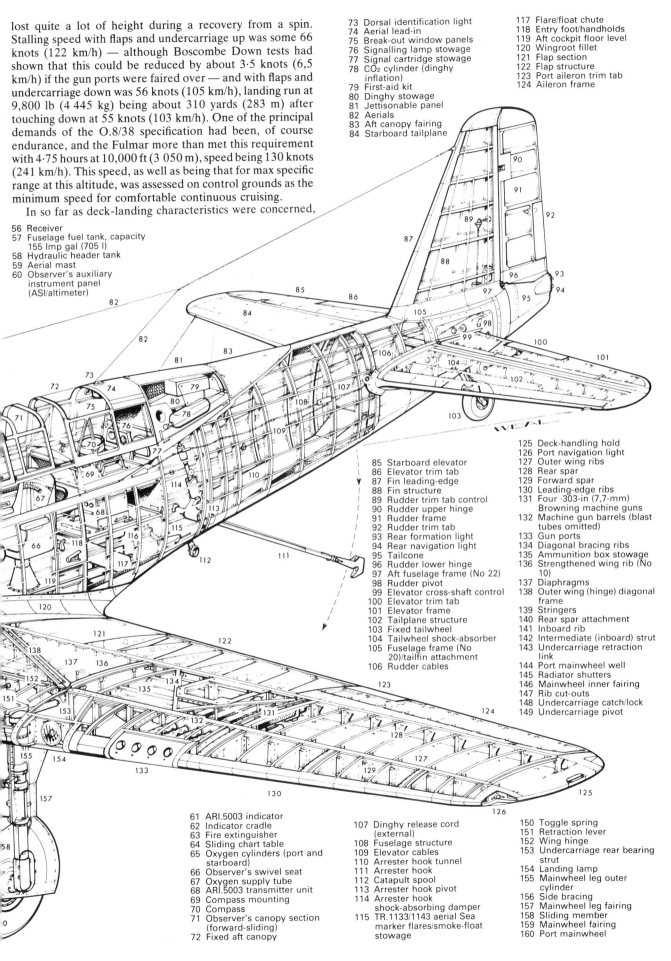

56 Receiver
57 Fuselage fuel tank, capacity 155 Imp gal (705 l)
58 Hydraulic header tank
59 Aerial mast
60 Observer's auxiliary instrument panel (ASI/altimeter)

61 ARI.5003 indicator
62 Indicator cradle
63 Fire extinguisher
64 Sliding chart table
65 Oxygen cylinders (port and starboard)
66 Observer's swivel seat
67 Oxygen supply tube
68 ARI.5003 transmitter unit
69 Compass mounting
70 Compass
71 Observer's canopy section (forward-sliding)
72 Fixed aft canopy

73 Dorsal identification light
74 Aerial lead-in
75 Break-out window panels
76 Signalling lamp stowage
77 Signal cartridge stowage
78 CO$_2$ cylinder (dinghy inflation)
79 First-aid kit
80 Dinghy stowage
81 Jettisonable panel
82 Aerials
83 Aft canopy fairing
84 Starboard tailplane

85 Starboard elevator
86 Elevator trim tab
87 Fin leading-edge
88 Fin structure
89 Rudder trim tab control
90 Rudder upper hinge
91 Rudder frame
92 Rudder trim tab
93 Rear formation light
94 Rear navigation light
95 Tailcone
96 Rudder lower hinge
97 Aft fuselage frame (No 22)
98 Rudder pivot
99 Elevator cross-shaft control
100 Elevator trim tab
101 Elevator frame
102 Tailplane structure
103 Fixed tailwheel
104 Tailwheel shock-absorber
105 Fuselage frame (No 20)/tailfin attachment
106 Rudder cables

107 Dinghy release cord (external)
108 Fuselage structure
109 Elevator cables
110 Arrester hook tunnel
111 Arrester hook
112 Catapult spool
113 Arrester hook pivot
114 Arrester hook shock-absorbing damper
115 TR.1133/1143 aerial Sea marker flares/smoke-float stowage

117 Flare/float chute
118 Entry foot/handholds
119 Aft cockpit floor level
120 Wingroot fillet
121 Flap section
122 Flap structure
123 Port aileron trim tab
124 Aileron frame

125 Deck-handling hold
126 Port navigation light
127 Outer wing ribs
128 Rear spar
129 Forward spar
130 Leading-edge ribs
131 Four ·303-in (7,7-mm) Browning machine guns
132 Machine gun barrels (blast tubes omitted)
133 Gun ports
134 Diagonal bracing ribs
135 Ammunition box stowage
136 Strengthened wing rib (No 10)
137 Diaphragms
138 Outer wing (hinge) diagonal frame
139 Stringers
140 Rear spar attachment
141 Inboard rib
142 Intermediate (inboard) strut
143 Undercarriage retraction link
144 Port mainwheel well
145 Radiator shutters
146 Mainwheel inner fairing
147 Rib cut-outs
148 Undercarriage catch/lock
149 Undercarriage pivot

150 Toggle spring
151 Retraction lever
152 Wing hinge
153 Undercarriage rear bearing strut
154 Landing lamp
155 Mainwheel leg outer cylinder
156 Side bracing
157 Mainwheel leg fairing
158 Sliding member
159 Mainwheel fairing
160 Port mainwheel

Fairey Fulmar I Cockpit Instrumentation Key:

1 Thermos flask
2 Cockpit lamp dimmer switch
3 Hydraulic system emergency handpump handle
4 Priming pump
5 Wireless remote control tuning lever
6 Main fuel cock
7 Arrester hook release
8 Fuel system priming cock
9 Heater control lever
10 Induction system priming pump
11 Wireless remote control volume control knob
12 R.1147 control lamp
13 Wireless remote control send/receive lever
14 R.3003 receiver switchbox
15 Elevator trim tab handwheel
16 Rudder trim tab handwheel
17 Undercarriage control lever
18 Flap control lever
19 Cockpit cooling control
20 Friction adjusting knob
21 Propeller control lever
22 Undercarriage warning horn press-button switch
23 Mixture control lever
24 Throttle control lever

25 Primary controls locking clips
26 Port instrument lamp dimmer switch
27 Elevator trim tab indicator
28 Rudder trim tab indicator
29 Spare bulb stowage
30 Brake pressure gauge
31 Slow-running cut-out control
32 Combined undercarriage position indicator/ignition switch
33 Hydraulic pressure gauge
34 Landing lamp switch
35 Landing lamp control lever
36 Canopy sliding hood release
37 Port instrument lamp
38 Boost cut-out control
39 Flap indicator
40 ASI correction card holder
41 Undercarriage and arrester hook indicator
42 Air temperature gauge
43 Reconnaissance flares firing push-switch
44 Clock
45 Engine starter push-switch
46 Engine starter master switch
47 Reflector gunsight dimmer switch

48 Fire extinguisher push-switch
49 Reflector gunsight
50 Gunsight mounting
51 ASI
52 Artificial horizon
53 Rate-of-climb indicator
54 Altimeter
55 Direction indicator
56 Turning indicator
57 Deviation cardholder
58 Control grip
59 Compass deviation cardholder
60 Compass
61 Brake lever
62 Gun fire press-button
63 Camera gun firing switch
64 Control column
65 Rudder pedals
66 Pilot's seat
67 Engine speed indicator
68 Oxygen regulator/contents meters
69 Headrest release
70 Starboard instrument lamp
71 Identification lamps switchbox
72 Intercommunication speaking tube

73 Oil pressure gauge
74 Oil temperature gauge
75 Boost pressure gauge
76 Radiator thermometer
77 Cartridge starter re-load control
78 De-icing pump
79 Camera unit wedge plate
80 Undercarriage emergency lowering handle
81 Starboard instrument lamp dimmer switch
82 Sutton harness release
83 Radiator shutter control lever
84 Radiator shutter control lever
85 Map box
86 Flare switchpanel
87 Camera gun switch
88 Pitot head heating switch
89 Air temperature indicator switch
90 Formation lights switch
91 Navigation lights switch
92 Identification lights switch
93 Signal cartridge stowage
94 Signal pistol
95 Seat adjustment lever
96 Coffman starter cartridge stowage
97 Oxygen bayonet socket

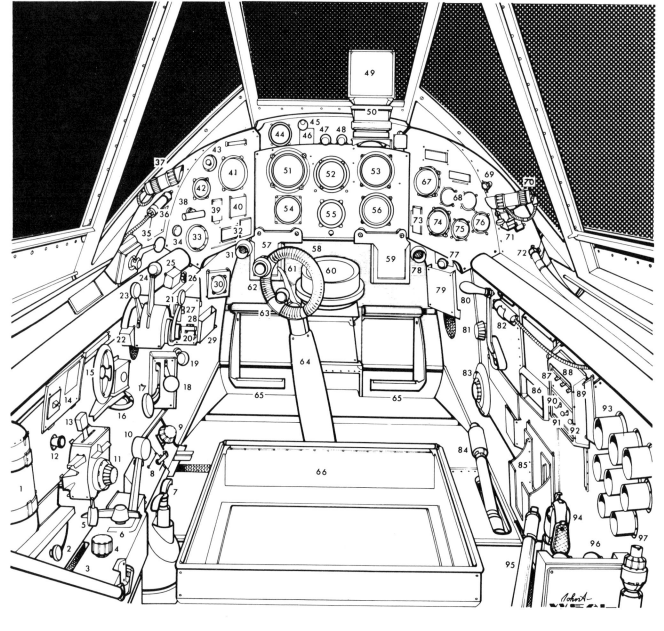

(Above) A late production Fulmar Mk II (DR673), being among the last 100 Fulmars built. The Mk II was tropicalised and had an uprated Merlin 30 engine and a new type Rotol propeller. (Below) A Fulmar Mk I (N4062) from the last but one production batch of this initial version of the fighter

the Fulmar came positively within the "easy" category. It was necessary to hold quite a lot of power so that the slipstream gave positive rudder and elevator effectiveness, but as with other aspects of its handling, the Fulmar was a forgiving aeroplane and even the most ham-fisted of pilots could usually put it onto the deck without bending anything, and for this I am eternally grateful as it was my fate, in mid-1942, to serve a short spell as a deck-landing instructor in *Argus*. At this time, the Fleet Air Arm had no dual-control deck-landing trainer and the instructional process usually began with the student standing beside a batsman at the end of an airfield runway while his instructor demonstrated the technique. It was then the student's turn, with the instructor seated in the back of the Fulmar, monitoring the approach on the rear airspeed indicator and altimeter, and giving instructions as necessary down the voice pipe. Then, horror of horrors, this process was repeated on the training carrier.

Now the *Argus* had not been built from the outset as a carrier and this was revealed all too clearly in its layout. On the credit side for deck landing training, *Argus* had no super-structure and so the deck offered a clear expanse. On the

debit side, her funnel gases exhausted through a large grille set in the round-down (i.e., the curved stern end of the flight deck). This meant that there was a built-in updraught at a critical point in the approach and since the carrier had only five arrester wires, many missed arrested landings were certain to result. Inevitably, after such an experience, students tended to come in too low and substantial numbers of arrester hooks were torn off as they grappled with the exhaust grille in the round-down as a result. Added to this hazard was the fact that the arrester wires on *Argus* were not of the self-centering type, so that an off-centre landing was usually accentuated by the reaction of the arrester wire.

During my back-seat periods, when I was supposed to be producing pearls of instructional wisdom for the enlightenment of the tyro in front intent on killing us both, I usually found myself speechless, having lapsed into some sort of fatalistic acceptance of what seemed at the time to be our inevitable decease. In retrospect, however, I suppose that I was reasonably chauffeured on most occasions — if one connotates "reasonably" with the fact that one was able to walk away from the aircraft at the end of the exercise. There was one outstanding exception — an off-centre landing which took us over the port side of *Argus* at a pace that ensured savouring every horrendous moment in slow motion. Unbelievably, the arrester wire did not break nor the hook disengage, and the Fulmar dangled vertically against the side of the carrier with its propeller barely brushing the sea below. A scrambling net was hurriedly lowered and the student and I performed like a pair of Olympic gymnasts. Somewhat to my surprise, the Fulmar was subsequently salvaged without extensive damage, but the damage to my nerves...!

The place and timing of the Fulmar's début on operations were most propitious. The Fulmar arrived in the Mediterranean theatre when convoys were fighting their way through to beleaguered Malta against the onslaught of Italy's yet-to-be-disenchanted *Regia Aeronautica*. The Italian bombers were just the new Fairey fighter's meat and the Fulmar pilots gobbled it voraciously — the Fulmars of No 806 Squadron embarked in *Illustrious* claimed the destruction of 10 bombers between 2 September and 14 October 1940, and while

covering Swordfish torpedo-bombers at Taranto in the following month claimed a further six "kills". No 806 had, meanwhile, been joined in the Mediterranean by No 808 Squadron, which, similarly equipped, was aboard *Ark Royal,* and a third squadron, No 807, had been formed at Worthy Down, three of its Fulmars going aboard *Pegasus* on 1 December 1940 to become the first aircraft to be used for the Catapult Fighter Ship scheme.

Five more Fulmar squadrons were to be formed during the following year — Nos 800, 804, 805, 809 and 884 — and the fighter first saw service at an overseas FAA shore station when No 805 Squadron was formed (on 1 January) at Dekheila, Egypt, this unit sharing in the defence of Crete a couple of months later. In the course of the year, Fulmars were to play a vital rôle (in May) in shadowing the battleship *Bismarck* and it was largely thanks to the outstanding night reconnaissance work performed by Fulmars that Swordfish were enabled to carry out a nocturnal torpedo attack on the vessel (on 25 May). Fulmars were active in providing fighter support in such actions as the attack on Petsamo, on the North Cape (in July), four Messerschmitt Bf 109s being shot down (by No 809 Squadron); others (of No 800X Squadron) mounted continuous nocturnal intrusion missions from Malta (from May to November); a Fulmar became one of the first aircraft to be catapulted from the armed merchantman *Ariquani* (in August) during Atlantic convoy duties, and the Fairey fighter was responsible for providing cover for most of the Malta reinforcement convoys.

This last-mentioned task continued into 1942 (with Nos 804, 809 and 884 squadrons); Fulmars (of No 889 Squadron) were to provide the fighter defence of the Suez Canal Zone (from February of that year); the Fairey fighter was active (with No 803 Squadron) in defence of what in those now far off days was known as Ceylon (now Sri Lanka), and Fulmars flew tactical reconnaissance and fighter cover sorties (with Nos 809 and 893 squadrons from *Victorious* and *Formidable* respectively) during the Allied invasion of North Africa (November). The year 1943 — by which time the Fulmar had passed the peak of its operational career and was being superseded by the Seafire — saw it participating in the invasion of Sicily (with No 893 Squadron) and providing protection for North Russian convoys (No 813 Squadron) —

(Above left) A Fulmar Mk II (X8641) photographed in October 1941 with a flush-fitting 60 Imp gal ventral fuel tank, and (below) a late production Fulmar Mk II (DR661) showing the tropical filters that were standardised for this model

(Above) A Fulmar Mk II (carrying the serial N8566 which should apparently be X8566) operating from the Royal Navy's shore base, HMS Phoenix, at Fayid, Egypt, and (below right) the first Fulmar (N1854) while serving as a two-seat communications aircraft with the Fairey company after World War II. The three-view general arrangement drawing depicts the Fulmar Mk II

altogether, Fulmars were to be operated by about a score of squadrons from eight fleet carriers and five escort carriers, as well as shore bases, yet their exploits were to be attended with singularly little publicity, at least, in so far as the participating aircraft was concerned. Perhaps the Fulmar lacked the glamour that attached to the single-seat fighters of the day, innate soundness and competence not being the stuff of headlines to set the public's adrenalin flowing.

The Fulmar was capable of absorbing its share of punishment and staying airborne, but it was at a decided disadvantage when tangling with enemy single-seaters and its observer must have felt particularly vulnerable. Some aircraft were, in fact, fitted with a single Vickers 'K' gun in the rear cockpit, but for the most part . . . one squadron is on record as having adopted the tactic of releasing sheets of toilet paper from the rear cockpit in an attempt to deter pursuing enemy fighters as nothing more potent was available to the observer!

After 250 Fulmars had been delivered, a 1,300 hp Merlin 30 supplanted the 1,080 hp Merlin VIII, a new Rotol propeller was fitted and the aircraft was tropicalised, becoming, with these changes, the Fulmar II. The added drag of the filters and the increased weight had to be offset against the 20 per cent increase in available power and the increment in level speed and climb rate was thus no more than nominal, while the greater fuel consumption reduced endurance.

By coincidence, my last command in the Royal Navy was HMS *Fulmar,* the Royal Naval Air Station at Lossiemouth, Scotland, where we were the proud possessors of the last surviving Fulmar, N1854, which had been the the first example off the line and initially flown on 4 January 1940. This aircraft had enjoyed quite a varied career by the time it reached us, having started off at the A&AEE, then at Boscombe Down, and subsequently being used for carrier trials with *Illustrious.* It had been retained by Fairey for development work, eventually being converted to Mk II standard, flying on into the 'fifties as a company communications and hack aircraft with the registration G-AIBE. It had finally reverted to service markings and its original serial and had been returned to the Navy, being delivered, appropriately enough, to HMS *Fulmar,* Lossiemouth was, of course, duly handed over to the RAF and our Fulmar was sent to end its days in the Fleet Air Arm Museum at RNAS Yeovilton where it is to be found today.□

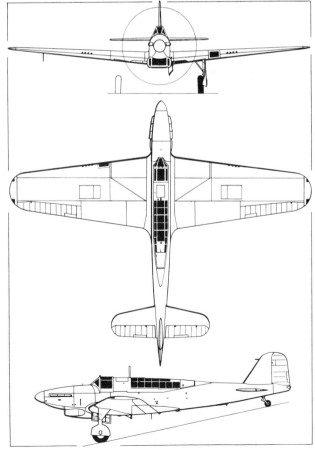

Vought Corsair

UNDENIABLY UNIQUE in appearance among single-seat fighters of its era, with its reverse-gulled wing, mighty Double Wasp engine and immense windmill of a propeller combining to impart an impression of brute strength, Chance Vought's F4U Corsair was not a comely aeroplane by any yardstick. It was an anathema to some pilots and shear ambrosia to others. There were those pilots that acclaimed it as the best single-seat fighter of any nation to emerge from WW II; there were pilots that pronounced it a vicious killer equally dispassionate towards killing its pilot as his opponent. Indeed, few fighters were capable of arousing within those that flew them such extremes of passion as was the Corsair.

Of course, in any shortlist drawn up of the most famous — as distinct from the most *efficacious* — fighters of World War II, this odd-looking warplane will inevitably rank among the classics near to the top. Yet, to my mind, the Corsair achieved such a level of distinction *despite* itself, but then I was never to be numbered among its more ardent admirers; those that apparently assessed the Corsair solely on the basis of its more glamorous attributes and disregarded the penalties that these invoked.

By the time I first encountered the Corsair in February 1944, almost exactly one year after this formidably large fighter's operational début with the US Marine Corps at Guadalcanal, Chance Vought's aeroplane had established something of a reputation in the South Pacific. Either this was an air superiority fighter *par excellence* or the enemy was providing something of a "Turkey Shoot" for, by the end of 1943, USMC Corsair pilots were being credited with no fewer than 584 "kills", a quite extraordinary figure in view of the known number of Marine Corps Corsair squadrons deployed to the South Pacific by that time. Admittedly, on the other side of the world, it was difficult to assess just how much credence could be placed in claims for the Corsair; how much of the credit for its reputation was to apportioned to the aircraft and how much to overly imaginative publicists whom, only a year or so earlier, had been referring to the Brewster F2A (Buffalo) as God's gift to naval aviators!

The Corsair had most certainly heralded a quantum leap in shipboard fighter performance, when, on 25 June 1942, the first production F4U-1 flew; the only problem was that a further two-and-a-half years were to elapse before the US Navy was to consider it suitable for *shipboard* operations! Whatever the Corsair was, it was certainly not a *natural* as a carrier-based combat aircraft, and that had, in the final analysis, been the task for which designer Rex B Beisel and his team had created the aircraft. In all fairness, however, Chance Vought's Engineering Department had broken an immense amount of new ground in creating this fighter following a 1 February 1938 US Navy request for single-seat shipboard fighter proposals.

The V-166B, as the company had designated the preliminary design, had been, in essence, the smallest practical airframe that could be built around the largest and most powerful air-cooled radial engine then under development. Promising almost twice the power of any then used by the US Navy, this engine had demanded a fuselage ground angle that would have made the Fieseler Storch look squat in order to achieve the requisite 18 in (46 cm) ground clearance for the propeller. Rex Biesel and his team had come up with a novel and extremely neat solution to this problem; the inverted gull wing that was to be the distinctive hallmark of the Chance Vought fighter thenceforth. Not only had this resolved the propeller clearance problem, it had simultaneously resolved the difficulty of keeping the undercarriage to a manageable length and, as a bonus, had minimised drag by offering the optimum right angle junction between wing and fuselage, eliminating the wetted area of a large fairing that would otherwise have been needed.

Determined to effect a major advance in the shipboard fighter-state-of-art, Chance Vought's Engineering Department had not been content with mating an innovatory airframe design with the world's first 2,000 hp engine and the largest propeller ever used by a fighter; it had elected to compound these advances with an entirely new spot-welding skin attachment technique to achieve a smoother surface finish than had been possible previously. The sum total of all these innovations was a very radical aeroplane, but a carrier-based fighter . . .?

On 11 June 1938, a contract had been issued for a prototype designated XF4U-1; the mock-up had been inspected by the US Navy's Bureau of Aeronautics between 8-11 February 1939, and on 29 May 1940, after several hours of taxying trials, the innovatory fighter had been flown by Chance Vought's Chief of Flight Test, Lyman A Bullard Jnr. The combination of an entirely new and untried power plant with an equally new airframe embodying a number of untried features had certainly tempted providence, and an incident during the brief initial flight test was a portent of problems ahead.

Powered by an XR-2800-4 Double Wasp engine and weighing in at 9,357 lb (4 245 kg), the XF4U-1 had just attained a 200 knot (370 km/h) cruise when the elevator tabs set up a high-frequency oscillation and then tore loose. Bullard had landed the prototype safely despite the exceedingly heavy control forces, but during the fifth flight, with Boone T Guyton, who had taken over as project pilot, at the controls, the XF4U-1 had forced-landed on a golf course, flipping over, losing a wing and writing off the vertical tail surfaces and propeller. Undeterred by this setback, Chance Vought had rebuilt the aircraft, which, on 1 October 1940, had demonstrated a ground speed of 404 mph (650 km/h) in a flight between Stratford and Hartford.

Despite the limited flight testing that had been conducted with the XF4U-1 and the handling problems that had revealed themselves from the outset and remained unresolved, time had by now begun to be considered of the essence, and on 28 November 1940, the US Navy had requested proposals for productionising the design; a process that was to result in changes that were to enhance some characteristics and exacerbate some problems, and in the latter category were the Corsair's manifest shortcomings as a shipboard aeroplane.

Engineering for production release had begun on 30 December, and flight test tempo had been accelerated in order that the prototype could be demonstrated to the US Navy at Anacostia at the earliest possible date. It now became apparent that the standard US Navy specification requirements would have to be rewritten to accommodate the Corsair and aircraft of its generation. One requirement was a vertical dive maintained for 10,000 ft (3 050 m) and during attempts to demonstrate this capability, a speed of 515 mph (829 km/h) had been clocked, but after landing it had been discovered that the fabric was stripping from the

rudder and elevators, the starboard flotation hatch had partly torn away and an access door had buckled. On 28 January 1941, in a final test dive from 20,000 ft (6 100 m), a speed of nearly 500 mph (885 km/h) had been reached when negative g in the hydraulic system allowed the propeller to overspeed, leading to a complete engine failure and a deadstick landing. This incident had rendered it obvious that the US Navy's dive requirement was no longer feasible; if the dive was initiated at 20,000 ft (6 100 m) unacceptably high g forces were encountered during recovery, while a dive begun from a higher altitude took the aircraft into compressibility effects. Another requirement that had to be waived was a 10-turn spin when it was ascertained that the control loads demanded for recovery exceeded human limits — during this test the pilot saved the XF4U-1 only by recourse to an anti-spin 'chute.

No fewer than 96 changes had to be made to the aileron control system alone during 110 successive flights early in 1941, but the XF4U-1 had still been decidedly immature on 21 April, when the Navy demonstration had been completed, and US Navy pilots that flew the prototype, while evincing enthusiasm over the XF4U-1's speed and climb rate, had mostly voiced reservations over its low speed characteristics, the lack of visibility over the nose during the landing approach, the landing performance itself and the unnerving predilection of the aircraft to drop a wing just before touching down. Had it not been for the extreme urgency that was by this time attached to the service introduction of a really high performance fighter, there can be little doubt that a production go-ahead would have been delayed pending a solution to these problems; as it was, on 30 June 1941, the first contract was confirmed for 584 F4U-1s, and the initial production aircraft was to fly five days short of a year later.

The production F4U-1 had embodied many changes and improvements, resulting both from prototype trials and changes in US Navy requirements; regrettably, none of these improvements had extended to the less glamorous attributes so vital to any effective deck-landing aircraft. In the light of European combat experience, it had become obvious that the

(Head of opposite page) The Corsair Mk I (JT118) in which the author checked out the diving characteristics of the Vought fighter with the undercarriage both retracted and extended. (Above right) The XF4U-1 photographed while undergoing testing at the Anacostia Naval Air Station in May 1941, and (below) the same aircraft photographed on 8 October 1940, a week after demonstrating a ground speed of 404 mph (650 km/h) between Stratford and Hartford

These photographs (above and below) of early production F4U-1 Corsairs show clearly the fighter's unique reverse-gulled wing and the very poor all-round vision offered the pilot from the cockpit.

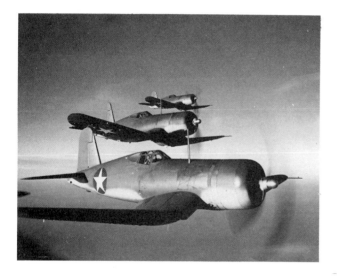

gun armament originally specified — a single 0·5-in (12,7-mm) gun in each wing plus a similar calibre weapon paired with a 0·3-in (7,62-mm) gun in the nose — was no longer adequate. The wing structure had accordingly been redesigned to accommodate three 0·5-in (12,7-mm) Brownings in each outer panel — although a few early production examples had mounted an interim armament of four wing guns — which had the incidental advantage of enabling the heavy synchronisation gear to be dispensed with.

Unfortunately, the integral wing leading edge tanks had been displaced by the revised armament and fuel capacity had had to be made up by installing a 237 US gal (897 l) self-sealing tank in the centre fuselage. This tank had of necessity to be as close as possible to the aircraft CG in order to minimise trim changes as fuel was consumed, but it so happened that this situation was already occupied by the cockpit! The design team had had no recourse but to relocate the cockpit 3 ft (0,92 m) farther aft. The forward view for take-off and landing offered by the prototype had come in for much criticism and that from the production model could only be described as appalling — some palliative measures were subsequently to be taken, but the fault was fundamental to the design and was to remain a major point of criticism throughout the Corsair's career. An early change had been the reintroduction of wing leading edge tanks, unprotected and situated outboard of the gun bays, each having a capacity of 62 US gal (235 l), these and the full armament taking the gross weight up to 12,694 lb (5 758 kg) from the 9,357 lb (4 244 kg) of the XF4U-1 and wing loading rising dramatically from 29·8 to 40·4 lb/sq ft (145,5 to 197,2 kg/m²). Understandably, the higher weights had an adverse effect on manoeuvrability, but a reduction in aileron span had served to improve roll rate.

The incipient bounce during landing resulting from overly stiff oleo action had been carried over from the prototype and was found to be most disconcerting by pilots fresh to the F4U-1, but not so disconcerting as the virtually unheralded torque stall that occured all too frequently in landing condition. Compounded by a serious directional instability immediately after touch-down and coupled with the frightful visibility from the cockpit during the landing approach, it was small wonder that the US Navy concluded that the average carrier pilot was unlikely to possess the necessary skill to master these unpleasant idiosyncrasies and that committing

By comparison with the XF4U-1, the cockpit of the series F4U-1 was located 3 ft (91 cm) further aft to allow additional fuel to be carried in the fuselage. This inevitably had an adverse effect on the pilot's view for deck landing and the F4U-1 was, in consequence, issued to land-based units.

A Corsair Mk I (JT162) of No 1830 Squadron, the Royal Navy's first Corsair unit, which was formed at Quonset on 1 June 1943. This squadron subsequently embarked aboard HMS Illustrious, typical operations including the provision of fleet defence patrols during attacks on targets in the Dutch East Indies in the summer of 1944

the Corsair to shipboard operations until these quirks had been at least alleviated would be the height of foolhardiness. Indeed, carrier qualification trials aboard the USS *Sangamon* in Chesapeake Bay on 25 September 1942 had been something of a fiasco, the pilot, Lt-Cdr S Porter, having to contend with windscreen contamination by oil from the hydraulically-operated cowl flaps and the valve push-rod mechanism, as well as the handling and visibility problems. Later trials were to be punctuated by a series of nose-overs, barrier-bounces and bent propellers.

A consequence of this lack of shipboard finesse on the part of the Corsair was the assignment of delivery priority in the fighter to the Marine Corps for shore-based operation, and the first Corsair-equipped combat squadron thus became VMF-124 formed on 7 September 1942, declared combat ready on 28 December and despatched post-haste to reinforce beleaguered US forces on the island of Guadalcanal. From here the first combat mission was flown on 11 February 1943 — escorting a PB2Y to Vella Lavella to pick up a downed pilot. On the following day, Corsairs flew escort to PB4Ys of VP-51 on a strike against enemy shipping in the Kahili area of Bougainville, being blooded during a similar mission two days later when intercepted by a large formation of Zero-Sen fighters. The Japanese force shot down a top cover of four P-38 Lightnings, two accompanying P-40 Warhawks, two of the PB4Ys and two of VMF-124's Corsairs, all for the loss of four Zero-Sens. This inauspicious opening of the Corsair's combat career was not, happily, an unfavourable augury for the future; with experience, the Marine Corps pilots learned to avoid mixing it with their more nimble Japanese opponents and take advantage of the Corsair's immensely superior level and dive speeds.

Within six months, all Marine Corps fighter squadrons in the South Pacific had been Corsair-equipped. Meanwhile, the US Navy had formed its first Corsair squadron, VF-12, which received its initial F4U-1 on 3 October 1942, but this

served primarily as trials unit and although it eventually became deck-qualified in April 1943 aboard the USS *Saratoga,* it was to turn its aircraft over to the Marines and relinquish the honour of being the first US Navy squadron to take the Corsair on operations to VF-17 formed on 19 April. This was the first squadron to receive F4U-1s fitted with full plexiglas canopies — retrospectively referred to as F4U-1As — which supplanted the confining "bird cage" canopy, with its numerous metal reinforcing strips against which a pilot's head could jar unpleasantly in turbulence owing to restricted width towards its apex. In the event, another year was to elapse before the US Navy was to clear the Corsair for shipboard operation, and VF-17 sailed aboard the USS *Bunker Hill* to New Georgia, which was reached in September, subsequently achieving conspicuous success as a shore-based unit.

Production tempo of the F4U-1 built up extremely rapidly — Chance Vought was to roll out its 1,000th aircraft on 22 August 1943 — and the parent company had been joined in the production programme by Brewster and Goodyear. In consequence, it was possible to offer supplies of this fighter to the Royal Navy which gladly accepted 95 early series F4U-1s as Corsair Mk Is, these being followed by a total of 510 "high-cabin" F4U-1s as Corsair IIs. The Royal Navy set up a procedure for forming and working-up squadrons on the type at either Quonset or Brunswick in North America, and then shipping the complete squadrons with their pilots to the UK aboard escort carriers. The first unit so formed was No 1830 Squadron, which, commissioned at Quonset on 1 June 1943, was subsequently to be attached to HMS *Illustrious.* Three more squadrons, Nos 1831, 1833 and 1834, formed in July, followed by two in August (Nos 1835 and 1836) and one each in September and October (Nos 1837 and 1838 respectively). A further eight squadrons were destined to form at a steady rate through 1944, and a final two in 1945 to give a total of 19 FAA Corsair squadrons.

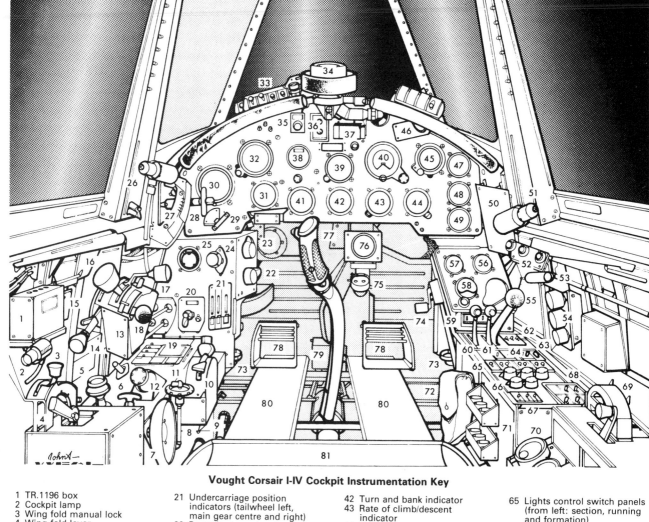

Vought Corsair I-IV Cockpit Instrumentation Key

1 TR.1196 box
2 Cockpit lamp
3 Wing fold manual lock
4 Wing fold lever
5 Rudder trimming tab control wheel
6 Tailwheel locking handle
7 Elevator trimming tab control wheel
8 Outer wing fuel tank CO_2 purging handle
9 Hydraulic handpump
10 Indercarriage and dive-brake control quadrant
11 Fuel tank selector
12 Aileron trimming tab control wheel
13 Engine control quadrant
14 Supercharger control lever
15 Engine limit data plate
16 Throttle
17 Propeller control lever and friction lock
18 Mixture control lever
19 Circuit breaker re-set buttons (armament, camera and water pump)
20 Hydraulic handpump check valve selector

21 Undercarriage position indicators (tailwheel left, main gear centre and right)
22 Port wing gun charging control knob
23 Starboard wing gun charging control knob
24 Alternate air control
25 Ignition switch
26 Instrument panel lamp
27 Flap position indicator
28 Flap position control lever
29 Auxiliary drop tank control (attach/release/flight lock)
30 Engine speed indicator
31 Boost gauge
32 Altimeter
33 Armament switches
34 Gunsight mount and protective padding
35 Water injection indicator light
36 Stall warning light (below) and test button (above)
37 Carburettor temperature warning light
38 Directional gyro
39 Compass indicator
40 Artificial horizon
41 ASI

42 Turn and bank indicator
43 Rate of climb/descent indicator
44 Cylinder temperature gauge
45 Clock
46 Data warning plate
47 Oil temperatrure guage
48 Oil pressure gauge
49 Fuel pressure gauge
50 Data card holder
51 Instrument panel lamp
52 Transmit key
53 Communications socket
54 Radio control box power supply
55 Cowling gill control lever
56 Hydraulic pressure gauge
57 Main tank fuel contents gauge (inc reserve)
58 Voltmeter
59 Oil cooler and intercooler flap indicators
60 Oil cooler flap control lever
61 Intercooler flap control lever
62 Upper and lower recognition lights control switch panel
63 Starter switch
64 Priming switch (right) and master heating switch (left)

65 Lights control switch panels (from left: section, running and formation)
66 Lights dimmer switches (top row: chart board, left and right console; bottom row: left and right instrument panel)
67 Fuel pump, pitot head heating, and defrosting switch panel
68 Lights, starter and IFF/radio buttons
69 Arrester hook control lever and lock
70 Oxygen contents and regulator
71 Signal cartridge clips (8)
72 Signal pistol holster
73 Brake pedal adjusters
74 Pressurising manual control
75 Cockpit ventilator control
76 Compass
77 Control grip and gun-firing button
78 Rudder pedals
79 Control column
80 Heel boards
81 Pilot's seat

Oddly enough, the Royal Navy was not quite so fastidious as the US Navy regarding deck landing characteristics and cleared the Corsair for shipboard operation some nine months before its American counterpart. The obstacles to the Corsair's shipboard use were admittedly not insurmountable, but I can only surmise that the apparently ready acceptance by their Lordships of the Admiralty of the Chance Vought fighter for carrier operation must have been solely due to the exigencies of the times, for the landing behaviour of the Corsair really was bad, a fact to which I was able to attest after the briefest acquaintance with the aircraft.

I had joined the Royal Aircraft Establishment at Farnborough in January 1944, and one of the first tasks to which I was assigned was that of checking out the diving characteristics of the Corsair with undercarriage both retracted and extended. The aircraft with which I was to perform the tests was an early Lend-Lease Corsair Mk I (JT118) and our encounter was certainly not a case of love at first sight. On the contrary, during my acquaintance with this impressively large and aesthetically unappealing fighter, which was to spread over several years, I was never to achieve any sort of rapport.

The Corsair's inordinately large proboscis was, I suppose,

its most outstanding feature — in the USA in later years I was to hear this fighter referred to by the sobriquet "Old Hog Nose" — and coupled with its fairly acute and most distinctive ground stance, it imparted an impression of rugged strength rather than aerodynamic refinement. The cockpit was, I discovered, inordinately spacious, and I was reminded of the suggestion of an RAF pilot on first seeing the P-47 Thunderbolt that its occupant might take evasive action by releasing his harness and dodging about the cockpit! It appeared to have been tailored for an extremely tall pilot — I subsequently learned that the principal Corsair project pilot was 6 ft 4 in (1,93 m) in height — and one of more modest stature such as myself inevitably experienced some discomfort keeping one's feet on the rudder with the seat adjusted to a height from which what little forward view existed could be gained. The layout of the cockpit was poor and on the ground the only reasonable view was *upward*!

The immense Pratt & Whitney R-2800-8 Double Wasp was turned over by hand four or five times, the fuel booster pump was switched ON, the priming switch was flicked several times, the ignition switch activated and the starter cartridge fired. The Double Wasp, which has take-off rating of 2,000 bhp at 2,700 rpm, usually burst into life immediately and with the firing switch depressed and the mixture control moved slowly to AUTO RICH was soon purring with all the smoothness and reliability so characteristic of this family of engines. The Double Wasp was opened up to 1,000 rpm to warm up, the usual temperature, pressure and magneto checks performed, the flaps lowered and raised, and the revs increased to 1,400, the operation of the two-speed supercharger being checked by moving the control from NEUTRAL to LOW and, after a pause of a few seconds to HIGH. With the propeller control fully down, the throttle was opened and take-off boost and static rpm checked, the stick being held hard back to contain a strong tendency for the tail to lift.

The feeling of not being at one with the aircraft was emphasised during taxying, when the totally inadequate forward view necessitated swinging that great nose from side to side, but to do this the tailwheel had to be unlocked and the Corsair was then very unstable directionally, necessitating constant use of the brakes with the danger of nosing over in the event of too harsh application. There could be no doubt that some practice was necessary to achieve satisfactory ground handling. For take-off, the trimmers had to be set six deg right rudder with six deg down on the right aileron and one deg nose up on the elevator. With mixture in AUTO RICH, fuel cock on RESERVE, booster pump ON, intercooler shutters

closed, the supercharger lever in NEUTRAL and the tailwheel locked, the engine was opened up to 54 in boost and 2,700 rpm. If trimming was correct, the Corsair demonstrated no tendency to swing and unstick was rapid. With the application of 30 deg of flap, such as would be employed for a carrier take-off, and about two-thirds normal fuel at a take-off weight of about 11,150 lb (5 058 kg), the Corsair would take-off within 185 yards (169 m) without wind and about 120 yards (110 m) into a 15 knot (28 km/h) wind.

The speed for maximum climb rate was 125 knots (232 km/h) from sea level up to 21,000 ft (6 400 m) and the intercooler shutters had to be opened fully, but the cowl gills were only half opened otherwise there was some buffet. Climb was certainly impressive, with that immense 13 ft 4 in (4,06 m) diameter Hamilton Standard propeller pulling the aircraft up like a high-speed lift, 10,000 ft (3 050 m) being passed in 4·6 minutes and 20,000 ft (6 095 m) in 9·6 minutes. Above 21,000 ft (6 400 m) climb speed was reduced three knots (5,5 km/h) per 2,000 ft (610 m), but the two-stage two-speed supercharger ensured good climbing capability well above 30,000 ft (9 145 m). Once in level flight, the Corsair could be trimmed to a very stable hands-off flying condition. Its stability was positive at all times in the cruise and at high speeds. It imparted a feeling of solidity; to compare it with, say, the Seafire, was like comparing a shire horse with a polo pony, and this feeling of solidness was combined with an impression of immense power.

The harmony of control was poor, the elevators being heavy but the ailerons being moderately light, enabling the Corsair to be rolled to its maximum rate even at fairly high diving speeds. This effective high-speed aileron control must certainly have been valuable in the South Pacific as the Corsair's principal opponent in that theatre, the Zero-Sen, had poor aileron control at high speeds at which it rolled sluggish-

(Above right) The F4U-1A (BuAer 55995) of US Navy "Ace" Ira Kepford of VF-17, the first US Navy Corsair-equipped squadron to see combat, and (below) and F4U-1D of VMF-111 "Devil Dogs" of the 4th Marine Air Wing.

Chance Vought (Vought-Sikorsky) F4U-1 Corsair II Cutaway Drawing Key

1 Spinner
2 Three-blade Hamilton Standard constant-speed propeller
3 Reduction gear housing
4 Nose ring
5 Pratt & Whitney R-2800-8 Double Wasp 18-cylinder two-row engine
6 Exhaust pipes
7 Hydraulically-operated cowling flaps
8 Fixed cowling panels
9 Wing leading-edge unprotected integral fuel tank, capacity 62 US gal (235 l)
10 Truss-type main spar
11 Leading-edge rib structure

12 Starboard navigation light
13 Wingtip
14 Wing structure
15 Wing ribs
16 Wing outer-section (fabric skinning aft of main spar)
17 Starboard aileron
18 Ammunition boxes (max total capacity 2,350 rounds)
19 Aileron trim tab
20 Aerial mast
21 Forward bulkhead
22 Oil tank, capacity 26 US gal (98 l)
23 Oil tank forward armour plate
24 Fire suppressor cylinder
25 Supercharger housing
26 Exhaust trunking
27 Blower assembly

28 Engine support frame
29 Engine control runs
30 Wing mainspar carry-through structure
31 Engine support attachment
32 Upper cowling deflection plate (0·1-in/0,25-cm aluminium)
33 Fuel filler cap
34 Fuselage main fuel tank, capacity 237 US gal (897 l)
35 Upper longeron
36 Fuselage forward frames
37 Rudder pedals
38 Heelboards
39 Control column
40 Instrument panel
41 Reflector sight
42 Armour-glass windshield
43 Rear-view mirror

44 Rearward-sliding cockpit canopy
45 Handgrip
46 Headrest
47 Pilot's head and back armour
48 Canopy frame

49 Pilot's seat
50 Engine control quadrant
51 Trim tab control wheels
52 Wing-folding lever
53 Centre/aft fuselage bulkhead
54 Radio shelf
55 Radio installation
56 Canopy track
57 Bulkhead
58 Aerial lead-in
59 Aerial mast
60 Aerials
61 Heavy-sheet skin plating
62 Dorsal identification light
63 Longeron
64 Control runs
65 Aft fuselage structure
66 Compass installation
67 Lifting tube
68 Access/inspection panels
69 Fin/fuselage forward attachment

70 Starboard tailplane
71 Elevator balance
72 Fin structure
73 Inspection panels
74 Rudder balance
75 Aerial stub
76 Rudder upper hinge
77 Rudder structure

78 Diagonal bracing
79 Rudder trim tab
80 Trim tab actuating rod
81 Access panel
82 Rudder post
83 Tailplane end rib
84 Elevator control runs
85 Fixed fairing root
86 Elevator trim tabs (port and starboard)
87 Tail cone
88 Rear navigation light
89 Port elevator

90 Elevator balance
91 Port tailplane structure

92 Arrester hook (stowed)
93 Tail section frames
94 Fairing
95 Tailwheel (retracted)
96 Arrester hook (lowered)
97 Tailwheel/hook doors

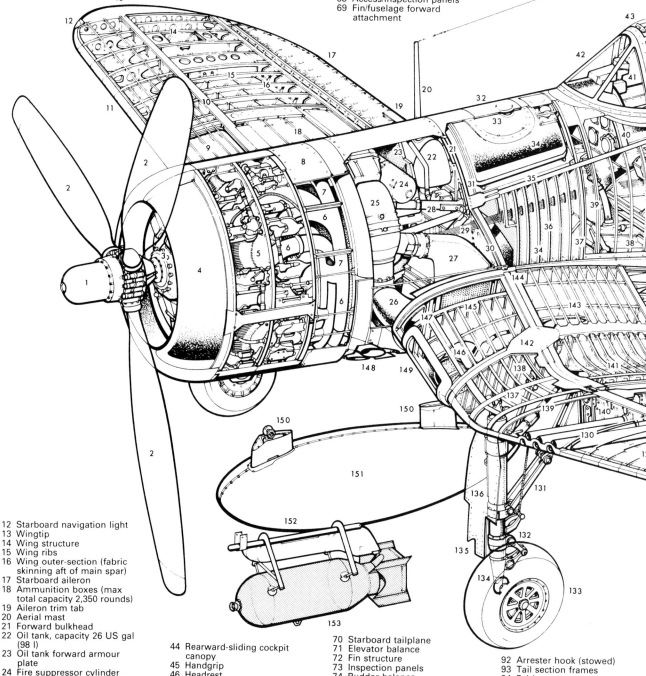

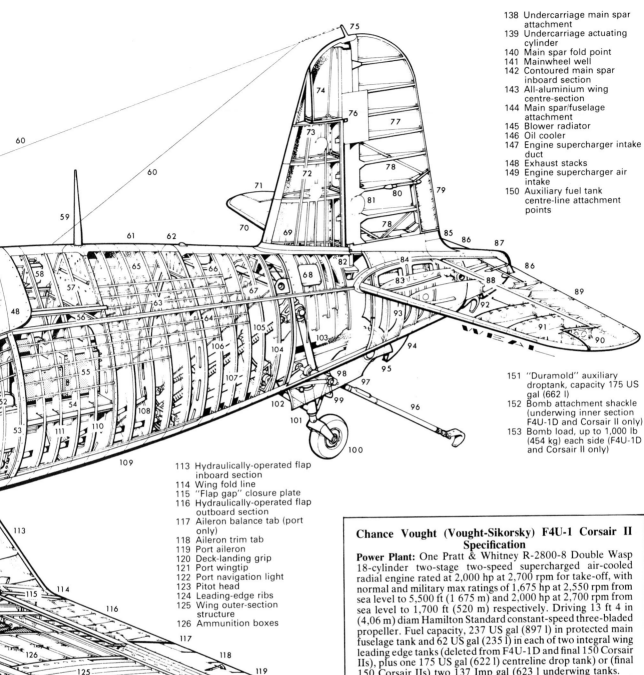

138 Undercarriage main spar attachment
139 Undercarriage actuating cylinder
140 Main spar fold point
141 Mainwheel well
142 Contoured main spar inboard section
143 All-aluminium wing centre-section
144 Main spar/fuselage attachment
145 Blower radiator
146 Oil cooler
147 Engine supercharger intake duct
148 Exhaust stacks
149 Engine supercharger air intake
150 Auxiliary fuel tank centre-line attachment points

151 "Duramold" auxiliary droptank, capacity 175 US gal (662 l)
152 Bomb attachment shackle (underwing inner section F4U-1D and Corsair II only)
153 Bomb load, up to 1,000 lb (454 kg) each side (F4U-1D and Corsair II only)

113 Hydraulically-operated flap inboard section
114 Wing fold line
115 "Flap gap" closure plate
116 Hydraulically-operated flap outboard section
117 Aileron balance tab (port only)
118 Aileron trim tab
119 Port aileron
120 Deck-landing grip
121 Port wingtip
122 Port navigation light
123 Pitot head
124 Leading-edge ribs
125 Wing outer-section structure
126 Ammunition boxes

98 Tailwheel/hook attachment/pivot
99 Mooring/tie-down lug
100 Rearward-retracting tailwheel
101 Tailwheel oleo
102 Support strut
103 Arrester hook actuated strut
104 Aft/tail section bulkhead
105 Arrester hook shock-absorber
106 Tailwheel/arrester hook cylinder
107 Arrester hook retraction strut
108 Bulkhead attachment points
109 Fuselage skinning
110 Bulkhead frame
111 Elevator/rudder control runs
112 Entry hand/foothold

127 Three 0·5-in (12,7-mm) Colt-Browning M-2 wing machine guns with 400 rpg (inboard pair) and 375 rpg (outboard)
128 Wing fold outboard cylinder
129 Wing leading-edge unprotected integral fuel tank, capacity 62 US gal (235 l) — deleted from final 150 Corsair IIs
130 Machine gun blast tubes
131 Mainwheel retraction strut
132 Torque links
133 Port mainwheel
134 Axle
135 Mainwheel leg fairing
136 Mainwheel oleo leg
137 Mainwheel leg pivot point

Chance Vought (Vought-Sikorsky) F4U-1 Corsair II
Specification

Power Plant: One Pratt & Whitney R-2800-8 Double Wasp 18-cylinder two-stage two-speed supercharged air-cooled radial engine rated at 2,000 hp at 2,700 rpm for take-off, with normal and military max ratings of 1,675 hp at 2,550 rpm from sea level to 5,500 ft (1 675 m) and 2,000 hp at 2,700 rpm from sea level to 1,700 ft (520 m) respectively. Driving 13 ft 4 in (4,06 m) diam Hamilton Standard constant-speed three-bladed propeller. Fuel capacity, 237 US gal (897 l) in protected main fuselage tank and 62 US gal (235 l) in each of two integral wing leading edge tanks (deleted from F4U-1D and final 150 Corsair IIs), plus one 175 US gal (622 l) centreline drop tank) or (final 150 Corsair IIs) two 137 Imp gal (623 l underwing tanks).
Performance: (At 11,878 lb/5 388 kg, fuel in main tank only) Max speed, 320 mph (515 km/h) at sea level, 392 mph (631 km/h) at 24,000 ft (7 315 m); max range, 1,070 mls (1,722 km) at 177 mph (285 km/h) at 5,000 ft (1 525 m); time to 10,000 ft (3 050 m), 5·1 min, to 20,000 ft (6 095 m), 10·7 min; service ceiling, 37,100 ft (11 310 m); (at 13,846 lb/6 280 kg with max internal fuel plus 175 US gal/662 l drop tank) Max speed, 310 mph (499 km/h) at sea level, 377 mph (606 km/h) at 24,000 ft (7 315 m); max range 1,735 mls (2 792 km) at 177 mph (285 km/h) at 5,000 ft (1 525 m); time to 10,000 ft (3 050 m), 6·2 min, to 20,000 ft (6 095 m), 13 min.
Weights: Empty equipped, 8,873 lb (4 025 kg); loaded (fuselage fuel only), 11,878 lb (5,388 kg), (max internal fuel), 12,694 lb (5,758 kg); max loaded, 13,846 lb (6 280 kg).
Dimensions: Span, 40 ft 11¾ in (12,49 m); span folded, 17 ft 0⅝ in (5,20 m); length, 32 ft 9½ in (9,99 m); height (propeller vertical), 15 ft 0¼ in (4,58 m); wing area, 314 sq ft (29,17 m²). Note: The Corsair II wing span was reduced to 39 ft 9³/₈ in (12,13 m).
Armament: Six 0·5-in (12,7-mm) Colt-Browning M-2 machine guns with total of 2,350 rounds (400 rpg inboard four guns and 375 rpg outboard two guns) plus two 1,000-lb (453,6-kg) bombs.

ly. I had heard that Marine Corps pilots used this high-speed roll capability as a standard evasive tactic, diving the Corsair and then rolling to port or starboard before recovery to shake off any pursuing enemy fighter. Acceleration was quite dramatic and a clean aeroplane with about two-thirds fuel in main tank only and 200 rounds for each of its six 'fifties could reach a maximum speed of 342 knots (634 km/h) at the Corsair's critical altitude of 24,000 ft (7,315 m) on normal maximum power, which, at that altitude was 1,550 hp at 2,550 rpm. At combat power of 1,650 hp at 2,700 rpm (limited to five minutes), maximum speed was 343 knots (636 km/h).

The flaps could be lowered 20 deg to assist manoeuvring at speeds up to 200 knots (370 km/h) and recommended speeds for aerobatics included 350-360 knots (650-670 km/h) for an upward roll, 330 knots (610 km/h) for a climbing roll, 300 knots (556 km/h) for a roll off the top of a loop and 260-280 knots (480-520 km/h) for a loop, but it was not recommended that the Corsair be held inverted for more than three seconds. The stalling characteristics were very poor, with little warning other than that afforded by the stall warning light on the instrument panel which was operated by the breakdown of airflow over the centre section. At the stall, the right wing dropped sharply and an incipient spin developed if the control column was not moved smartly forward. If the Corsair stalled in a steep turn it would normally flick out, but recovery was rapid if control column pressure was relaxed quickly. At about 11,500 lb (5 216 kg) with engine off and all up, the Corsair would stall at 90 knots (167 km/h), and with flaps and undercarriage down at 76 knots (141 km/h), the warning light coming on at 80 knots (148 km/h).

My initial task with the Corsair was, as previously mentioned, to check out the diving characteristics. We had had reports of Marine Corps Corsairs losing the fabric from their elevators, and I could well imagine this because, due to the combination of relative aerodynamic cleanliness, high power and weight, the Corsair accelerated very rapidly in a dive with the aircraft clean, and relatively inexperienced pilots working off some exuberance by diving steeply from high altitudes without close regard to structural limitations could easily have found themselves in trouble. In clean condition, accel-

eration was rapid to 400 knots (740 km/h) below 10,000 ft (3 050 m), but with the undercarriage extended to serve as a dive brake it took about the same height loss to reach 350 knots (650 km/h). Any attempt to exceed these limiting speeds produced pronounced elevator buffeting. Lowering the undercarriage as a brake was done by using the dive brake control, the tailwheel remaining retracted otherwise damage to the tailwheel doors would have resulted. Lowering the mainwheels produced a strong nose down trim change, and the elevators heavied up in diving and a pull-out called for plenty of height in consequence. Buffeting of the elevators could occur during the recovery, dictating easing off the pull-out and reducing g. Prior to the dive, the supercharger was set to NEUTRAL, the mixture in AUTO RICH, the throttle was set one-third open, the cowling flaps, oil and intercooler shutters were shut and the rudder was trimmed six deg left with the elevator set one-and-a-half deg nose down. As no automatic boost control was fitted, care had to be exercised in avoiding overboosting.

I was well aware that the US Navy had found the Corsair's deck-landing characteristics so disappointing in trials that it had been assigned for shore duties while an attempt was being made to iron out the problems, and although the FAA *was* deck-landing the aircraft, I knew that, by consensus, it had been pronounced a brute and assumed that shipboard operations with the Corsair were something of a case of needs must when the devil drives. The fact that experienced US Navy pilots *could* deck-land the Corsair had been demonstrated a couple of months earlier, in November 1943, when VF-17, providing high cover for the carriers *Essex* and *Bunker Hill,* had run short of fuel after decimating an attacking torpedo-bomber force and had landed safely aboard the carriers. All in all, I was most anxious to discover for myself if the Corsair was the deck-landing dog that it was reputed to be. It was!

In the deck-landing configuration with approach power, the Corsair could demonstrate a very nasty incipient torque stall with dangerously little warning, the starboard wing usually dropping sharply. With the large flaps fully extended the descent rate was rapid, and a simulated deck-landing at 80 knots (148 km/h) gave very poor view and sluggish aileron

The Corsair saw extensive use with the Royal New Zealand Air Force, no fewer than 425 fighters of this type being supplied to become standard RNZAF equipment and equipping all 12 of the service's fighter squadrons. One of the first two RNZAF squadrons to form on the Corsair was No 21, and an F4U-1 of this unit (NZ5218) is illustrated below

(Above) Three F4U-1 Corsairs with late-production style cockpit canopies seen in No 17 Squadron, RNZAF, service. This unit was operational over Guadalcanal late in 1944. (Below left) Corsair Mk Is of No 738 Squadron, a training unit at Lewiston, Maine

and elevator control. A curved approach was very necessary if the pilot was to have any chance of seeing the carrier, let alone the batsman! When the throttle was cut, the nose dropped so that the aircraft bounced on its mainwheels, and once the tailwheel made contact, the aircraft proved very unstable directionally, despite the tailwheel lock, swinging either to port or starboard, and this swing had to be checked immediately with the brakes. On one approach, I tried a baulked landing and discovered that the sudden opening of the throttle at 80 knots (148 km/h) also produced the previously-mentioned torque stall, but this time the port wing dropped. I needed no more convincing of the wisdom of the US Navy in withholding the Corsair from shipboard operation! Oh yes, the Corsair could be landed on a deck without undue difficulty by an experienced pilot in ideal conditions, but with pilots of average capability, really pitching decks and marginal weather conditions, attrition simply had to be of serious proportions.

Changes were being continuously applied to the Corsair on the assembly lines, among the first that could be seen externally being the introduction of the higher, single-piece canopy as distinct from the original "bird cage" hood. This vastly improved canopy was accompanied by the elimination of the cut-outs for aft-vision behind the headrest and the raising of the seat by about seven inches (18 cm), and the combination did marginally improve forward view. Although these modifications did not apparently warrant any change in US Navy designation at that time, their application produced the designation Corsair Mk II in the Royal Navy. Oddly enough, somewhat more significant changes in later batches of aircraft did not result in mark number changes, despite the addition of at least a suffix letter to the US Navy designation. For example: all Royal Navy Corsairs could carry the 142 Imp gal (646 l) centreline tank and with the 361st Corsair II this could be augmented by a 137 Imp gal (623 l) tank under the starboard wing only (in lieu of a bomb), but with the 441st aircraft, the unprotected integral wing leading edge tanks were discarded and a 137 Imp gal (623 l) tank could be carried under each wing. Thus, the last 150 Corsair Mk IIs were basically F4U-1Ds, but unlike their US Navy counterparts they carried no distinctive designation. To make nonsense of the whole mark number system, identical aircraft produced by Brewster and Goodyear were assigned the designations Corsair Mk III and Mk IV respectively.

Other changes included the provision of longer-stroke oleos to take some of the bounce out of the landing and, peculiar to FAA Corsairs, the clipping of eight inches (20 cm) from each wingtip to reduce the folded height for stowage in the cramped below-decks hangars of escort carriers, this latter, somewhat rudimentary modification incidentally improving lateral control. The Corsair II was, of course, a heavy aircraft for escort carrier work and reports soon began to reach us at Farnborough of a disturbing accident rate and of excessive wear on arrester wires. It was not just the sheer bulk of the Corsair, but the fact that the pilots were throwing it onto the deck too fast, the lack of aerodynamic stall warning making for a tendency to approach at too high a speed. The real trouble, of course, lay in the fact that the modifications characterised by the Corsair Mk II had made little positive improvement in its deck-landing qualities except that there was less tendency to bounce over the wires after the mainwheels' first deck contact.

In general, the arrester wires were only surviving about four landings before having to be replaced. Inevitably, a Corsair II came to the RAE to be tried out in the arrester gear fitted on the short runway. These trials included a series with the aircraft carrying two 1,000-lb (453,6-kg) bombs which gave an all-up weight of 14,000 lb (6 350 kg). At 2·4 g and a deliberate 15 ft (4,57 m) off centre contact, the arrester wire was being destroyed at each landing. These were extreme conditions, of course, but arrester wire wear and tear remained excessive and the number of accidents escalated in proportion to the number of Corsairs deployed. Later, with a Corsair IV, we were to perform a number of tests with arrester wires fitted with heavy 1-in (2,54-cm) centre spans (ie, the piece contacted by the arrester hook). The very first landing that I made into this heavy span whipped the tail-wheel oleo clean off the aircraft, so this was obviously no

Showing clearly the clipped wingtips adopted by the Royal Navy to aid shipboard stowage, the photograph below depicts Corsair Mk I JT172 of No 1835 Squadron in 1943, which was one of the first Royal Navy Corsair units and later became No 732 Squadron

solution to the problem. Indeed, no solution was to be found by the time the problem disappeared with the disembarkation of the last FAA Corsair squadron in August 1946.

In the meantime, the FAA had taken its Corsairs into action, their operational début in the European theatre having taken place on 3 April 1944 when No 1834 Squadron aboard HMS *Victorious* flew fighter cover in concert with Hellcat, Wildcat and Seafire squadrons for Barracudas attacking *Tirpitz* lying in Kaafiord, northern Norway. In further attacks on *Tirpitz* in July and August, the Corsairs of Nos 1841 and 1842 squadrons from HMS *Formidable* were also in action. April also witnessed the operational début of the FAA Corsair in the Pacific area, when, on the 19th of that month, Nos 1830 and 1833 squadrons escorted Barracudas attacking Sabang.

Despite the fact that the FAA was flying the Corsair from carriers in several theatres, the original design aim of shipboard operation was not achieved by the US services until 28 December 1944, and then it was a Marine Corps squadron that first flew combat sorties from a carrier. The F4U-1 had been finally cleared for shipboard service with the US Navy in the previous April, after VF-103 had completed 113 uneventful landings in succession aboard the USS *Gambier Bay*, its Corsairs having been fitted with the longer-stroke oleos mentioned earlier. The Marine Corps squadron that initiated shipboard Corsair operations. VMF-124, flew from the USS *Essex,* the first USMC unit to be deployed aboard a fast carrier specifically to meet the increasing threat of Japanese *Kamikaze* attacks, and by the end of the Okinawa campaign, nearly every US Navy carrier was equipped with Corsairs.

There can be no doubt that the Corsair was one of the fastest naval aircraft of WW II and few of its pilots criticised it from the performance standpoint. It had a good range, adequate firepower, an extremely reliable engine and it could absorb a lot of punishment. However, in my view it left much to be desired as a fighter from the viewpoint of manoeuvrability and this same shortcoming was apparent in the dive bombing rôle in which it saw widespread use. Finally, it had a very dreary track record as a deck-landing aircraft; many were the pilots that lauded its high-speed performance but decried its lack of affinity with a carrier deck.

It was with this unenthusiastic regard for the Corsair lingering in my memory that I found myself faced with the same aircraft in slightly different guise a number of years later, in 1951, when I was posted on attachment as a test pilot to the US Naval Air Test Center at Patuxent River. On the inventory of Flight Test was the AU-1, a dedicated low-level ground support derivative of the original Corsair evolved specifically for Marine Corps use in the Korean War. Fitted with a single-stage two-speed R-2800-83WA version of the Double Wasp with a sea level combat rating of 2,800 hp, a lot more armour in the cockpit and engine sections and a built-in armament of four 20-mm Mk 6 cannon with 231 rpg, the AU-1 had taken on a lot of weight by comparison with the WW II Corsairs with which I was familiar. With a pair of 150 US gal (568 l) drop tanks, a 1,000-lb (453,6-kg) bomb and six 500-lb (226,8-kg) bombs, the AU-1 weighed in at no less than 19,398 lb (8,799 kg).

Understandably, performance had suffered, the maximum speed attainable when laden in the fashion described being 207 knots (384 km/h) at 8,800 ft (2,680 m), but combat range was 715 nm (1 325 km) cruising at 165 knots (306 km/h) at 15,000 ft (4 570 m). It was the handling of the AU-1 that served to heighten my distaste for the Corsair, however, for if its ancestor had proffered some unendearing characteristics, they had been multiplied in the descendant. The AU-1 had developed some highly undesirable directional stability and control characteristics, such as requiring almost full right rudder on a deck-landing approach, thus rendering baulked landing the most hazardous of operations. It also displayed a directional oscillation in diving with external stores, thus setting up wing rocking and seriously affecting the aiming accuracy. The manoeuvring forces were high — 13 lb (5,9 kg) per g at 200 knots 370 km/h) at mid c_G — and aileron overbalance occurred above 265 knots (491 km/h). These shortcomings were compounded by the old fault of inadequate stall warning and, if anything, the forward view appeared to have worsened. Whether any of these defects were eventually remedied I know not, but unless they were, I sympathise with any pilots that operated the AU-1 from a carrier.

The Corsair is a difficult aircraft to assess for, as I have already said, it was operationally successful in spite of itself. Designed essentially as a shipboard air superiority weapon, it was only a qualified success when operated from carriers, but when operated from shore bases by the US Marine Corps it built up an excellent record. The Corsair has, of course, a sentimental place in the hearts of FAA pilots because it gave us our only fighter VC, Lt Robert Hampton Gray, RCanNVR, who, leading a force of Corsairs attacking Japanese naval vessels in Onawaga Bay on 9 August 1945, attacked a destroyer despite his aircraft having suffered damage from anti-aircraft fire, and scored a direct hit before his aircraft was struck once more and burst into flames.□

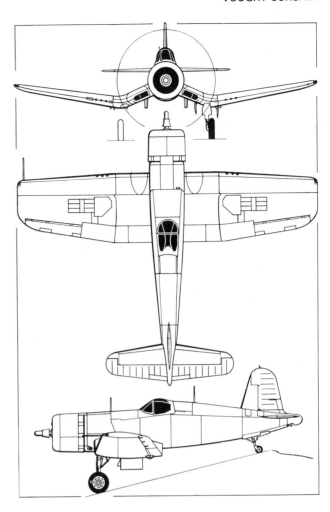

The general arrangement drawing (above right) depicts the Royal Navy's Corsair Mk II with clipped wingtips (to permit accommodation in British carrier hangars with wings folded), and the photographs (above right and below) illustrate a Corsair Mk IV (KD178) prior to acceptance by the Royal Navy, this being a Goodyear-built FG-1D equivalent to the Vought-Sikorsky-built F4U-1D

Curtiss Helldiver

"HELLDIVER", as an aircraft appellation, had very strong Hollywood connotations for those of us in the Fleet Air Arm in World War II, conjuring visions of a tensely dramatic Wallace Beery against a colourful pre-war US Navy backdrop, replete with Curtiss dive-bombing aeroplanes, all bracing wires, struts and eye-dazzling insignia. It had become effectively a generic name for *all* Curtiss naval aircraft assigned to the dive-bombing rôle since applied at the beginning of the 'thirties to the F8C-4, the first US Navy aeroplane designed from the outset to include dive-bombing in its repertoire. Thanks to the efforts of the Californian film capital, it had also become an emotive, adrenalin-stirring epithet, though not a part of *official* US Navy nomenclature until the advent of the first monoplane in the series and, in the event, the last of the genus.

Oddly enough, the application of the name "Helldiver" to this last dive bomber was, from one aspect at least, the most apposite. To the American ornithologist, helldiver is the popular name for the diving birds of the family *Podicipedidae,* known in Europe as grebes and characterised by their *short bodies.* It was the sharing of this physical trait with its namesake that was to contribute most to the exceedingly poor handling characteristics inherent in the misbegotten Curtiss brute that was to be the last Helldiver. On the other hand, it might be said that the appellation was singularly *inappropriate* as another characteristic of the ornithic helldiver is its mere gesture of a tail, whereas the Curtiss aero-

plane ended up with what was, proportionately, just about the largest tail in the business!

It was later to be said of the Curtiss Helldiver monoplane that it was a beast at birth and gathered beastliness along with maturity. At Farnborough, we had little knowledge of the unenviable reputation that had already earned for it the derisory nickname of the "Beast" when, late in October 1944, the Helldiver made its début at the RAE. We were certainly unaware that this aeroplane had come within an ace of causing one of the biggest fiascos in naval aviation history; that in the previous year, when US Navy squadron VS-9 had taken Helldivers aboard the newly-commissioned *Essex*-class carrier USS *Yorktown* for pre-operational deployment trials, the carrier's commander, Capt J J Clark, after witnessing an horrific series of structural failures, arrester wire misses and collapsing tailwheels, had urged the US Navy to cut its losses and abandon the Helldiver production programme.

Nor did we know that, four months prior to the Helldiver's appearance at Farnborough, when Task Force 58 had launched a strike against the retreating Japanese Fleet, on 20 June, following the Battle of the Philippine Sea, 90 per cent of the 50 Helldivers participating had been lost — by far the worst attrition suffered by any US shipboard aircraft since the Battle of Midway. We did know however, that FAA squadron No 1820 had formed on Helldivers at Squantum on 1 April that its aircraft had been shipped back to the UK aboard HMS *Arbiter* and that the squadron was already awaiting disbandment. We were not tardy in discovering the reason: the handling characteristics of the "Beast" were such that it would never have been allowed *near* a British carrier deck!

The Helldiver had been conceived to surpass by handsome margins the capabilities of the Douglas SBD Dauntless in every respect, yet ironically, when it was finally — and very belatedly — to achieve operational status, it was to offer only marginal performance advantages over its predecessor, coupling these with some *very* serious disadvantages. Indeed, some 30 years later, Lt Cmdr James E Vose, who commanded VB-17 when that squadron was responsible for nursing the Helldiver through its carrier qualification trials and for the operational début of the dive bomber from the USS *Bunker Hill,* was to say of the Helldiver*, "The SB2C offered little improvement on the SBD . . . the SBD would be my choice!"

The Curtiss SB2C Helldiver had been conceived in 1938, a US Navy specification intended to bring about a quantum advance in the state of the art of the carrier-based dive bomber being translated into hardware by a team led by Raymond C Blaylock. The estimated performance of the proposed aircraft had been impressive and would certainly have produced the immense capability enhancement sought by the US Navy in its dive-bombing force had paper promise been fulfilled by the aeroplane that materialised. Perhaps, as was later to be suggested in mitigation of what was to follow, the US Navy had been too rigid in its specification, allowing the design team insufficient flexibility; perhaps the pressures imposed by the need to maintain the movement of production lines once the aircraft had been committed only permitted palliatives for the dive bomber's more serious shortcomings, disallowing the thoroughgoing redesign that was manifestly necessary. Whatever the cause, the gestation and infancy of the aircraft were to be more noteworthy for their failures than for their successes; the faults that were inherent in the design were never to be eradicated with maturity.

A single prototype of the new dive bomber had been

In correspondence with Barrett Tillman, author of "The Dauntless Dive Bomber of World War Two", United States Naval Institute, Annapolis, Maryland.

ordered by the US Navy as the XSB2C-1 on 15 May 1939, Raymond Blaylock and his team having conceived a somewhat corpulent but aerodynamically clean low-wing cantilever monoplane representing the very latest thinking in dive bomber design. On the surface, the proposed aeroplane appeared to accomplish successfully the exacting task of mating the large Wright R-2600 Cyclone 14 engine, stipulated by the Bureau of Aeronautics, and the very substantial internal fuel capacity that its use implied, plus an integral weapons bay and a new standard of internal equipment, with the compactness dictated by the arbitrary demands of carrier lift sizes, hangar space, etc. The future Helldiver was both a compact and a dense aeroplane and the seeds of its subsequent problems had been sown.

In so far as Curtiss-Wright was concerned factory floor space and design office space were at a premium owing to large export contracts for the Hawk 75A and the newly placed Army Air Corps contract for the P-40. Work had begun on a new manufacturing facility at Columbus and this had been earmarked for production of the new dive bomber, but meanwhile, detail design of the XSB2C-1 had to be pursued in a nearby cattle barn on the Ohio State University Fairgrounds. The programme had first begun to run into trouble in February 1940, when wind tunnel testing of models revealed potentially excessive stalling speeds, necessitating major wing redesign, gross area being increased by 10 per

(Head of opposite page) SBW-1B Helldiver JW117, one of 26 CCF-built aircraft assigned to the Royal Navy under Lease-Lend. (Below) The prototype Helldiver, the XSB2C-1 (BuAer No 1758) photographed shortly after the commencement of flight testing, and (above right) after the lengthening of the forward fuselage, the enlarging of the tail surfaces and the resumption of flight testing in October 1941.

cent, but by the autumn, the major components of the prototype, which had been *built* in the barn, were being transported to the Curtiss-Wright factory at Buffalo, New York, for final assembly, and from here the aircraft was to fly for the first time on 18 December 1940.

From the outset, it could be seen that the XSB2C-1 was facing serious problems, yet, three weeks *before* the initial flight a production contract had been awarded for 200 SB2C-1s which were to be built at the new Columbus facility, and such was the importance now attached to the aircraft by the US Navy that tooling up, the hiring of labour and the purchase of long-leadtime items and materials had begun, the aim being to start the delivery of production aeroplanes in December 1941! Initial flight testing made it obvious that the design was anything *but* ready to be committed to production. But misgivings notwithstanding, the wheels of large-scale production had been set in motion and a temporary lack of co-operation on the part of the aircraft that they involved was evidently viewed as insufficient justification for exercising caution.

The Curtiss Electric propeller was troublesome both on the ground and in the air, and the new R-2600-8 engine had major teething problems, but these difficulties could obvi-

ously be ironed out with time. The most serious shortcoming demonstrated by the XSB2C-1 was its extremely poor stability. Its stalling characteristics were very bad indeed and low-speed handling was marginal throughout. Then, in February 1941, the prototype's engine cut on finals and the aircraft broke its back just aft of the wing in the ensuing crash. The utmost urgency was attached to rebuilding the prototype, the opportunity being taken to lengthen the forward fuselage by 12 in (30,5 cm) and redesign and enlarge the vertical tail surfaces to alleviate the stability problem. For eight months, the SB2C Helldiver programme proceeded without benefit of a prototype, the flight test programme not being resumed until 20 October 1941.

The rebuilt prototype displayed barely less pernicious handling characteristics than it had before reconstruction, but these apart, the performance of the Helldiver at this very early stage in its evolution appeared promising. Powered by an R-2600-8 Double Cyclone with a normal rating of 1,500 hp at 2,400 rpm from sea level to 5,800 ft (1 768 m) and a military rating of 1,700 hp at 2,600 rpm from sea level to 3,000 ft (915 m), the XSB2C-1 attained maximum speeds ranging from 252 knots (467 km/h) at sea level to 280 knots (519 km/h) at 14,600 ft (4 450 m). Initial climb was a very respectable 2,380 ft/min (12,1 m/sec) and range on normal maximum internal fuel of 270 US gal (1 022 l) and toting a 1,000-lb (453,6-kg) bomb internally was 865 nm (1 603 km) at 1,500 ft (457 m).

Then, on 21 December, two months after flight testing had recommenced, test pilot Baron T Hulse was forced to bail out after the XSB2C-1 suffered a structural failure in the starboard wing and the tail collapsed when pulling out of a dive from 22,000 ft (6 705 m). The programme was thus once more without a prototype.

During the largely abortive and decidedly brief flight test career of the XSB2C-1, Raymond Blaylock and his team were working frantically to cope with both the changes dictated by flight trials and the stream of modifications and alterations to the production SB2C-1 demanded by the Bureau of Aeronautics. The assembly lines in the new Columbus factory were commited; the Helldiver had been pro-

(Above left) An early production SB2C-4 (BuNo 19924), this being the version of the Helldiver built in largest quantities. (Below) SB2C-1 Helldivers of US Navy Squadron VB-8 taking off from the USS Bunker Hill in June 1944. VB-8 followed VB-17 aboard the Bunker Hill, the former having introduced the Helldiver to combat

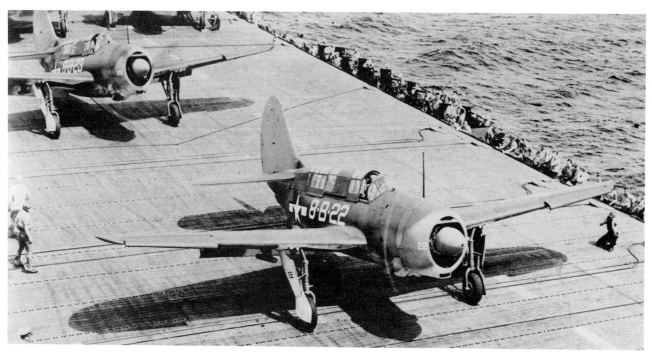

(Above and below right) The SBW-1B Helldiver was found to be generally unsatisfactory in the UK, failing to attain the minimum deck landing standards acceptable to the Royal Navy. The photograph below right illustrates clearly the inordinately short fuselage of the Helldiver by comparison with its wing and tail surfaces

nounced the first US Navy bomber to be really *mass* produced and immense backing had been organised for the quantity manufacture of the aircraft. Far-reaching design changes were obviously desirable, but the production programme could not be slowed and far less halted to permit such: the SB2C-1 had to be delivered come hell or high water!

The tail assembly was again redesigned and dramatically enlarged, resulting in the immense surfaces that were to become the hallmark of the production aeroplane, flap actuation speed was tripled and general strengthening of the structure was undertaken. The weight of the production SB2C-1 began to escalate, but the principal factors in the impressive weight growth from prototype to production model were the potential user service's demands for changes made in the light of British and French operational experience in Europe. Self-sealing fuel tanks were introduced and their capacity increased by 50 US gal (189 l), the fuel and oil lines were protected, 195 lb (88,5 kg) of armour protection was provided for the pilot and gunner, fixed armament was doubled to four 0·5-in (12,7-mm) machine guns and transferred from the engine cowl to the wings, and wet points were provided in the wings for two 58 US gal (219,5 l) long-range tanks, optional external loads being two 100-lb (45,36-kg) bombs or 325-lb (147,4-kg) depth charges. The empty weight rose from the 7,122 lb (3 320 kg) of the prototype to 10,114 lb (4 588 kg) for the production SB2C-1, normal loaded weight rising from 10,261 lb(4 654 kg) to no less than 14,958 lb (6 785 kg), and all without any commensurate increase in power. The effect of this escalation on performance and handling may be left to the imagination.

Understandably, the production programme *did* fall behind schedule and was to be slow in gathering momentum, the first SB2C-1 commencing its flight test programme in June 1942. By that time, the Columbus plant was recipient of further production orders and added Helldiver production capacity was being provided by Canadian Car & Foundry's Fort William plant with which a licence contract was being negotiated, this to be followed in October by the placing of a further licence contract with Fairchild Aircraft at Longueuil. Trials with the SB2C-1 posed even more problems than had the testing of the XSB2C-1, some of them inherited from the prototype and others the direct result of the weight escalation. The first production example was sent to Anacostia for

US Navy trials as rapidly as possible, but, after testing there and at Philadelphia, was returned to Columbus for major rework. During the autumn, six SB2C-1s were each assigned to different phases of the test programme, producing sufficient complaints to fill a sizeable tome and the one assigned to Langley being lost after suffering a structural failure during a high-speed pullout.

The subsequent development programme was a saga in itself; there can be little doubt that, had it not been for the exigencies of the times, the production lines *would* have been halted pending satisfactory solutions to the most serious shortcomings of the aeroplane that they were now turning out in *hundreds,* and it suffices to say that, between June

Curtiss SB2C-4 Helldiver Cutaway Drawing Key

1 Curtiss Electric four-bladed constant-speed propeller
2 Spinner
3 Propeller hub mechanism
4 Spinner backplate
5 Propeller reduction gearbox
6 Carburettor intake
7 Intake ducting
8 Warm air filters
9 Engine cowling ring
10 Oil cooler intake
11 Engine cowling
12 Wright R-2600-20 Cyclone 14 radial engine
13 Cooling air exit louvres
14 Exhaust collector
15 Exhaust pipe fairing
16 Oil cooler
17 Engine accessories
18 Hydraulic pressure accumulator

33 Starboard navigation light
34 Formation light
35 Starboard aileron
36 Aileron aluminium top skin
37 Aileron control mechanism
38 Starboard dive brake (open position)
39 Windshield
40 Bullet proof internal windscreen
41 Reflector gunsight
42 Instrument panel shroud
43 Cockpit coaming
44 De-icing fluid tank
45 Instrument panel
46 Pilot's pull-out chart board
47 Rudder pedals
48 Control column
49 Cockpit floor level
50 Engine throttle controls
51 Pilot's seat
52 Oxygen bottle
53 Safety harness
54 Armoured seat back

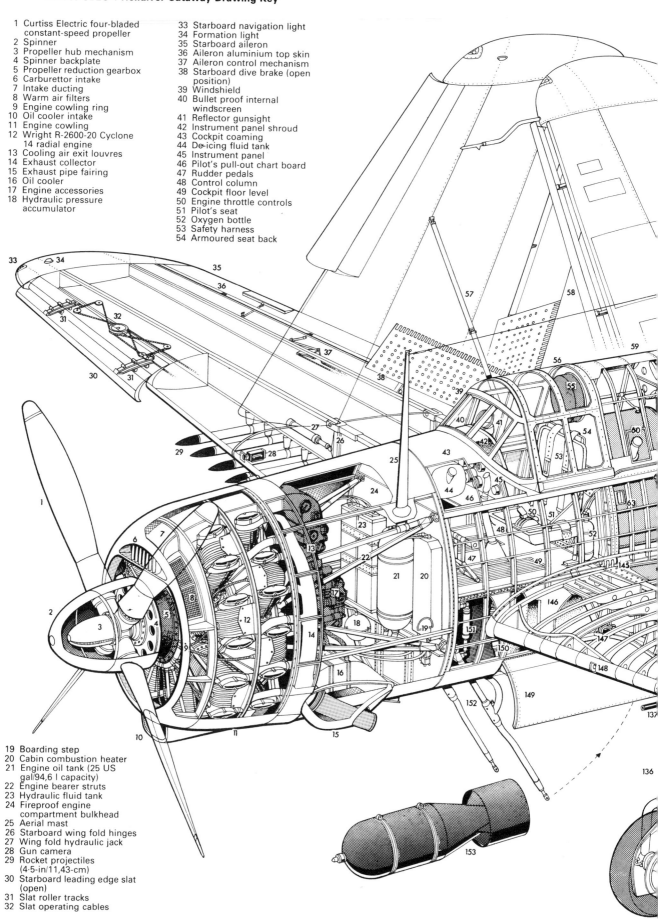

19 Boarding step
20 Cabin combustion heater
21 Engine oil tank (25 US gal/94,6 l capacity)
22 Engine bearer struts
23 Hydraulic fluid tank
24 Fireproof engine compartment bulkhead
25 Aerial mast
26 Starboard wing fold hinges
27 Wing fold hydraulic jack
28 Gun camera
29 Rocket projectiles (4·5-in/11,43-cm)
30 Starboard leading edge slat (open)
31 Slat roller tracks
32 Slat operating cables

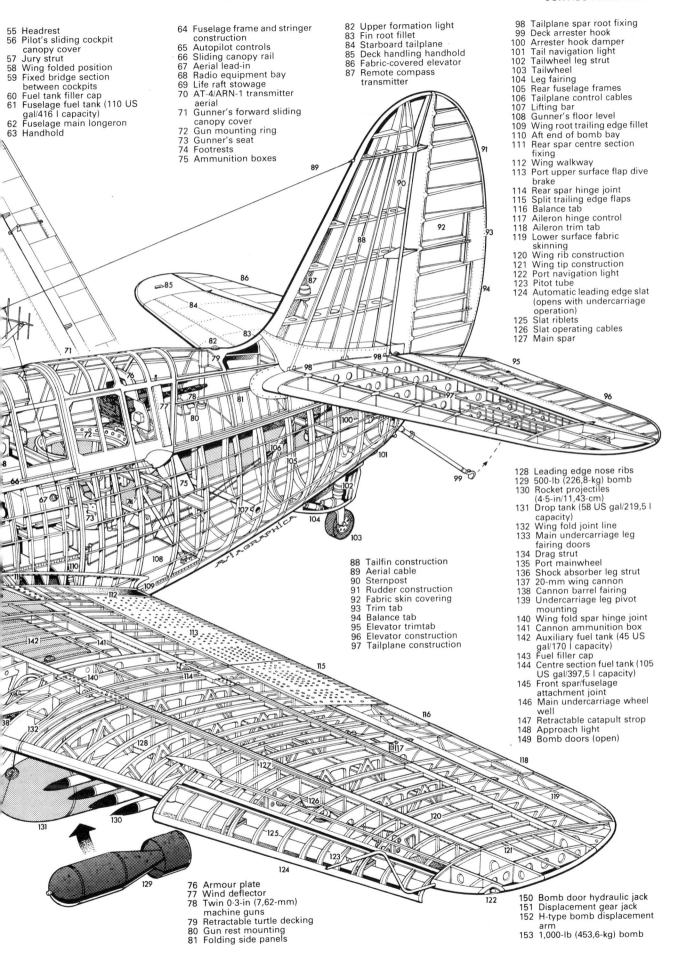

55 Headrest
56 Pilot's sliding cockpit canopy cover
57 Jury strut
58 Wing folded position
59 Fixed bridge section between cockpits
60 Fuel tank filler cap
61 Fuselage fuel tank (110 US gal/416 l capacity)
62 Fuselage main longeron
63 Handhold

64 Fuselage frame and stringer construction
65 Autopilot controls
66 Sliding canopy rail
67 Aerial lead-in
68 Radio equipment bay
69 Life raft stowage
70 AT-4/ARN-1 transmitter aerial
71 Gunner's forward sliding canopy cover
72 Gun mounting ring
73 Gunner's seat
74 Footrests
75 Ammunition boxes

82 Upper formation light
83 Fin root fillet
84 Starboard tailplane
85 Deck handling handhold
86 Fabric-covered elevator
87 Remote compass transmitter

98 Tailplane spar root fixing
99 Deck arrester hook
100 Arrester hook damper
101 Tail navigation light
102 Tailwheel leg strut
103 Tailwheel
104 Leg fairing
105 Rear fuselage frames
106 Tailplane control cables
107 Lifting bar
108 Gunner's floor level
109 Wing root trailing edge fillet
110 Aft end of bomb bay
111 Rear spar centre section fixing
112 Wing walkway
113 Port upper surface flap dive brake
114 Rear spar hinge joint
115 Split trailing edge flaps
116 Balance tab
117 Aileron hinge control
118 Aileron trim tab
119 Lower surface fabric skinning
120 Wing rib construction
121 Wing tip construction
122 Port navigation light
123 Pitot tube
124 Automatic leading edge slat (opens with undercarriage operation)
125 Slat riblets
126 Slat operating cables
127 Main spar

88 Tailfin construction
89 Aerial cable
90 Sternpost
91 Rudder construction
92 Fabric skin covering
93 Trim tab
94 Balance tab
95 Elevator trimtab
96 Elevator construction
97 Tailplane construction

128 Leading edge nose ribs
129 500-lb (226,8-kg) bomb
130 Rocket projectiles (4·5-in/11,43-cm)
131 Drop tank (58 US gal/219,5 l capacity)
132 Wing fold joint line
133 Main undercarriage leg fairing doors
134 Drag strut
135 Port mainwheel
136 Shock absorber leg strut
137 20-mm wing cannon
138 Cannon barrel fairing
139 Undercarriage leg pivot mounting
140 Wing fold spar hinge joint
141 Cannon ammunition box
142 Auxiliary fuel tank (45 US gal/170 l capacity)
143 Fuel filler cap
144 Centre section fuel tank (105 US gal/397,5 l capacity)
145 Front spar/fuselage attachment joint
146 Main undercarriage wheel well
147 Retractable catapult strop
148 Approach light
149 Bomb doors (open)

76 Armour plate
77 Wind deflector
78 Twin 0·3-in (7,62-mm) machine guns
79 Retractable turtle decking
80 Gun rest mounting
81 Folding side panels

150 Bomb door hydraulic jack
151 Displacement gear jack
152 H-type bomb displacement arm
153 1,000-lb (453,6-kg) bomb

1942, when the first production model was tested, and November 1943, when the first Helldiver offering no serious problems other than those fundamental to its basic design came off the line — the 601st production aircraft — no fewer than 889 major design changes had been made, which, in turn, had necessitated many thousands of minor changes.

The dominating physical characteristic of the SB2C-1 was the inordinate size of the wing and tail surfaces by comparison with that of the fuselage. The two-spar stressed-skin aluminium-alloy wing was built in four sections, two of these being bolted to the fuselage and comprising the centre section, and the outer panels folding manually upwards immediately outboard of the main undercarriage attachment points. The ailerons were dynamically and statically balanced, and the remainder of the trailing edge of the wing was occupied by split plain flaps which opened both upward and downward to serve as dive brakes, hydraulic locks for the upper portions permitting the lower flaps to operate in orthodox fashion for landing. These flaps set up tremendous tail buffet when serving as dive brakes and were, in fact, to be perforated from the SB2C-4 (and equivalent CCF and Fairchild) model to alleviate this highly disconcerting phenomenon. Slats mechanically linked with undercarriage actuation extended from the outer third of the wing leading edge to aid lateral control at low speeds. A 105 US gal (397,5 l) self-sealing fuel tank was housed between the spars of the centre section on each side, and whereas the first production aircraft carried a pair of 0·50-in (12,7-mm) machine guns with 1,600 rounds in each centre section half, these were replaced in subsequent aircraft (SB2C-1C) by a 20-mm cannon on each side with a combined total of 800 rounds, this installation reducing gross weight by 228 lb (103,4 kg).

The oval-section fuselage was an aluminium-alloy semi-monocoque structure with a flush-riveted smooth Alclad skin. The pilot, who was provided with an armourglass windscreen and back armour, was seated immediately forward of the fuselage fuel tank of 110 US gal (416,4 l) capacity which could be supplemented by a jettisonable 130 US gal (492 l) weapons bay tank. he weapons bay was equipped with hydraulically-operated doors and normally accommodated a single 1,000-lb (453,6-kg) bomb or two 500-lb (226,8-kg) bombs, although it could house a 1,600-lb (725,75-kg) bomb or two 1,000-lb (453,6-kg) bombs, and if the weapons bay doors were removed and a supporting truss installed a Mk 13-2 torpedo could be carried. The gunner was provided with a single 0·50-in (12,7-mm) gun in early production aircraft,

but this was replaced at an early stage by a pair of 0·3-in (7,62-mm) guns on an armoured mount with 2,000 rounds. The tail had aluminium-alloy frames and the fixed surfaces were covered by flush-riveted Alclad skin, the movable surfaces being fabric covered.

The massive increase in weight by comparison with the prototype had exacted a commensurate toll on performance and it was quickly ascertained that maximum and cruise speeds of the production SB2C-1 Helldiver were scantly better than those of the SBD Dauntless that it was intended to succeed, the older aeroplane being appreciably more manoeuvrable and suffering none of the adverse stall characteristics and marginal low-speed handling of the new Curtiss dive bomber. The Helldiver had been designed to haul a very much larger bomb load over a very much greater range at appreciably higher speed than the Dauntless, but much had happened between drawing board and production aeroplane, and although the SB2C-1 was finally committed to combat by VB-17 which flew its first operational sortie from the USS *Bunker Hill* in the second strike against Rabaul on 11 November 1943, it was tacitly admitted that the Helldiver was still far from operationally effective. As one VB-17 pilot is recorded as having commented at the time, "The SB Deuce has more bugs than an oriental flophouse!"

As the numbers of Helldivers aboard US Navy carriers increased, serviceability improved — although never to be considered good — and the growing familiarity of US Navy pilots with the unpleasant nature of the Curtiss dive bomber reduced accident attrition to acceptable levels, but there was little to endear the Helldiver to its crews, air or ground, to whom it had become the "Beast". However, the production lines were continuing to churn out this least attractive of all US Navy production combat aeroplanes and the output from Columbus was being supplemented by Canadian production Canadian Car & Foundry having flown its first Helldiver (as the SBW-1) on 29 July 1943, with Fairchild Aircraft having followed suit (as the SBF-1) on 28 August of the same year. The 26 Helldivers assigned to the FAA under Lease-Lend arrangements were, in fact, CCF-built SBW-1Bs the suffix letter indicating Britain) and equivalent to the Curtiss-built SB2C-1C.

One of the FAA's SBW-1B Helldivers (JW115) duly arrived at Farnborough, as previously recounted, late in October 1944, the intention being to assess its dive-bombing qualities in particular and its handling characteristics in general in comparison with the Douglas SBD-5 Dauntless and

Despite its stubby, porcine fuselage contours, the Helldiver was not unpleasant to the eye, but few of its handling characteristics were pleasing. Nevertheless, it was built in very large numbers, the version built in the greatest quantities being the SB2C-4 illustrated here.

the Vultee Vengeance IV, and as deck landing assessment was also involved, I was inevitably assigned the task. The Helldiver was an aggressively stolid aeroplane and once one had become accustomed to the imensity of its wing and tail surfaces by comparison with its stubby, porcine fuselage, it was not unpleasing to the eye.

The big Wright R-2600-8 Cyclone 14, which, by this time, had overcome most of the problems that had plagued its early mating with the Helldiver airframe, growled healthily, its tone reminiscent of that of the smaller single-row Cyclone that I had known so well in the Wildcat. While warming up, I had time to look around the cockpit, the layout of which could best be described, in Irish parlance, as organised chaos! There was no evidence of constructive planning, yet one could not complain that anything was not to hand — except for the rudder trimmer which was a somewhat vital exception. It was simply a case of knowing where to look. The cockpit was, in typical American fashion, both roomy and comfortable, but I found that the rudder pedals and control column were at full reach.

Control movement produced noticeable friction in all three control circuits which was fairly bad in the aileron circuit and very bad in the elevator circuit. Taxying was unpleasant owing to the combination of poor forward view, particularly with the cowl gills open, and weather-cocking tendencies in crosswinds, although the wide-track undercarriage, tailwheel lock and harsh brakes were all helpful in countering ground swing. Take-off was straightforward enough, although the view over the nose with cowl gills half open left much to be desired until the tail was raised, this calling for a firm push on the control column to overcome the friction in the control circuit. There appeared to be little or no aileron control response until a speed of at least 90 knots (167 km/h) had been reached. On raising the undercarriage and flaps there was virtually no noticeable change of trim, and climb at 130 knots (241 km/h) revealed marginal longitudinal stability and positive lateral instability. The aircraft was lightly loaded and the initial climb rate was over 2,000 ft/min (10 m/sec), but with full fuel in clean condition and without bombs at a loaded weight of 13,674 lb (6 202 kg), the maximum sea level climb rate at normal power (ie, 1,500 hp at 2,400 rpm) was 1,620 ft/min (8,23 m/sec), and with a pair of 1,000-lb (453,6-kg) bombs was only 1,270 ft/min (6,45 m/sec).

In level flight cruise at 190 knots (352 km/h) the instability characteristics persisted and harmony of control was spoiled by the heavy elevator. In bumpy air very hard work on the rudder and ailerons was called for to control the aircraft which wallowed continuously, and I rapidly concluded that the Helldiver was decidedly one of the worst aircraft that I had ever flown in turbulence, and I had flown a few bad ones! By the same token, it was a *terrible* aircraft to fly on instruments, and it was hardly surprising, therefore, that an autopilot was fitted.

Lightly loaded, the Helldiver had a maximum speed of about 220 knots (408 km/h) at sea level and could just about reach 240 knots (445 km/h) at its critical altitude of 13,400 ft (4 085 m). Its practical combat radius with a 1,000-lb (453,6-kg) bomb and maximum standard internal fuel was only 240 nm (445 km), this being based on 20 min warm-up and idling, a minute for take-off at military power, 10 min rendezvous at 60 per cent normal sea level power, climb to 15,000 ft (4 570 m) and cruise at that altitude, five minutes of combat at full military power at 1,500 ft (460 m) plus 10 min at full normal power, and then return flight at 1,500 ft (460 m) at 60 per cent normal power, 60 min rendezvous and landing. This was *inferior* to the SBD-5 Dauntless and cruise speed was only 12 knots (22 km/h) higher!

The all-up stall at a weight of 9,500 lb (4 309 kg) occurred at 77 knots (143 km/h) with no warning whatsoever,

The SB2C-4 version of the Helldiver, an example of which (BuNo 20722) is seen above, was the first version to have perforated wing flaps to inhibit tail buffeting

although admittedly this was no more than a gentle nose drop. The all-down stall at 66 knots (122 km/h) was very difficult to achieve unless the aircraft was trimmed well back and the control column was pulled right back. Heavy elevator buffeting set in well before the stall when the nose and wing dropped sharply. The wing tank fuel load dictated which wing dropped at the all-down stall.

A primary interest at Farnborough lay, of course, in comparing the dive bombing characteristics of the Helldiver with those of the Dauntless and the Vengeance. In unbraked dives to 320 knots (593 km/h) there was no buffeting and the Helldiver was easy to hold on target, although constant rudder trimming was necessary above 280 knots (519 km/h), and corrections to line by aileron turns were very hard work. The pull-out forces were fairly high. The operational technique was to open the split flaps in a gentle pull up at 150 knots (278 km/h), which gave a slight nose-down change of trim, and wing over onto the target. In the braked dive there was constant tail buffeting, although no adverse effects on control resulted from the use of the split flaps. The pull out gave fairly high forces and set up extra buffet. The flaps were normally retracted at 180 knots (333 km/h) after recovery and gave a slight nose-up trim change. Of the three American dive bombers tested at Farnborough, the Helldiver was by far and away the worst owing to its buffet characteristics, its high elevator pull-out forces, and the very heavy rudder and aileron forces which rendered aiming corrections difficult.

The landing circuit was joined at 120 knots (222 km/h), speed then being reduced to 100 knots (185 km/h) for lowering the undercarriage, the leading-edge slats extending simultaneously and producing a negligible nose-down trim change, but the poor aileron control was already very much in evidence. At 95 knots (176 km/h) the flaps were lowered and the first one-third of travel was accompanied by a violent nose-up change in trim, this being cancelled out by the nose-down trim change that resulted from the remaining two-thirds of flap travel. At the approach speed of 85 knots (157 km/h) the ailerons were very sluggish in their effect, the elevator fairly heavy but effective and the rudder light and effective.

The view from the cockpit on the approach was fairly acceptable until hold-off and then the rise of the nose blanked off most of the view dead ahead and slightly to each side. On cutting the throttle there was an acute nose-down change of trim, meaning that a wheely landing was inevitable, but the delightfully soft undercarriage absorbed all bounce. There was no swing on the landing run, presumably due to the combination of stabilising effect of the wide undercarriage and the tailwheel lock. The baulked landing case revealed that the trim change on application of engine power was most emphatically excessive. I found that I could just hold the nose-up change of trim with as much forward pressure on the column as I could apply at a mere 30 in Hg

Curtiss SB2C-1C (SBW-1B) Helldiver Specification

Power Plant: One Wright R-2600-8 Cyclone 14 14-cylinder radial air cooled engine rated at (military) 1,700 hp at 2,600 rpm from sea level to 3,000 ft (915 m) and 1,450 hp at 2,600 rpm from 7,800 ft (2 375 m) to 12,000 ft (3 660 m), and (normal) 1,500 hp at 2,400 rpm from sea level to 5,800 ft (1,770 m) and 1,350 hp at 2,400 rpm from 8,900 ft (2 710 m) to 13,000 ft (3 960 m). Driving 12-ft (3,66-m) diam three-blade Curtiss Electric constant-speed propeller. Total internal fuel tankage, 320 US gal (1 211 l), comprising one 110 US gal (416. l) fuselage tank and two 105 US gal (397,5 l) wing root tanks. Provision for one 130 US gal (492 l) jettisonable weapons bay tank and two 58 US gal (219,5 l) wing drop tanks.
Performance: (At 14,720 lb/6,677 kg with max standard internal fuel and 1,000-lb/453,6-kg bomb) Max speed (military power), 265 mph (426 km/h) at sea level, 281 mph) 452 km/h) at 12,400 ft (3 780 m), (normal power), 252 mph (405 km/h) at sea level, 275 mph (442 km/h) at 13,400 ft (4 085 m); range cruise, 158 mph (254 km/h) at 1,500 ft (455 m); initial climb (military power), 1,750 ft/min (8,9 m/sec), (normal power), 1,440 ft/min (7,3 m/sec); time to 10,000 ft (3,050 m) at military power, 7·7 min, to 20,000 ft (6 095 m), 22·9 min; service ceiling, 24,200 ft (7 375 m); max range, 1,110 mls (1 786 km); combat radius, 276 mls (445 km); take-off distance (calm), 382 yds (349 m), (15-knot wind), 243 yds (222 m), (25-knot wind) 167 yds (152 m).
Weights: Empty, 10,114 lb (4 588 kg); loaded (clean), 13,674 lb (6,202 kg); max take-off (Mk 13-2 torpedo and two drop tanks), 16,812 lb (7 626 kg).
Dimensions: Span 49 ft 8⅝ in (15,14 m); length, 36 ft 9 in (11,20 m); height (tail down), 14 ft 9 in (4,49 m); span folded, 22 ft 6½ in (6,87 m); height folded, 16 ft 10 in (5,13 m); wing area, 422 sq ft (39,20 m²).
Armament: Two fixed forward-firing 20-mm cannon with 800 rounds and two 0·3-in (7,62-mm) machine guns on flexible mounting with 2,000 rounds. (Internal) one 1,000-lb (453,6-kg) or 1,600-lb (725,76-kg) bomb, or two 1,000-lb (453,6-kg) or 500-lb (226,8-kg) bombs, or one Mk 13-2 torpedo, or one 650-lb (294,8-kg) or two 325-lb (147,4-kg) depth charges. (External under wing) Two 100-lb (45,36-kg) bombs or two 325-lb (147,4-kg) depth charges.

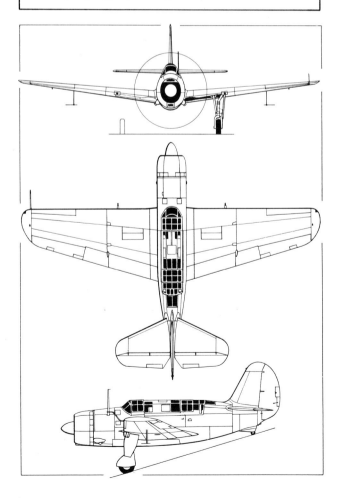

manifold pressure. Quite frankly, with the terrible aileron control at approach speed and the excessive longitudinal trim change with engine power, the Helldiver would *never* have been acceptable for decklanding by British standards, and, indeed, was never flown onto a British carrier by an FAA pilot. One could only sympathise with the US Navy pilots flying this unpleasant aircraft from carriers in the Pacific, wonder that their accident attrition was tolerable and understand their choice of nickname for the Helldiver. For my money, all the effort that Curtiss-Wright and the US Navy had put into an attempt to turn what was so obviously a wrong'un from birth into at least a reasonably acceptable shipboard aircraft had been wasted. The Helldiver was a *beast!*

By the time we had completed our evaluation of the SBW-1B Helldiver at Farnborough, the SB2C-3 had been under test and placed in production with an R-2600-20 offering a military rating of 1,900 hp at 2,800 rpm for take-off, and military and normal (low blower) ratings of 1,750 hp at 2,600 rpm at 3,200 ft (975 m) and 1,600 hp at 2,400 rpm at 5,000 ft (1 525 m). Equipped with cast aluminium cylinder heads and the new Wright "W" cylinder barrel fins, this uprated engine drove a four-bladed Curtiss Electric propeller in place of the three-blader of the SB2C-1, and the additional "horses" that the -20 engine offered were at least a gesture in the right direction, this power plant being standardised for all succeeding Helldiver versions. In other respects, the SB2C-3 was essentially similar to the -1, production following on 978 of the earlier model from Columbus (plus 66 of the equivalent SBW-1s and 50 SBF-1s) and totalling 1,112 aircraft (plus 413 SBW-3s and 150 SBF-3s).

Further minor changes, such as the perforation of the wing flaps to inhibit tail buffeting and the provision of racks under the outer wings for 4·5 in (11,43-cm) rockets, resulted in the SB2C-4 as Curtiss-Wright and the US Navy continued to endeavour to extract the best possible from a bad job. No fewer than 2,045 SB2C-4s were to roll off the lines, including a number equipped with radar as SB2C-4Es (plus 270 SBW-4Es and 100 SBF-4Es). Meanwhile, the Helldiver was playing an increasingly important rôle in the Pacific War, although, in truth, the really critical phases of the conflict had passed, having been fought out by the Dauntless. However, WW II was approaching its end and with it the production career of the Helldiver. Only one other production model was to appear, the SB2C-5 with 35 US gal (132 l) more fixed internal fuel which began to leave the the Columbus line in February 1945, a total of 970 being produced (plus 86 of the equivalent CCF-built SBW-5).

If the 900 examples of the land-based equivalent of the SB2C-1 built for the US Army Air Force as A-25As under the Army-Navy standardisation programme with naval equipment and wing-folding mechanism deleted — although, in the event, 410 of these were reassigned to the Marine Corps as SB2C-1As — are added to the shipboard models built for the US Navy, the grand total of Helldivers completed is some 7,140 aircraft. This quantity is far greater than that of any other dive bomber built by any nation, yet, ironically, in the rôle for which it was created, the Helldiver was one of the least efficaceous aircraft. Its production life had been plagued by innumerable problems, many of which were inherent in its basic design and incapable of solution. Yet, despite manifestly inauspicious characteristics, production was persisted with. There can be no doubt that the Helldiver was committed to quantity manufacture before the true nature of the beast had been ascertained and once the machinery for mass production had begun to turn, none was willing to admit the mistake and bring it to a halt. Those US Navy mechanics swearing that SB2C really stood for "Son-of-a-Bitch Second Class" had, for what it was worth, my profound sympathy! □

Fairey Barracuda

THE SWORDFISH, so the records say, was responsible for the sinking of a greater tonnage of enemy shipping during WW II than most other Allied aircraft. There is no gainsaying the records, but such success attributed to a relic of an era long past — the Swordfish was assuredly an anachronism long before Adolf Hitler cast covetous glances in the direction of Poland — is difficult to reconcile today with such total obsolescence. Its intended successor, the Albacore, was hardly the advance the Navy's aircrew had a right to expect, being, as was suggested at the time of its début, no more than a "tarted up Swordfish", offering its crew reasonable means of answering one of the calls of nature and less likely to encourage pneumonia. Romantic of appearance through these bestrutted and braced biplanes were to some, evoking nostalgia, as they did, for the days when the tempo of aeronautical development was more leisurely, they must surely have had any *Luftwaffe* fighter pilot that encountered them rubbing his eyes in disbelief.

Inevitably, therefore, the TSR — torpedo-spotter-reconnaissance — boys awaited with bated breath the arrival of the long-promised and much-vaunted monoplane that sported the highly emotive appellation of Barracuda and promised to enable them to vault the decade or so between the concept of their antiquated and supremely vulnerable biplanes and the early 'forties. I assume that they were to be just as astonished as I was at first sight of the monster that was in due course to materialise as the fulfilment of their anticipation. Could this *really* have been spawned by Marcel Lobelle's drawing boards where such aesthetically appealing creations as the delectable little Fantôme and pleasingly handsome if somewhat ineffectual Fulmar had seen birth?

I was serving with the Service Trials Unit at Arbroath in

September 1942, when our first Barracuda arrived. As it entered the airfield circuit, it could be seen that its contours were nothing if not unprepossessing. Here were no rakish lines such as those of its namesake, that voracious West Indian fish. Then it turned on to the approach and disgorged a mass of ironmongery from wings and fuselage transforming the pedestrian and unappealing into what could only be described as an "airborne disaster"! The old adage, "If it looks right . . .", inevitably sprung to mind and I concluded

The first prototype Barracuda (P1767) seen above with the low tail-plane with which it was originally flown and below with the high-set tailplane subsequently adopted to deal with a buffeting problem. (Head of page) The first Barracuda Mk II (P9667)

(Above) The first production Barracuda Mk II (P9667) toting a torpedo, although, in so far as is known, this weapon was never used by the Barracuda in action. Note characteristic level-flight nose-down sit. (Immediately below left) A series production Barracuda Mk II (LS789) and (extreme bottom left) a Blackburn-built Mk II (BV760) showing clearly the Fairey-Youngman flaps

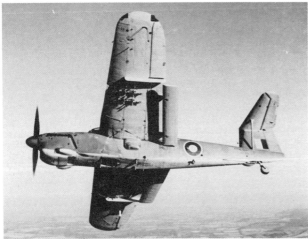

ical surfaces) tailplane. Yet a further unorthodox feature of the aircraft was the design of its mighty undercarriage. The main legs were inverted L-shaped assemblies pivoted near to the base of the fuselage and raised or lowered by jack struts attached at the elbows, the base of each inverted L assembly retracting complete with fairing into the fuselage side and the remaining portion of the leg with wheel and fairing retracting into a wing well.

All in all, this large and relatively heavily-loaded aeroplane appeared to call for a degree of circumspection, a view that remained with me when, a few days after the arrival of Barracuda Mk I P9645, the fourth production example, I clambered into the cockpit for an initial air test and for what was to be my second experience of an underpowered aircraft, the first having been the Blackburn Roc. The Barracuda had been conceived for the 1,200 hp Rolls-Royce Exe 24-cylinder X-type pressure-air-cooled sleeve-valve engine, but further work on this power plant had been halted and the initial production Barracuda had been provided with a Rolls-Royce Merlin 30 of 1,300 hp — eight per cent more power than originally envisaged but hardly commensurate with the weight that had meanwhile been taken on. The result was that the Merlin and the three-bladed Rotol propeller that it drove provided a woefully insufficient combination to lift off the Barracuda in anything like a reasonable distance and take-off was to prove a nail-biting business on the short runways at Arbroath.

After what seemed an eternity, this monstrosity eventually unstuck and the anxiety of parting company with a rapidly diminishing portion of runway gave place to a few perspiration-evoking moments until those gangling undercarriage legs laboriously tucked themselves out of sight. Matters then began to improve, but the rate of climb was anything but inspiring and I could not help wondering what effect on climb would result from a torpedo being slung underneath. Once cruise altitude had been reached, I found that the Barracuda was quite pleasantly manoeuvrable, being particularly light on the ailerons but displaying a mild suspicion of rudder overbalance. It surprisingly revealed a good turn of speed in diving; a characteristic certainly to be appreciated by the TSR boys, whose survival often depended on a fast descent from cruise level to sea level to reduce vulnerability to ships' flak and fighter defences. Equally important with fast dive capability was, of course, the ability to dive steeply to give maximum deflection angle changes to the opposing

that there were events that I could await with rather more pleasure than taking this quaint contraption into the air.

A high-shoulder-wing all-metal stressed-skin monoplane, the Barracuda was something of an abortion on the ground. Indeed, with everything folded it gave the impression of having been involved in a very nasty accident. Its most distinctive feature was provided by the Fairey-Youngman flaps — effectively separate aerofoil surfaces mounted inboard of the ailerons and below and behind the wing trailing edge — which were lowered some 20 degrees to increase take-off lift and about 30 degrees for fast descents. When in neutral they merely augmented the wing area. The strut-braced high-set tailplane was another curiosity of the Barracuda, this feature having been adopted when it had been ascertained during prototype trials that the wake from the flaps buffeted a normally-positioned (ie, at the junction of fuselage and vert-

Numerous items of special equipment were developed for and/or carried by the Barracuda. The underwing containers shown above appended to Barracuda Mk II P9795, for example, were each intended to accommodate two paratroops who departed the containers via trap-doors. Successful live drops were made at the AFEE before the entire scheme was abandoned

anti-aircraft guns. Both Swordfish and Albacore could dive steeply but with little acceleration. On the other hand, a monoplane offered the diving speed but angle could not be steep if pull-out at low level was to be effected safely, a problem that Marcel Lobelle and his team had not-so-neatly solved by means of the previously-mentioned Fairey-Youngman flaps. During my initial flight I made only a perfunctory check of these flaps, which seemed very effective, but I was to make much closer acquaintance with them later on the Barracuda II.

When it came to landing — and particularly deck landing — the Barracuda's characteristics were the exact antithesis of those that it displayed as it struggled to get airborne. In short, while take-off could only be described as very poor, the landing could be said to be very good. With everything down, there was so much drag that the Merlin 30 demanded about +4 lbs boost on the approach and when the throttle was cut at

From whatever angle the Barracuda was viewed it provided little in the way of aeronautical pulchritude, and seen from the rear with wings folded (above left) its appearance was quite extraordinary. Trials with an air-sea rescue lifeboat beneath the fuselage were undertaken with at least one Barracuda Mk II (MX613) seen below

Fairey Barracuda Cockpit Instrumentation Key:

1 VHF (ARI 5403/5272) control unit
2 Intercom selector switch (VHF/mix/beacon)
3 Intercom 'Press to call' switch
4 Cockpit lights switchgear
5 Ultra-violet lamps dimmer switch
6 General (red) lights dimmer switch
7 Emergency lights switch
8 General (red) lights master switch
9 Undercarriage emergency release handle stowage
10 Dinghy emergency release lever
11 Port mainwheel unit emergency release handle
12 Altitude limit lamps
13 Pilot's speaking tube
14 Ultra-violet cockpit lamp
15 Sliding hood release catch
16 ZBX control unit
17 Ship's speed control
18 Elevator trim tab control (stall-dive)
19 Rudder trim tab control (left-right)
20 Aileron trim tab control
21 Brakes pressure gauge
22 Arresting hook release lever
23 Flaps selector lever (normal-neutral-land)
24 Undercarriage selector lever
25 Undercarriage interlock lever (subsequently deleted)
26 Friction adjusting nut
27 Priming cock
28 Propeller speed control lever
29 Clock mounting

30 Throttle lever
31 Rocket-firing (RATOG) push-button
32 IFF detonator switches (masked)
33 Radio altimeter indicator lights
34 Air temperature gauge
35 Landing light switch
36 Fire warning lamp
37 Carburettor air intake control handle (hot: pull/cold: push)
38 Landing lamp control
39 Ignition switches
40 Undercarriage indicator switch
41 Flap position indicator
42 IFF control switches
43 Cylinder priming pump
44 Undercarriage warning lamp
45 Radio altimeter
46 Ventilator control
47 Reflector sight bracket
48 ASI
49 Artificial horizon
50 Rate of climb/descent indicator
51 Altimeter
52 Directional gyro
53 Turn and bank (slip) indicator
54 Automatic boost control cut-out
55 Slow-running cut-out control
56 DR compass switches
57 DR compass card holder
58 Fuel pressure warning lamp (partially obscured by control grip)
59 Fuel cock control
60 Fire-extinguisher push-buttons

61 Compass heading indicator
62 DR compass repeater
63 Engine starter reloading control
64 P.8/P.11 compass correction card holder
65 Underwing handling rail release switch
66 Oil dilution push-button
67 Compass lamp dimmer switch
68 Undercarriage and arresting hook indicator
69 P.8/P.11 compass
70 Rudder pedals
71 Pilot's seat
72 Control column
73 Starter and booster-coil push-button
74 Engine starter master switch
75 Brake lever (contol grip mounting)
76 Recognition (resin) lights switch
77 Navigation lights switches
78 Formation lights switch (off/morse/steady)
79 Downwards recognition lights selector switch (clear/green/red)
80 Oil pressure gauge
81 Boost gauge (obscured by control grip)
82 Intercom 'Press to speak' switch (mounted on control grip)
83 Bomb/torpedo firing button (mounted on control grip)
84 Pitot head heater switch
85 Windscreen de-icing pump
86 Engine speed indicator
87 Radiator temperature gauge
88 Oil temperature gauge
89 Fuel contents gauge (port tank)
90 Fuel contents gauge (starboard tank)

91 Reflector sight supply socket
92 Ultra-violet cockpit lamp
93 Identification and recognition lights switchbox
94 Headrest release
95 Reflector sight stowage clip
96 Bomb containers jettison switch
97 Bomb fusing switches
98 Starboard mainwheel unit emergency release handle
99 Speaking tubes
100 Undercarriage emergency release handle stowage
101 Oxygen regulator
102 Cockpit lamp and dimmer switch
103 Fire extinguisher
104 Oxygen regulator light dimmer switch
105 Bomb selector/torpedo switch panel
106 Bomb gear master switch
107 Undercarriage emergency gear control (handles clip-stowed)
108 F.46 camera switch
109 Radiator shutter control
110 Radio altimeter limit switch (subsequently repositioned fig. 117)
111 Flying controls locking-stays eyebolt
112 Radiator shutter indicator
113 Navigation lights dimmer (rheostat) switch
114 Signal cartridge stowage ports
115 Signal pistol
116 Seat adjustment lever
117 Radio altimeter limit switch position
118 16-point automatic bomb distributor

the *moment critique* the Barracuda sank like a stone and remained glued on the deck. The view from the cockpit for this process was good.

I was destined to have little to do with the Barracuda Mk I, of which, in fact, only 30 examples were built, for, by the time I came into contact with this angular ugly Fairey product, the prototype of the rather more powerful Mk II was already flying and this was to be the first service version. The Barracuda II differed from its predecessor primarily in having a Merlin 32 affording 1,640 bhp at 3,000 rpm and driving a four-bladed Rotol propeller. The boost gauge now registered +18 lbs on take-off rather than the +12 lbs of the ealier model and the result was a respectable improvement in getting airborne.

I had not entirely parted company with the sadly underpowered Barracuda Mk I, however, for, on 12 June 1943, I was to find myself in one low over Dunino airfield, a little grass satellite just south of St Andrews of golf fame, the purpose of the flight being radio altimeter trials. The readouts from the altimeter were being checked against a system which involved trailing an aerial to which was attached a substantial lead weight and as the runs got progressively lower, the aerial was wound in by the observer. The final stages of the trial called for slow runs so low that it had been decided to lower the flaps and undercarriage so that ground contact would warn me to climb higher without, hopefully, damaging the aircraft. A slight power loss caused by boost capsule trouble ensured that ground contact was indeed made. I hurriedly opened up to full power but, to my astonishment, Barracuda and ground remained in contact! By this time, we had reached and passed the airfield boundary, proving the point in no uncertain terms by passing through some telephone wires and a small tree, bouncing on a hillock and settling gracefully into a ploughed field where a combination of Scottish stone dyke and a series of anti-invasion glider stakes finally halted our progress but removed the Barracuda's mighty undercarriage. Subsequent investigation revealed that the trailing aerial had contacted the ground and the combined coefficient of friction of the undercarriage wheels and trailing aerial had been just enough to tip us over the backside of the depleted power curve.

That was to be my last experience with the initial model of the Barracuda. I had first flown its production successor, the Mk II, during the previous April, and unfortunately for my

assessment of this more powerful version, I had flown the Grumman Avenger some two weeks previously and had been so favourably impressed that it had left me rather appalled by the equivalent state of the art in the UK. Of course, the TSR boys were, by this time, working up on the Barracuda II, No 827 Squadron at RNAS Stretton, in Cheshire, having received its aircraft at the beginning of the year, and the first reports had begun to reach us of aircraft diving into the sea, sometimes inverted, while simulating torpedo attacks. As the frequency of such accidents increased, it became progressively more difficult to simply attribute such disasters to the unfamiliarity of ex-biplane crews with monoplane performance, as was the initial tendency.

Meanwhile, I had moved on to the Royal Aircraft Establishment at Farnborough, where I found myself up-to-the-neck in investigating these Barracuda losses, which , by now, totalled five. I was well aware that the torpedo attack technique was to dive to low altitude using the dive flaps, level out, launch the torpedo, retract the flaps and make a rapid and evasive breakaway to one side. This latter phase of the manoeuvre seemed the obvious area for suspicion, and I recollected the rudder overbalance that I had sensed during my first flight in a Barracuda. I therefore performed a series of sideslips at height and at various speeds, deliberately stalling the rudder. When the rudder overbalanced, the nose dropped quite sharply. I also checked the change of trim when the dive brakes were retracted at the bottom of a high-speed dive and this was markedly nose down.

The next stage was to try out the combination manoeuvre. I alerted the flight observer to switch on the cameras recording the instruments giving airspeed, altitude, and elevator, rudder and aileron angles, and then put the aircraft into a dive to 210 knots (389 km/h) with the flaps in the dive position and with the elevator trimmed to hold it steady. I then simulated levelling out at sea level, and when the speed

The Barracuda Mk III was intended primarily for anti-submarine reconnaissance tasks for which it carried an ASV (Air-to-Surface Vessel) Mk X radar scanner in a radome under the rear fuselage as seen in these photographs (above left and below) of the definitive prototype Mk III (DP855), originally the first Boulton Paul-built Mk II

Fairey Barracuda Mk II Cutaway Drawing Key:

1 Spinner
2 Four-blade Rotol propeller
3 Coolant header tank
4 Generator cooling intake
5 Radiator intake
6 Oil cooler radiator (centre)
7 Engine coolant radiators (left and right)
8 Debris guard
9 Carburretor air intake filter fairing
10 Starboard mainwheel
11 Mainwheel door
12 Exhaust outlet
13 Engine bearer assembly
14 Coolant pipes
15 Exhaust shroud
16 Rolls-Royce Merlin 32 engine
17 Angled firewall
18 Oil tank
19 Engine bearer/bulkhead attachment
20 Entry foot/handholds
21 Strengthening plate
22 Rudder pedal bar
23 Throttle lever quadrant
24 Control column grip
25 Down-view panel
26 Pilot's seat

37 Aileron trim tab control linkage
38 Starboard outer fuel cell
39 Bomb gear access panels (3)
40 Hinged trailing edge
41 Scrap view showing underwing panels plus

46 Pilot's headrest
47 Incendiary bomb
48 Frame members
49 Seat frame mounting
50 Underfloor control runs
51 Mainwheel unit operating jack

42 Hinged (Fairey-Youngman diving brake) flap, and
43 Outer wing section handling rail (stowed)
44 Starboard inner fuel cell
45 Pilot's sliding canopy section

27 Windscreen hot-air/de-icing pipe
28 Windscreen
29 Wing skinning
30 Gun camera housing
31 Wing main front spar
32 Starboard navigation light
33 Outer wing section locking plunger
34 Starboard recognition light
35 Starboard aileron
36 Aileron hinge box covers (3)

52 Mainwheel unit torsion box well
53 Main spar centre-section carry-through
54 Navigator's Vickers gun (stowed)
55 Decking cut-out
56 Main slinging point
57 Navigator's tilting canopy section

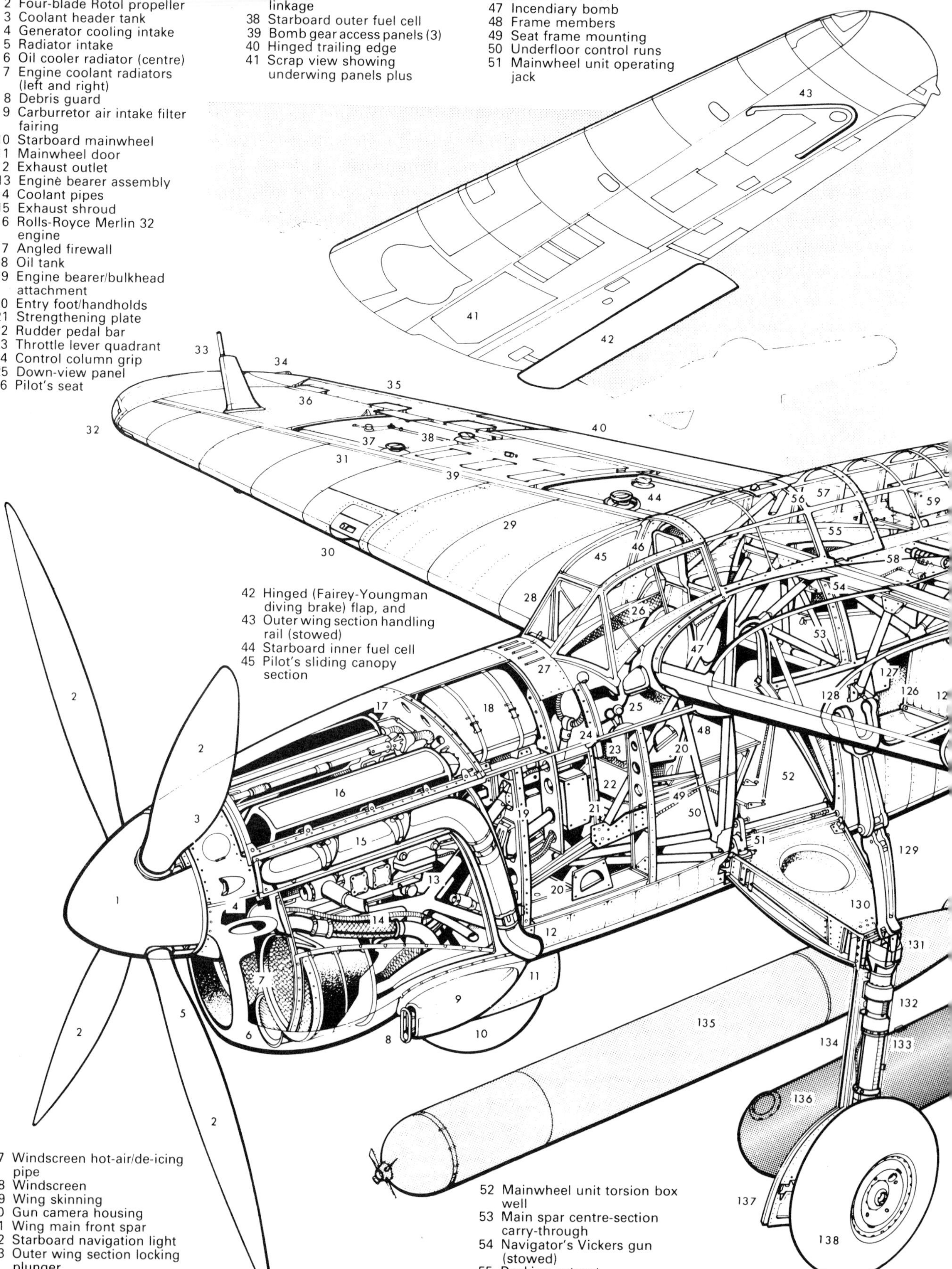

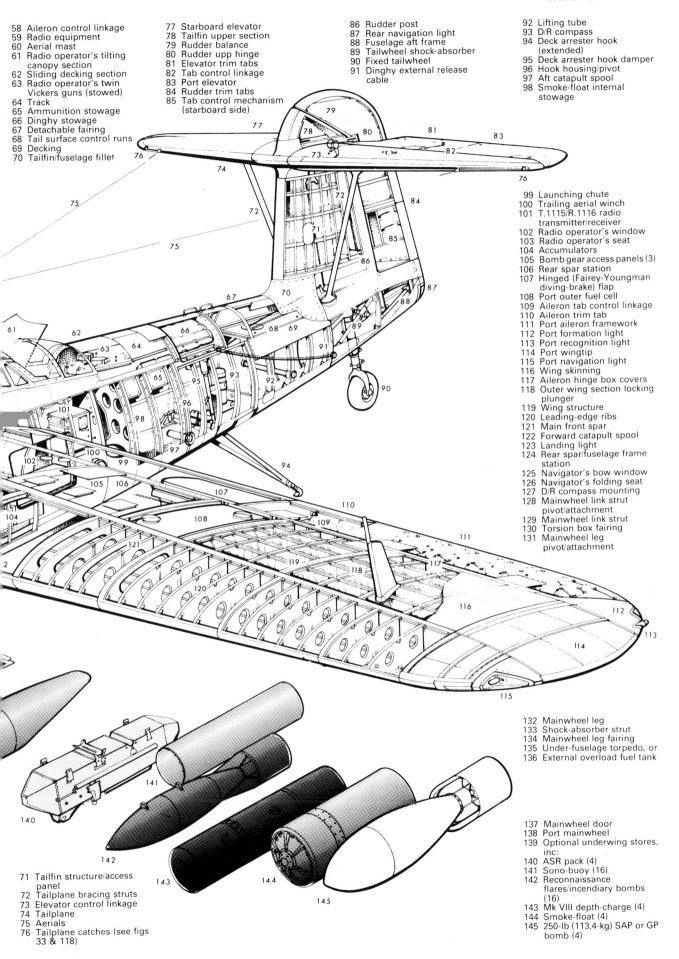

58 Aileron control linkage
59 Radio equipment
60 Aerial mast
61 Radio operator's tilting canopy section
62 Sliding decking section
63 Radio operator's twin Vickers guns (stowed)
64 Track
65 Ammunition stowage
66 Dinghy stowage
67 Detachable fairing
68 Tail surface control runs
69 Decking
70 Tailfin/fuselage fillet

77 Starboard elevator
78 Tailfin upper section
79 Rudder balance
80 Rudder upp hinge
81 Elevator trim tabs
82 Tab control linkage
83 Port elevator
84 Rudder trim tabs
85 Tab control mechanism (starboard side)

86 Rudder post
87 Rear navigation light
88 Fuselage aft frame
89 Tailwheel shock-absorber
90 Fixed tailwheel
91 Dinghy external release cable

92 Lifting tube
93 D/R compass
94 Deck arrester hook (extended)
95 Deck arrester hook damper
96 Hook housing/pivot
97 Aft catapult spool
98 Smoke-float internal stowage

99 Launching chute
100 Trailing aerial winch
101 T.1115/R.1116 radio transmitter/receiver
102 Radio operator's window
103 Radio operator's seat
104 Accumulators
105 Bomb gear access panels (3)
106 Rear spar station
107 Hinged (Fairey-Youngman diving-brake) flap
108 Port outer fuel cell
109 Aileron tab control linkage
110 Aileron trim tab
111 Port aileron framework
112 Port formation light
113 Port recognition light
114 Port wingtip
115 Port navigation light
116 Wing skinning
117 Aileron hinge box covers
118 Outer wing section locking plunger
119 Wing structure
120 Leading-edge ribs
121 Main front spar
122 Forward catapult spool
123 Landing light
124 Rear spar/fuselage frame station
125 Navigator's bow window
126 Navigator's folding seat
127 D/R compass mounting
128 Mainwheel link strut pivot/attachment
129 Mainwheel link strut
130 Torsion box fairing
131 Mainwheel leg pivot/attachment

132 Mainwheel leg
133 Shock-absorber strut
134 Mainwheel leg fairing
135 Under-fuselage torpedo, or
136 External overload fuel tank

137 Mainwheel door
138 Port mainwheel
139 Optional underwing stores, inc:
140 ASR pack (4)
141 Sono-buoy (16)
142 Reconnaissance flares/incendiary bombs (16)
143 Mk VIII depth-charge (4)
144 Smoke-float (4)
145 250-lb (113,4-kg) SAP or GP bomb (4)

71 Tailfin structure/access panel
72 Tailplane bracing struts
73 Elevator control linkage
74 Tailplane
75 Aerials
76 Tailplane catches (see figs 33 & 118)

The Barracuda Mk V, an example of which (RK588) is seen above and below left in service with No 783 Squadron at Lee-on-Solent, appeared too late to see action and contracts for this re-engined and extensively modified version of the aircraft were dramatically reduced with the end of hostilities

Fairey Barracuda Mk II Specification

Power Plant: One Rolls-Royce Merlin 32 12-cylinder 60-Vee liquid-cooled engine rated at 1,600 hp at 3,000 rpm for take-off, with max output of 1,640 hp at 3,000 rpm at 1,750 ft (535 m) and internationally rated at 1,360 hp at 2,850 rpm at 5,500 ft (1 676 m). Rotol four-bladed constant-speed propeller of 11 ft 9 in (3,58 m) diameter. Total internal fuel capacity of 226 Imp gal (1 027 l) with provision for additional 116 Imp gal (527 l) fuel in crutch tank.
Performance: (Clean at 12,600 lb/5 715 kg) Max speed, 210 mph (338 km/h) at 2,000 ft (610 m); max cruise, 193 mph (311 km/h) at 5,000 ft (1 525 m); econ cruise, 172 mph (277 km/h) at 5,000 ft (1 525 m); range, 724 mls (1,165 km) at 145 mph (233 km/h) at 5,000 ft (1 525 m); service ceiling, 21,600 ft (6,585 m); at 14,080 lb/6 386 kg with four 450-lb/204-kg Mk VII depth charges) max speed, 160 mph (257 km/h) at sea level, 165 mph (265 km/h at 2,000 ft (610 m); range 455 mls (732 km) at 131 mph (211 km/h); service seiling, 16,400 ft (5 000 m); (at 13,916 lb/6313 kg with torpedo) max speed, 194 mph (312 km/h) at sea level, 199 mph (320 km/h) at 2,000 ft (610 m); range, 604 mls (972 km) at 150 mph (241 km/h); service ceiling, 17,500 ft (5 335 m).
Weights: Empty, 9,350 lb (4 445 kg); loaded (clean), 12,600 lb (5 715 kg); max loaded, 14,080 lb (6 386 kg).
Dimensions: Span, 49 ft 2½ in (14,50 m); length, 39 ft 11⁹/₁₆ in (12,18 m); height, 15 ft 0½ in (4,58 m); width folded, 18 ft 3 in (5,56 m); wing area, 405 sq ft (37,62 m²).
Armament: Two 0·303-in (7,7-mm) Vickers K gas-operated machine guns on Fairey flexible mount in rear cockpit, plus one 18-in (45,72-cm) torpedo, six 250-lb (113,4-kg) bombs, three 500-lb (226,8-kg) bombs, or four 285-lb (129-kg) Mk XI or 450-lb (204-kg) Mk VII depth charges.

had dropped below 190 knots (352 km/h) — the restriction speed for retracting the dive flaps — I raised the flaps to cruise position and kicked on rudder as I pulled away to starboard. In a flash the aircraft was in an inverted dive! Fortunately, I had plenty of altitude in which to sort out the recovery, but I shuddered at the thought of what the inevitable consequences would have been had I actually performed the test at sea level.

The results of this and a number of similar flights were quickly analysed and an appropriate warning issued to all TSR aircrew, the epidemic of crashes ending immediately, but I cannot leave this accident investigation without paying tribute to one of the flight observers involved in these tests — Mrs Gwen Alston. Mrs Alston was a truly remarkable "lady boffin", who, despite having lost her scientist husband in a fatal crash while on similar duty, never flinched at any risky flight and in all circumstances displayed the essence of courage. She had been my observer on the first flight in which we ascertained the true cause of the Barracuda crashes.

Over the next two years, I was to fly the Barracuda spasmodically in its various versions up to the final Mk V, but throughout it was to remain for me a singularly uninspiring aircraft. We had a number of Barracuda IIs at the RAE on various tasks, but we were largely preoccupied with the continuingly poor take-off characteristics of the aircraft which were causing particular concern in connection with operations from small escort carriers. We therefore launched a series of trials utilising RATOG (rocket-assisted take-off gear).

Three solid-fuel rockets were fitted on each side of the fuselage angled inboard to direct their thrust through the Barracuda's CG and thus avoid any violent trim changes. The rockets were fired electrically by the pilot at a point indicated by an external white marker and calculated to give the optimum acceleration effect by the rockets petering out just as the aircraft was comfortably airborne, the entire contraption then being jettisoned. After the usual proving trials on the Farnborough runways, I made the first such rocket-assisted take-off with a Barracuda II (P9791) from a carrier (HMS *Pretoria Castle*) on 1 August 1944. Tests were reasonably successful and RATOG was subsequently to be used on numerous occasions to get heavily-loaded Barracudas safely off the escort carrier decks.

A Boulton Paul-built Barracuda II (DR126) was assigned

to the RAE for catapulting and arresting trials with various combinations of armament and stores, and I was to fly this aircraft at times festooned like a Christmas tree with bombs, depth charges, radomes and even an air-sea rescue lifeboat. With such loads, the catapult take-off could be a very tottering affair, the British four-point system being used whereby the aircraft was supported in a cradle by four metal spools protruding from the sides of the fuselage and thus left the catapult in almost level-flight attitude from which it had to be carefully rotated once airborne in order to obtain the necessary lift to climb. It was decided, therefore, to adopt the American two-point system employing a wire strop attached at one end to a single hook under the belly of the aircraft and at the other to a shuttle in the catapult slot on the deck. The tail was also secured by a hold-back with a breaking ring inserted in it between deck attachment and aircraft attachment, the aircraft thus sitting in a normal tail-down ground position. When the catapult fired, the breaking ring held the aircraft until maximum pressure had built up, and when the ring broke, the shuttle moved forward along the catapult slot until it reached the end of its stroke. It was then braked and the strop was held so that its top end slid clear of the belly hook as the aircraft became airborne in the climb attitude. I was to make the first such two-point catapult launches of a British aircraft (ie, the Barracuda II DR 126) at sea from the *Pretoria Castle* on 3 April 1945, the trials comprising six launches, some with a torpedo fitted and others with an external load of four 500-lb (226,8-kg) bombs.

Another interesting trial conducted with the Barracuda II concerned the experimental use of a dive-braking propeller. This four-bladed Rotol unit had a fine pitch stop well advanced to give a braking effect in a dive, the technique prior to entering the dive being to close the throttle and reduce speed to a maximum of 150 knots (278 km/h) before moving the pitch lever to the fully fine position in order to avoid overspeeding. The immediate effect of this action was a

The Barracuda Mk V LS479 (above) was a conversion of a Mk II, as was also the prototype Mk V P9976 (below). A small number of such conversions were followed by about 30 genuine production Mk Vs. The general arrangement drawing at the foot of the opposite column represents the Barracuda Mk II

strong nose-down pitch and rapid deceleration. In the dive, speed was slow in building up and a very steep angle — 70-80 degrees — was possible to reach the terminal velocity of 225 knots (417 km/h) in 8,000 ft (2 438 m). The pull-out load proved to be much higher but not unacceptably so. Indeed, the propeller did all that was expected of it in the dive, but it imposed serious handling limitations on the other phases of flight, such as take-off and cruise fuel consumption.

The Barracuda Mk III was intended primarily for anti-submarine reconnaissance tasks and in consequence, carried an ASV (Air-to-Surface Vessel) Mk X radar scanner in a radome under the rear fuselage, and the effect of this excrescence on performance may be imagined, but the definitive model, the Barracuda Mk V*, did at least eradicate one or two of the more troublesome shortcomings of preceding versions. Much modified and re-engined with a 2,020 hp Rolls-Royce Griffon 37, the Mk V was structurally strengthened and had 3 ft 10 in (1,17 m) of additional wing span which gave it a further 30 sq ft (2,79 m²) of area. The first Mk Vs, which were conversions of Mks II and III airframes, retained the original vertical tail surfaces, but the true production aircraft had a large dorsal fin and, eventually, a very much larger rudder of increased aspect ratio which finally cured the disastrous rudder overbalance that had haunted the aircraft from its earliest days. The performance was certainly improved by installation of the Griffon, but forward view deteriorated and lateral control was certainly heavier.

The Barracuda was to receive some prominence as a result of its dive-bombing attack on the battleship *Tirpitz* lying in Kaafjord on 3 April 1944, this being performed by 42 aircraft from Nos 827, 829 and 830 squadrons from *Victorious* and No 831 Squadron from *Furious,* but, in general, the career of this aesthetically unappealing aircraft made a valuable yet unspectacular contribution to Fleet Air Arm wartime operations. Since I was destined never to fly the Barracuda operationally, I am not qualified to comment on that aspect, except to say that its crews seemed to appreciate its ruggedness, and perhaps that is about the nicest thing that can be said of this "mighty monster". □

The designation Barracuda Mk IV was originally assigned to the prototype Griffon-engined aircraft, a converted Mk II (P9976) which flew on 16 November 1944.

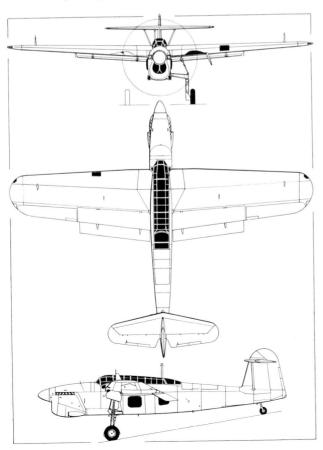

Hawker Sea Hurricane

S HORT ON RANGE, with the ditching propensities of a submarine, harsh stalling characteristics, a very mediocre view for deck landing and an undercarriage that was as likely as not to bounce it over the arrester wires. What less likely a candidate for deployment aboard aircraft carriers as a naval single-seat fighter than the Hurricane could have been imagined when, more than two score years ago, the Fleet Air Arm found itself at war! Yet, legacy of parsimony, expediency and shortsightedness inflicted on British naval aviation of the 'thirties though its seagoing assignment two years later undoubtedly was, the Hurricane was to take to the nautical environment extraordinarily well. Its shipboard début was to give the FAA an enormous fillip, and while no fighter designed solely with shore-based operation in mind could have expected unqualified success at sea, it was to acquit itself with distinction during its brief naval first-line career.

Aircraft development costs and the prospects for their amortisation are of the essence today, but they exerted barely less influence a half-century since when it came — in so far as the UK was concerned — to single-seat shipboard fighter evolution. The Navy rarely had more than four or five dozen such aircraft distributed between fewer than a half-dozen carriers; there was little prospect of acceptably amortising the development costs of a specialised naval interceptor over so small a potential production run. Thus, their Lordships of the Admiralty too readily accepted the ill-founded postulation of the Air Ministry that there was no likelihood of the Fleet having to face land-based aircraft other than of the long-range patrol type; that the RAF was competent to provide protection in the event of the Fleet coming within range of other shore-based aircraft.

With these assurances and believing no more than a gesture towards single-seat naval fighters to be necessary, a process of extemporisation had begun. The Nimrod, introduced by the FAA in 1932, was no more than a derivative of the RAF's Fury, and its successor, seven years later, the Sea Gladiator, was but another adaptation of an RAF fighter with even fewer concessions to the nautical rôle.

The mating of Hurricane with carrier deck, it might therefore be said, was no more than the continuation of what had become a time-honoured, economical and reasonably successful practice. In truth, it was symptomatic of the aforesaid neglect that naval fighter development had suffered in the UK 'tween the wars; when the other major naval powers, Japan and the USA, were placing emphasis on effectiveness rather than economy and experience rather than expediency in equipping their shipboard fighter elements. The *Sea* Hurricane was, thus, like the Seafire that was to follow it aboard British carrier decks, very much a product of desperation, albeit a product that, despite its inevitable shortcomings, was *very* welcome indeed and was, for a year, to reign as the fastest fighter in the FAA's inventory.

Adaptation of the Hurricane for naval use had been set in train as a result of the experience of No 46 Sqdn, RAF, which, during the ill-fated Norwegian campaign of May 1940, had successfully flown its Hurricanes off the carrier HMS *Glorious* with the intention of setting up base in Norway, and, when the campaign went awry, had landed them back aboard the carrier in a windspeed of 40 knots (74 km/h) over the deck. The subsequent loss of the aircraft with *Glorious* to the guns of the German battlecruisers *Scharnhorst* and *Gneisenau* was incidental to the fact that the Hurricane had proved itself not merely amenable to taking-off from a carrier at sea but *landing back on again* and with squadron pilots inexperienced in shipboard operations to boot.

The stimulation was thus provided Hawker Aircraft to explore the deck-operating potential of the Hurricane by fitting a V-frame arrester hook and catapult spools, and one aircraft so modified was delivered to the RAE at Farnborough in March 1941. Two distinct lines of development for the seagoing Hurricane were now pursued simultaneously: one embraced the conventional operation of the fighter from carrier decks and the other — to which the greater urgency was attached — involved its launching from a simple rocket-driven catapult mounted on the fo'c'sle of a converted merchant vessel. The latter, the so-called "Catafighter" scheme, was a masterpiece of improvisation conceived as an interim measure to overcome the lack of escort carriers and provide at least a partial antidote to the menace of the long-range German maritime aircraft that were inflicting such grievous losses on the Atlantic convoys.

Fitted with catapult spools only, 50 well-worn Hurricane Is, some of which had already been discarded by the squadrons, were reassigned for adaptation at Hamble as "Catafighters" under the designation Sea Hurricane Mk IA — although these aircraft were soon to become known less officially as *Hurricats* — and at the same time, 35 merchant vessels of all sorts and sizes and all now categorised as CAM (Catapult Aircraft Merchantman) ships were fitted with catapults, while four former banana boats that were in process of fitting out as auxiliary naval vessels were adapted as Fighter Catapult Ships. Whereas the manning of the CAM ship *Hurricats* was to be the responsibility of the RAF, and a Merchant Ship Fighter Unit (MSFU) was set up by that service at Speke to provide the necessary personnel, the Fighter Catapult Ships were to be the responsibility of the Navy and their *Hurricats* operated by FAA personnel. These naval vessels were to each have one catapult-mounted fighter and a second stored as a reserve, No 804 Sqdn being given the task of manning the aircraft.

In so far as the CAM ships were concerned, it was intended that two or more, laden with their normal cargoes, would form integral components of each convoy, launching their *Hurricats* in the event that the convoy was directly threatened by enemy aircraft. It was proposed that, after engaging in combat and assuming that insufficient fuel remained to enable the pilot to reach the nearest land, the aircraft would be ditched in the path of the convoy and, all things being equal,

one or another vessel would heave to and pick up the pilot. The *Hurricats* were essentially expendable, each flying but one mission, and the high wastage was considered to be fully justified by the dramatic nature of the circumstances. It was widely believed that the "Catafighter" scheme involved a suicidal, one-way-ticket mission, although, in the event, this notion was to prove false. It was nevertheless extremely hazardous and that it was to result in the loss of so few pilots was purely fortuitous.

The catapult was propelled by banks of 3-in (7,62-cm) rockets, and with flaps set for take-off and engine at full throttle, the *Hurricat* accelerated from 0 to 65 knots (120 km/h) within 70 ft (21,3 m) — the launching approaching an alarming 3·5 g as compared with the more modest 2·5 g of an hydraulic catapult — at the end of which the catapult was arrested by an hydraulic buffer. The first of the CAM ships to set sail was the SS *Michael E* which weighed anchor in Belfast on 27 May 1941. In the event, this vessel was to be torpedoed before its *Hurricat* could be launched, and the honour of gaining the first "kill" with a catapulted Sea Hurricane was to go to Lt R W H "Bob" Everett of No 804 Sqdn who intercepted and destroyed an Fw 200C Condor on 3 August 1941

(Above right) A Sea Hurricane Mk IB taking-off from and (head of opposite page) picking up the arrester wires on the veteran carrier HMS Argus, and (below) being take up to the flight deck on Argus's lift. This carrier, which celebrated its 25th year of Royal Navy service in 1943, served primarily for training and trials purposes

after launching from the Fighter Catapult Ship HMS *Maplin*.

There can be no doubt that this initial seagoing Hurricane performed a vitally important rôle as a deterrent to the Condors, although how much shipping it in fact saved as a result of its deterrence value is impossible to determine. The CAM ships, themselves, undertook 175 voyages averaging 2,600 nm (4 820 km) over a little more than two years, 12 of the 35 vessels involved being lost as a result of enemy action. During the period, there was a total of eight *Hurricat* operational launchings of which six resulted in the destruction of an enemy aircraft, and only one of the "Catafighter" pilots lost his life.

The major problem of the "Catafighter" scheme was, of course, its relative inflexibility, and the parallel development of the Sea Hurricane to operate not only from conventional carriers but from small escort carriers known as MAC (Merchant Aircraft Carrier) ships had very much more potential. Successful trials had been conducted with an aircraft equipped with both V-frame hook and catapult spools, and some 300 Hurricane Mk Is were scheduled for adaptation — mostly by General Aircraft Limited — as Sea Hurricane Mk IBs, this consisting only of the provision of hook and spools and the necessary local structural reinforcement to absorb the loads imposed by catapult acceleration and the deceleration accompanying arrested landings, and the replacement of RAF radio equipment by that used by the FAA.

From early 1941, FAA squadrons began forming or reforming on the Sea Hurricane Mk IB, the first of these being destined for the Fleet carriers, commencing with No 880, which was eventually to embark on HMS *Furious* and, subsequently, HMS *Indomitable*, followed closely by Nos 803 and 806, the former, which had flown Skuas from HMS *Ark Royal*, being assigned, in the event, to shore-based duties in Palestine and the Western Desert, and the latter

converting from Fulmars and embarking in HMS *Formidable*. No 801 Sqdn, which had flown Sea Gladiators in concert with Skuas from *Courageous*, took Sea Hurricane Mk IBs aboard HMS *Argus* before reassignment to HMS *Eagle*, but No 883 Sqdn, formed at Yeovilton during October, was to become one of the first two squadrons to take Sea Hurricanes aboard one of the Navy's escort carriers, the US-built HMS *Avenger*, in the following summer.

No 883 Sqdn was to operate from *Avenger* in concert with No 802 Sqdn, both embarking a complement of six aircraft. The latter unit, with which I had fulfilled the rôle of Squadron Armament Officer, had flown Wildcats with noteworthy success from the Royal Navy's first escort carrier, the tiny HMS *Audacity* until it was sunk on 21 December 1941, and when I rejoined No 802 at Yeovilton on 1 February 1942, I found that henceforth we were to fly Sea Hurricane Mk IBs. I had first flown the Hurricane in 1940, and remembered well how very exhilarating an experience I had found it then. But at that time, there had been no thought of adapting Hawker's fighter for the shipboard rôle and in consequence I now viewed it in a somewhat different light.

Certainly the Sea Hurricane Mk IB looked every bit a fighter; if lacking the aesthetically appealing sleekness of the Spitfire, it nevertheless possessed pleasing lines and gave an impression of greater robustness. For a year I had been flying Wildcats, however, first from Donibristle and then from *Audacity*, developing a deep affection for this barrel-like little warplane in the process, and it was natural that I should make comparisons between the portly Grumman and this improvised Hawker shipboard fighter. Comparison was perhaps not entirely fair as, unlike the Sea Hurricane, the Wildcat had been designed from scratch as a carrier aircraft and for such use it had much to commend it over the fighter to which No 802 Sqdn was now converting. For example, the Wildcat offered markedly better endurance and its cockpit offered a better all-round view for deck landing, combining this with excellent slow flying characteristics and a very robust undercarriage. Its initial climb rate was better than that of the Sea Hurricane but, being more stable to fly, it was heavier to manoeuvre. The ditching characteristics of the Wildcat were excellent — a fact for which I could vouch from personal experience — but it needed only half an eye to see that as soon as the sea churned into the Sea Hurricane's immense ventral bath it would turn turtle!

(Above left and below) One of the last Gloster-built Hurricane Mk Is (Z4852) after conversion as a Sea Hurricane Mk IA, known unofficially as the 'Hurricat', for deployment aboard the CAM ships and the Fighter Catapult Ships of the Royal Navy

(Above and below right) A Sea Hurricane Mk IC (V6741) converted from a Hurricane Mk I of the third Gloster production batch by the introduction of new four-cannon outer wing panels, arrester hook and other naval equipment

However, if the Sea Hurricane was bested by the Wildcat in features most desirable in a deck-landing fighter, it possessed other intrinsic qualities and once our squadron work-up really got into its stride, I recaptured some of the exhilaration that I had experienced when flying the Hawker fighter some 18 months before. Starting the Merlin III engine was easy except when the temperature really dropped. The fuel distributor cock was turned to RESERVE the primer pump given four or five strokes, the main and starting magnetos switched ON, and the electric starter button depressed. As soon as the Merlin fired, the starting magneto was switched OFF and the fuel cock turned to MAIN TANKS.

The usual checks were made of fuel and oil pressures, magnetos, propeller constant speed operation, flaps and pneumatic brake pressure during warm up, and taxying was easy owing to the wide track undercarriage, although it was necessary to swing the aircraft from side to side slightly in order to get a clear view ahead. For take-off all trim tabs were set NEUTRAL, mixture control to RICH, the propeller fully fined and the flaps set UP. Once the tail was raised during the take-off run, the view ahead was good and the swing could be held easily on rudder till unstick at 70 knots (130 km/h) at 6¼ lb boost and 2,600 rpm. The radiator flap, which was normally open for take-off, had to be operated on the climb to keep the coolant temperature below 120 deg C (248 deg F) and above 70 deg C (158 deg F).

In cruise the Sea Hurricane was stable about all three axes, but in a dive it became tail heavy and it was important not to trim this out with the tabs, otherwise difficulty could be experienced in recovery. It was generally accepted that single-seat day fighters should be just on the stable side of the borderline between positive and neutral stability. There is usually a relationship between subsonic speed and stability, so that the greater the speed the greater the stability and *vice versa*; the borderline with the Sea Hurricane was 139 knots (258 km/h). The all-up stall occured at 68 knots (126 km/h), preceded by fore and aft instability before a sharp wing drop to the vertical attitude, so care was necessary to avoid a spin developing. The all-down stall at 57 knots (106 km/h) exhibited similar characteristics. While deliberate spinning was prohibited, a spin could result from too tight a turn in combat and while normal recovery action was effective a considerable amount of height could be lost.

Aerobatics in the Sea Hurricane were certainly pleasant and easy to execute. Loops could be effected comfortably at

260 knots (482 km/h), although they were possible at much lower speeds, and rolls could be performed down to 156 knots (290 km/h), adding up to a very manoeuvrable fighter with fairly good harmony of control throughout the speed range. The ailerons were the lightest control and the rudder the heaviest. The controls heavied up with increases in speed but remained effective. The split trailing edge flaps could be used for added manoeuvrability as they could be set at any position throughout their range. They were somewhat slow in deploying, taking 8-10 seconds to fully down. Above 104 knots (193 km/h) they were raised partially by the airflow if fully lowered.

For landing the canopy was opened at about 120 knots (222 km/h), the undercarriage lowered and the selector lever returned to NEUTRAL, propeller pitch set fully fine and the turn onto the final approach made. The flaps were then lowered at a speed below 104 knots (193 km/h) and the approach speed eased off to 78 knots (145 km/h), view being reasonable for an airfield landing and a three-point touchdown easy to execute. For deck landing the approach could be made at 70 knots (130 km/h), but the Sea Hurricane was far outside the deck landing class of the Wildcat; then it was to be remembered that it was not tailormade for this job.

There was no question of adopting the crabbed approach with the Sea Hurricane as was later to be developed for the Seafire to improve forward vision. The use of rudder on the approach in the Sea Hurricane produced a considerable increase in nose-heaviness which was quite unacceptable in this delicate situation, so it was a straight approach or nothing and the inadequate view forward simply had to be accepted. Its harsh stalling characteristics were anything but suited for deck landing and the undercarriage had a lot of bounce in it which could prove embarrassing on occasions. At least it was more robust than the Seafire that was to succeed it and could withstand quite a lot more deck landing punishment.

The squadron work-up was thoroughly enjoyable and I

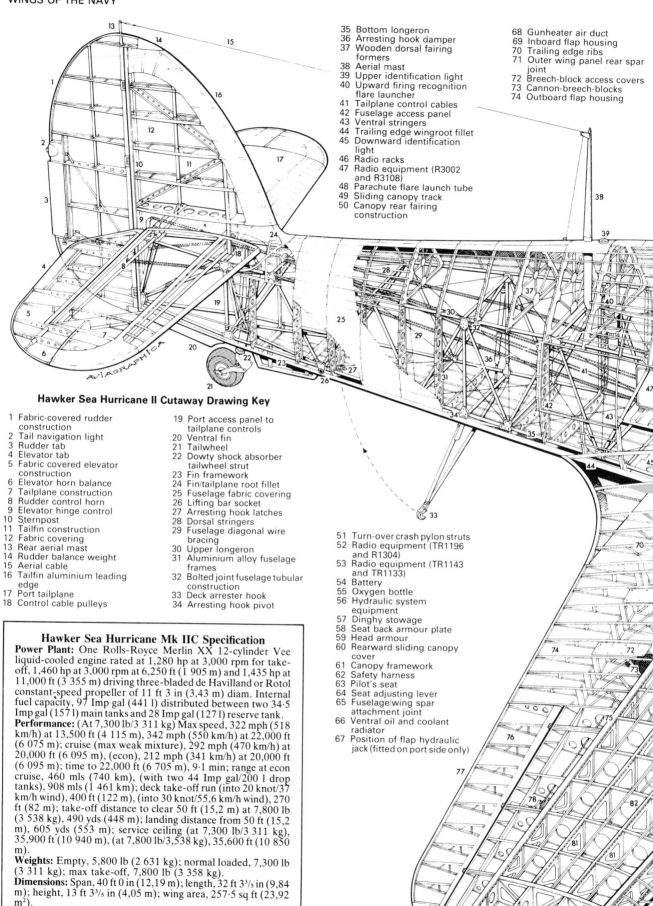

Hawker Sea Hurricane II Cutaway Drawing Key

35 Bottom longeron
36 Arresting hook damper
37 Wooden dorsal fairing formers
38 Aerial mast
39 Upper identification light
40 Upward firing recognition flare launcher
41 Tailplane control cables
42 Fuselage access panel
43 Ventral stringers
44 Trailing edge wingroot fillet
45 Downward identification light
46 Radio racks
47 Radio equipment (R3002 and R3108)
48 Parachute flare launch tube
49 Sliding canopy track
50 Canopy rear fairing construction

68 Gunheater air duct
69 Inboard flap housing
70 Trailing edge ribs
71 Outer wing panel rear spar joint
72 Breech-block access covers
73 Cannon-breech-blocks
74 Outboard flap housing

1 Fabric-covered rudder construction
2 Tail navigation light
3 Rudder tab
4 Elevator tab
5 Fabric covered elevator construction
6 Elevator horn balance
7 Tailplane construction
8 Rudder control horn
9 Elevator hinge control
10 Sternpost
11 Tailfin construction
12 Fabric covering
13 Rear aerial mast
14 Rudder balance weight
15 Aerial cable
16 Tailfin aluminium leading edge
17 Port tailplane
18 Control cable pulleys

19 Port access panel to tailplane controls
20 Ventral fin
21 Tailwheel
22 Dowty shock absorber tailwheel strut
23 Fin framework
24 Fin/tailplane root fillet
25 Fuselage fabric covering
26 Lifting bar socket
27 Arresting hook latches
28 Dorsal stringers
29 Fuselage diagonal wire bracing
30 Upper longeron
31 Aluminium alloy fuselage frames
32 Bolted joint fuselage tubular construction
33 Deck arrester hook
34 Arresting hook pivot

51 Turn-over crash pylon struts
52 Radio equipment (TR1196 and R1304)
53 Radio equipment (TR1143 and TR1133)
54 Battery
55 Oxygen bottle
56 Hydraulic system equipment
57 Dinghy stowage
58 Seat back armour plate
59 Head armour
60 Rearward sliding canopy cover
61 Canopy framework
62 Safety harness
63 Pilot's seat
64 Seat adjusting lever
65 Fuselage/wing spar attachment joint
66 Ventral oil and coolant radiator
67 Position of flap hydraulic jack (fitted on port side only)

Hawker Sea Hurricane Mk IIC Specification
Power Plant: One Rolls-Royce Merlin XX 12-cylinder Vee liquid-cooled engine rated at 1,280 hp at 3,000 rpm for take-off, 1,460 hp at 3,000 rpm at 6,250 ft (1 905 m) and 1,435 hp at 11,000 ft (3 355 m) driving three-bladed de Havilland or Rotol constant-speed propeller of 11 ft 3 in (3,43 m) diam. Internal fuel capacity, 97 Imp gal (441 l) distributed between two 34·5 Imp gal (157 l) main tanks and 28 Imp gal (127 l) reserve tank.
Performance: (At 7,300 lb/3 311 kg) Max speed, 322 mph (518 km/h) at 13,500 ft (4 115 m), 342 mph (550 km/h) at 22,000 ft (6 075 m); cruise (max weak mixture), 292 mph (470 km/h) at 20,000 ft (6 095 m), (econ), 212 mph (341 km/h) at 20,000 ft (6 095 m); time to 22,000 ft (6 705 m), 9·1 min; range at econ cruise, 460 mls (740 km), (with two 44 Imp gal/200 l drop tanks), 908 mls (1 461 km); deck take-off run (into 20 knot/37 km/h wind), 400 ft (122 m), (into 30 knot/55,6 km/h wind), 270 ft (82 m); take-off distance to clear 50 ft (15,2 m) at 7,800 lb (3 538 kg), 490 yds (448 m); landing distance from 50 ft (15,2 m), 605 yds (553 m); service ceiling (at 7,300 lb/3 311 kg), 35,900 ft (10 940 m), (at 7,800 lb/3,538 kg), 35,600 ft (10 850 m).
Weights: Empty, 5,800 lb (2 631 kg); normal loaded, 7,300 lb (3 311 kg); max take-off, 7,800 lb (3 358 kg).
Dimensions: Span, 40 ft 0 in (12,19 m); length, 32 ft 3³/₈ in (9,84 m); height, 13 ft 3³/₈ in (4,05 m); wing area, 257·5 sq ft (23,92 m²).
Armament: Four 20-mm British Hispano Mk I or Mk II cannon with 100 rpg.

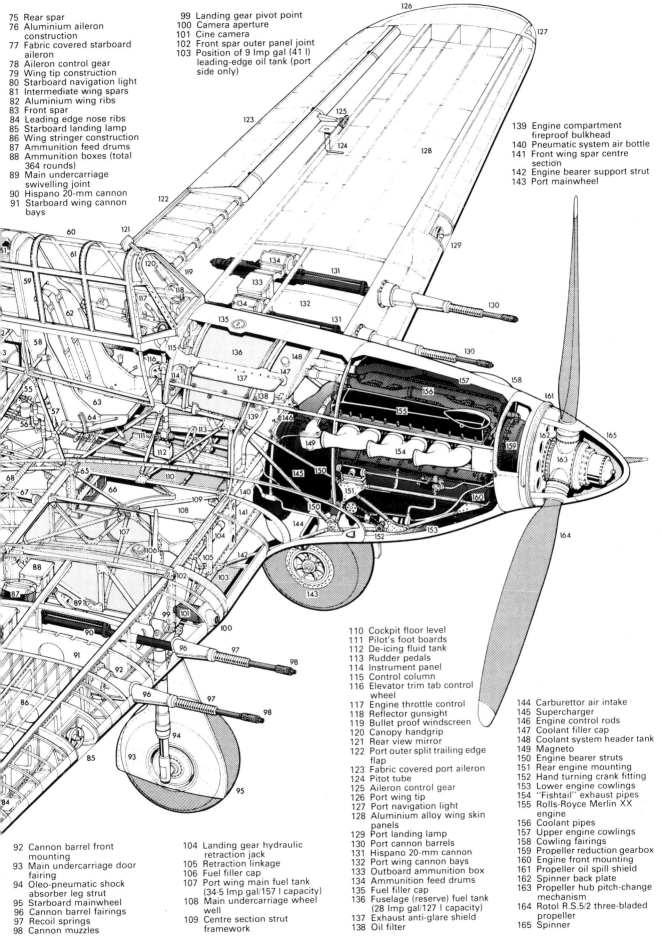

75 Rear spar
76 Aluminium aileron construction
77 Fabric covered starboard aileron
78 Aileron control gear
79 Wing tip construction
80 Starboard navigation light
81 Intermediate wing spars
82 Aluminium wing ribs
83 Front spar
84 Leading edge nose ribs
85 Starboard landing lamp
86 Wing stringer construction
87 Ammunition feed drums
88 Ammunition boxes (total 364 rounds)
89 Main undercarriage swivelling joint
90 Hispano 20-mm cannon
91 Starboard wing cannon bays

99 Landing gear pivot point
100 Camera aperture
101 Cine camera
102 Front spar outer panel joint
103 Position of 9 Imp gal (41 l) leading-edge oil tank (port side only)

139 Engine compartment fireproof bulkhead
140 Pneumatic system air bottle
141 Front wing spar centre section
142 Engine bearer support strut
143 Port mainwheel

110 Cockpit floor level
111 Pilot's foot boards
112 De-icing fluid tank
113 Rudder pedals
114 Instrument panel
115 Control column
116 Elevator trim tab control wheel
117 Engine throttle control
118 Reflector gunsight
119 Bullet proof windscreen
120 Canopy handgrip
121 Rear view mirror
122 Port outer split trailing edge flap
123 Fabric covered port aileron
124 Pitot tube
125 Aileron control gear
126 Port wing tip
127 Port navigation light
128 Aluminium alloy wing skin panels
129 Port landing lamp
130 Port cannon barrels
131 Hispano 20-mm cannon
132 Port wing cannon bays
133 Outboard ammunition box
134 Ammunition feed drums
135 Fuel filler cap
136 Fuselage (reserve) fuel tank (28 Imp gal/127 l capacity)
137 Exhaust anti-glare shield
138 Oil filter

144 Carburettor air intake
145 Supercharger
146 Engine control rods
147 Coolant filler cap
148 Coolant system header tank
149 Magneto
150 Engine bearer struts
151 Rear engine mounting
152 Hand turning crank fitting
153 Lower engine cowlings
154 "Fishtail" exhaust pipes
155 Rolls-Royce Merlin XX engine
156 Coolant pipes
157 Upper engine cowlings
158 Cowling fairings
159 Propeller reduction gearbox
160 Engine front mounting
161 Propeller oil spill shield
162 Spinner back plate
163 Propeller hub pitch-change mechanism
164 Rotol R.S.5/2 three-bladed propeller
165 Spinner

92 Cannon barrel front mounting
93 Main undercarriage door fairing
94 Oleo-pneumatic shock absorber leg strut
95 Starboard mainwheel
96 Cannon barrel fairings
97 Recoil springs
98 Cannon muzzles

104 Landing gear hydraulic retraction jack
105 Retraction linkage
106 Fuel filler cap
107 Port wing main fuel tank (34·5 Imp gal/157 l capacity)
108 Main undercarriage wheel well
109 Centre section strut framework

A Sea Hurricane Mk IA making a practice launch from a CAM ship in the Clyde, accelerating from 0 to 65 knots (120 km/h) within 70 ft (21 m) propelled by banks of 3-in (7,62 cm) rockets

most vividly recall the spell at our armament camp at RN Air Station St Merryn, by which time we were thoroughly conversant with the handling characteristics of the Sea Hurricane. After our successes in the Atlantic using Wildcats for head-on attacks against Condors, it was decided to try to teach this method of attack against towed sleeve drogue targets. I was selected to make the trial firing runs and was strictly forbidden to open fire until the Hurricane was actually *above* the towing Skua. This left precious little aiming and firing time against a small sleeve target and on the first two sorties I flew slap through the drogue, actually bringing it back to base wrapped around the starboard wing on the second sortie. However, by allowing slightly earlier time for opening fire we got it right, although the Skua tug pilots understandably never waxed enthusiastic about this exercise.

In May, I was sent to RN Air Station Arbroath to prepare for deck landing trials aboard the escort carrier HMS *Avenger.* The Sea Hurricane was being hurriedly committed to a gap filling programme. It was already providing the backbone of the fleet fighter element fielded by the FAA from the Royal Navy's Fleet carriers; the precarious operation of Sea Hurricanes from CAM ships on the North Atlantic convoy routes was giving place to more orthodox — if at times barely less hazardous — operation from MAC ships, and now it was being readied for embarkation on the growing number of British- and US-built escort carriers. Nos 802 and 883 squadrons were to be in the vanguard of this last-mentioned deployment.

The characteristics of the Sea Hurricane were hardly the ideal for the 12,000-ton escort carriers, but even less so for the MAC ships. These mini-carriers — merchantmen with superstructure removed and bridge offset amidships, providing a simple, unobstructed flight deck on which a mix of fighters and ASW aircraft, usually a half-dozen each Sea Hurricanes and Swordfish, could be ranged aft — were, nevertheless, rapidly proving themselves an effective means of providing close air cover for convoys, particularly when such were beyond the range of RAF Coastal Command's land-based aircraft. In fact, the Sea Hurricanes aboard these vessels had to be viewed as barely less expendable than those

aboard the CAM ships as the MAC ships possessed no hangar accommodation and therefore only the most superficial maintenance could be effected aboard. The Sea Hurricanes were thus exposed to the elements continuously, be they Atlantic gale or the deep frost of the Barents Sea, with the hardly surprising result that few completed more than 30 or so flying hours before airframe or engine was rendered suspect by salt water corrosion.

The Sea Hurricane Mk IB had meanwhile been joined by the Mk IC, first issued to No 811 Sqdn at Lee-on-Solent in January 1942, this being a shore-based unit previously equipped principally with Chesapeakes. The Sea Hurricane Mk IC was essentially a marriage of new four-cannon Hurricane Mk IIC outer wing panels with a Merlin III-engined late-series Hurricane Mk I, the nuptials being accompanied by the usual navalisation. Although lacking any compensation for the added armament weight in the form of increased power, the Sea Hurricane Mk IC could still clock 256 knots (474 km/h) at around 15,000 ft (4 570 m) and the improved effectiveness resulting from the cannon armament was very welcome. This version soon began to reach Nos 802 and 883 squadrons at Yeovilton, other recipient units that were to follow including No 801 Sqdn aboard HMS *Eagle,* No 880 Sqdn aboard HMS *Furious* and No 885 Sqdn aboard HMS *Victorious.*

The Mk IC was to be followed into service late in 1942 by the similarly-armed Sea Hurricane Mk IIC which benefited from the installation of the Merlin XX engine rated at 1,460 bhp at 6,250 ft (1 905 m) and 1,435 bhp at 11,000 ft (3 355 m), this model being capable of 297 knots (550 km/h) at 22,000 ft (6 705 m). The Mk IIC was originally intended as a new-build aeroplane, although, in the event, it too was to produced with the aid of conversion kits by General Aircraft, these kits being made available from mid-1942, by which time the Royal Navy had almost 600 Sea Hurricanes in its inventory. Another version that was to follow on in small numbers was the Canadian-built Sea Hurricane Mk XIIA which reverted to the octet of Browning guns and had a Packard-built Merlin 29 engine.

In so far as the Sea Hurricanes embarked in the Fleet

carriers were concerned, the Mediterranean was destined to be their most important operational venue. This had dated from March 1942, when the old HMS *Eagle* had reached Force "H" as a replacement for the ill-fated HMS *Ark Royal* and including in its aircraft complement four Sea Hurricanes attached to No 813 Sqdn. These, so it is alleged, had the engine manifold pressure control modified to raise maximum boost from +6¼ lb to +16 lb to wring a few more knots out of the aircraft at the altitude at which combat was most likely to take place, although the effect on engine life of the use of such boost can best be left to the imagination. By the time *Eagle* provided the primary air cover for Operation *Harpoon* — six fast merchantmen headed for Malta and met by Force "H" as escort on 12 June — the four Sea Hurricanes of No 813 Sqdn had been joined aboard the carrier by No 801's dozen Sea Hurricanes and these provided very effective air cover, but the inadequate endurance of the Sea Hurricane was rendered manifestly obvious as was also the need for the cannon armament that had still to become available with delivery of the Mk IC.

The most noteworthy action of the Sea Hurricane in the Mediterranean and the last major action in which Sea Hurricanes were to operate from Fleet carriers was Operation *Pedestal*, the object of which was to get 14 merchantmen, including the tanker *Ohio*, through the Sicilian Narrows under cover of a very powerful escort consisting of two battleships, seven cruisers, 24 destroyers and the Fleet carriers HMS *Eagle*, HMS *Indomitable* and HMS *Victorious*. Between them, these carriers fielded 72 fighters, including 47 Sea Hurricanes. Nos 801 (12 Sea Hurricanes plus four spares) and 813 (four Sea Hurricanes) squadrons were aboard *Eagle*, No 885 (five Sea Hurricanes) was aboard *Victorious*, and Nos 800 (12 Sea Hurricanes) and 880 (10 Sea Hurricanes) squadrons were aboard *Indomitable*. By FAA standards at that time this was a massive use of air power but it was to prove vital in the hard-fought battles that were to

accompany the bitterly-contested voyage that commenced in the Straits of Gibraltar on 10 August and ended in Valetta five days later.

Much has since been written about this epic operation in which *Eagle*, together with all but four of her Sea Hurricanes, was to be lost to the torpedoes of U-73 almost as soon as battle was engaged, and it suffices to say that *Pedestal* succeeded — but only just! The élan displayed by the FAA fighters during almost four days of continuous air attack was a primary factor in the prevention of the destruction of the entire convoy — five of the merchantmen, including the all important tanker *Ohio*, got through to save Malta from what seemed inevitable starvation and surrender. As for the Sea Hurricanes, despite the loss of 16 of their number with *Eagle* almost at the outset, they were to claim 25 of the 38 confirmed "kills" — one Sea Hurricane pilot, Lt R J Cork, alone claiming the destruction of three German and three Italian aircraft — for the loss of but three.

Meanwhile, Nos 802 and 883 squadrons, having completed working up, had embarked on the escort carrier HMS *Avenger* to play a vital rôle in protecting convoy PQ 18 which sailed for Murmansk from Loch Ewe on 2 September. The convoy's predecessor, PQ 17, had been cut to pieces in the Arctic in July, and PQ 18 was subjected to incessant air attack from the moment that it came within range of *Luftwaffe* bases in northern Norway. But the attackers soon discovered *this* convoy to be different in having fighter cover in the shape of the dozen Sea Hurricanes of Nos 802 and 883 squadrons aboard *Avenger*. Five enemy aircraft were positively destroyed before the convoy reached Murmansk relatively unscathed and a further 17 aircraft of the *Luftwaffe* had been damaged, four of the Sea Hurricanes being lost of which three of the pilots were saved.

I had not accompanied No 802 Sqdn when it departed aboard *Avenger*, September having seen me posted to the Service Trials Unit at Arbroath where I was to fly Sea Hur-

Sea Hurricane Mk IBs of Nos 800 and 880 Squadrons aboard HMS Indomitable during a refuelling stop at Freetown prior to participation in Operation Pedestal. Wildcats of No 806 Squadron may be seen behind the Sea Hurricanes

ricane Mks IC and IIC on a variety of trials, including night deck landings. The Sea Hurricane was not really suited to the night environment, however, owing to the combination of relatively poor forward view and exhaust glare from the engine even with glare shields fitted. But by this time, the Sea Hurricane's brief career as the mainstay of the FAA fighter squadrons was already drawing to a close and little serious consideration was being given to the expansion of its operational repertoire.

The Sea Hurricane had been seen from the outset as no

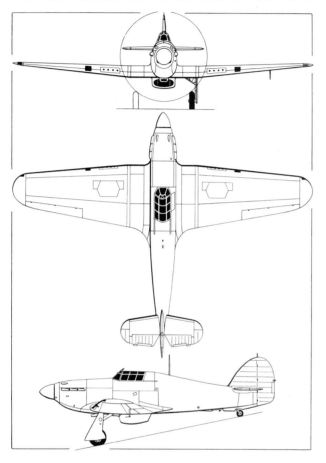

more than a stopgap and it was becoming seriously outclassed by enemy fighters which were appearing in ever increasing numbers as escorts for bombers attacking our convoys. Fortunately, the more efficacious Seafire had now begun to appear and the Hellcat was in prospect. Nos 880 and 885 squadrons, after returning from *Pedestal,* had begun working up on the Spitfire at Stretton in August preparatory to Seafire IIC conversion, with No 801 Sqdn following suit in September. The Sea Hurricane was, nevertheless, to continue to give valuable service with the escort carriers, the MAC ships and ashore — as late as April 1943, No 877 Sqdn was to be formed on Sea Hurricanes for the defence of Tanga, East Africa — and it was to contribute substantially to Operation *Torch,* the Allied invasion of North Africa in November 1942. Sea Hurricanes operating from the escort carriers *Avenger* (No 802 Sqdn), *Biter* (No 800 Sqdn) and *Dasher* (Nos 804 and 891 sqdns) during *Torch.* Indeed, although by the close of 1943, the Sea Hurricane had largely disappeared from frontline FAA units, the Seafire having achieved predominance from the beginning of that year, it was not until April 1944, when No 824 Sqdn aboard HMS *Striker* re-equipped with Wildcat Mk Vs, that the last Sea Hurricanes to serve afloat were finally disembarked.

It was aboard *Striker,* in October 1943, that I had had my final acquaintance with the Sea Hurricane, having been despatched to this escort carrier in a Mk IIC for low windspeed deck-landing trials and off-centre landings. The sturdy Sea Hurricane withstood this harsh treatment splendidly down to a windspeed over the deck of 16 knots (30 km/h).

Critical examination of an aircraft that was manifestly a stopgap in so far as the Fleet Air Arm was concerned yet had enjoyed a starring rôle in that epic aerial conflict of all aerial conflicts, the "Battle of Britain", is by no means easy. Can one justifiably criticise features and characteristics created for a task totally dissimilar to that for which it was conscripted as a result of *force majeure?* Perhaps it is sufficient to say that, contrary to logic, it took to the naval environment remarkably well. A thoroughly competent Fleet fighter it was not and could never have been, but it was a great dogfighter with, in its cannon-armed versions, plenty of punch and, most important, it reached the Fleet Air Arm at a time when that service desperately needed a relatively fast and reasonably modern single-seat fighter embarked in its carriers. □

The general arrangement drawing above left depicts the Sea Hurricane Mk IB. (Below) A Sea Hurricane Mk IIC (NF717) originally built as a late series Hurricane Mk IIC but retained at Langley after completion for naval conversion whereupon it was assigned a new serial, the original serial being in the KW batch

Grumman Avenger

A DASH OF AUDACITY can be perceived in the design of every truly successful combat aircraft. Indeed, audaciousness may even be considered synonymous with progress in aircraft design, for, without its infusion, the end product is inevitably pedestrian and how better could be described the carrier-based aeroplanes with which Britain's Fleet Air Arm went to War! The need for the Royal Navy's aviators to fly such antediluvial types as the Swordfish and Sea Gladiator when hostilities began was a direct result of the pedetentous approach of the naval staff to the operational requirements of the Fleet Air Arm; a lack of boldness and imagination hardly calculated to inspire British naval aircraft designers of the day.

Fortunately for the Allied cause, this lack of enterprise had not been emulated in the USA, where audacity had been displayed in no small measure by aircraft manufacturers in their efforts to meet more far-sighted shipboard combat aircraft requirements, outstanding among the companies that had created a new generation of carrier-based aeroplanes being the Grumman Aircraft Engineering Corporation of Bethpage. It was to this Long Island-based company that the British Fleet Air Arm was to contract an immense debt for boosting the service's morale at a time when it was very much the poor cousin to the RAF in the matter of frontline aircraft. It was not simply the fact that British naval aviation was restored to the first division by this company's progeny; Grumman aircraft gave the Fleet Air Arm an insight into how purpose-built naval aeroplanes could really perform,

(Below) Avenger Mk Is of the Royal Navy's No 849 Squadron shore-based at Hatston being loaded with Mk 13-2 torpedoes, and (head of page) an Eastern Motors-built TBM-3E Avenger, the suffix letter in the designation signifying the installation of APS-4 search radar.

General Motors-built TBM-3E Avengers photographed during pre-US Navy acceptance trials. The TBM-3 differed from earlier production models of the Avenger primarily in having an uprated engine. All production was undertaken by the Eastern Aircraft Division of General Motors

reorientating much of the naval staff thinking on operational requirements in the process.

Perhaps in some way this change of attitude in which they resulted was symbolised by the way in which the abstruse thinking of their Lordships of the Admiralty, which had led to the bestowal of the unimaginative appellations of Tarpon and Martlet on two pugnacious Grumman combat aircraft, performed a volte-face and accepted the vastly more emotive American names of Avenger and Wildcat.

These classic Grumman products embodied their fair share of design audacity and the Avenger perhaps more so than the Wildcat. The Avenger had stemmed from an invitation distributed among US aircraft manufacturers by the US Navy in

1939 soliciting design proposals for a new shipboard torpedo-bomber which had to meet exacting and far-sighted requirements. In its attempts to meet the demands of the outline specification, the Grumman team, headed by Bob Hall assistant chief engineer in charge of experimental work, and A R Koch, test and project engineer, had made no concessions to aesthetics; they had retained the corpulence of line characteristic of all preceding Grumman shipboard warplanes, accentuating this corpulency in order to accommodate a capacious internal weapons bay — itself a novel feature for a shipboard aeroplane — able to house a 22-in (56-cm) torpedo or up to four 500-lb (226,8-kg) bombs, with a 275 US gal (1 042 l) long-range tank as an optional store. To this innovatory aspect of the design was added the first power-operated dorsal turret ever to be toted by a US single-engined warplane, some thought having been given to the self-defence capability of a warplane of this category for the first time. The pilot was provided with a 0·3-in (7,62-mm) machine gun in the starboard side of the engine cowling, the gunner in his turret wielded a 0·5-in (12,7-mm) gun, while the bombardier, who sat between the two, could climb down inside the deep fuselage to a compartment behind the weapons bay from which he could operate an aft-firing ventral 0·3-in (7,62-mm) weapon.

(Above left) A General Motors-built TBM-1E Avenger under test at the company's Trenton, New Jersey, facility, and (below) one of the first batch of TBF-1 Avengers prior to delivery to the Norfolk NAS in May 1942 for US Navy Squadron VT-8

One of the initial batch of Avenger Mk Is (FN767) supplied to the Royal Navy and photographed in April 1943. At this time, Royal Navy Avengers were about to be flown operationally (with No 832 Squadron) for the first time, their initial deployment being aboard the USS Saratoga

Assigned the designation XTBF-1, the new torpedo-bomber had been the recipient of a contract for two prototypes on 8 April 1940, and the US Navy was evidently sufficiently impressed with the potential of the projected aircraft to order "off the drawing board" 286 production TBF-1s on the following 23 December. One week short of 16 months from the issuing of the prototype contract, on 1 August 1941, the first XTBF-1 had flown, with Bob Hall himself at the controls. Regrettably, this prototype was lost four months later when an uncontrollable fire developed in the weapons bay, but within barely more than three weeks, on 20 December, the second XTBF-1 had flown to continue the test programme. Earlier, on 7 December, the second aeroplane was to have been shown to the public for the first time during an "open day" at the Bethpage factory — the announcement of the news of the attack on Pearl Harbor on that day immediately resulted, so it is alleged, in the new torpedo-bomber being named "Avenger".

The first production TBF-1 Avenger had followed closely on the heels of the second prototype, on 3 January 1942, and some idea of the impetus placed behind its production programme may be gathered from the fact that no fewer than 145 of the torpedo-bombers had been delivered in the first half of the year which also saw the first operational deployment of the new Grumman. Six crews from Torpedo Squadron Eight (VT-8) had been assigned to an Avenger conversion course at Norfolk NAS, the remainder of the squadron with TBD-1 Devastators remaining with the USS *Hornet*. After completion of conversion, the six crews flew their Avengers to Pearl Harbor. The *Hornet* had already put to sea, however, and the Avengers therefore continued on across the Pacific to Midway. From here, on 4 June, the half-dozen torpedo-bombers had taken-off to attack Admiral Chuichi Nagumo's carrier force. Five failed to return and the sixth regained the island with only the trim tab for longitudinal control, one mainwheel dangling, the weapons bay doors agape, and with one gunner dead and the other wounded.

Happily, this discouraging start to its service career had not proved an inauspicious augury, for, by the beginning of 1943, when the first Fleet Air Arm squadron to equip with the Grumman torpedo-bomber, No 832, took on its aircraft at Norfolk NAS, the Avenger had thoroughly redeemed itself and was established as a capable, dependable and trouble-free warplane, the combination of inherent structural ruggedness and effective defensive armament endowing it with a good chance of survival in fulfilling a mission for which the survivability rate was notoriously low.

In April 1943, No 832 Squadron took its newly-acquired Grummans aboard the USS *Saratoga* for the first operational deployment of the Avenger in British service, three other FAA squadrons, Nos 845, 846 and 850, having by this time converted or being in process of conversion to this torpedo-bomber, and it was during the course of this month that I was to first make acquaintance with the Avenger.

"The grand-daddy of all Wildcats!" This was our initial reaction at the Service Trials Unit at Crail, on the Firth of Forth, when our first Avenger was flown in early in the spring of 1943. Here again were the rotund yet efficient-looking fuselage, the large radial engine and angular wings and tail assembly; it was so obviously related to the Wildcat, even down to the small, solid-tyre tailwheel, that there could be no doubt of its origin. Indeed, at first sight the Avenger could well have been a scaled-up Wildcat, but the resemblance had to be confined to external contour owing to its sheer size and rôle, and I hardly expected this torpedo-bomber to offer in the air any of the exhilaration that I had experienced with its smaller stablemate.

On 12 April, soon after its arrival at Crail, I was hoisting myself over the cockpit sill of the Avenger and speculating on the reaction of the FAA boys to the roominess and luxury offered by its "front office" by comparison with the aircraft to which they were accustomed and even by comparison with its nearest British equivalent, the Barracuda, which was only just entering FAA service. The big 14-cylinder two-row Wright R-2600-8 Cyclone 14 engine was started on the 147 US gal (557 l) of the three-tank set with mixture set to RICH and the booster pump ON, the inertia starter then being energised and engaged while the priming switch was held on PRIME. The Cyclone 14, which turned an immense 13-ft (3,96-m) diameter Hamilton Standard propeller, came to life with an even deeper and throatier roar than the single-row nine-cylinder Cyclone of the Wildcat with which I was familiar, and was warmed up at between 1,000 and 1,200 revs with the booster pump off. The fuel selector was then moved to either the port or starboard 94 US gal (356 l) side tank for run up. The cowl gills and the oil cooler shutters were retained fully open throughout all ground running, the revs being steadily increased to 1,800, at which the two-speed supercharger was exercised, the operation of the constant-speed propeller checked and the magnetos tested.

View for taxying was acceptable, despite the bulk of the engine and the not inconsiderable ground angle, and taxying

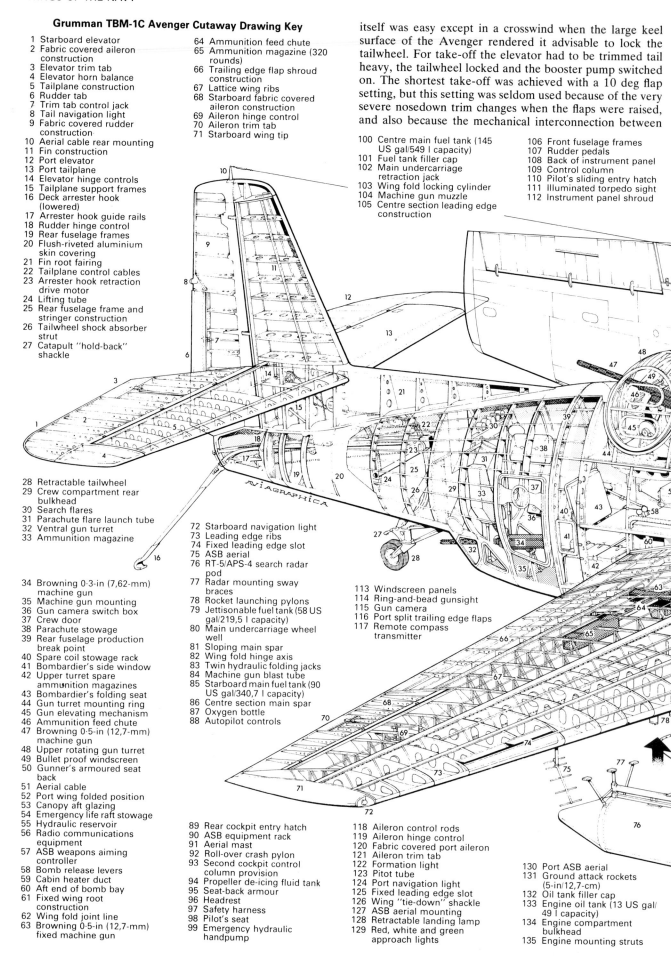

Grumman TBM-1C Avenger Cutaway Drawing Key

1 Starboard elevator
2 Fabric covered aileron construction
3 Elevator trim tab
4 Elevator horn balance
5 Tailplane construction
6 Rudder tab
7 Trim tab control jack
8 Tail navigation light
9 Fabric covered rudder construction
10 Aerial cable rear mounting
11 Fin construction
12 Port elevator
13 Port tailplane
14 Elevator hinge controls
15 Tailplane support frames
16 Deck arrester hook (lowered)
17 Arrester hook guide rails
18 Rudder hinge control
19 Rear fuselage frames
20 Flush-riveted aluminium skin covering
21 Fin root fairing
22 Tailplane control cables
23 Arrester hook retraction drive motor
24 Lifting tube
25 Rear fuselage frame and stringer construction
26 Tailwheel shock absorber strut
27 Catapult "hold-back" shackle

28 Retractable tailwheel
29 Crew compartment rear bulkhead
30 Search flares
31 Parachute flare launch tube
32 Ventral gun turret
33 Ammunition magazine

34 Browning 0·3-in (7,62-mm) machine gun
35 Machine gun mounting
36 Gun camera switch box
37 Crew door
38 Parachute stowage
39 Rear fuselage production break point
40 Spare coil stowage rack
41 Bombardier's side window
42 Upper turret spare ammunition magazines
43 Bombardier's folding seat
44 Gun turret mounting ring
45 Gun elevating mechanism
46 Ammunition feed chute
47 Browning 0·5-in (12,7-mm) machine gun
48 Upper rotating gun turret
49 Bullet proof windscreen
50 Gunner's armoured seat back
51 Aerial cable
52 Port wing folded position
53 Canopy aft glazing
54 Emergency life raft stowage
55 Hydraulic reservoir
56 Radio communications equipment
57 ASB weapons aiming controller
58 Bomb release levers
59 Cabin heater duct
60 Aft end of bomb bay
61 Fixed wing root construction
62 Wing fold joint line
63 Browning 0·5-in (12,7-mm) fixed machine gun

64 Ammunition feed chute
65 Ammunition magazine (320 rounds)
66 Trailing edge flap shroud construction
67 Lattice wing ribs
68 Starboard fabric covered aileron construction
69 Aileron hinge control
70 Aileron trim tab
71 Starboard wing tip

72 Starboard navigation light
73 Leading edge ribs
74 Fixed leading edge slot
75 ASB aerial
76 RT-5/APS-4 search radar pod
77 Radar mounting sway braces
78 Rocket launching pylons
79 Jettisonable fuel tank (58 US gal/219,5 l capacity)
80 Main undercarriage wheel well
81 Sloping main spar
82 Wing fold hinge axis
83 Twin hydraulic folding jacks
84 Machine gun blast tube
85 Starboard main fuel tank (90 US gal/340,7 l capacity)
86 Centre section main spar
87 Oxygen bottle
88 Autopilot controls

89 Rear cockpit entry hatch
90 ASB equipment rack
91 Aerial mast
92 Roll-over crash pylon
93 Second cockpit control column provision
94 Propeller de-icing fluid tank
95 Seat-back armour
96 Headrest
97 Safety harness
98 Pilot's seat
99 Emergency hydraulic handpump

100 Centre main fuel tank (145 US gal/549 l capacity)
101 Fuel tank filler cap
102 Main undercarriage retraction jack
103 Wing fold locking cylinder
104 Machine gun muzzle
105 Centre section leading edge construction

106 Front fuselage frames
107 Rudder pedals
108 Back of instrument panel
109 Control column
110 Pilot's sliding entry hatch
111 Illuminated torpedo sight
112 Instrument panel shroud

113 Windscreen panels
114 Ring-and-bead gunsight
115 Gun camera
116 Port split trailing edge flaps
117 Remote compass transmitter

118 Aileron control rods
119 Aileron hinge control
120 Fabric covered port aileron
121 Aileron trim tab
122 Formation light
123 Pitot tube
124 Port navigation light
125 Fixed leading edge slot
126 Wing "tie-down" shackle
127 ASB aerial mounting
128 Retractable landing lamp
129 Red, white and green approach lights

130 Port ASB aerial
131 Ground attack rockets (5-in/12,7-cm)
132 Oil tank filler cap
133 Engine oil tank (13 US gal/ 49 l capacity)
134 Engine compartment bulkhead
135 Engine mounting struts

itself was easy except in a crosswind when the large keel surface of the Avenger rendered it advisable to lock the tailwheel. For take-off the elevator had to be trimmed tail heavy, the tailwheel locked and the booster pump switched on. The shortest take-off was achieved with a 10 deg flap setting, but this setting was seldom used because of the very severe nosedown trim changes when the flaps were raised, and also because the mechanical interconnection between the flaps and the undercarriage selector lever allowed both flaps and undercarriage to be raised when the undercarriage lever was set to UP. With standard internal fuel but without any warload at some 14,000 lb (6 350 kg), the Avenger I, alias TBF-1B, could take-off within about 240 yards (220 m) in nil wind, or about 140 yards (130 m) with a 15 knot (28 km/h) headwind.

As the Double Cyclone had no automatic boost control, the throttle had to be opened only as far as was required to give 44½ in Hg at 2,600 revs in the climb at 115 knots (213 km/h). This power setting was then reduced to 38 in and 2,400 revs in the climb at 115 knots (213 km/h) to give a rate of climb of about 1,000 ft/min (5,08 m/sec). At 60 per cent normal sea level power with mixture set to LEAN, the normal cruise altitude of 15,000 ft (4 570 m) was reached in about 18 minutes, and above this altitude, the

supercharger was changed from LOW to HIGH gear by throttling back to about 1,700 rpm, and once in HIGH gear the throttle could be opened up to 41 in Hg at 2,400 rpm to continue the climb, reducing climbing speed by two knots (3,7 km/h) per thousand feet up to the service ceiling of 22,600 ft (6,890 m).

At cruising speeds the Avenger was stable about all axes, but the controls were heavy at all speeds. Even as the stall was approached the elevator became noticeably heavier and less effective, the stall itself occurring suddenly and without warning, either port or starboard wing dropping. Lightly loaded, the Avenger stalled with all up at 76 knots (141 km/h) and

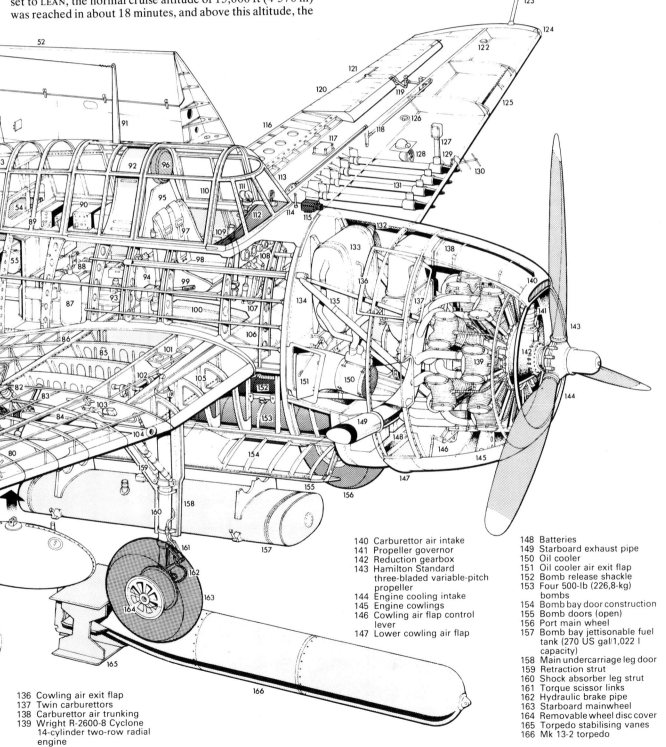

140 Carburettor air intake
141 Propeller governor
142 Reduction gearbox
143 Hamilton Standard three-bladed variable-pitch propeller
144 Engine cooling intake
145 Engine cowlings
146 Cowling air flap control lever
147 Lower cowling air flap

148 Batteries
149 Starboard exhaust pipe
150 Oil cooler
151 Oil cooler air exit flap
152 Bomb release shackle
153 Four 500-lb (226,8-kg) bombs
154 Bomb bay door construction
155 Bomb doors (open)
156 Port main wheel
157 Bomb bay jettisonable fuel tank (270 US gal/1,022 l capacity)
158 Main undercarriage leg door
159 Retraction strut
160 Shock absorber leg strut
161 Torque scissor links
162 Hydraulic brake pipe
163 Starboard mainwheel
164 Removable wheel disc cover
165 Torpedo stabilising vanes
166 Mk 13-2 torpedo

136 Cowling air exit flap
137 Twin carburettors
138 Carburettor air trunking
139 Wright R-2600-8 Cyclone 14-cylinder two-row radial engine

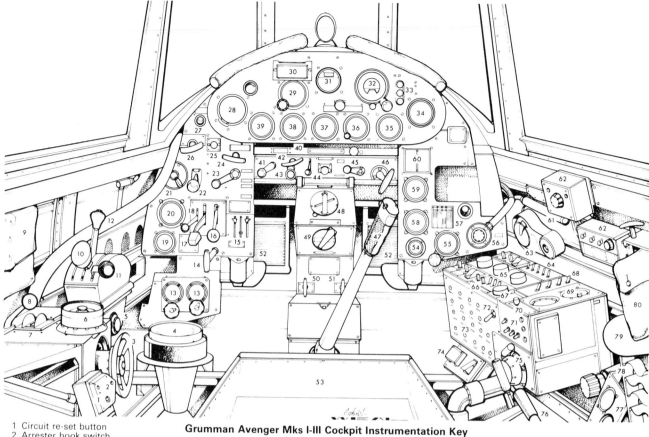

Grumman Avenger Mks I-III Cockpit Instrumentation Key

1 Circuit re-set button
2 Arrester hook switch
3 Elevator trimming tab control
4 Compass
5 Control quadrant friction adjustment
6 Rudder trimming tab control (aileron trimming tab control mounted on forward face of box)
7 Booster pump switch
8 Tailwheel lock
9 Map/document case
10 Throttle control lever
11 Mixture control
12 Supercharger control
13 Oxygen contents/flow gauges
14 Landing gear emergency release lever
15 Flap and undercarriage indicators
16 Flap lever
17 Undercarriage lever
18 Undercarriage locking lever
19 External air temperature gauge

20 Cylinder head temperature gauge
21 Ignition switch
22 Propeller control
23 Oil cooler shutters control
24 Emergency bomb release lever
25 ABA warning button
26 Carburettor air intake control
27 Bomb doors warning light
28 Boost gauge
29 Altimeter
30 Correction card holder
31 Directional gyro
32 Artificial horizon
33 Radio altimeter indicator lights
34 Radio altimeter
35 Radio altimeter limit switch
36 Rate of climb indicator
37 Turn-and-bank indicator
38 ASI
39 RPM indicator
40 Sliding chart board
41 Cowling gill control

42 Arrester hook manual control
43 Fuel strainer drain control
44 Bomb door control lever
45 Wing folding control
46 Wing folding mechanical lock
47 Control column
48 Compass direction indicator
49 Fuel cock control
50 De-icer control
51 Cockpit heat control
52 Rudder pedals
53 Pilot's seat
54 Fuel gauge
55 Clock
56 Propeller anti-icer control
57 Data plate
58 Fuel gauge selector
59 Fuel pressure/oil temperature and pressure triple gauge
60 Take-off/landing instructions
61 Fluorescent lighting
62 Radio control boxes (2)
63 Main electrical panel, inc:
64 Lights/pitot tube heating ON/OFF switches

65 Dimmer switches (compass/chart board/electrical panel)
66 Gun camera/armament/torpedo (smoke) bomb switches
67 Tell-tale lights switches
68 Control surface ON/OFF power switches
69 Ammeter
70 Recognition light keying switch
71 Recognition lights ON/OFF switches (white/red/green/amber)
72 Battery ON/OFF master switch
73 Circuit breaker switch panel
74 Destruct switch
75 R1147 tuning unit
76 Hydraulic hand pump
77 Hydraulic pressure gauges
78 Signal cartridges stowage clips
79 Oxygen bottle
80 Signal pistol holster

with all down at 68 knots (126 km/h). But all in all, Grumman's torpedo-bomber was an amiable enough aeroplane. Relative lack of manoeuvrability was to be expected in an aircraft of its size and purpose, but then, it was not designed to turn with a Zero-Sen but to provide a rock-steady platform for launching a torpedo. It gave a comforting impression of vicelessness., yet the Pilot's Notes indicated that the Avenger did have an Achilles heel, affording a warning that intentional spinning was prohibited and that, should an unintentional spin occur, normal recovery action should be applied immediately. I was to be forcibly reminded of that warning a number of years later by the Avenger's descendant, the AF-2 Guardian.

The TBF-1B Avenger I, which was the Lend-Lease equivalent of the initial production TBF-1 for the US Navy, had a practical combat radius of 225 nm (417 km) with a Mk 13-2 torpedo or four 500-lb (226,8-kg) bombs and standard internal fuel, this being based on 20 min warm-up and idling,

a minute for take-off, 10 min for rendezvous at 60 per cent normal sea level power, climb to cruise altitude of 15,000 ft (4 570 m), five minutes combat at 1,500 ft (457 m) with full military power plus 10 min at full normal power, return cruise at 1,500 ft (457 m) at 60 per cent NSLP and 60 min for rendezvous, landing and reserve. This action radius could be boosted to 340 nm (630 km) by the provision of two 58 US gal (220 l) underwing tanks, the maximum range of 1,105 mls (1 778 km) at a 133 knot (246 km/h) cruise at 5,000 ft (1 525 m) being extended to 1,390 mls (2 236 km), such being just right for the Avenger's primary operational arena of the Pacific.

I was particularly interested in the Avenger's diving characteristics as it was intended as a torpedo-*bomber* and "bomber" in US Navy parlance of those days was synonymous with "dive-bomber". The undercarriage could be used as a dive brake if required and could be lowered prior to the dive at any speed up to 200 knots (370 km/h). From the trimmed

(Above) Avenger Mk II JZ570 flying with 58 US gal (219l) drop tanks during trials at the A & AEE in August 1944. The ASB aerial may be seen beneath the outer wing panel and may also be seen beneath the wings of the TBF-1E (below right)

fast cruise condition, the Avenger had to be trimmed nose heavy during the dive and left rudder trim was also required as the controls were heavy indeed. The maximum diving speed at 16,000 lb (7 725 kg) was 285 knots (528 km/h) and the weapons bay doors could be opened at this speed, but the pull-out was a two-handed, somewhat phrenetic affair, with one hand pulling with all its strength and the other retrimming frantically. Somehow, I do not think that the Grumman team had *dive* bombing much in mind when creating the Avenger. From a relatively shallow dive such as normally preceded a torpedo run, the Avenger stabilised almost immediately, a characteristic that was crucially important if a clean and accurate drop was to be achieved. For an evasive breakaway from a torpedo run, the use of both hands on the stick and a heavy push on the rudder pedal were necessary to cope with the control loads.

The amiability of the Avenger really showed itself in landing which was extremely easy. The undercarriage was lowered and the speed reduced to 110 knots (204 km/h). The mixture was set RICH and the propeller fully fine, booster pump selected ON and supercharger checked in LOW. Flaps were then lowered fully and the engine-assisted approach made at 85 knots (158 km/h). Landing the Avenger on a carrier was about as easy as that difficult art is ever likely to be. The view was good with the cowl gills closed, the aircraft was superbly steady at 78 knots (144 km/h) and the huge sting-type arrester hook grappled even the most ill-judged landing attempts to convert them into safe arrivals, the mighty undercarriage apparently being capable of absorbing vertical velocities of up to 16 ft/sec (4,9 m/sec), which is a fair thump. The tailwheel had to be unlocked for deck landing in case the arrest was effected off centre, thus imposing side contact loads on the tailwheel.

The Avenger early distinguished itself in the Pacific, a theatre in which the opposing fighter pilots were particularly tenacious and mounted on the magnificent Zero-Sen. Of course, it usually had the good fortune to be protected by its stablemate, the Wildcat, and later, the Hellcat, and in anyone's book the Grumman pairings were formidable, but the Avenger had brought a new dimension to naval strike aircraft in the matter of defensive capability. The fuel tanks were self-sealing and protected in strategic areas by armour; all crew members were provided with some armour protection and with the phase in by Grumman of the TBF-1C, the single forward-firing 0·3-in (7,62-mm) gun operated by the pilot gave place to a pair of 0·5-in (12,7-mm) weapons with 600 rpg. Thus, the Avenger could give a good account of itself even without fighter protection, a fact to which many surviv-

ing Japanese fighter pilots will attest. As used to be said. "If you're slow you're bound to go unless you have the might to fight!"

Apart from its defensive capabilities, the Avenger offered outstanding sturdiness which was much appreciated by its crews. When ditching at sea was necessary it rarely broke up on impact and almost invariably floated for sufficient time for its crew to vacate the aircraft without undue haste. Records abounded of Avenger pilots making dead stick landings and walking away from their aircraft after it had ploughed through telegraph poles, fences and even barns.

Preoccupation with development and production of the F6F Hellcat and growing production requirements led to the General Motors Corporation establishing a second source for Avenger production at its Eastern Aircraft Division, the Eastern-built equivalent of Grumman's TBF-1 and -1C being the TBM-1 and 1C, which, when delivered to the Royal Navy, became Avenger IIs. Grumman production continued

(Above) An Avenger Mk III (JZ691) with ASH radar under the starboard wing, the RT-5/APS-4 search radar installation being common with the US Navy's TBM-3E. (Immediately below left) An Avenger Mk III (KE461) in post-WW II Royal Navy service. The general arrangement drawing illustrates the Avenger Mk I

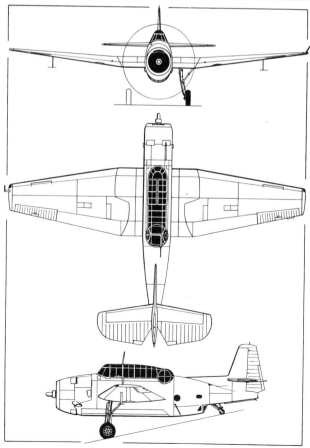

until early 1944, when the last of 2,290 left the Bethpage line of which 395 TBF-1Bs had been assigned to the Royal Navy, Eastern producing 2,882 TBM-1s, of which the Royal Navy was recipient of 334, and going on to produce 4,664 TBM-3s of which 192 entered the Royal Navy inventory to become Avenger IIIs. This last-mentioned model differed only in having an R-2800-20 engine in place of the -8, this affording 100 hp more at normal maximum power between sea level and 5,000 ft (1 525 m) and 50 hp more at military power between sea level and 3,200 ft (975 m).

While designed primarily for the torpedo-launching rôle and employed for this task extensively by the US Navy, the 900 plus Avengers supplied to the Fleet Air Arm rarely employed torpedoes, serving mostly as a bomber with bombs, mines or depth charges, and as a strike aircraft with rocket projectiles. No 832 Squadron, that had taken its Avengers into action from the *Saratoga* during the landings in the Middle Solomons, embarked in both *Victorious* and *Illustrious* during subsequent service with the East Indies Fleet, its last commission being aboard the escort carrier *Begum*. No fewer than 14 other FAA first-line squadron received Avengers, eight of these being with the service by the end of 1943. Most of these formed at the US Navy bases at Norfolk, Quonset and Squantum, and were then ferried to the UK aboard escort carriers.

Initially, the FAA's Avengers served chiefly from escort carriers or shore bases on anti-submarine patrol and, less frequently, on mine laying sorties in home waters. Some Avenger squadrons flew from escort carriers engaged in escorting Russian convoys, but one of their most important rôles was that of anti-shipping strike as part of Operation "Channel Stop" from April 1944, during the build-up for D-Day, this operation being intended to deny the English Channel to enemy shipping. However, the most spectacular exploits of the FAA's Avengers took place in the Pacific, one of the first major operations in which they participated being the attack on the Japanese naval base at Surabaja on 19 May 1944, during which Nos 832 and 845 Squadrons from *Illustrious* flew in concert with US Navy units from *Saratoga*. Avengers operated first with the East Indies Fleet and subsequently with the British Pacific Fleet during the final phases of the war against Japan, playing major rôles in many outstanding actions, such as the attack on the Japanese oil refineries at Palembang, Sumatra, in January 1945, the Avengers being drawn from Nos 820, 849, 854 and 857 Squadrons operating from *Indefatigable, Victorious, Illustrious* and *Indomiatable*. Between March and May 1945, Avengers from these carriers and *Formidable* performed

A standard Avenger Mk II (JZ574) built by General Motors and equivalent to the US Navy's TBM-1C. Three hundred and thirty-four of these followed 395 Avenger Mk Is into the Royal Navy's inventory, preceding 192 Avenger Mk IIIs, and by concensus the Avenger was the most efficaceous shipboard torpedo-bomber of World War II

intensive attacks on Japanese fighter bases in Formosa and islands to the south of Japan to support the US Okinawa landings, and on 24 July, Avengers of No 848 Squadron flying from *Formidable* became the first FAA bombers to attack the Japanese homeland which was to remain under attack from FAA Avengers until 15 August.

The Avenger was to be the recipient of many uncomplimentary epithets during its wartime career, such as the "Turkey" and the "Pregnant Beast", but these were mostly generated by its corpulence and used with affection, for the Grumman torpedo-bomber *earned* the confidence of its crews and this is an important yardstick when measuring the relative success of an aeroplane. The Grumman Avenger was one of the truly great shipboard aircraft of World War II, and it was destined to soldier on in a variety of rôles other than that for which it was specifically designed for many postwar years. Ironically, the last Avengers to be retired from service were those operated by its primary wartime enemy, the Japanese. □

Grumman TBF-1C Avenger Specification

Power Plant: One Wright R-2600-8 (Cyclone 14)) two-row 14-cylinder air-cooled radial engine rated (military) at 1,700 hp at 2,600 rpm from sea level to 3,000 ft (915 m) and 1,450 hp at 2,600 rpm between 7,800 ft (2,375 m) and 12,000 ft (3 660 m), or (normal) 1,500 hp at 2,400 rpm from sea level to 5,800 ft (1 770 m) and 1,350 hp at 2,400 rpm between 8,900 ft (2 715 m) and 13,000 ft (3 960 m). Three-bladed Hamilton Standard constant-speed propeller of 13 ft (3,96 m) diameter. Standard internal fuel capacity of 335 US gal (1 269 l) comprising 147 US gal (557 l) main tank with 94 US gal (356 l) port and starboard. Provision for two 58 US gal (220 l) underwing tanks and (ferry) 275 US gal (1 042 l) jettisonable weapons bay tank.
Performance: (At 16,412 lb/7 444 kg); Max speed, 249 mph (401 km/h) at sea level, 257 mph (414 km/h) at 12,000 ft (3,660 m); range cruise, 153 mph (246 km/h); time to 10,000 ft (3 050 m), 13 min, to 20,000 ft (6 095 m), 41·6 min; service ceiling, 21,400 ft (6 525 m); max range (internal fuel), 1,105 mls (1 778 km), (with two drop tanks), 1,390 mls (2 236 km); ferry range (with weapons bay and underwing tanks), 2,685 mls (4 320 km).
Weights: Empty equipped, 10,555 lb (4 788 kg); loaded (one Mk 13-2 torpedo), 16,412 lb (7 444 kg), (four 500-lb/226,8-kg bombs), 16,426 lb (7 450 kg), (Mk 13-2 torpedo and underwing tanks), 17,364 lb (7 876 kg).
Dimensions: Span, 54 ft 2 in (16,51 m), folded, 19 ft 0 in (5,79 m); length, 40 ft 9 in (12,42 m); height (tail down), 13 ft 9 in (4,19 m); wing area, 490 sq ft (45,52 m²); wheel track, 10 ft 10 in (3,50 m).
Armament: (Defensive): Two fixed forward-firing 0·5-in (12,7-mm) machine guns with 600 rpg, one 0·5-in (12,7-mm) machine gun with 400 rounds in power-operated dorsal turret and one 0·3-in (7,62-mm) machine gun with 500 rounds firing aft from ventral position (Offensive): One Mk 13-2 torpedo, one 1,000-lb (453,6-kg) bomb or four 500-lb (226,8-kg) bombs.

(Above left and below) An Avenger AS Mk 4 (XB444) operating from RNAS Ford as interim anti-submarine equipment in 1954 pending availability of the Fairey Gannet

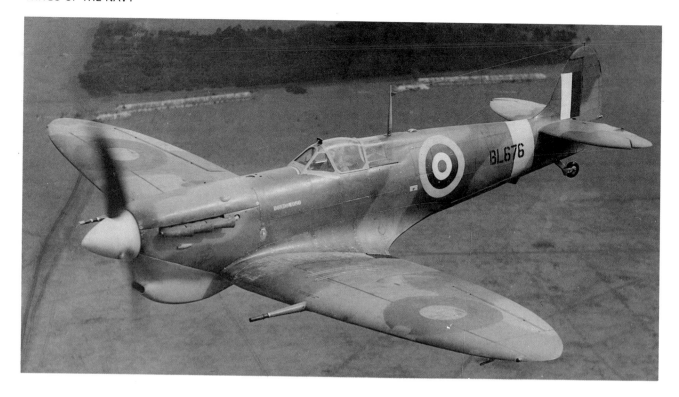

Supermarine Seafire

THE VENUE WAS YEOVILTON AIRFIELD: the time was a drably grey and blustery winter's afternoon more than a quarter-century ago and the event was the disbanding of a Royal Navy fighter squadron. The brief ceremony held at that Somerset airfield on that afternoon of 23 November 1954 did not mark *solely* the dissolution of No 764 Squadron after a mere 18 months of existence as a training unit; it signified the closing of the final chapter of a saga that had opened more than a dozen years earlier, when the war at sea was at its nadir in so far as the Allies were concerned, for No 764 had enjoyed the distinction of flying the last Supermarine Seafires serving with the Royal Navy.

The Seafire, certainly aesthetically the most elegant fighter ever to grace a carrier deck, was the product of adversity; it might be said to have been born of desperation. The rôle of naval air power was expanding with the course of the war, but its full potential could not be exploited without a shipboard fighter capable of a performance at least comparable with contemporary enemy shore-based fighters by which it was likely to be opposed. In so far as the Royal Navy was concerned, the Grumman Wildcat was placing the service's carrier-borne fighter element back in business, but outstanding naval fighter though this purpose-built and rugged American product undoubtedly was, it lacked the performance necessary to take on the shore-based opposition on equal terms.

As a result of a brilliant piece of improvisation, the Navy had been presented with the Sea Hurricane which had proved that a high-performance shore-based fighter *could* be operated with relative safety from a carrier, but the Hawker fighter's chances of survival against a Bf 109G or Fw 190 were anything but good. Nevertheless, its successful adaptation for the shipboard rôle had at least brought about something of a revolution in naval thinking, and logically enough,

in 1941, the Admiralty began to demand a similar adaptation of what was then the highest performing fighter available — the Spitfire.

This scheme was received with mixed feelings by those naval pilots in the know. Everyone admired the Spitfire and itched to fly it — but from an aircraft carrier? That was a horse of a very different colour! None needed convincing of the performance or handling attributes of this magnificent fighter, which was, surely, one of the greatest warplanes ever conceived, but there was a certain air of fragility about the aeroplane; a ballerina-like delicacy that seemed inconsistent with the demanding, muscle-taxing scenario of shipboard operations. Could that slender fuselage stand the harsh deceleration of an arrested landing; would that frail undercarriage absorb the shock of 15 ft/sec (4,57 m/sec) vertical velocity and could those wafer-like wings take the acceleration forces of a catapult launch? What of the Spitfire's high landing speed, but, above all, would the pilot ever be able to see the carrier deck on the approach?

Obviously, there were many technical difficulties, but the feasibility or otherwise of the scheme was only to be determined by practical trials and, accordingly, having obtained the somewhat, reluctant agreement of the Air Ministry for the transfer of a number of Spitfires, both existing and to be produced, the Admiralty initiated late in 1941 preliminary trials with a Spitfire VB (AB205). An A-frame arrester hook had been introduced on the centre longerons aft of the firewall and at the rear of the cockpit.

The task of carrying out the trials was assigned to Lt Cdr H P Bramwell, CO of the Service Trials Unit at RNAS Arbroath, who, after spending two weeks practising ADDLs (Aerodrome Dummy Deck Landings), took his "hooked" Spitfire aboard HMS *Illustrious* in the Clyde during Christmas week of 1941. Peter Bramwell made twelve successful deck landings, seven take-offs and four catapult launches. Generally satisfied with the results, he did have reservations, however, and as little of the deck could be seen during a normal straight final appraoch, recommended that a curving approach technique be adopted so that the pilot could keep the batsman (Deck Landing Control Officer) in sight for as long as possible. He also expressed some doubt as to the Spitfire's suitability for operation from US-built "Woolworth" escort carriers.

His report was sufficiently encouraging to warrant Admiralty confirmation of a programme covering the transfer and adaptation of 250 Spitfires for naval use. It was proposed that these would comprise 48 existing Spitfire Mk VBs with the remainder being new-production Mk VCs and as the name "Sea Spitfire" was somewhat dissonant-sounding, the contraction "Seafire" was officially adopted for the "hooked" Spitfire. Adaptation for shipboard use was to be the essence of simplicity, and, apart from changes to internal equipment, such as the introduction of naval HF R/T and IFF, and a homing beacon receiver, was to comprise provision of a hydraulically-damped and faired A-frame arrester hook released by means of a Bowden cable, and slinging points, with the necessary local strengthening. The reworking of the Spitfire Mk VBs was undertaken by Air Service Training Limited as Seafire Mk IBs, but these were intended for use as trainers and they lacked the slinging points and homing beacon receiver which were introduced on a further 166 Seafire Mk IBs that were later to be delivered to the Navy by both Air Service Training and Cunliffe-Owen Aircraft.

The Seafire Mk IB was viewed as an interim model with which squadrons would be enabled to work up pending delivery of the assembly line adaptations of the new-production Spitfire Mk VCs, which had been assigned the designation Seafire Mk IIC, but owing to alacrity on the part of Supermarine in delivering Seafire Mk IICs, the first example of each version reached the Navy on the same day, 15 June 1942. The Seafire Mk IIC differed from the Mk IB essentially in having the universal or 'C' wing — although the extra pair of 20-mm cannon that could be accommodated by this wing was never to be fitted in service as the weight penalty was to be found unacceptable — and catapult spools, the spigots for which called for some local beefing up. Some further strengthening was provided by an external fishplate between the forward cockpit bulkhead and the radio bay, the CG change resulting from the new installations and strengthening being restored by balance weights.

My first acquaintance with the Seafire was made in August 1942, when I was serving with No 897 Squadron at RNAS Stretton. At that time we were operating Fulmars, and I was somewhat puzzled at being instructed to proceed to Donibristle to bring back two Seafire Mk IBs which were then allocated to me to build up some experience. At the beginning of September, I was abruptly sent off to RNAS Machrihanish in a Hurricane which was exchanged for a Wildcat upon my arrival. After a 15-minute refamiliarisation flight in the Wildcat the next morning, I was sent off to the escort carrier HMS *Biter* for a series of deck landings and catapult launches, ostensibly to proof the ship's catapult. On returning to Stretton, I found myself a member of No 801 Squadron, which had reformed on 7 September with a complement of a dozen Seafire Mk IBs and was, in fact, destined to be the only operational FAA squadron to be fully equipped with this mark. At Stretton, the object of all my to-ing and fro-ing was finally revealed to me: I had been selected to undertake the first Seafire deck trials on an escort carrier!

It was back to Machrihanish again, and at 1330 hours on 11 September I was flying a Seafire towards HMS *Biter* — the time being significant as it turned out. As I approached *Biter*, I confidently assumed that all would be breached up for this momentous occasion — the first landing of a Seafire on one of these postage stamp-sized platforms — and I did a quick circuit at 400 ft (120 m) and settled into my approach. Contrary to Peter Bramwell's earlier recommendations, I adopted a straight final approach with the aircraft crabbed to starboard so that I had a good clear view to port of both the deck and, supposedly, the batsman, of whom, in the event I saw no sign.

Nevertheless, all went smoothly and I touched down on *Biter*, picking up the second wire. I came to a stop somewhat smartly and cut the engine, and it was only then that I realised

(Above right, below and head of opposite page) A Castle Bromwich-built Spitfire Mk VB (BL676) "Bondowoso" fitted with arrester hook and slinging points by Air Service Training Limited, this, together with three other Mk VBs having been delivered to the company's Hamble works on 10 January 1942 for conversion to Seafire Mk IB standards as the first of a batch of 48 aircraft

that the deck was completely deserted! Then striding from the island came a lone figure — the Captain. He stepped up on the wing and said, with a pleasant smile, "I say old boy, you were not expected so early and everyone's at lunch!" It was only then that the truth dawned on me: I had landed with the carrier 25 deg out of wind, only 13 knots (24 km/h) windspeed over the deck, the arrester wires lying flat and unsupported, and no batsman!

Since the programme called for me to start with 32 knots (59 km/h) of wind and work down to 20 knots (37 km/h), I felt that, albeit inadvertently, I had proved something. The Captain agreed that much of the programme could be taken as read and forthwith sent a signal to the Admiralty announcing successful completion of the trials! Perhaps this was a little premature as, after lunch, it was decided that I should make a landing with 10-12 knots (18-22 km/h) wind over the deck. With the help of the batsman, the landing was perfectly straightforward, but as the arrester wire reached the end of its pull-out, my arrester hook parted company with my aircraft. Since no crash barrier was being used for the trials and it was obvious that my brakes would not prevent me trickling over the bows and being run over by the carrier, I swung the Seafire gently into the island, bringing it to an abrupt halt with surprisingly little damage.

I was, of course, totally unaware at the time that the panic to get a Seafire aboard an escort carrier was a part of the preparation for Operation *Torch*, the Allied invasion of North Africa that was to commence in the early hours of 8 November, two months later. As it turned out, the three escort carriers involved, *Biter, Dasher* and *Avenger,* were all to be armed with Sea Hurricanes for this assault, the Seafires operating primarily from the elderly *Argus* and *Furious* — carriers with T-shaped elevators capable of accommodating the non-folding fighters — while the more modern *Formidable* and *Victorious*, with lifts too small to accept these early

Seafires, were each to stow a half-dozen of the fighters in permanent deck-parks where they were exposed to the elements.

The tempo at which squadrons had been converting to the Seafire had meanwhile been building up. No 807 had received its first Seafire Mk IIC at Lee-on-Solent towards the end of June, and late in August, three other squadrons, Nos 880 and 885 formerly on Sea Hurricanes, and No 884 previously equipped with Fulmars converted to Seafire Mk IICs, the last mentioned unit at Stretton and the others at Lee, while in the following month, No 801 began, as previously mentioned, working up on the Seafire Mk IB. During its six weeks' work-up, No 801, incidentally, succeeded in landing-on at sea all 12 of its Seafires with only 23 seconds interval between aircraft.

The first of the new Seafire squadrons to embark for *Torch* was No 880 assigned to the old and slow HMS *Argus* with a complement of 18 Mk IICs, followed a few days later by No 801 with a dozen Mk IBs and No 807 with a similar number of Mk IICs, both embarked aboard HMS *Furious,* while Nos 884 and 885, with a half-dozen Seafire IICs apiece, joined the Fleet carriers HMS *Victorious* and HMS *Formidable* respectively. The first Seafire actions of *Torch* were an unsuccessful strafing attack by No 885 Squadron, which was frustrated by thick ground haze, and a sweep over the Tafaroui naval air base by No 807 Squadron. While returning to *Furoius,* No 807 was bounced by Dewoitine 520s, Sub-Lt G C Baldwin obtaining the first *confirmed* "kill" for the Seafire (a New Zealander, Sub-Lt A S Long of No 885 Squadron, had earlier been credited with a "probable" after attacking a Martin 167 over Mers el Khebir harbour). One unusual story involving a Seafire on this first day of *Torch* concerned Sub-Lt L P Twiss of No 807 Squadron, later to become a well-known test pilot. Twiss landed alongside a US Army tank column to give warning of a hidden anti-tank battery and subsequently made two reconnaissance flights at the special request of the commander of the column. Short on fuel, he was forced to land at Tafaroui, which had still to be taken by the Allies, spent the night under the wing of his aircraft and next morning persuaded the French to refuel his Seafire and then returned to *Furious.*

Operation *Torch* had provided the first large-scale blooding of the Seafire, and if there was some little disappointment among personnel at the lack of vigorous opposition, the début had been by consensus successful. Nevertheless, there was some concern over performance shortcomings, initial

(Above left and below) Seafire Mk IIC MA970 used as a development aircraft and photographed in September 1942 while fitted with a Merlin 46 engine and four-bladed propeller. Supermarine's first production Mk IIC, MA970 was retained by the manufacturer and subsequently fitted with the folding wing developed for the Mk III with which it flew in November 1942

A Seafire L Mk IIC fitted with four-bladed propeller serving as a trials aircraft for 60-lb (27-kg) rocket projectiles. The strengthened undercarriage of the Mk IIC permitted reasonable external ordnance loads to be carried but no squadron used this type in the attack role

climb rate and low-altitude speed particularly leaving something to be desired. The Seafire Mk IIC was some 13-15 knots (24-27 km/h) slower than the Mk IB at all altitudes owing to the heavier "C" wing and the added weight of local strengthening coupled with the greater drag of the wing to which could be added that of the catapult spools. Prior to *Torch,* Seafire Mk IBs of No 801 Squadron flying from *Furious* and participating in Operation *Train* had failed to overhaul Ju 88s shadowing the force in which the carrier was included, and the German bomber had proved capable of outdistancing the Seafire Mk IICs of No 807 Squadron with some ease.

These frustrating encounters were primarily responsible for the decision to test the Merlin 32 in the Seafire, this differing from the Merlin 45 or 46 in having a cropped supercharger impeller, max boost being raised to +18 lb and max output rising by 430 hp at 3,000 ft (915 m) to 1,640 hp, full advantage of the increase being taken by means of a four-bladed propeller which replaced the standard three-blader. With this engine change, the fighter became the Seafire L Mk IIC and I was to become familiar with this variant when it first arrived in November 1942 at the Service Trials Unit at Arbroath, to where I had been posted on 12 September, after my brief sojourn aboard *Biter.*

The Seafire L Mk IIC was the most exciting aircraft that I had flown to that time. Its initial climb rate and acceleration were little short of magnificent, and at maximum boost it could maintain 4,600 ft/min (23,36 m/sec) up to 6,000 ft (1 830 m). The fully-supercharged Mk IIC took at least two minutes longer to attain 20,000 ft (6 095 m) and was markedly slower at all altitudes up to 25,000 ft (7 620 m). Later, some Seafire L Mk IICs were to have their wingtips clipped to boost roll rate and incidentally, add another four knots (7,5 km/h) to maximum speed, although these advantages were to be obtained at some cost in take-off run and service ceiling. Another result of the installation of the Merlin 32 was a quite dramatic reduction in take-off distance and, in fact, the L Mk IIC without flaps could get airborne in a shorter distance than the standard Mk IIC using full flap! My enthusiasm for this new Seafire variant was such that, one afternoon, in sheer exhilaration, I looped it around both spans of the Forth Bridge in succession — court-martial stuff nowadays but during a war nobody has the time to bother with such formalities.

On 15 December 1942, I took the Seafire L Mk IIC aboard HMS *Activity* and performed a series of 15 deck-landing and take-off tests to a limit run of 360 ft (110 m) which was reached in 25 knots (46 km/h) of wind at an all-up weight of 7,183 lb (3 258 kg). There was little doubt of the efficacy of

the Merlin 32-engined Seafire and as a result of these and other trials, the decision was taken to convert all Merlin 46-engined Seafire Mk IICs to L Mk IIC standard, the conversion programme commencing during the following March and the first unit selected to operate this type being No 807 Squadron.

It was about this time that I witnessed a very unusual incident at Machrihanish when the airfield was alerted that a Seafire being flown by Lt David Wilkinson (later to be killed in a flying accident) had a mechanic wrapped around its rear end! The mechanic, a rating appropriately enough named Overhead, had apparently been lying on the tail of the Seafire to hold it down while running up on the deck of a carrier in the Clyde area. Wilkinson had throttled back to let the mechanic off, but due to a misunderstanding, the mechanic had remained where he was and the Seafire had taken-off with him clinging on for dear life. The pilot could not account for the extraordinary tail-heaviness of his Seafire until he was alerted by radio of the situation. He promptly headed for Machrihanish at low level and slow cruise, the slipstream clamping the unfortunate mechanic in position. A straight-in approach to the runway and a wheeler landing to keep the tail up as long as possible, and the mechanic's ordeal was over — he suffered shock and the effects of cold, but was otherwise totally unhurt.

The further expansion of the Navy's Seafire component began in December 1942, when two more Fulmar squadrons Nos 808 and 887, converted to Mk IICs, and No 880 Squadron was spilt to provide the nucleus of another squadron, No 889. The equipment of these units, the provision of replacements for squadrons that had participated in *Torch* and the establishment of adequate reserves absorbed all production — by now primarily from Westland Aircraft, which had been allocated responsibility for Merlin-engined Seafire development, with Cunliffe-Owen as the company's sub-contractor — until the spring of 1943, when a further half-dozen squadrons were re-armed with the Seafire IIC (Nos 809, 879, 886, 894, 895 and 897) to bring the total complement of first-line Seafire squadrons to 14 and giving the Seafire the distinction of being the most numerous combat aircraft type in Royal Navy operational service.

Between 29 December 1942 and 3 January 1943, I had had the task of giving Seafire deck landing instruction to No 65(F) "East India" Squadron, RAF, and on 15 January, I was again despatched to *Activity* for a further series of 15 deck-landings and take-offs with a Mk IIC, this time to a limit run of 370 ft (113 m) reached in a 20 knots (37 km/h) wind. In the following month, a Mk IIC equipped with RATOG (rocket-assisted take-off gear) from the RAE Farnborough carried out trials aboard HMS *Illustrious* and, for comparison purposes, I joined in with an L Mk IIC, which, as usual, took-off like a scalded cat with 175 ft (53 m) in 30 knots (55 km/h) of wind. The RATOG trials were the direct result of the fact that, other than Fleet carriers of the *Illustrious* class, the Navy's carriers did not have catapults compatible with the spigots and spools of the Seafire, rockets thus being the only readily available means of shortening take-offs. Although the trials aboard *Illustrious* were pronounced successful and subsequent production Seafires were provided with RATOG attachment points, this rather dramatic means of reducing take-off distances possessed some obvious operational disadvantages and was never, in fact, to be used by Seafires during the war.

Soon afterwards, the Service Trials Unit moved from Arbroath to Crail on the Firth of Forth, and from here I was sent to give deck-landing instruction to Nos 411(F) and 416(F) squadrons at Kenley, and No 402(F) Squadron at Digby, all Royal Canadian Air Force units. There was an incidental bonus for me at Kenley as the extroverted Canadians would only agree to a session of ADDLs if I, in turn, agreed to accompany them on a fighter sweep over France, and so a most illicit swop system was initiated with me as an admittedly willing victim.

In June 1943, the Navy's latest carrier, HMS *Indomitable,* having been completed with an enlarged forward lift, embarked no fewer than 40 Seafire Mk IICs and L Mk IICs, but there was no gainsaying that the lack of wing folding had been a serious nuisance as, apart from *Argus* and *Furious*, no Royal Navy carrier had previously possessed elevators large enough to enable them to strike down their Seafires undismantled. The problem had, of course, been seen from the outset and work had been proceeding apace on providing the Seafire with a wing fold system. At first sight, the folding of such a thin wing appeared to present virtually insoluble problems if loss of stiffness and excessive weight were to be avoided, but with commendable speed. Supermarine had devised a system of two straight fore and aft folds, a break being introduced at the outer wheel well extremities from which the wing hinged upward manually, a second fold at the wingtip joint turning downward to afford an acceptable stowage height. It was ascertained that at least 90 per cent of the "C" wing's torsional rigidity factor could be maintained

and in the event, the weight penalty was restricted to 125 lb (56,7 kg).

The prototype conversion (MA970) — actually an adaptation of Supermarine's first production Seafire Mk IIC — commenced its test programme mid-November 1942, and came to us at Crail in June 1943, barely three months before Westland was due to initiate production deliveries as the Seafire Mk III, and at the Service Trials Unit we were more concerned with its deck handling rather than its flight characteristics, although I carried out one check flight with the prototype on 16 June. In fact, the production Seafire Mk III differed from preceding versions in one respect other than its folding wing; it had a Merlin 55 engine with automatic boost control and barometrically-governed full throttle height which relieved the pilot of the need to use his judgement in order to get the most out of his engine. The Merlin 55 had the same combat rating of 1,415 hp at 11,000 ft (3 350 m) as the earlier Merlin 45 of the Mk IIC but drove a similar four-bladed propeller to that of the L Mk IIC.

The Seafire Mk III displayed almost identical handling qualities to those of the Mk IIC but it was 17 knots (32 km/h) faster at all altitudes. Deliveries were to begin to No 894 Squadron late in November 1943, but by that time production was already to have given place to that of the L Mk III, this having a low-altitude Merlin 55M with a cropped supercharger impeller like that of the Merlin 32, the collector pipes being supplanted by individual exhaust stacks which both reduced weight and provided a modicum of thrust. The Seafire L Mk III, which was to be built in larger numbers than any other Seafire variant, began to reach the squadrons in quantity during the spring of 1944.

The month of July 1943 saw further operational deployment of Seafires in support of a major Allied assault, the newly-commissioned *Indomitable* carrying what was at that time the largest fighter complement ever embarked by any Royal Navy carrier, comprising the Seafire L Mk IICs of No 807 Squadron and the Mk IICs of Nos 880 and 899 squadrons, intended as a major part of the fighter cover for Force H mounting Operation *Husky,* the invasion of Sicily launched on 10 July. For me, the month involved intensive Seafire development flying and culminated in instructions to undertake a series of landings on escort carriers to ascertain the minimum acceptable wind speed at which a Seafire could be

A Seafire L Mk IIC of No 899 Squadron taking-off from HMS Hunter during the Salerno Bay operations in September 1943. Known as Operation Avalanche, the Salerno Bay operations were provided with air cover almost exclusively by Seafires flying from five escort carriers

(Above) Seafire L Mk IICs of Nos 879 and 886 squadrons flying off HMS Attacker during the opening phase of the Salerno Bay operations. Nine squadrons and two flights of Seafires totalling 106 aircraft participated in this action but deck-landing attrition proved unacceptably high.

operated, bearing in mind, so my instructions informed me, that RAF pilots might also have to make landings with "hooked" Spitfires and without the benefit of previous deck-landing experience.

Thus, on 3 August, I completed 10 low-wind-speed landing aboard HMS *Fencer* and, on 11 August, 20 similar landings aboard HMS *Tracker,* rounding these off on 14 August with another five landings on HMS *Pretoria Castle,* all with a Seafire Mk IB and without any untoward problems. The next month, the real purpose behind these trials emerged when Operation *Avalanche* was mounted on the morning of the 9th to put Allied forces ashore in the Bay of Salerno, the bulk of the air cover being provided by Seafire L Mk IICs from no fewer than five escort carriers, which, between them, carried nine squadrons and two flights with 106 aircraft. The carriers were the *Attacker* (Nos 879 and 886 squadrons), the *Battler* (Nos 807 and 808 squadrons), the *Hunter* (No 899 Squadron and No 834 Flight), the *Stalker* (No 880 Squadron and No 833 Flight) and the *Unicorn* (Nos 809, 887 and 897 squadrons). The weather was calm with very little wind and the escort carriers were operating at windspeeds which were virtually those created by their own speed of about 18 knots (33 km/h). Small wonder that the Admiralty had been anxious about low-wind-speed landings. As it was, there were a large number of "prangs" as hooks pulled out or pilots missed the wires and hurtled into crash barriers, no fewer than 42 Seafires being written off.

The unexpectedly high incidence of deck-landing accidents during the first day of *Avalanche* — Seafire availability dropping by something of the order of 38 per cent by the second day as a result — was largely responsible for the fact that the escort carriers had only 39 serviceable Seafires at dawn on D-Day plus Two! The problem was promptly dumped back in our laps for further solution, one result being that, on 30 September, I carried out 15 landings into the arrester wires on the dummy deck at Arbroath while photos were taken of each stage of each landing. These tests led to some hook-strengthening modifications and I was sent off on 26 November with a Seafire L Mk IIC with strengthened hook for landing trials aboard HMS *Ravager*.

On my way to *Ravager* from Arbroath, I landed at Abbotsinch to refuel. On take-off the throttle jammed at full power and since Abbotsinch was in a built-up area, I headed for Ayr airfield, reaching it in four minutes flat like a bat out of hell,

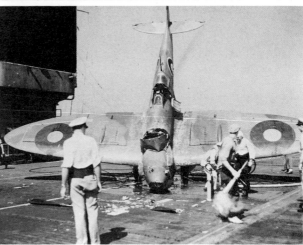

The Salerno operations were noteworthy for the high incidence of Seafire deck landing accidents, the photographs above and below recording accidents aboard HMS Attacker. Seafire availability had dropped by some 38 per cent by the second day of the operations

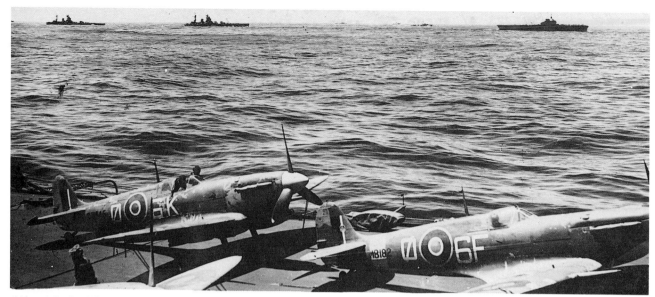

(Above) Seafire Mk IICs of No 885 Squadron (MB182 in foreground) aboard HMS Formidable in July 1943 as part of Force H mounting the invasion of Sicily, and (immediately below left) Seafire Mk IIC of No 885 Squadron on the deck of HMS Formidable during Operation Torch. Flown by S/Lt J. D. Buchanan, this aircraft, together with MB146 flown by S/Lt A. S. Long, destroyed a Martin 167 over Mers el Khebir on 8 November 1942

cutting the magneto switches and gliding in. The fault was soon cured and I resumed the flight to the carrier. I made 10 landings on *Ravager*, starting at 17 knots (31,5 km/h) windspeed and reducing ship's speed by one knot per landing until the propeller tips clipped the deck at a recorded retardation of 2·03 g's. I was flown ashore to pick up a replacement L Mk IIC, and the next day was back aboard *Ravager*. Over the course of two days, I carried out a further 30 landings at various low windspeeds and combinations of arrester wire settings. At first, the batsman gave me three successive wave-off's so I landed any way, and after a parley among the trials team, it was decided that would be fairer to remove the batsman, who was not used to the Seafire, to my crabbed approaches, or to the fast approach speeds that we were recording.

These trials were intended to produce answers which were required before the mounting of Operation *Dragoon*, the invasion of the South of France in which it was hoped that

(Immediately left and above) A Seafire L Mk IIC (MB293) seen with small practice bombs on a centreline rack for trials purposes, this aircraft later going to No 879 Squadron aboard HMS Attacker. (Below) An early Westland-built Seafire Mk III (LR785) with Merlin 50A engine and three-bladed propeller

Seafires launched from escort carriers would once again play a major rôle. The *Avalanche* operation had undoubtedly tarnished the Seafire's reputation and the attrition that it had suffered was totally unacceptable. Although we believed that we had resolved the hardware problems reasonably satisfactorily, the Fifth Sea Lord, Rear-Admiral D W Boyd, now wanted to know something of the pilot problems asociated with the Seafire. He felt that I was too experienced in deck-landings to give him the answers, so he made Jeffrey Quill, the most experienced Spitfire pilot in the UK, an RNVR Lieutenant-Commander in the Fleet Air Arm and sent him deck landing in the Seafire with a directive to report back on his experiences.

Jeffrey Quill was an inspired choice as he had the analytical mind of a superb test pilot trained to find answers to any flight problems. He submitted his report on 29 February 1944, and it made four main observations: (1) Pilots had to be trained to employ a curved approach to the deck as the crabbed approach was acceptable only for skilled and experienced pilots; (2) multi-ejector type exhaust manifolds should be fitted to all Seafires and the pilots trained to land with their heads out of the cockpit and looking along the portside of the engine cowling; (3) the Seafire had inherent poor speed controllability, and (4) the Seafire lacked the necessary robustness for carrier landings, but the fitting of a sting-type hook would probably reduce the accident rate.

This report was not entirely encouraging and the sour reputation that the Seafire was acquiring was in no way relieved by common knowledge of the greater sturdiness, better endurance and markedly superior deck-landing and ditching qualities offered by the new Grumman Hellcat. Furthermore, the less tractable side of the Seafire's nature

(Above) A Westland-built Seafire Mk III (NF545) with standard Merlin 55 engine and four-bladed propeller. This aircraft was later assigned to No 899 Squadron. The general arrangement drawing (right) depicts the Seafire Mk III

Supermarine Seafire L Mk III Specification
Power Plant: One Rolls-Royce Merlin 55M twelve-cylinder 60 deg Vee liquid-cooled engine rated at 1,600 hp at 3,000 rpm for take-off and military power of 1,585 hp at 3,000 rpm at 2,750 ft (840 m) driving Rotol four-bladed constant-speed propeller. Internal fuel capacity, 85 Imp gal (386,4 l), plus jettisonable 30 Imp gal (136 l), 45 Imp gal (204,5 l) or 90 Imp gal (409 l) tank.
Performance: ((At 6,784 lb/3 077 kg) Max speed, 331 mph (533 km/h) at sea level, 348 mph (560 km/h) at 6,000 ft (1 830 m), 331 mph (533 km/h) at 19,000 ft (5 790 m); normal range cruise, 172 mph (277 km/h); max range (with 90 Imp gal/409 l drop tank), 513 mls (825 km); radius of action (with 45 Imp gal/204,5 l drop tank), 140 mls (225 km), (with 90 Imp gal/409 l drop tank), 200 mls (322 km); patrol endurance (time on station), 2·05 hr with 45 Imp gal/204,5 l tank, 3·10 hr with 90 Imp gal/409 l tank; max initial climb, 4,160 ft/min (21,13 m/sec); time to 5,000 ft (1 525 m), 1·9 min; service ceiling, 24,000 ft (7 315 m).
Weight: Empty equipped, 6,204 lb (2 814 kg); loaded (clean), 6,784 lb (3 077 kg); max take-off, 7,640 lb (3 465 kg).
Dimensions: Span, 36 ft 10 in (11,23 m); length, 30 ft 2½ in (9,21 m); height (propeller vertical, tail down), 13 ft 0 in (3,96 m); wing area, 242 sq ft (22,48 m²).
Armament: Four 0·303-in (7,7-mm) Browning machine guns with 350 rpg and two 20-mm Hispano cannon with 120 rpg, plus one 500-lb (226,8-kg) bomb or (late production) four 60-lb (27-kg) rocket projectiles on Mk VIII launchers.

was prone to exaggeration and the result was that many pilots were unduly apprehensive of deck-landing this fighter.

By the time Jeffrey Quill's report was rendered, I had become Chief Naval Test Pilot at RAE Farnborough, my predecessor having been killed landing a Seafire aboard a carrier at the beginning of 1944, and I was now to be heavily committed to test programmes involving the second-generation Griffon-engined developments of this shipboard fighter. However, these were to be interspersed with trials involving the earlier Merlin-engined models, such as a new series of RATOG tests with a Seafire L Mk IIC, these being a continuation of the earlier trials at the RAE and aboard *Illustrious,* and directly connected with the forthcoming Operation *Dragoon.*

For rocket-assisted take-offs, it was necessary to set the elevator trimmer one division more nose up than for normal take-off in order to counteract the nose-down thrust produced by the rockets on firing. Eighteen degrees of flap was set by getting the groundcrew to insert wedges when the flaps were down, these being held secure once the flaps were raised. The wooden wedges had been found necessary as the Seafire's flaps could be only fully lowered or fully housed and this improvisation produced a take-off setting, the wedges being discarded once the Seafire was airborne by selecting flaps down, the wedges falling away and the flaps then being fully raised. The throttle friction nut had to be screwed up tightly to counteract acceleration effect, as the firing button was depressed on the throttle handgrip. On receiving the take-off signal, the pilot turned the firing button to FIRE, ran up fully on the brakes and applied rudder to counteract swing as the brakes were released.

On drawing abeam of the firing-point flag, the firing button

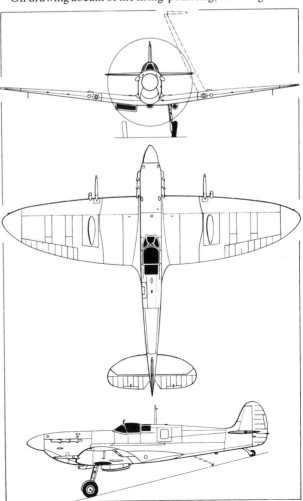

Supermarine Seafire Mk XV/XVII Cockpit Instrumentation Key

1 Power failure warning light
2 Switch panel (from front: cine-camera master switch, pressure head heater switch, navigation lights switch)
3 Radiator ground test pushbutton
4 Oil dilution pushbutton
5 Rudder trimming tab handwheel
6 Elevator trimming tab handwheel
7 Carburettor air intake filter control
8 Fuel transfer selector cock
9 Fuel tank pressure cock
10 Friction damper
11 Throttle control lever
12 Crowbar stowage clip
13 Two-position door catch lever
14 Camera switch
15 Bomb selector switch
16 Bomb distributor switch
17 Bomb fusing switch
18 Supercharger control
19 Propeller speed control lever

20 Pneumatic pressure gauge
21 Elevator tab indicator
22 Tailwheel indicator light
23 Arrester hook indicator light
24 Electrical master switch
25 Ignition switches
26 Floodlight
27 Radio pushbutton controller
28 Undercarriage indicator
29 Oxygen supply regulator/contents gauge
30 Flap control
31 Gyro gunsight ON/OFF switch
32 Gunsight mounting bar
33 Dimmer switch
34 Airspeed indicator
35 Artificial horizon
36 Rate of climb/descent indicator
37 Altimeter
38 Gun-firing and bomb-release pushbutton
39 Brake lever
40 Direction indicator

41 Turning indicator
42 Cine-camera pushbutton
43 Compass deviation card holder (with jettison tank)
44 Compass deviation card holder (without jettison tank)
45 Cockpit floodlight switches (obscured by control grip)
46 Starter pushbutton
47 Fuel cock control
48 Control column
49 Rudder pedals
50 Rudder pedal leg-reach adjustment starwheels
51 Pilot's seat
52 Drop tank jettison control grip
53 Drop tank ON/OFF cock
54 Cylinder priming pump
55 Starter breach re-indexing control
56 Slow-running cut-out control
57 Fuel low-level warning light
58 Fuel contents dual gague
59 Oil pressure gauge
60 Oil temperature gauge

61 Coolant temperature gauge
62 Boost gauge
63 Fuel pressure warning light
64 Engine speed indicator
65 Cockpit ventilation control
66 Gunsight spare lamp stowage
67 Signalling switchbox
68 Gyro gunsight selector switch
69 R.1147 controller
70 R.1147 wave tuner
71 Flap emergency lowering CO_2 cylinder and lever
72 Data plate
73 Harness control
74 Undercarriage emergency lowering CO_2 cylinder and lever
75 IFF distress switch
76 IFF main switch
77 IFF pushbutton (2)
78 Undercarriage selector lever
79 Windscreen de-icing cock
80 Windscreen de-icing needle valve
81 Windscreen de-icing pump

was depressed and the torque swing then tended to damp out. The Seafire had to be held in the three-point attitude during the entire take-off run if full benefit was to be obtained from the thrust line of the rockets. Ideally, the rockets died just after the Seafire became airborne, the undercarriage then being retracted and the expended RATOG units being jettisoned while airspeed was still low. Asymmetric rocket failures were explored and, for realism, I was not informed as to which side the rocket had been disconnected. Since the Seafire had only one rocket on each side the effect was minimal. Night take-offs were also made, and these necessitated the immediate transfer of attention to the blind-flying instruments as the

rockets were fired in order to avoid risk of momentary blindness as a result of rocket glare. The pilots of aircraft on a carrier deck ranged aft of the Seafire taking-off had to close their eyes for about five seconds as soon as they saw it signalled off as otherwise the flash dazzled them for quite a while.

By mid-summer of 1944, the tempo of Griffon-engined Seafire development was accelerating, but I still had occasion to fly its Merlin-engined predecessor from time to time. One of the tasks that I had enjoyed most from the outset of my tenure at the RAE was being launched in a Seafire from the 20-ft (6,1-m) high rocket-powered catapult, usually to amuse — or alarm — visiting dignitaries. On 10 July, I was giving such a demonstration in my trusty Seafire L Mk IIC, which had been loaded on the heavy metal cradle by means of four metal spools attached to the aircraft and engaging claws on the cradle legs. After a very short run under the power of the battery of rockets attached to the bottom rear of the cradle, two long, pointed prongs on the front of the cradle theoretically engaged two tubes filled with water and sealed by fibre discs, penetration of the discs allowing the prongs to expel the water under pressure and bring the cradle to a standstill within its own length, the aircraft automatically disengaging for free flight. On this particular occasion, someone had forgotten to fill the water tubes, and with a rending crash of metal, I left the end of the catapult with the cradle still firmly attached to my Seafire, which, understandably, was descending fast under all that extra weight. By extraordinary luck, the cradle and my Seafire parted company at the moment critique!

The Seafire Mk III had by now entered service, although the only unit operating this more extensively navalised Merlin-engined model outside the United Kingdom was No 889 Squadron, which was serving aboard the escort carrier HMS *Atheling* in the Indian Ocean, and which, at this time, was endeavouring to distract Japanese attention from the American landings in the Marianas in concert with *Illustrious,* the fighter element aboard which comprised Corsairs. It was on this side of the world that the Seafire was to see most action, although it was to fail to eradicate the unfavourable impression that it had created during *Avalanche* and attrition resulting from landing accidents remained high, despite the growing experience of its pilots. Indeed, those that had doubted the wisdom of adapting the Spitfire for shipboard operations from the outset saw more than fulfilled many of their misgivings concerning the structural integrity of this fighter operating in a scenario for which it had not been designed.

The potential of the Griffon-engined Spitfire had meanwhile impressed their Lordships of the Admiralty sufficiently for them to have expressed keen interest in a similarly-powered Seafire, and on 21 February 1943, Jeffrey Quill had dropped in to Arbroath in a Griffon-engined Spitfire Mk XII, staying for a couple of days of deck landing instruction on our dummy deck which had been laid out with arrester wires on a short runway. I had been moved on to this more powerful Spitfire at once and if I had thought flying the Seafire L Mk

IIC to be an exhilarating experience, it had been as nothing compared with this; the throaty growl of the Griffon III engine, the superlative low-level speed and the very fine roll rate, owing much to its clipped wings, combined to produce sheer magic. I had taken this beauty aboard HMS *Indomitable* on 9 March, and had completed the routine series of 15 deck landings with no trouble at all.

One year and five weeks later, on the afternoon of 26 March 1944, I landed the first prototype (NS487) of the Griffon-engined Seafire aboard HMS *Indefatigable* for the first time — I had landed on a Mosquito during the course of the morning of the same day, such being the panic of that period of the war. This, the Seafire Mk XV, which had been evolved to Specification N.4/43 and the mark number of which reflected an attempt on the part of officialdom to introduce some logic into the designating of members of the closely related Spitfire and Seafire lines of development, its immediate predecessor having been the Spitfire Mk XIV was something of a mongrel if such may be said of any member of so thoroughbred a family

The Seafire Mk XV utilised the L Mk III airframe to which had been added the wing root fuel tanks of the Spitfire Mk IX, and the retractable tailwheel and enlarged vertical surfaces of the Spitfire Mk VIII. This amalgam had been mated with a naval version of the Griffon engine, the Mk VI, offering combat ratings of 1,815 hp at 4,500 ft (1 370 m) and 1,730 hp at 13,000 ft (3,960 m) at 2,740 rpm and with +15 lb boost. The fuel tankage had been rearranged to produce a slight gain in internal capacity at 100 Imp gal (454,6 l), and the heavier — and rather thirstier — engine permitted provision of a weightier, more highly-stressed hook, though still

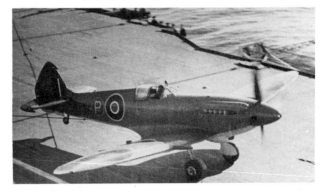

(Below) The first prototype of the Griffon-engined Seafire Mk XV (NS487), this having a Seafire L Mk III airframe which had been mated with the wing root fuel tanks of the Spitfire Mk IX, the enlarged vertical tail surfaces of the Spitfire Mk VIII and a Griffon VI engine. (Above right) NS487 being landed aboard HMS Indefatigable by the author for the first time on 26 March 1944

Supermarine Seafire XVII Cutaway Drawing Key

1 Starboard wingtip
2 Navigation light
3 Starboard aileron
4 Browning 0·303-in (7,7-mm) machine guns
5 Machine gun ports (patched)
6 Ammunition boxes (350 rounds per gun)
7 Aileron control rod
8 Bellcrank control hinge
9 Starboard wing folded position
10 Jury strut
11 Aileron cables
12 Cannon ammunition box, 120 rounds
13 Starboard 20-mm Hispano cannon
14 Ammunition feed drum
15 Cannon barrel

16 Starboard leading edge fuel tank (9·75 Imp gal/44 l capacity)
17 Cannon barrel support fairing
18 Engine cowling fairing
19 Spinner
20 Rotol four-bladed constant-speed propeller
21 Propeller hub mechanism
22 Spinner backplate
23 Coolant system header tank
24 Coolant filler cap
25 Rolls-Royce Griffon VI engine
26 Exhaust stubs
27 Front engine mounting
28 Engine bottom cowling
29 Radio suppressor
30 Engine bearer

31 Coolant pipes
32 Carburettor air intake
33 Engine bearer lower strut
34 Main spar stub attachment
35 Engine bearer attachment
36 Fireproof bulkhead
37 Engine accessories
38 Hydraulic reservoir
39 Oil tank (8 Imp gal/36 l capacity)
40 Oil tank filler cap
41 Top main fuel tank (32·5 Imp gal/148 l capacity)
42 Fuel filler cap
43 Instrument panel
44 Compass mounting
45 Fuel tank/longeron attachment fittings
46 Bottom main fuel tank (48 Imp gal/218 l capacity)
47 Rudder pedal bar
48 Sloping fuel tank bulkhead
49 Fuel cock control

50 Control column hand grip
51 Engine throttle and propeller controls
52 Radio controller
53 Bullet proof windscreen
54 Gyro gunsight

55 Windscreen side panels
56 Port wing folded position
57 Folding wing tips
58 Pitot tube
59 Spent cartridge case ejector chute
60 Sliding bubble-type canopy
61 Headrest
62 Head armour plate
63 Pilot's seat
64 Safety harness
65 Side entry hatch
66 Back armour
67 Seat support frame
68 Air bottles
69 Sliding canopy rails
70 T.R.5043 radio transmitter/receiver
71 Radio rack

72 Fuselage main longeron
73 Radio access hatch
74 Whip aerial
75 Fuselage skin plating
76 Fin root fairing

77 Starboard tailplane
78 Starboard elevator
79 Fin front spar
80 Tailfin construction
81 Stern post

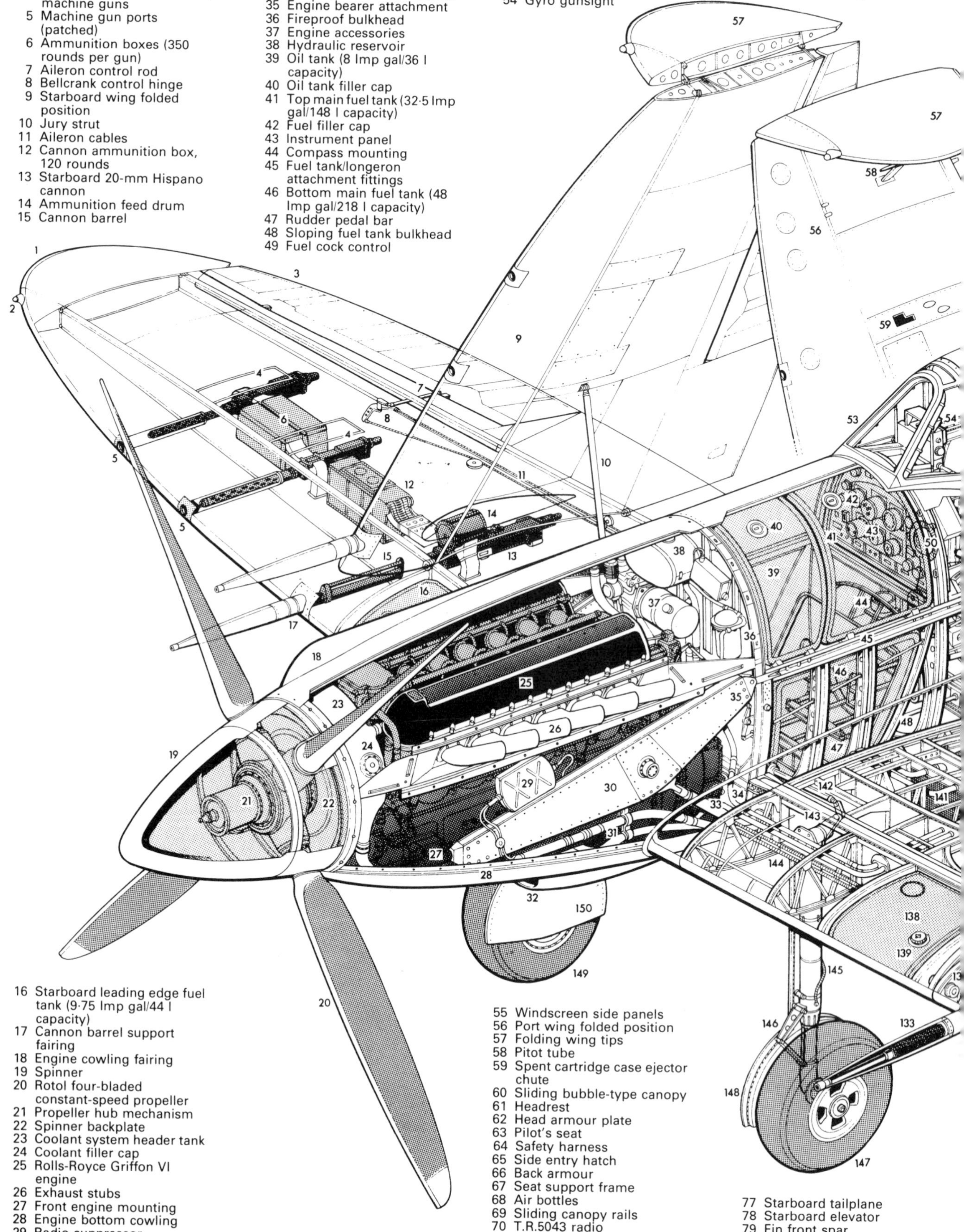

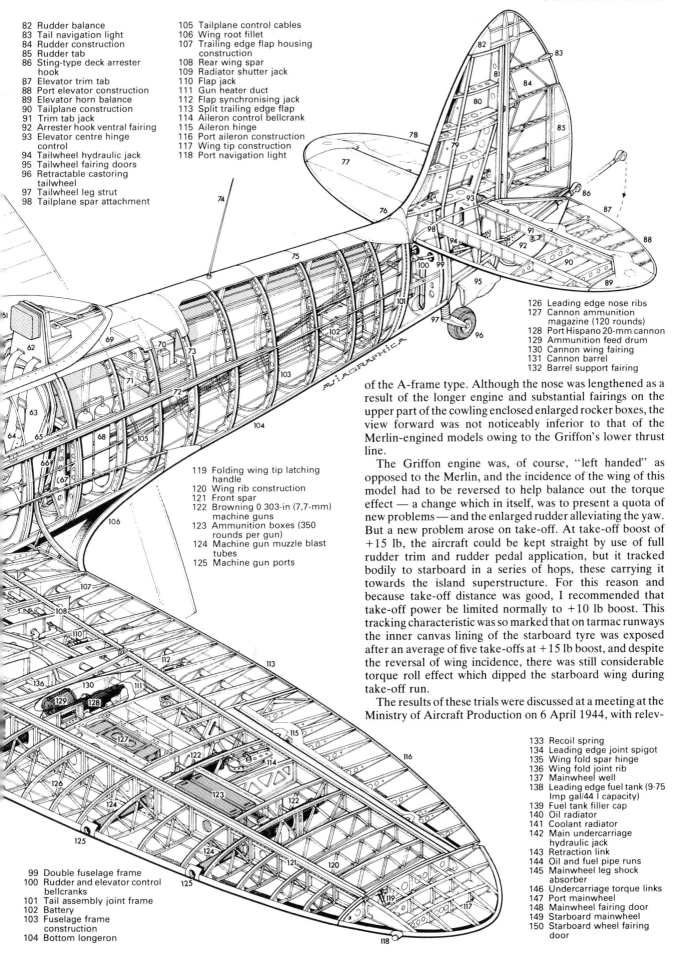

82 Rudder balance
83 Tail navigation light
84 Rudder construction
85 Rudder tab
86 Sting-type deck arrester hook
87 Elevator trim tab
88 Port elevator construction
89 Elevator horn balance
90 Tailplane construction
91 Trim tab jack
92 Arrester hook ventral fairing
93 Elevator centre hinge control
94 Tailwheel hydraulic jack
95 Tailwheel fairing doors
96 Retractable castoring tailwheel
97 Tailwheel leg strut
98 Tailplane spar attachment

105 Tailplane control cables
106 Wing root fillet
107 Trailing edge flap housing construction
108 Rear wing spar
109 Radiator shutter jack
110 Flap jack
111 Gun heater duct
112 Flap synchronising jack
113 Split trailing edge flap
114 Aileron control bellcrank
115 Aileron hinge
116 Port aileron construction
117 Wing tip construction
118 Port navigation light

119 Folding wing tip latching handle
120 Wing rib construction
121 Front spar
122 Browning 0 303-in (7,7-mm) machine guns
123 Ammunition boxes (350 rounds per gun)
124 Machine gun muzzle blast tubes
125 Machine gun ports

126 Leading edge nose ribs
127 Cannon ammunition magazine (120 rounds)
128 Port Hispano 20-mm cannon
129 Ammunition feed drum
130 Cannon wing fairing
131 Cannon barrel
132 Barrel support fairing

99 Double fuselage frame
100 Rudder and elevator control bellcranks
101 Tail assembly joint frame
102 Battery
103 Fuselage frame construction
104 Bottom longeron

of the A-frame type. Although the nose was lengthened as a result of the longer engine and substantial fairings on the upper part of the cowling enclosed enlarged rocker boxes, the view forward was not noticeably inferior to that of the Merlin-engined models owing to the Griffon's lower thrust line.

The Griffon engine was, of course, "left handed" as opposed to the Merlin, and the incidence of the wing of this model had to be reversed to help balance out the torque effect — a change which in itself, was to present a quota of new problems — and the enlarged rudder alleviating the yaw. But a new problem arose on take-off. At take-off boost of +15 lb, the aircraft could be kept straight by use of full rudder trim and rudder pedal application, but it tracked bodily to starboard in a series of hops, these carrying it towards the island superstructure. For this reason and because take-off distance was good, I recommended that take-off power be limited normally to +10 lb boost. This tracking characteristic was so marked that on tarmac runways the inner canvas lining of the starboard tyre was exposed after an average of five take-offs at +15 lb boost, and despite the reversal of wing incidence, there was still considerable torque roll effect which dipped the starboard wing during take-off run.

The results of these trials were discussed at a meeting at the Ministry of Aircraft Production on 6 April 1944, with relev-

133 Recoil spring
134 Leading edge joint spigot
135 Wing fold spar hinge
136 Wing fold joint rib
137 Mainwheel well
138 Leading edge fuel tank (9·75 Imp gal/44 l capacity)
139 Fuel tank filler cap
140 Oil radiator
141 Coolant radiator
142 Main undercarriage hydraulic jack
143 Retraction link
144 Oil and fuel pipe runs
145 Mainwheel leg shock absorber
146 Undercarriage torque links
147 Port mainwheel
148 Mainwheel fairing door
149 Starboard mainwheel
150 Starboard wheel fairing door

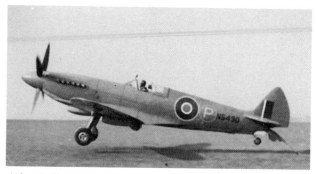

(Above) The second prototype Seafire Mk XV (NS490) with new hook of 'sting' type photographed during trials at High Post, and (below) NS490 being landed aboard HMS Pretoria Castle by the author on 20 November 1944

ance to the possible conversion of the Spitfire Mk 21 for naval use, and it was agreed that a contra-rotating propeller should be introduced at the earliest opportunity to eliminate the tracking, while throttle travel should be increased to afford coarser engine control.

A further stage in the refinement of the Seafire Mk XV was reached a month later, on 12 May, when I made the first tail-down catapult launch with the first prototype. The tail-down launching system meant that we could do away with the ugly and weighty catapult spools, which protruded from the flanks of the aircraft like knobs form the neck of Frankenstein's monster, and replace them with a single hook under the centre section and a holdback point at the tail. It offered the added advantage that the aircraft took-off in optimum three-point attitude as opposed to an attitude parallel to that of the line of flight.

While the strengthened A-frame hook was to be retained for the first few hundred production Seafire Mk XVs in the event, the second prototype (NS490), which arrived at the RAE Farnborough during July, was fitted with a new hook of "sting" type which lay horizontally beneath the base of the rudder and moved aft when lowered before adopting the trailing position. The hook was now fitted in the optimum position, permitting a marked increase in the range of aircraft attitude when deck landing, and shortly after the arrival of NS490 at Farnborough, I took NS487 — by now also fitted with a "sting" type hook — aboard HMS *Implacable*. On 28 August, I performed a series of 15 deck landings, by this time the aircraft having been fitted with a new throttle control box which had the quadrant increased by 80 per cent so that the greater travel reduced the sensitivity of power increase with throttle movement. The throttle was also gated TAKE-OFF (+10 lb boost) and COMBAT (+15 lb boost) as recommended at the MAP meeting in the previous April.

With its increased (11 per cent) horn balance on the elevators, which improved speed control on the approach, and the markedly enhanced safety factor of the "sting" hook, we were getting much nearer in our quest for a Seafire with reasonably good deck landing characteristics. I felt that the

hook could be lengthened further with benefit, but the Seafire was, like its land-based stablemate, a very clean aircraft and lack of drag allowed it to float over the arrester wires if approach speed was imprecise. I suggested, therefore, that, in addition to lengthening the hook, a five-bladed propeller be adopted to produce more braking effect on cutting the throttle. Of course, the Seafire would never have been remotely acceptable for deck landing but for its innocuous stalling characteristics. For example, the Seafire Mk XV all-down stall occurred at 57 knots (106 km/h) with only a gentle drop of the nose preceded by mild buffeting and a slight twitch on the ailerons.

In mid-October, I was aboard *Pretoria Castle* with two of the Seafire Mk XV prototypes, one with a lengthened "sting" hook and the other with the earlier A-frame hook but with an extra fine pitch propeller to assist braking in the landing configuration by presenting more of a "disc". The longer hook was a great success and the finer-pitch propeller partially successful. A month later, I took three Seafire Mk XVs aboard *Pretoria Castle,* each embodying some modifications previously advocated. The second prototype (NS490) had the "sting" hook and fined-off propeller (the fine pitch stop being advanced two degrees), the fourth prototype (PK240) retained the A-frame hook but had been fitted with a five-bladed propeller, and a production example (SR448) — actually the third off the Westland line — mated A-frame hook and fined-off propeller with controllable radiator flaps and stronger wheels and tyres. These trials really finalised the "sting" hook as standard for all future Seafires, together with the increased throttle quadrant as fitted to all the trials aircraft and the two-deg fine pitch stop, the five-bladed propeller eventually being adopted for the somewhat abortive Seafire Mk 45.

While production tempo of the Seafire Mk XV was building up, the fighter had been going through yet further stages in its evolution which was, of course, now firmly wedded to the Griffon engine, although no Seafires with this power plant were destined to see service in World War II. Westland had been busily refining the basic Mk XV, the company's attention being directed primarily towards further improvements to the undercarriage, enhanced all-round pilot vision and increased internal fuel capacity. The third prototype Seafire Mk XV (NS493) had been used by Westland to test various modifications, the most obvious being the cutting down of the aft fuselage decking to the level of the upper longerons and the application of a frameless "bubble" canopy, and this change was to be applied to the final 30 Mk XVs off the assembly line and to be standardised for the next variant, the Seafire Mk XVII.

The Seafire Mk XVII was more noteworthy, however, for the markedly superior undercarriage that it was eventually to introduce. In November 1945, before the application of the new undercarriage, I took the Mk XVII through its RATOG proofing tests. Like the Mk XV, this aircraft tracked bodily to starboard, and I suspected that this characteristic would become heavily accentuated when asymmetric firing was attempted with the starboard rocket failed. Indeed, I was convinced that under such circumstances a collision with the carrier's island structure would be inevitable. In the following March, I was to have the opportunity to confirm my conviction concerning the behaviour of the Seafire Mk XVII, and, for that matter, the Mk XV, under conditions of asymmetric RATOG firing and, as a result, these "first generation" Griffon-engined Seafires were never to use RATOG at sea unless ranged forward of the first crash barrier position on the carrier flight deck.

Subsequently, in January 1946, the first Seafire Mk XVII fitted with the long-stroke undercarriage was to come to the RAE for checking out before application of this new gear on the production line. All previous Seafires had been fitted with undercarriages that, apart from minor beefing up, were essentially similar to that of the Spitfire Mk VC, which was, of course, almost 1,700 lb (770 kg) lighter than the Seafire Mk XV. The new undercarriage was markedly stronger and in consequence, less prone to breaking under the strain of Seafire weights, but, more important, the oleo stroke had been lengthened. This not only provided greater propeller clearance on the deck and thus markedly reduced the Seafire's propensity to "peck" — the blade tips hitting the deck during arresting; it offered a lower rebound ratio which was a boon for deck landing as it absorbed the bounce that could carry Seafires fitted with the earlier undercarriage over the arrester wires and into the crash barrier.

As previously mentioned, another feature of the (later) production Seafire Mk XVII was an increase in its potential internal fuel capacity. The reduction in the weight aft resulting from the lowered rear decking had permitted the installation of a 33 Imp gal (150 l) fuel tank behind the cockpit, adding some 60 miles (96 km) to the radius of action, and this tank could be replaced by a pair of F 24 cameras, a facility not available in the Mk XV. A futher change in the fuel system of the Mk XVII was the introduction of fuel lines in the mainplanes which enabled 22·5 Imp gal (102 l) jettisonable slipper-type tanks to be fitted under the outer mainplanes. Known as "combat tanks", these could be retained for all manoeuvres and their application was a bonus stemming from the beefed-up mainspar necessitated by the new undercarriage. The ability to carry heavier underwing loads — the "combat tanks" could be replaced by 250-lb (113,4-kg) bombs or twice as many rocket projectiles as could be toted before — certainly enhanced the tactical flexibility of the Seafire Mk XVII, but it was viewed somewhat as an interim model pending availability of a Seafire fitted with a two-stage Griffon 60-series engine.

Specification N.7/44 had earlier been formulated for a Seafire equivalent to the Spitfire Mk 21 which mated wings that were entirely new in both plan and profile with the new two stage Griffon. Assigned the designation Seafire Mk 45, a prototype (TM379) was produced by the adaptation of a standard Spitfire Mk 21, the only concession to its nautical rôle consisting of modified mainwheel fairing plates to increase arrester wire clearance, the installation of naval R/T and the application of "sting" type hook and slinging points. In mid-November 1944, TM379 had come to Farnborough for arresting proofing. This had gone splendidly and on the

23rd of that month, I had taken the Griffon 61-powered aeroplane aboard *Pretoria Castle* for its initial deck trials, landing on at 9,250 lb (4 196 kg), some 1,200 lb (544 kg) more than the clean loaded weight of the Seafire Mk XVII.

I found the Seafire Mk 45 prototype easier to deck land than, say, the Mk XV, but forward view had deteriorated slightly and aileron control was less effective. Approach speed was 75 knots (139 km/h) and the stalling characteristics had certainly worsened, there being virtually no warning before a wing dropped and the all-down stall occurring at 58 knots (107 km/h). The performance increase with the two-stage Griffon was, of course, significant — one of the 50 production examples later built (LA494) was to attain the equivalent of Mach = 0·88 in a dive at 35,000 ft (10 670 m) a year or so later — and a very high roll rate was possible, but this improved performance had been achieved at some cost to handling. Substantial trim changes were demanded with variations of power and the very much greater output of the two-stage engine combined with the five-bladed propeller to produce an unpleasant swinging tendency during take-off. In fact, the throttle had to be advanced somewhat gingerly and then no more than +7 lb of boost could be used, and even with full left rudder a predilection for swinging to starboard and crabbing remained.

Whereas the Seafire Mk XVII had been considered somewhat in the light of an interim model pending introduction of the two-stage Griffon, so the Mk 45 was viewed as a development aircraft rather than as a potential embarked operational fighter pending availability of the six-bladed contra-prop intended for application to the ultimate Seafire development. Thus, only 50 Seafire Mk 45s were built, these being produced at Castle Bromwich during the latter part of 1945, and subsequently giving the maintenance people

(Above right and below) The third prototype Seafire Mk XV (NS493) utilised by Westland to test various modifications, the most obvious being a cut-down rear fuselage and 'bubble' type cockpit canopy, a change applied to the final 30 Mk XVs off the assembly line and standardised for the Mk XVII

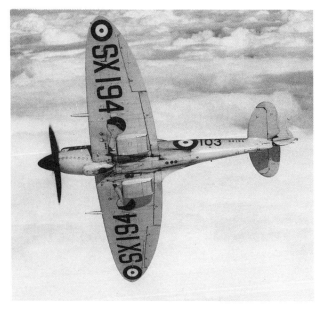

(Above and below left) A Seafire Mk XVII (SX194) in post-WW II service with No 781 Squadron at Lee-on-Solent. The permanent camera ports just aft of the wing trailing edge may be clearly seen in the lower photo. With the change from Roman to Arabic numerals for mark numbers in 1947, this version of the fighter became the Seafire FR Mk 17

innumerable headaches owing to their inordinate demands on servicing time.

The contra-prop had duly appeared on TM379 which had returned to the RAE as the prototype Seafire Mk 46 in June 1945, but the Mk 46 was destined to be yet another interim model as the folding arrangement for the new wing introduced with the Mk 45 had still to be finalised. Thus, like its immediate predecessor, the Mk 46 embodied minimum "navalisation", although it did incorporate more of the features that were to be standardised on the definitive Seafire Mk 47 which was to bring the production career of the sea-legged Spitfire to a close. For example, the frameless "bubble" canopy reappeared together with the wing "wet" points permitting "combat" tanks to be carried, and RATOG points were provided. Of course, the most important innovation was the Griffon 87 engine driving two three-bladed contra-rotating propellers which quite transformed the characteristics of the fighter, eliminating most of the more "uncomfortable" aspects of the Mk 45.

After completing arresting proofing with the prototype Mk 46, I took it aboard *Pretoria Castle* on 12 July 1945, making 10 landings down to a windspeed of 16 knots (30 km/h).

From the outset, I became aware that this was by far the easiest Seafire of them all to operate from a deck. Full power up to +18 lb boost could be applied for take-off with rudder neutral and the aircraft ran straight as a die, the run itself being so short as to render catapulting superfluous. It was indeed a delightful machine; variations of power were no longer demanding on trim — loops and rolls could be effected without any call for rudder corrections if the aircraft was properly trimmed — and the contra-prop gave very powerful braking on cutting the throttle. In fact, so strong was this braking effect that the stick had to be pulled back as the throttle was cut because the nose otherwise pitched down sharply.

The war now being over, little sense of urgency was attached to getting the fully-navalised two-stage Griffon-powered Seafire Mk 47 into carrier service and, indeed, the first production example was not destined to appear until early 1947, but between April 1946 and October of the following year, a succession of all marks of Griffon-engined Seafire nevertheless passed through my hands on RATOG, arresting and catapult trials at overload weights festooned with a bewildering variety of external stores. There were occasional problems when hardware broke loose, but after a short spell of "back to the drawing board", these were invariably resolved. Overload weights attained during these trials included 9,775 lb (4 434 kg) with the Seafire Mk XVII and 12,490 lb (5 665 kg) with the Mk 47. When one considers that the normal loaded weight of the Seafire Mk IB had been 6,718 lb (3 047 kg), some measure may be gained of the dramatic development of this fighter that had taken place over a few short years.

It has been said of the Spitfire 20 series and their sea-legged offspring that they were no longer *true* 'fires, but this I cannot really accept. It is true that very few details remained unaltered during their production lives, but the design principles and basic configuration on which they were originally based persisted throughout. Really fundamental changes were proposed from time to time, but the advantages that such offered were too nebulous to render worthwhile any radical departure from the tried and proven, and the final production versions of both Spitfire and Seafire, end products of a continuous process of incremental design development though they undoubtedly were, remained, in my view at least essentially refinements of Reginald Mitchell's original design. Despite the innumerable changes, surprisingly little

(Above) The first prototype Seafire Mk 45 (TM379) was an adaptation of a Spitfire Mk 21, which, with 'sting' hook and slinging points, was taken aboard HMS Pretoria Castle by the author for initial deck trials on 23 November 1944. (Immediately below right) One of the 50 Seafire Mk 45s (LA432) with five-bladed propeller built at the Castle Bromwich plant

aesthetic beauty of line had been lost — although, admittedly, the tail suffered somewhat — and none of the beautiful harmony of control.

The Seafire Mk 47 differed little externally from its immediate predecessor, but featured hydraulically — apart from the first dozen or so off the line which had manually — operated wing folding, the actual fold consisting of a single break immediately outboard of the cannon bay and the outboard panel folding upward through 90 deg. A Griffon 88 was standardised, this differing from the Griffon 87 in having a Rolls-Royce-developed injection system in place of the original Bendix-Stromberg fuel-metering carburettor. Large-area flaps were provided, their deflection being reduced by 10 deg to improve arrester wire clearance, and immense vertical tail surfaces similar to those evolved for the Spiteful made their appearance.

Seated in the cockpit of the Seafire Mk 47, an impressive length of nose stretched ahead, but, unlike that of, say, the Firebrand, it did not seem obtrusive. Despite the growth in sophistication of the Seafire's equipment with the passage of

(Immediately above right) One of two Seafire Mk 45s (LA444, the other being LA442) which commenced trials with contra-rotating propellers at the end of 1945, and (below) the second production Seafire Mk 46 (LA542), 24 being built at South Marston

the years, the layout of the instrumentation remained neat, although the cockpit was perhaps austere by American shipboard fighter standards of the day. No provision was made for cockpit heating, for example, and there was certainly not overmuch space for a pilot of even my relatively compact stature, while a pilot of more than average height would surely have experienced discomfort during protracted sorties.

The Griffon 88 was started on the lower main (48 Imp gal/218 l) fuel tank. Incidentally, as a result of the progressive increases in total fuel capacity — with overload fuel the Mk 47 had an endurance of four hours and a range in excess of 800 nm (1 480 km) — and the number of tanks involved (which could total as many as 10), fuel management procedures had become rather more complex than was the case with preceding Seafire models. The cock just below the centre of the instrument panel was turned to ON, the fuel booster pump was switched to MAIN and activated for 10-15 seconds, a single stroke of the priming pump, the ignition was switched ON, the Coffman starter cartridge was fired, the starter pushbutton being kept depressed to operate the booster coil, and the Griffon usually burst into life with a delightful throaty roar.

During the warm-up at 1,200-1,400 rpm after oil pressure had steadied, the normal checks of constant-speed propeller, two-speed supercharger, generator, magnetos and brake pressure were carried out. Taxying was effortless, as with all Seafires, but the Mk 47 was very nose heavy and care had to be exercised when applying the brakes in consequence. From a carrier deck the take-off was made with the elevator trim-

med one division nose up, the radiator shutters switched OPEN and the flaps at TAKE-OFF. The surge of acceleration at +18 lb boost and 2,750 rpm was electrifying, and the climb at this power to 1,000 ft (305 m) was so rapid that the pilot was hard pushed to retract the undercarriage and flaps before passing this altitude at which power had to be reduced to +9 lb and 2,600 rpm.

The maximum climb speed was 150 knots (278 km/h) IAS, with the supercharger changing automatically into high gear at around 10,000 ft (3 050 m) so that this speed was maintained up to 25,000 ft (7 620 m) which was reached in a little over nine minutes. Thereafter, speed was reduced by three knots (5,6 km/h) per thousand feet, but the Seafire was still climbing at something of the order of 3,000 ft/min, passing 30,000 ft (9 145 m) in round about 10·5 minutes. This definitive Seafire model certainly excelled in climbing and few other production piston-engined fighters could match it let alone surpass it.

The supreme feature of the Mk 47, as with all Seafires, was its superlative control harmony, which, combined with its performance, rendered it an outstanding combat fighter. Control response and manoeuvrability could hardly be faulted, and a 360 deg turn entered at 270 knots (500 km/h) IAS at 10,000 ft (3 050 m) was effected within 25 seconds. All normal aerobatics could be performed with ease — although inverted flight had to be restricted owing to the rapid fall in oil pressure — and recommended IAS for a loop was 300-320 knots (556-593 km/h), with 180-220 knots (333-408 km/h) for a roll, 320-340 knots (593-630 km/h) for a roll off a loop and 350-400 knots (649-741 km/h) for an upward roll. True, the rate of roll was marginally lower than achieved by earlier Seafires, and particularly those with clipped wings, but it was impressive nonetheless and superior to most contemporaries.

Acceleration was good and from 200 knots (370 km/h) at 10,000 ft (3 050 m) it would reach 270 knots (500 km/h) at full power within a minute, while, in level flight at 20,500 ft (6 250 m) a speed of 392 knots (726 km/h) was attainable. Although longitudinally and directionally stable, it was somewhat unstable laterally owing to friction in the aileron control circuit. It was very fast indeed in a dive and with the Rolls-Royce injector pump that had supplanted the Bendix-Stromberg carburettor of earlier versions of the two-stage Griffon it could be bunted straight into a vertical dive without a trace of engine falter, but the immense rudder

(Above left) The prototype Seafire Mk 47 (PS944), this photograph illustrating the wing-fold arrangement, and (below) the fourth Seafire Mk 47 (PS947) seen picking up the arrester wire. The first 14 fighters of this type were produced with manually-operated wing folding, the folding process on subsequent aircraft being actuated hydraulically

The definitive Seafire, the FR Mk 47, had few serious competitors in speed and rate of climb among contemporary piston-engined fighters, the climb capability endowing it with a defensive superiority over early naval jet fighters whose limiting Mach numbers barely exceeded that of this final Seafire model. The general arrangement drawing on the following page illustrates the Seafire FR Mk 47, the top sideview depicting the Mk XV for comparison purposes

and the rudder trim tab had to be handled with some care as sudden application produced violent skidding.

The mild stalling characteristics although not perhaps as completely innocuous on the Mk 47 as on early Seafires, made it an aircraft that could be flown to the limits of manoeuvrability with complete impunity, but vision, which had been reduced laterally as a result of the introduction of curved sidescreens, left a lot to be desired in inclement weather, and the lack of windscreen wiper aggravated the condition which was still further impaired at low speeds by the tail-down attitude adopted by the aircraft. Nevertheless, it was still the easiest of all Seafires to deck land, although, anomalously enough, it was probably the most difficult to land ashore.

Circuit speed was 170 knots (315 km/h), at which the hood could be opened, the booster pump switched on for the tank in use and the radiator shutters opened. The undercarriage was lowered at about 150 knots (278 km/h) and the selector lever returned to IDLE. The propeller rpm were set to 2,600 and the flaps were lowered. The turn on to the final approach on an airfield was made at 120 knots (222 km/h) and the propeller rpm control lever set fully forward while speed was gradually reduced to 90 knots (167 km/h). The aircraft normally wheeled onto the runway to give improved view and avoid the possibility of a bounce as the throttle was cut, for the nose of the Seafire Mk 47 then tended to drop unless positively corrected.

In the three-and-a-half years that had elapsed between the Navy taking on charge the first of its folding-wing Seafire Mk IIIs late in 1943, and the delivery of the first of its Seafire Mk 47s early in 1947, the navalised Spitfire had covered a great deal of water, both from carriers and shore bases. Seafires had played an important rôle in the air operations immediately preceding and during the Normandy invasion of June 1944 as part of the 2nd TAF, flying from bases on the English south coast. At this time, the only Seafire-armed carrier with the Home Fleet was *Furious* (Nos 801 and 880 squadrons), which had been engaged in a series of Norwegian coastal strikes, but it had been joined by *Indefatigable* (Nos 887 and 894 squadrons) in Norwegian strikes and fighter sweeps by the beginning of August, in which month four escort carriers with Seafires — *Attacker* (No 879 Sqdn), *Khedive* (No 899 Sqdn), *Hunter* (No 807 Sqdn) and *Stalker* (No 809 Sqdn) — had played a major part in Operation

Supermarine Seafire Mk 47 Specification

Power Plant: One Rolls-Royce Griffon 88 twelve-cylinder 60 deg Vee liquid-cooled engine rated at 1,935 hp at 2,750 rpm for take-off, 2,350 hp at 2,750 rpm at 1,250 ft (380 m) and 2,145 hp at 15,500 ft (2 745 m), driving two Rotol three-blade constant-speed contra-rotating co-axial propellers of 11 ft 3,35 m) diam. Internal fuel capacity, 152 Imp gal (691 l) divided between upper (36 Imp gal/163,6 l) and lower (48 Imp gal/218,2 l) main tanks, (32 Imp gal/145,5 l) rear tank, two (5·5 Imp gal/25 l) wing root tanks and two (12·5 Imp gal/56,8 l) wing tanks, and provision for two (22·5 Imp gal/102,3 l) underwing "combat" tanks and one (30 Imp gal/136,4 l, 50 Imp gal/227,3 l or 90 Imp gal/409 l) auxiliary drop tank beneath fuselage.
Performance: Max speed, 353 mph (568 km/h) at sea level, 376 mph (605 km/h) at 5,000 ft (1 525 m), 405 mph (652 km/h) at 9,500 ft (2 895 m), 452 mph (727 km/h) at 20,500 ft (6 250 m); normal range cruise, 215-235 mph (346-378 km/h) at 20,000 ft (6 095 m); radius of action (internal fuel), 200 mls (322 km); max range (with "combat" tanks and 90 Imp gal/409 l centreline drop tank), 940 mls (1,513 km) at 20,000 ft (6 095 m); max initial climb 4,800 ft/min (24,38 m/sec); time to 20,000 ft (6 095 m), 4·9 min; service ceiling, 43,100 ft (13 135 m).
Weights: Empty equipped, 8,680 lb (3 937 kg); loaded (clean), 10,700 lb (4 853 kg); limiting (for unrestricted flying), 11,070 lb (5 021 kg); max take-off ("combat" tanks, 50 Imp gal/227,3 l centreline drop tank and two 500-lb/226,8-kg bombs), 12,530 lb (5 683,5 kg).
Dimensions: Span, 36 ft 11 in (11,25 m); length, 34 ft 4 in (10,46 m); height (over propeller, tail down); 12 ft 9 in (3,88 m); wing area, 243·6 sq ft (22, 63 m²); width folded, 19 ft 1 in (5,82 m); height folded, 13 ft 10 in (4,52 m).
Armament: Four 20 mm British Hispano Mk 5 cannon with 175 rpg for inner and 150 rpg for outer, plus provision for eight 60-lb (27-kg) rocket projectiles on zero-length launchers or up to three 500-lb (226,8-kg) bombs.

Dragoon, the invasion of the South of France, these vessels and their Seafires subsequently operating in the Aegean.

As previously mentioned, the escort carrier *Atheling* operating in the Indian Ocean had been the first to receive the folding-wing Seafire Mk III when No 889 Sqdn embarked in May 1944, although this unit was to be disbanded three months later, when, there no longer being a requirement for a fighter escort carrier in the Indian Ocean, *Atheling* proved too slow to serve with the main Fleet. There had followed a hiatus of more than three months before Seafires had again joined the Eastern Fleet, *Indefatigable* arriving at Trincomalee in November, still with Nos 887 and 894 squadrons aboard.

The strict range limitations of the Seafire Mk III now began to make themselves increasingly felt; the availability of aircraft such as the Avenger with greatly enhanced operational radii had resulted in a major change in offensive doctrine and the distances now covered by carrier-launched strikes were extended accordingly. The range being called for was well beyond the capability of the Seafire, which, perforce, was restricted to Fleet defence, but a rôle in which its excellent acceleration and fast climb placed it second to none, and this remained its primary mission after *Indefatigable* commenced operations in the Far East at the beginning of 1945.

The escort carriers *Hunter* and *Stalker*, with Nos 807 and 809 squadrons respectively, joined the East Indies Fleet in April 1945, to participate in the following month's Operation *Dracula,* the assault on Rangoon. These carriers were later joined by *Attacker* with No 879 Squadron. Meanwhile, Nos 887 and 894 squadrons flew in support of the Okinawa invasion from *Indefatigable,* and in June, Nos 801 and 880 squadrons from *Implacable* were in action at Truk, these two carriers with their four Seafire squadrons mounting strikes on the Japanese home islands with the US Third Fleet during July and August.

With the end of the war in the Pacific and the reduction in the strength of the Royal Navy's air component in consequence, the number of Seafire squadrons diminished rapidly, but this fighter's career was far from over. The last Seafire Mk

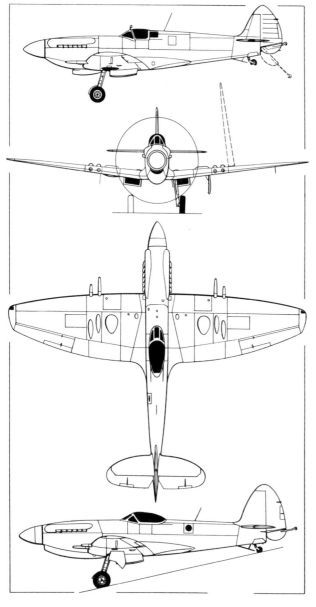

III-equipped first-line squadron, No 801, disbanded in June 1946, with the return from the Far East to the UK of *Implacable,* but the newer generation of Griffon-engined Seafires that had just been entering service as the conflict came to an end was to equip the postwar nucleus, which, by August 1946, comprised only four first-line fighter squadrons — Nos 802, 805, 806 and 807 — all but the last-mentioned being equipped with the Seafire Mk XV, No 807 having the Mk XVII.

The Mk XV squadrons were deployed aboard *Venerable* (No 802), *Ocean* (No 805) and *Glory* (No 806) during the course of 1946, while the Mk XVIIs of No 807 Squadron, which was not allocated to a Carrier Air Group, were deployed for some three months from November 1946 to Lübeck, Germany, where the unit was attached to the 2nd TAF. Nos 802 and 805 squadrons were disbanded in the following year, but two other squadrons had meanwhile reformed on Seafires, No 800 with Mk XVIIs and No 804 with Mk XVs, these embarking on *Triumph* and *Teseus* respectively in February 1947. Although reformed once more, in April 1947, with Seafire Mk XVIIs for service aboard *Ocean,* No 805 Squadron was subsequently transferred to the Royal Australian Navy and re-equipped with Sea Furies in August 1948. In the same month, No 807 also converted to the Sea Fury and the Navy was left with only two first-line Seafire squadrons, No 800 aboard *Triumph* and No 804 aboard *Ocean,* both eventually converting to Mk 47s in February 1948 and April 1949 respectively.

No 800 Squadron was to gain the distinction of being the only unit to take the Seafire Mk 47 into action. A month after *Triumph* arrived in Singapore, in September 1949, No 800 mounted a number of rocket attacks against Communist terrorist hide-outs from RNAS Sembawang, and when, in the following June, hostilities broke out in Korea, *Triumph* soon arrived off the west Korean coast, No 800 making its first rocket attack — the target being the airfield at Haeju — on 4 July 1950. The Seafires continued their participation in the Korean conflict until *Triumph* was finally withdrawn to Hong Kong on 25 September, at which time just one fully-serviceable Seafire remained. When the carrier arrived back in the UK two months later, No 800 Squadron was disbanded and the Seafire finally passed from first-line Royal Navy service. Of course, it was to linger on with reserve and training units until, as recounted earlier, the last training squadron to operate this type, No 764, was disbanded at RNAS Yeovilton on 23 November 1954.

The Seafire had seen more than eight years of first-line service and the number of combat sorties that it flew in that time must surely have approached five figures. For my own part, I regretted its passing as, for me, it marked the end of an era. Nobody would pretend that the Seafire had been the ideal carrier fighter, but I had probably deck-landed it more than any other pilot and had never felt anything but exhilaration at the challenge that it presented. It was an aeroplane which seemed tailormade for the pilot and I cannot imagine any other aircraft that would have permitted the liberty of the crab-type approach that I and many other pilots used for deck landing. True, it left much to be desired with regard to robustness, particularly in its early versions, but then it was doing something that it was never meant for in the first place. It is also true that it was a lousy ditcher and I witnessed a number of fatal accidents resulting from its emulation of the diving characteristics of a submarine, but it had been designed for fighting not ditching.

There were undoubtedly pluses and minuses, but the Fleet Air Arm owes the Seafire an enormous debt of gratitude, because it gave the Royal Navy's intake of young wartime fighter pilots the experience of flying the best that there was — an incalculable morale booster at a critical moment in World War II.□

Fairey Firefly

APPELLATIONS assigned to combat aircraft have ranged, over the years, the full gamut from sublime to ridiculous, but there can have been few more truly appropriate examples of aeronautical nomenclature than that assigned to Fairey's final fighter, the Firefly. The *lampyrinae* from which the name was borrowed have the property of emitting phosphorescent light, and if their Fairey-built namesakes were not exactly luminiferous, they were luminaries in the sense that, among shipboard aircraft of their day, the combination of supreme versatility, tractability and reliability that they coupled with performance, handling qualities and firepower was unrivalled. Indeed, the extraordinary amenability that the Firefly was to reveal to an unprecedentedly broad rôle spectrum was to endow it with a life span of almost a quarter-century.

The two-seat shipboard fighter, a class considered *passé* from the early 'thirties by the navies of other maritime powers, had been persisted with by the Royal Navy alone, bringing the formula to the apex of its evolution — in piston-engined form at least — in the autumn of 1943, when No 1770 Squadron began forming on Fireflies at Yeovilton. There was nothing radical about the Firefly. Rather it represented the synthesis of the Fairey Aviation Company's years of expertise in combining the demands of the nautical with those of the aeronautical. But if lacking radicality of concept, it was not devoid of the innovatory, not least of its innovative features being its fully-retractable Fairey-patented Youngman area-increasing flaps.

It represented a very real advance on anything that had gone before from virtually every aspect; it lacked little of the agility of its single-seat contemporaries and, if unable to deliver level speeds considered spectacular by standards then appertaining, it could trade firepower with its potential opponents on a basis of at least equality and offered significant advances in range and endurance. As first delivered to the Fleet Air Arm in that autumn of the early 'forties, the Firefly was good; the promise inherent in the basic design ensured that it would eventually transcend the very good.

Bearing a superficial resemblance to the Fulmar, to which it was a successor in only the broadest genealogical signification, the Firefly was conceived from the outset as a *multi-rôle* aircraft, albeit with emphasis on hard-hitting fighter capabilities, and perhaps the most remarkable aspect of its evolution was the brevity of its gestatory period. Conceived under the leadership of H E Chaplin as an amalgam of features of two specifications, N.8/39 and N.9/39, the Fairey submission that was to give birth to the Firefly and around which a new specification, N.5/40, was to be written envisaged a marginally smaller aeroplane than the Fulmar, but one possessing an empty weight barely less than the *fully loaded* weight of the preceding warplane. The approval of the Admiralty was most noteworthy in the rapidity with which it was forthcoming. From submission of the proposal in September 1939, less than nine months elapsed to the acceptance, on 6 June 1940, of the mock-up and a contract, six days later, for an initial production batch of 200 aircraft!

The first drawings were issued on 16 November 1940, the name Firefly being officially adopted during the following month, and although no prototype aircraft had been contracted for, it was decided to assemble the first four aircraft from production components in the experimental shop at

Hayes to serve in the development rôle. Several innovatory features along the lines eventually to result in Fairey's envelope jigging system of construction were introduced into the manufacture of the Firefly. The fuselage, built in halves subsequently joined along the vertical centre-line, embodied no longitudinal stringers, deriving its strength from a large number of heavy "U" frames and the outer skin, and the Rolls-Royce Griffon IIB engine being mounted as a quickly-detachable "power egg" — the Firefly being among the first British aircraft to utilise such an installation. The most important design feature of the Firefly, however, was the use that it made of Youngman area-increasing flaps, which, it might be said, were an early form of variable-geometry. Fully retracted for high-speed flight, these flaps extended on tracks to increase wing area in the cruise, a function performed in addition to their more orthodox task in taking-off and landing. Mating the necessary flap linkage with the required wing fold demanded no little ingenuity on the part of the Fairey team, but the Youngman flaps were to radically reduce the Firefly's turn radius and make a major contribution to the very good manoeuvrability and, in consequence, self-defence capability of the aeroplane.

The first development Firefly (Z1826) was rolled out of the experimental shop and flown for the first time from the Great West airfield by C S "Chris" Staniland, Fairey's Chief Test Pilot, on 22 December 1941, a mere 13 months after the issue of the first drawings to the shops. The second development aircraft (Z1827) followed the first into the air within six months, on 4 June 1942, but three weeks later, on 26 June, the tail assembly collapsed at low altitude following elevator

over-balance and this aircraft was destroyed, "Chris" Staniland losing his life. The third aircraft, Z1828, flew on 26 August, and this was followed in September by the fourth, Z1829, originally intended as a structural test specimen but completed for flight testing as a replacement for the second aircraft.

It was the arrival of this fourth development machine at Arbroath, the base of the Fleet Air Arm's Service Trials Unit, that gave me my first opportunity to examine the new naval débutante. The date was 1 February 1943, and the Firefly had been sent to Arbroath, together with a prototype Firebrand and a Barracuda II, for some practice on the dummy carrier deck prior to deck trials aboard HMS *Illustrious*. As I knew that the Firefly would shortly pass into the STU's care, I examined the aircraft with particular interest.

My first impression was one of beautiful proportions; a careful mating of smoothly-cowled Griffon engine blending with cleanly-contoured fuselage and aesthetically pleasing elliptical wings. All similarity to the preceding Fulmar was confined to the general configuration, with its tandem seating for two crew members, nose radiator and inward-retracting main undercarriage members. All the elegance of the Fulmar remained, but this had, in some indefinable fashion, been infused with an air of pugnacity; its ground stance seemed more businesslike, an impression strengthened by the quartette of 20-mm Hispano cannon barrels protruding from the wing leading edges. One retrogressive step by comparison with the Fulmar that I noted, though, was the situation of the forward cockpit which was marginally further aft in relation to the wing leading edge. This, in itself, was a fairly minor point, but when coupled with some very obtrusive metal framing and decidedly restricted canopy headroom, plus a shallow raked windscreen, forward view was obviously deficient and bid fair to become a critical shortcoming at high angles of approach incidence.

By the time I was nominated as Firefly project officer in May 1943, the Service Trials Unit had transferred to Crail, on the northern mouth of the Firth of Forth, the first pre-production aircraft (Z1830) had left the Hayes line in the previous January, the original production contract had twice been increased — to 300 on 3 September 1941, and to 600 on

(Above left) The first prototype Firefly (Z1826) in its original form (compare with photograph below) with horn-balanced rudder and dummy cannon (Below) The first development Firefly (Z1826) in its definitive form

(Above) A Firefly F Mk I of No 1772 Squadron from HMS Indefatigable in the Pacific, and (below right) a Firefly F Mk I of No 1770 Squadron returning to the same carrier after a strike against Sumatran oil refineries. No 1770 was the first Firefly squadron, forming at Yeovilton 1 October 1943 and embarking on HMS Indefatigable in the following year

20 June 1942 — and delivery tempo was building up rapidly. Indeed, the Firefly in which I had made my first flight on 4 June was Z1839, the *tenth* aeroplane off the production line.

For me, the deep-throated growl of the superlative Rolls-Royce Griffon engine had epitomised sheer power from the moment, a few weeks earlier, that I had first experienced its exhilarating surge — and awesome thirst — pulling the Spitfire XII off the ground at Arbroath, and it was with pleasurable anticipation that I first hoisted myself over the cockpit sill of the Firefly. Offering maximum ratings of 1,735 hp at 1,000 ft (305 m) and 1,495 hp at 14,500 ft (4 420 m), the Griffon IIB was provided with 145·5 Imp gal (661 l) of fuel in the main tank immediately aft of the cockpit and 23 Imp gal (104,5 l) in each of the wing centre-section leading-edge tanks. With the wing tanks empty, main tank fuel was limited to 116 Imp gal (527 l) to keep the CG within the permissible limits, and with max internal fuel, at least 30 Imp gal (136 l) had to be drawn off the main tank before switching to the wing tanks. After priming the engine and depressing the starter button, the Griffon fired immediately and was opened up slowly to 1,200 rpm for warm-up. With oil at 15°C (59°F) and coolant at 40°C (104° F), the throttle was opened fully to 2,750 rpm and +12 lb boost for a brief check, the engine giving vent to a very impressive roar which died down as I eased back and commenced taxying. The Firefly was very stable on the ground, thanks to its wide-track undercarriage, and the brakes proved smooth and positive.

A quick check that all three trim tabs were zeroed, the propeller was fined, the fuel cock set on MAIN and the flaps selected one notch down for take-off, the Firefly accelerated with commendable rapidity but demanded strong rudder movement to control a marked tendency to swing to star-goard. The initial climb out was at 120 knots (222 km/h) IAS, the flaps being raised at about 300 ft (90 m), climbing speed rapidly building up to 135 knots (250 km/h) which was recommended for max climb rate up to 16,000 ft (4 875 m), the retraction of undercarriage and flaps having produced a measure of nose-up trim. I soon discovered that all changes of power and speed demanded attention to the trim tabs as they were accompanied by marked changes in lateral and directional trim, and the Firefly was not overly stable either in the climb or in level flight, being just about possible to fly "hands-off" by dint of very careful trimming.

Nevertheless, the Firefly was a pilot's aeroplane and its handling characteristics were good, although the controls tended to heavy up with speed, this being particularly notice-able on the ailerons, but it could be thrown about with

reasonable élan, although spinning was not recommended. In fact, the Firefly responded to standard spin recovery action extremely well, recovery normally being effected in half a turn, but an IAS of at least 160 knots (296 km/h) was neces-sary before pulling out of the ensuing dive. In diving the aircraft became very tail heavy as speed built up, also tending to yaw to port, and in order to avoid high g in recovery, it was adviseable to trim the Firefly into a dive. Stall warning came in the form of a modicum of elevator buffet three or four knots before the onset of the stall, the nose and port wing tending to drop quite sharply, stalling speed in clean condi-tion being about 90 knots (167 km/h) IAS. In a steep turn a sudden reduction in elevator feel gave warning of an approaching stall and if the pull force was not immediately

Firefly F Mk I (Z1844) of the initial production batch after coming to grief on 9 September 1943 aboard HMS Pretoria Castle after the arrester hook failed to lower while the aircraft was being landed by the author

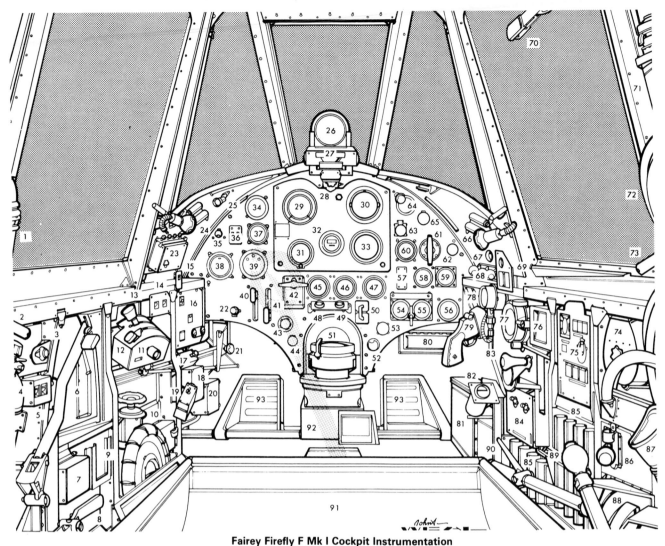

Fairey Firefly F Mk I Cockpit Instrumentation

1 Vacuum flask
2 Floodlight
3 Floodlight dimmer switch
4 Fire-extinguisher
5 RP switches
6 Flap control lever
7 RP auto-selector box
8 Front catapult spool lever
9 Data card holder
10 Trimming tabs control unit
11 Friction lock
12 Propeller control lever
13 Throttle lever
14 RP and bomb switches
15 Gunsight master switch
16 Port switch panel
17 Supercharger control switch
  and warning lamp
18 ARI 5245 (or 5307) controller
19 ARI 5245 (or TR 5043) junction
  box
20 Bomb auto-distributor box
21 Supercharger light
  barometric switch
22 Arrester hook indicator
23 TR 1196 (or TR 5043)

24 Panel floodlights
25 Undercarriage warning light
26 Gunsight
27 Gunsight mounting
28 Gunsight lamp switch
29 ASI
30 Artificial horizon
31 Altimeter
32 Direction indicator
33 Turn-and-bank indicator
34 Engine speed indicator
35 Floodlight switch
36 Ignition switches
37 Boost pressure gauge
38 Brakes and supply pressure
  gauge
39 Undercarriage position
  indicator
40 Arrester hook control lever
41 Undercarriage control lever
42 Fuel tank cock control
43 Slow-running cut-out control
44 Cockpit heating control
45 Fuel gauge (port wing)
46 Fuel gauge (stbd wing)
47 Fuel gauge (main tank)

48 Fuel pressure warning light
49 Wing tank pumps warning
  light
50 Wing tank fuel pump
  change-over switch
51 Compass
52 Compass floodlight switch
53 Carburettor air-intake heat
  control
54 Oxygen delivery gauge
55 Oxygen supply gauge
56 Air temperature gauge
57 Oil pressure gauge
58 Oil temperature gauge
59 Clock
60 Radiator temperature gauge
61 Cylinder priming pump
62 Floodlight switch
63 Engine starter push-button
64 Windscreen de-icing pump
65 Starter re-loading control
66 Panel floodlights
67 Gunsight supply socket
68 Gunsight spare bulbs (3)
69 Long-range tanks and bombs
  switch panel

70 Hood jettison control lever
71 Incendiary bomb
72 Speaking tube
73 Floodlight
74 Rheostat type 'H'
75 Starboard switch panel
76 Engine data plate
77 Identification lights
  switchbox
78 Camera footage indicator
79 Signal pistol
80 Map case
81 Junction box
82 Ammunition rounds counter
83 Hood operating handle
84 Fllodlight switch panel
85 Signal cartridge stowage
  racks
86 Oxygen master valve
87 Speaking tube mouthpiece
88 Ground/flight switch
89 Seat-raising handle
90 Hydraulic handpump
91 Pilot's seat
92 Control column (shaded)
93 Rudder pedals

relaxed the Firefly would flick out of the turn. Recommended speeds for aerobatics were 180-220 knots (333-408 km/h) for a roll, 260-280 knots (480-520 km/h) for a loop and 280-300 knots (520-556 km/h) for a half-roll off the top.

At this stage, I was most interested in the landing characteristics of the Firefly, for my immediate task was to carry out a series of deck landing and catapult trials aboard *Illustrious*. Speed was reduced to 175 knots (324 km/h) in the circuit at which cruise flap setting was selected, the wheels coming down at about 155 knots (287 km/h) and full flap being

applied below 125 knots (232 km/h). The initial approach in lightly loaded condition was made at some 90 knots (167 km/h) on land — or about 10 knots (18 km/h) higher without-outflap — reducing to 85 knots (157 km/h) on finals, and such was the power available from the Griffon that, in the event of a mislanding, the Firefly would climb away easily on climbing power, the use of full take-off power being unnecessary. The drill was to open the throttle to +9 lb, increase the airspeed to 90 knots (167 km/h), raise the undercarriage and retrim.

The Firefly handled well on the approach, but view was

seriously impaired by the previously-mentioned windscreen and canopy faults. Furthermore, at the critical point at which the throttle was cut for touchdown, the stick had to be pulled back to counteract the tendency for the heavy nose to drop. This was obviously to be particularly important on the carrier, as the arrester hook was mounted midway between the wing trailing edge and the tailwheel. The touchdown itself had a nice solid feel to it and once on the ground the Firefly, ran straight and steady, and the brakes could be applied reasonably fiercely without fear of nosing over.

During the take-off for my third flight, the open canopy suddenly detached itself just after unstick, draping itself around the leading edge of the port tailplane where it severed the mainspar, producing violent stick flutter from the blanked-off elevator. I completed a very shaky circuit and landed at a high rate of knots, and from that moment, the jettisoning characteristics of the canopy were suspect and became the subject of wind tunnel testing.

The trials aboard *Illustrious* took place on 8-9 June with a replacement aircraft, Z1844, and were very successful indeed, although they did highlight the deficiency in forward view during the approach. It was found that the best approach speed for a deck landing was 78-80 knots (144-148 km/h), a curved approach being necessary to obtain a reasonable view of the deck. The combination of poor forward view and the jettisoning problem promptly led to the introduction of a taller windscreen which improved the view in rain so much that the wind-driven windscreen wiper could be deleted. The new screen, which featured the minimum of framing, necessitated a raised canopy with the incidental advantage that the pilot was afforded more headroom.

The next stage in the programme was to get the Firefly aboard a smaller carrier, and this was accomplished with HMS *Pretoria Castle* on 8 September. On the following day, however, I had a somewhat hairy experience when the Firefly was launched from the catapult at 65 knots (120 km/h) into a windspeed of only 8 knots (15 km/h) over the carrier deck, with the unnerving result that the aircraft dropped to within 15 ft (4,5 m) of the sea! Having sorted this one out and still

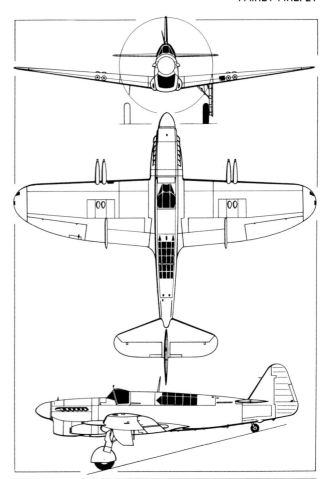

The general arrangement drawing depicts the standard Firefly F Mk I. (Immediately above) The first Firefly NF Mk II prototype (Z1831) and (immediately below) the second NF Mk II prototype (Z1875). These featured a lengthened forward fuselage and wing-mounted radar pods

(Below) The prototype Firefly NF Mk I (DT933) with the radar pod under the engine. The NF Mk II actually preceded the NF Mk I

Fairey Firefly F Mk I Specification

Power Plant: One Rolls-Royce Griffon IIB 12-cylinder Vee liquid-cooled engine rated at 1,735 hp at 2,750 rpm at 1,000 ft (305 m) and 1,495 hp at 2,750 rpm (5 min limit) at 14,500 ft (4 420 m) driving three-bladed Rotol wooden constant-speed propeller of 13 ft (3,96 m) diam. Internal fuel capacity comprising 145·5 Imp gal (661 l) in main fuselage tank and 23 Imp gal (104,5 l) in each of two wing tanks. Provision for two 45 Imp gal (204,5 l) Sea Hurricane-type or 90 Imp gal (409 l) US-type drop tanks.

Performance: (Clean) Max speed, 284 mph (457 km/h) at sea level, 273 mph (439 km/h) at 3,500 ft (1 070 m), 319 mph (513 km/h) at 17,000 ft (5 180 m), (with two 90 Imp gal/409 l drop tanks), 257 mph (413 km/h) at sea level, 266 mph (428 km/h) at 3,500 ft (1 070 m), 288 mph (463 km/h) at 17,000 ft (5 180 m); climb (at 12,200 lb/5 534 kg) to 5,000 ft (1 525 m), 2·5 min, to 10,000 ft (3 050 m), 5·75 min; range (internal fuel), 774 mls (1 245 km) at 233 mph (375 km/h), (with two 45 Imp gal/204,5 l drop tanks), 1,088 mls (1 750 km) at 207 mph (33 km/h), (with two 90 Imp gal/409 l drop tanks), 1,364 mls (2 195 km) at 204 mph (328 km/h); service ceiling (clean), 29,000 ft (8 840 m); take-off distance (at 12,200 lb/5 534 kg), 685 yds (749 m) into 10-knot (18,5-km/h wind, 505 yds (552 m) into 20-knot (37 km/h) wind.

Weights: Empty equipped, 8,925 lb (4 048 kg); loaded (clean), 12,250 lb (5 556 kg); max take-off (with two 90 Imp gal/409 l drop tanks), 13,656 lb (6 194 kg), (with two 1,000-lb/453,6-kg bombs), 14,288 lb (6 481 kg).

Dimensions: Span 44 ft 6 in (13,56 m); width folded, 16 ft 0 in (4,88 m); length, 37 ft 0 in (11,28 m); length folded, 37 ft 7½ in (11,47 m); height, 15 ft 5½ in (4,74 m); wing area, 328 sq ft (30,47 m²).

Armament: Four wing-mounted 20-mm Hispano Mk II or Mk V cannon with 160 rpg. Provision for eight 60-lb (27,2-kg) rockets, or two 500-lb (227-kg) or 1,000-lb (453,6-kg) bombs, or two 1,000-lb (453,6-kg) mines.

(Above) A standard Firefly F Mk I (DT985) seen flying with a pair of 1,000-lb (454-kg) bombs, the carriage of which initially posed a number of problems at the RAE Farnborough, and (below left) a Firefly FR Mk I (PP425) with the ASH radar pod slung beneath the engine cowling

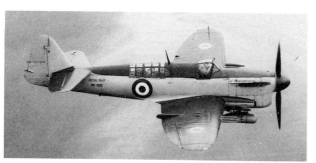

feeling decidedly shaken, I came into land, checking that the arrester hook green light was showing the hook to be lowered, and landed on nicely, getting a "Roger" from *Pretoria Castle's* batsman all the way. The next thing I knew was violent contact with the crash barrier, which smartly wiped off the undercarriage, and the Firefly slithering along on its belly in a shower of wood splinters from the shattering propeller. The Firefly slid on to the catapult track and came to a grinding halt. A soon as I clambered out of the cockpit I could see that the hook had not lowered despite the fact that the green indicator light was *still* glowing on the panel! Investigation revealed that only one of the two hook unlocking latches had released, although this had activated the hook signal light. In spite of this failure there should never have been an accident as the batsman, whose responsibility it was to check that undercarriage, flaps and hook were all down, should never have given the final "cut" signal to land. Thus, a technical fault had been compounded by human error.

As a result of this incident, a modification was introduced to the hook release mechanism and I was back on *Pretoria Castle* with another Firefly Z1880, on 22 November for a two-day series of sidewind catapult launchings and landings at weights up to 12,160 lb (5 516 kg). These trials went well and so it was decided to test the Firefly in a further series of low windspeed trials, again on *Pretoria Castle*, in December, with the primary object of ascertaining the suitability of the new two-seat fighter for the "Woolworth" carriers, the small escort carriers which were being received from the USA. In the event, no particular problems were encountered, although the anticipated limit was reached when that arrester wire pulled out to its maximum and the retardation was so violent that the propeller tips clipped the deck. Although the Firefly could not be considered above average for ease of landing on a carrier, it was a *good* average, and so deck landing clearance was given to the first operational unit, No 1770 Squadron, which had formed with 12 aircraft on 1 October 1943.

At this point in time, the Firefly developed a land runway

problem, namely violent tailwheel shimmy, which bid fair to cause structural damage to the tail. By the time I moved on to the Royal Aeronautical Establishment at Farnborough, in January 1944, the problem had been handed on there for solution. A tailwheel lock was tried, but there was a simpler answer in the ingenious Marstrand anti-shimmy tailwheel tyre which had a very wide and deep groove in the middle. This proved completely efficaceous and the problem was resolved.

Many other relatively minor changes and modifications were meanwhile being introduced as a result of parallel test programmes. A mass balance had replaced the original rudder horn balance at an early stage, and metal skinning had replaced a fabric on the ailerons; the 20-mm gun barrels had been faired in and the two-man dinghy in the rear fuselage had been replaced by individual K-type dinghies. The Firefly was, by consensus, a thoroughly sound basic design and was beginning to reveal something of the development potential inherent in its concept. It was not a "hot number" in the level speed stakes, but then a large single-engined two-seater was hardly expected to compete on even terms with similarly-powered, smaller and lighter single-seat contemporaries. Its level speed capability was, nonetheless, thoroughly respectable, a clean aircraft clocking 247 knots (458 km/h) at sea level and reaching 277 knots (513 km/h) at 17,000 ft (5 180 m). Although the controls called for moderate physical effort, the Firefly was a very manoeuvrable aeroplane, thanks largely to its Youngman flaps, and with these flaps at take-off setting, it could turn with the best of its single-seat contemporaries near the stall and turn inside most of them. But it was in range and endurance that the Firefly excelled, again thanks in part to the Youngman flaps.

These flaps, which were operated by a lever to the left of the pilot, had three positions in addition to the "housed" or full-retracted setting. They could be extended at near-zero incidence beneath the trailing edge to improve manoeuvrability at low and medium speeds; they could be moved aft and lowered to improve take-off and they could be moved further aft and rotated through a maximum angle for landing. Extended but undrooped, they provided an invaluable increment of lift in the cruise, which, for maximum range, was 155 knots (287 km/h) at high altitude and 175 knots (324 km/h) at low altitude.

Meanwhile, the Firefly was being readied for operational initiation. The first squadron, No 1770, was flying from Grimsetter pending the final working up aboard the new HMS *Indefatigable,* a second squadron, No 1771, formed at Yeovilton on 1 February 1944, and a third, No 1772, at Burscough in May. No 1770 Sqdn embarked on *Indefatigable* in time to participate in Operation *Mascot* against the *Tirpitz* which was once again nearing combat readiness in Altenfiord, on Norway's northern coast, after sustaining damage as a result of Operation *Tungsten* on 3 April 1944. The British carrier force, including *Indefatigable,* reached the position from which it was to launch the first strike of *Mascot* on 17 July, the primary tasks of the Fireflies being reconnaissance of Altenfiord and the strafing of the anti-aircraft gun positions protecting *Tirpitz.* In the event, the first strike of *Mascot* proved a singular failure as the German warship was shrouded by smoke, and the second strike was frustrated by fog. On 22 and 29 August, No 1770's Fireflies flew reconnaissance misions for further FAA strikes against *Tirpitz,* but these strikes, too, failed to inflict any serious damage.

The Fireflies of No 1771 Sqdn in the meantime embarked aboard another new carrier, HMS *Implacable,* and flew armed reconnaissance and anti-shipping sorties along the Norwegian coast in October, but no opportunity was presented to the Firefly to demonstrate its mettle in fighter-versus-fighter combat and, in fact, this operational teeth-cutting process over Norwegian waters did little to confirm the capabilities of the new shipboard warplane. It was the Far East that was to provide the venue in which the Firefly was really to prove itself operationally, and here it was still too close to the threshold of its service career to demonstrate to any extent the supreme versatility for which it was to achieve a measure of fame in later years.

Whereas the first production series aeroplanes had been straight Firefly F Mk I two-seat day fighters, work had been proceeding on the complementary NF Mk II two-seat night fighter for which the second pre-series airframe, Z1831, had been assigned as a prototype. Initially, the NF Mk II had been envisaged as a relatively straightforward adaptation of the basic F Mk I, with AI Mk X radar housed in two small radomes mounted on the wing leading edges, close to the fuselage, CG balance being restored by the weight of the AI operator's equipment in the rear cockpit. In the event, it was to be ascertained that the CG had moved too far aft and an 18-in (45,70 cm) bay had to be inserted aft of the engine firewall to set matters to rights. These changes, quite understandably, had a deleterious effect on aircraft performance, and when it was ascertained that, now a quite separate type, the NF Mk II could not be conveniently produced by the introduction of modifications on the F Mk I assembly line, the contract was cancelled, only 37 being completed and these being reconverted to Mk I standard.

Another factor motivating the abandoning of the NF Mk II was the development of more compact radar equipment, enabling versions of the basic F Mk I to be offered in both fighter-reconnaissance and night fighting variants as the FR Mk I and NF Mk I, carrying ASH and AI radar respectively in a cannister beneath the forward fuselage, the latter having shrouded exhausts or an anti-dazzle shield above the exhaust pipes. For NF Mk I trials purposes, DT933 was to be used during the summer of 1945, and 140 Fireflies were delivered in this form, as compared with 236 FR Mk Is and 459 straight F Mk Is (132 of which were produced by General Aircraft at Hanworth), plus 37 NF Mk IIs which subsequently reverted to Mk I standard.

By the beginning of 1945, *Indefatigable* had arrived in the Indian Ocean and, between 1 and 7 January, flew rocket sorties against the Pangkalan Brandan refinery, Sumatra, with considerable effect. It was during one of these sorties, on 4 January, that the Fireflies of No 1770 Sqdn drew first blood in air-to-air combat, Lt D Levitt claiming the destruction of one Ki.43 Hayabusa and a second fighter of this type being claimed by Sub Lts Redding and Stott. Two more Hayabusas were claimed by No 1770 on 24 January, during the first of two strikes against Palembang refineries through balloon barrages and intensive anti-aircraft fire. It was now that the Firefly began to establish the enviable reputation for sturdiness and reliability that it was to retain throughout its long post-WW II career. On 29 January, before leaving the Indian Ocean for the Pacific where *Indefatigable* was to participate in the Okinawa invasion, No 1170 Sqdn added three more Hayabusas to its score. By the time Task Force 57, of which *Indefatigable* was a part, sortied from its advanced base at Manus Island, in the Admiralties, on 19 March, some of the crews of No 1772 Sqdn, which had meanwhile arrived in the Far East, were incorporated into No 1770, and from the first British fighter sweeps and strikes against airfields on Mikayo, five days before the US Marines began their assault on

(Above right and below) The prototype Firefly Mk III (Z1835), essentially the 10th Mk I airframe with a Griffon 61 engine and a beard radiator, proved to possess unsatisfactory handling characteristics and was eventually modified to Mk IV standards involving more extensive redesign, Z1835 becoming one of three prototypes of the later model

Fairey Firefly FR Mk 4 Cutaway Drawing Key

1 Spinner
2 Rotol four-bladed propeller
3 Propeller hub pitch-change mechanism
4 Spinner backplate
5 Ignition cooling air intake
6 Coolant header tank
7 Supercharger air intake
8 Front engine mounting
9 Intake trunking
10 Engine bearer struts
11 Exhaust stubs
12 Rolls-Royce Griffon 74 V-twelve engine
13 Detachable engine cowlings
14 Auxiliary fuel tank (90 Imp gal/409 l capacity)
15 Front spar wing fold latches
16 Inboard ammunition box
17 Gun bay blister fairings
18 Hispano 20-mm cannon
19 Outboard ammunition box
20 Cannon barrel mountings
21 Cannon barrel fairings
22 1,000-lb (453,6-kg) mine
23 ASH radar housing
24 Radar scanner
25 Gun camera
26 Starboard navigation light
27 Wing tip fairing
28 Formation keeping lights
29 Starboard aileron
30 Aileron hinge control
31 Fairey-Youngman flap (cruise setting)
32 Flap hinge fairing
33 Outboard flap hinge linkage
34 Rear spar wing fold latch

35 Oil tank (11·5 Imp gal/52 l capacity)
36 Rotol engine auxiliary gearbox
37 Engine control rods
38 Fireproof bulkhead
39 Heater duct
40 Rudder pedals
41 Control column
42 Fuselage lifting bar attachment
43 Hydraulic fluid tank
44 Windscreen de-icing fluid tank
45 Instrument panel
46 Windscreen
47 Gyro gunsight
48 Pilot's rear view mirror
49 Sliding canopy cover
50 Headrest
51 Safety harness
52 Pilot's seat
53 Throttle and propeller controls
54 Catapult spool release
55 Flap lever
56 Fire extinguisher
57 Thermos flask
58 Fuselage double frame
59 Wing spar attachment joint
60 Tailplane control push-pull rods
61 Fuselage top longeron

62 Canopy sliding rail
63 Main fuel tank (146 Imp gal/664 l capacity)
64 Fuel filler cap
65 Starboard wing folded position
66 Aerial mast
67 Aerial cable lead-in
68 Air scoop
69 Radar director
70 Radio racks
71 Kick-in step
72 Observer's swivelling seat
73 Observer's entry hatch
74 Radio and electronics racks
75 Signal lamp
76 Observer's cockpit aft glazing
77 Rear equipment bay
78 Rear fuselage decking
79 Wing fold jury strut
80 Remote compass transmitter

81 Port jury strut, stowed position
82 Fin root fillet
83 Starboard tailplane
84 Starboard elevator
85 Elevator tab
86 Fin construction
87 Sternpost
88 Aerial cable
89 Rudder balance
90 Fabric-covered rudder construction
91 Rudder tab
92 Tail-navigation lights
93 Rudder hinge control

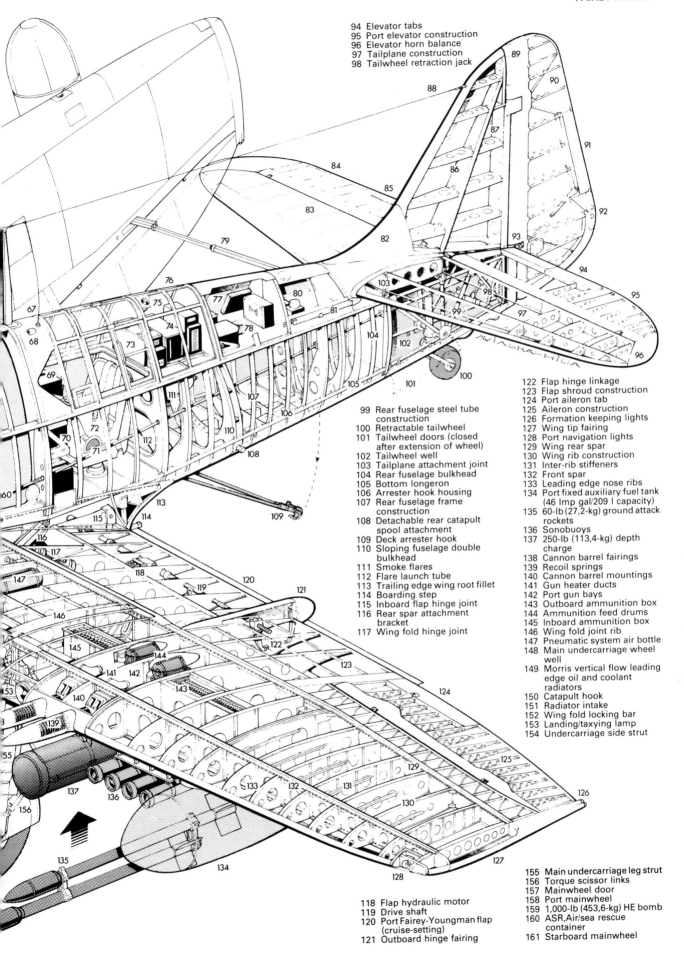

94 Elevator tabs
95 Port elevator construction
96 Elevator horn balance
97 Tailplane construction
98 Tailwheel retraction jack

99 Rear fuselage steel tube construction
100 Retractable tailwheel
101 Tailwheel doors (closed after extension of wheel)
102 Tailwheel well
103 Tailplane attachment joint
104 Rear fuselage bulkhead
105 Bottom longeron
106 Arrester hook housing
107 Rear fuselage frame construction
108 Detachable rear catapult spool attachment
109 Deck arrester hook
110 Sloping fuselage double bulkhead
111 Smoke flares
112 Flare launch tube
113 Trailing edge wing root fillet
114 Boarding step
115 Inboard flap hinge joint
116 Rear spar attachment bracket
117 Wing fold hinge joint

118 Flap hydraulic motor
119 Drive shaft
120 Port Fairey-Youngman flap (cruise-setting)
121 Outboard hinge fairing

122 Flap hinge linkage
123 Flap shroud construction
124 Port aileron tab
125 Aileron construction
126 Formation keeping lights
127 Wing tip fairing
128 Port navigation lights
129 Wing rear spar
130 Wing rib construction
131 Inter-rib stiffeners
132 Front spar
133 Leading edge nose ribs
134 Port fixed auxiliary fuel tank (46 Imp gal/209 l capacity)
135 60-lb (27,2-kg) ground attack rockets
136 Sonobuoys
137 250-lb (113,4-kg) depth charge
138 Cannon barrel fairings
139 Recoil springs
140 Cannon barrel mountings
141 Gun heater ducts
142 Port gun bays
143 Outboard ammunition box
144 Ammunition feed drums
145 Inboard ammunition box
146 Wing fold joint rib
147 Pneumatic system air bottle
148 Main undercarriage wheel well
149 Morris vertical flow leading edge oil and coolant radiators
150 Catapult hook
151 Radiator intake
152 Wing fold locking bar
153 Landing/taxying lamp
154 Undercarriage side strut

155 Main undercarriage leg strut
156 Torque scissor links
157 Mainwheel door
158 Port mainwheel
159 1,000-lb (453,6-kg) HE bomb
160 ASR, Air/sea rescue container
161 Starboard mainwheel

(Above) A pair of Firefly Mk IVs (TW735 in foreground and TW734 in background) from the first major production batch, the first service deliveries of this model commencing late September 1946. Development of the extensively revised Mk IV version gave the Firefly something of a new lease on life

(Above and below) Two of the Mk I airframes employed in the Firefly Mk IV development programme, Z2118 above and MB649 below, the former still retaining elliptical wingtips and Mk I vertical tail surfaces at this time

Okinawa, this unit was constantly engaged in offensive sorties.

The main body of the British Pacific Fleet left the Okinawa area on 25 May, returning to Sydney for repairs and replenishment, and shortly afterwards it was joined by *Implacable* which included the Fireflies of No 1771 Sqdn in its complement. During 14/15 June, this squadron participated in series of air strikes against Truk in the Carolinas and, on 10 July, acquired the distinction of being the first FAA aircraft to fly over mainland Japan. On 24 July, No 1771 was joined in attacks on shipping and shore targets by No 1772 from *Indefatigable* (this unit having succeeded No 1770

aboard the carrier), and during these operations, the Fireflies became the first British aircraft to fly over Tokyo. Prior to V-J day, a fourth Firefly squadron, No 1790 formed in January at Burscough, had joined the British Pacific Fleet and was operating from *Implacable* in the night fighting rôle. Two further squadrons, Nos 1791 and 1792, were home-based on Fireflies, having formed at Lee-on-Solent in March and May respectively, and two more squadrons, No 816 and 822, had relinquished Barracudas and were working up on the Firefly.

When WW II finally came to an end, the Firefly was far from having reached the apex of its evolution, and development and testing tempo was to continue apace. At this time, I was taking the Firefly through its RATOG (Rocket Assisted Take-Off Gear) trials, which included asymmetric firing to simulate rocket failure on one side. The Firefly proved, in fact, to have an ideal RATOG configuration, with the rockets set at a shallow angle to the fuselage and firing nearly through the CG and almost parallel to the thrust line of the engine. A few months later, in November 1945, a series of overload trials was initiated with the Firefly at the RAE. These included catapulting, arresting, rocket-assisted take-offs and overload landings. Problems were immediately encountered with the carriage of two 1,000 lb (453,6-kg) bombs, and I had these fall off twice on catapult launches and once during arrested landings. It was to take the best part of the year to modify the Firefly bomb carriage satisfactorily, and the culmination of these much extended trials was the series of rocket take-offs and overload landings at 14,000 lb (6 350 kg) AUW.

From a very early stage in the production career of the Firefly, work had been in progress on the mating of the airframe with the appreciably more powerful two-stage Griffon 61 engine. Firefly Mk Is were eventually to replace the 1,735 hp Griffon IIB with the 1,990 hp Griffon XII, and the application of the two-stage engine was expected to have a very useful if not an overly dramatic effect on performance. An early Mk I airframe, Z1835, had been fitted with a Griffon 61 as a Mk III prototype and had sported a heavy, semi-annular chin radiator which was soon found to be aerodynamically unsound, this somewhat cumbersome front end adversely affecting fore-and aft control and stability. Trials were promptly abandoned and a more extensive redesign initiated involving the introduction of leading-edge radiators in forward extensions of the wing centre section, these being tested on a Mk I airframe, Z2118, during 1944.

The prototype Mk II was duly modified with the new radiator arrangement and, fitted with a Griffon 72, became one of three prototypes of the Firefly Mk IV, the others being two ex-Mk I airframes (MB469 and PP482) which were similarly modified. The first Mk IV development aircraft, Z2118, initially flew with the semi-elliptical wings and the fin-and-rudder assembly of the Mk I, but early flight testing revealed that the extra torque produced by the four-bladed propeller necessary to absorb the power of the two-stage Griffon produced some control problems and the tail fin was therefore enlarged and a dorsal extension introduced to afford better directional stability. The centre section extensions housing the new leading-edge radiators had resulted in a not unsubstantial increment of wing area and the original area was restored simply by clipping the wingtips, the reduced span usefully increasing the rate of roll. The intake for the supercharger was relocated immediately behind the spinner, thus allowing a clean sweep of the bottom cowling line, and the centre section fuel tanks were discarded in favour of a nacelle fitting flush beneath the port wing and balanced under the starboard wing by another nacelle which could house either fuel — in which case total capacity was 255·5 Imp gal (1 161 l) — or a radar scanner and its associated gear.

The first production Firefly Mk 4* did not make its initial

The use of Roman numerals for aircraft mark numbers from I to XX was abandoned soon after the end of WWII and Arabic numerals substituted.

Fairey Firefly FR Mk 4 Specification

Power Plant: One Rolls-Royce Griffon 74 12-cylinder Vee liquid-cooled two-speed two-stage engine rated at 2,004 hp at 2,750 rpm for take-off, 2,245 hp at 2,750 rpm at 9,250 ft (2 820 m), 1,510 hp at 2,600 rpm at 7,500 ft (2 280 m) and 1,405 hp at 2,600 rpm at 20,500 ft (6 250 m) driving Rotol four-bladed constant-speed propeller. Fuel capacity comprising 145·5 Imp gal (661 l) in main fuselage tank and 55 Imp gal (250 l) in port wing fairing. Provision for two 90 Imp gal (209 l) drop tanks.
Performance: (Clean) Max speed, 316 mph (509 km/h) at sea level, 345 mph (555 km/h) at 12,500 ft (3 810 m), (with two 90 Imp gal/409 l) drop tanks), 282 mph (454 km/h) at sea level, 310 mph (499 km/h) at 12,500 ft (3 810 m); time to 5,000 ft (1 525 m), 3·6 min, to 10,000 ft (3 050 m), 7·15 min, to 20,000 ft (6 095 m), 15·5 min; service ceiling, 29,200 ft (8 900 m); range (standard fuel), 582 mls (937 km) at 233 mph (375 km/h), (with two 90 Imp gal/409 l drop tanks), 1,070 mls (1 722 km) at 228 mph (367 km/h); take-off distance (at 12,770 lb/5 792 kg), 675 yds (738 m) into 10-knot (18,5-km/h) wind, 504 yds (551 m) into 20-knot (37 km/h) wind.
Weights: Empty equipped, 9,859 lb (4 472 kg); loaded (clean), 13,500 lb (6 124 kg); max take-off, 15,615 lb (7 083 kg).
Dimensions: Span, 41 ft 0 in (12,49 m); width folded, 16 ft 0 in (4,88 m); length, 37 ft 0 in (11,28 m); length folded (tail up), 37 ft 7½ in (11,47 m); height, 15 ft 5½ in (4,74 m); wing area, 330 sq ft (30,66 m²).
Armament: Four 20-mm Hispano cannon with 160 rpg and provision for two 1,000-lb (453,6-kg) bombs or eight 60-lb (27,2-kg) rockets, or eight 25-lb (11,34-kg) rockets and two 500-lb (227-kg) bombs.

(Above left) A Firefly AS Mk 5 anti-submarine, reconnaissance and strike aircraft with underwing sonobuoy containers, and (below) a Firefly AS Mk 6 (WD917) operating from RNAS Ford. The AS Mk 6 was to become the last representative of the prolific Firefly family to retain an operational role

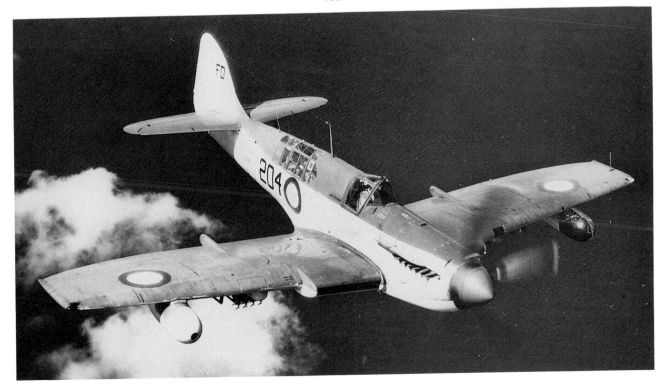

flight until 25 May 1946, delivery following four months later, on 29 September, and a further five months were to elapse before, in February 1947, a Mk 4 arrived at the RAE for arresting proofing trials which commenced on 1 March and immediately ran into a mound of problems. These were caused by unsatisfactory snap gear which should have kept the arrester hook locked into the fuselage after it had picked up the arrester wire and so prevented excessive forward pitching. For most of March, I kept demolishing propeller tips as test after test failed.

This was a somewhat inauspicious start to the Farnborough stay of this new mark of Firefly, which at first sight, appeared to have undergone so radical a metamorphosis as to be virtually a new aircraft type. The previously related changes did radically alter the appearance of the aircraft, and to my mind it was sleeker and more elegant, although the whole effect was marred by the two large underwing fairings. There were numerous less obvious changes, such as the provision of tailwheel lock, primarily to avoid excessive crabbing during

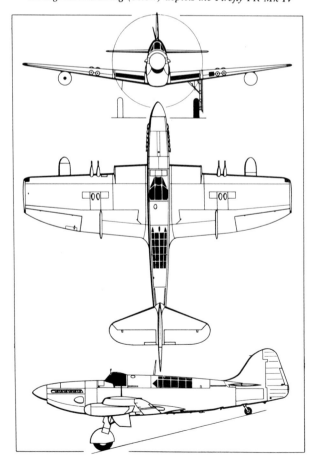

(Above) A Firefly AS Mk 5 landing aboard HMS Vengeance during exercises off the Portuguese coast in the early 'fifties. The general arrangement drawing (below) depicts the Firefly FR Mk IV

catapult launching due to the high torque effect of the Griffon 74 now standardised, but it was still very much a Firefly for all that. For all the redesign that had betokened this very different Firefly and its greater power notwithstanding, it handled very much as did the preceding variants, offering the same handling shortcomings and advantages, with a modicum more control heaviness but displaying more zest on the climb and in acceleration.

With the advent of the Mk 4, the Firefly took something of a new lease on life, revealing a quite extraordinary amenability to new rôles to which were soon to be added that of anti-submarine warfare, and with commendable perspicacity, the Fairey company, provided by the Firefly with a sound basis for continuing business through the leanest of the immediate postwar years, evolved what it referred to as a "universal" airframe, capable of accepting the various equipment demanded by the anti-submarine, day fighter-reconnaissance and night fighting rôles. This, the Firefly Mk 5, first flew on 12 December 1947, and production contracts for the aeroplane continued to flow at a time when the level of military aircraft production in the UK was still sharply declining in the postwar euphoria. Deliveries of the new model to the Navy commenced in January 1948 and continued until May 1950, and a very important modification introduced onto the Mk 5 production line at the beginning of 1949 — some of the Fireflies already delivered being retrospectively modified — was a long-needed refinement to the breed, namely power-folding wings which replaced the manual folding arrangement which was nothing short of a feat of endurance to accomplish on the deck of a carrier under way.

At this time, however, the Firefly was involved in a new war, hostilities having commenced in Korea during 1950. Six Firefly squadrons were to be involved in Korean operations, the first being No 810 from HMS *Theseus,* a light fleet carrier on station off the Korean coast within days of the start of the fighting. From then until the end of the conflict, at least one British or Commonwealth carrier was in Korean waters. The Firefly Mks 4 and 5 involved over Korea operated primarily in a close support rôle, although minelaying missions and shipping strikes were also flown. Carrying mixed loads of bombs and rockets up to a maximum of 2,000 lb (907 kg) per aircraft, the Fireflies operated at an intensive sortie rate — up to 120 sorties per day from a single carrier — frequently in inclement weather. The squadrons involved were No 810 embarked in HMS *Theseus,* Nos 812 and 820 in HMS *Glory,* No 825 in HMS *Ocean,* No 827 in HMS *Triumph* and No 817 in HMAS *Sidney.*

A further and final step in the utilisation of the Firefly in the anti-submarine rôle came in 1950 with the development of the AS Mk 6 which was optimised for the ASW task, the first prototype of which was to fly on 22 May 1951 and the first production aircraft five months later, on 16 October, But the production life of the Firefly as an operational aircraft was now drawing to its close. The availability of the Avenger AS Mk 4 through MDAP resulted in cutbacks in AS Mk 7 production and the redevelopment of the aircraft as the T Mk 7 trainer for anti-submarine observers, and the final aircraft off the line were U Mk 8 radio-controlled target drone versions of the Firefly which made use of components put in hand for cancelled Mk 7s, the last of these being delivered on 20 April 1956, bringing Firefly production finally to an end, a total of 1,702 aircraft of this type having been manufactured in all its versions.

The Firefly was well loved by the Fleet Air Arm; what other than affection could be felt for a pilot's aeroplane that combined good handling characteristics with a sound performance, tremendous reliability and outstanding versatility. It was an excellent example of the shipboard aircraft designer's art and one that served the Royal Navy long and well.□

Blackburn Firebrand

A WELL-CHOSEN, emotive name for a military aircraft can, in my view, be charismatic; it may even afford a psychological advantage in combat. Such aircraft as the Spitfire, Wildcat and Hornet — all truly great fighters — undoubtedly owed something of their charismata to the aggressive associations of their appellations. There have been, of course, the occasional noteworthy exceptions; the aircraft that failed to match up to fine fighting names. Firebrand, for example, had a nice ring to it as a name for a combat aircraft, but rather than being charismatic in so far as concerned the warplane on which it was bestowed, it proved prophetic, though hardly in a fashion envisaged by those responsible for its adoption.

A firebrand is, according to the *Oxford English Dictionary,* one who or that which kindles strife or mischief, inflames the passions, etc. There was no gainsaying that the Blackburn recipient of the name Firebrand kindled its share of strife, but regrettably between customer and contractor, and while pilots used rather stronger adjectives than mischievous apropos the less endearing characteristics of the aircraft, it certainly demonstrated the ability to inflame *their* passions!

Whatever attributes the publicists of the day may have claimed for the Blackburn Firebrand, in the final analysis, this welterweight of a single-seat shipboard torpedo-fighter was a failure. It was never a pilot's aircraft — how could it be when he sat nearer the tail than the nose; as a deck-landing aeroplane it was a disaster and it was incapable of fulfilling competently either the rôle of torpedo-bomber or that of fighter, but it was built like a battleship — and there were to be those that would say that it flew like one!

In view of the British aircraft industry's leadership in the design of shipboard combat aircraft for a substantial period

between the two World Wars, it is perhaps odd that no British *purpose-designed* single-seat propeller-driven fleet fighter monoplane ever saw carrier service. It was to fill just such a need that Blackburn's chief designer, C E Petty, and his team created the Firebrand, but the rugged and not inelegant warplane that saw birth on the Brough drawing boards in 1940, in response to specification N.11/40, was to suffer such a protracted succession of changes in its intended rôle, its power plant and its structure, that some seven years were to elapse before it was to achieve operational status aboard a carrier, by which time it was to bear little more than a configurational similarity to the prototype that had flown for the first time on 27 February 1942.   For its intended rôle of fleet fighter, the Firebrand was a formidably large aeroplane of extraordinarily robust construction, with a heavy-duty centreline frame around which was built a massive two-spar wing centre section into which folded the proportionately immense main undercarriage members and forward extensions of which accommodated the coolant radiator for the compact 2,305 hp Napier Sabre III 24-cylinder H-type engine around which this fighter had been designed. The forward fuselage was a circular-section tubular-steel structure, which housed both main and auxiliary fuel tanks, and aft of the pilot's cockpit the fuselage was an oval-section stressed-skin semi-monocoque. The entire wing trailing-edge, from root to Frise-type aileron, was occupied by hydraulically-operated Fowler and subsidiary flaps, and each outer wing panel was intended to accommodate a pair of 20-mm Hispano cannon with 200 rpg. It was indeed a very substantial collection of ironmongery for the rôle that it was intended to fulfil, and by the time Flt Lt Arthur Thompson took the first prototype, DD804, into the air for its maiden

(Above) The unarmed first prototype Firebrand (DD804) landing at Brough early in 1942, and (immediately below) the four-cannon second prototype (DD810)

(Immediately above) The third prototype Firebrand (DD815) which was to be rebuilt after suffering damage in a forced landing, becoming the Mk II prototype (NV636). (Below) The first production Firebrand Mk I (DK363) at Luton in 1943

flight from RAF Leconfield — the airfield at Brough being in a water-logged state — it was tacitly accepted that the Firebrand was *too* substantial a warplane for the task for which it had been created and had, in any case, been outmoded by the successful adaptation of the Spitfire for the shipboard rôle.

Hindsight suggests that further development of the Firebrand should have been abandoned at this stage, but two further prototypes were by now virtually complete and series production of the Firebrand I was already in its initial stages, and if this large aeroplane lacked the nimbleness necessary for mixing it with its shore-based contemporaries, it did offer formidable load-carrying potential. Thus, the idea of reworking the basic design for the rôle of torpedo-carrying strike fighter was conceived, a transformation posing no mean task for Blackburn's design team.

Meanwhile, the unarmed first prototype, with some modifications to the horizontal tail surfaces as a result of contractor's trials, had undergone full performance trials at the A&AEE at Boscombe Down, the principal recommendations resulting from which being some increases in flap and

rudder areas to improve low-speed handling, and the fully-armed second (DD810) and third (DD815) prototypes had joined the flight test programme on 15 July and 15 September 1942 respectively. The second prototype was delivered to the Navy on 11 October, initial trials being performed by the service from RNAS Machrihanish, Kintyre, and I first came in contact with the aircraft on 1 February 1943, when it arrived at Arbroath, where I was serving in the Service Trials Unit, prior to its initial deck landing trials aboard HMS *Illustrious* in the Clyde Estuary.

The Firebrand prototype was impressively big and grossly oversized for the fighter mission, which, in so far as we were aware at that time, was still its *raison d'être*; perhaps powerful burliness best describes the principal impression that it imparted, but it was aesthetically not unappealing. When it landed on *Illustrious* a few days later, it presented an awesome sight and seemed likely to tear the arrester wires clean out of the ship, but, in fact, the landing speed proved very reasonable, thanks to the extensive trailing-edge flappery. The pilot, Cmdr D R F Cambell, obviously had problems with the view ahead, which was hardly surprising, taking into account the aft positioning of the cockpit and the length of nose interposed between windscreen and propeller. Once the Firebrand was on the deck, wing folding also posed a quota of problems. The wings were folded manually to lie parallel to the fuselage, leading edge uppermost, latch pins being withdrawn from forged-steel fork-end fittings at the extremities of the centre-section spars, but coping with this in the wind that always blows over a carrier's deck demanded a large squad of aircraft handlers.

More than a year was to pass before I was actually to get my hands on a Firebrand, an event that was to take place at the Royal Aircraft Establishment at Farnborough on 19 May 1944, and much had happened to this aircraft in the interim. After its trials aboard *Illustrious,* the second prototype had been returned to the contractor but had suffered damage in a forced landing. While being flown by Arthur Thompson, the aircraft had had an engine seizure about a mile short of the approach to Brough airfield as a result of an oil pipe fracture. In attempting a wheels-up landing with his view obscured by oil on the windscreen, the pilot had flown into the inch-and-a-quarter (3,2-cm) thick cable of the Earle's Cement overhead bucket system, this arresting the aircraft in flight in no uncertain fashion, breaking and then lashing back through the fuselage structure immediately behind the pilot. Surprisingly, Thompson had suffered the most minor of injuries, and it had been decided to rebuild the prototype and simultaneously incorporate the design changes that "Jim" Petty and his team had concluded were necessary to transform the Firebrand for its newly-proposed torpedo-carrying rôle.

The centre section had been widened by 15·5 in (39,4 cm) and strengthened along its centreline to allow an 18-in (45,7-cm) torpedo weighing 1,850 lb (839 kg) to be slung between the wheel well doors, and re-serialled NV636, this aircraft had re-emerged as the prototype Mk II and had flown at Brough on 31 March 1943, flying two days later with a dummy torpedo for the first time and, on 3 April, being looped and rolled with this appendage for the benefit of the then Minister for Aircraft Production, Sir Stafford Cripps. Time was to reveal that the hanging of "tin-fish" from an aircraft, presupposing adequate power and lift, was a relatively simple matter by comparison with ensuring its effective launching.

The structural changes and the torpedo, which boosted gross weight by 1,424 lb (646 kg) to 15,049 lb (6 826 kg), had not had as dramatically deleterious an effect on performance as might have been supposed: maximum speed at its best altitude of 18,000 ft (5 485 m) was reduced from the 310 knots (574 km/h) clocked by the Mk I to 302 knots (560 km/h), sea level climb rate was down from 2,250 ft/min

(11,43 m/sec) to 1,900 ft/min (9,65 m/sec) and take-off run into a 20 knot (37 km/h) wind had been stretched from 515 ft (157 m) to 680 ft (207 m).

Meanwhile, an assembly line had been gathering momentum at Brough and the first nine production aircraft (DK363-371), having reached too advanced a stage to be modified for the torpedo-dropping rôle, had been completed in the original straight fighter configuration as Firebrand Mk Is — all of these subsequently being utilised for various experimental tasks — but, the priority in the supply of Sabre engines having been assigned to the Hawker Typhoon by this time, the Blackburn team had been faced with the ingenuity-taxing task of mating the existing airframe with the two-row 18-cylinder sleeve-valve Bristol Centaurus VII radial.

The tenth and eleventh Firebrand Mk I airframes (DK372-373) had been assigned for conversion as prototypes of what was to be defined by Specification S.8/43, issued on 3 October 1943, as the Centaurus-powered Firebrand Mk III. Despite the magnitude of the rework, Blackburn, with commendable despatch, had succeeded in getting the first of these prototypes flying on 21 December 1943, and although the next dozen aircraft on the assembly line (DK374-385) had been perforce completed with the Sabre engine, these incorporating the modifications necessary for torpedo carrying and being known as Firebrand Mk IIs, all the remaining 27 aircraft (DK386-412) built against the original Firebrand contract for 50 aircraft (excluding the three Mk I prototypes) were to be delivered to Mk III standard.

The first production Firebrand Mk III was, in fact, to be almost another year in coming off the line, commencing its flight test programme in November 1944, and the fourth production example (DK389) arrived at Farnborough in February 1945, followed in May by the second example (DK387). These aircraft had been delivered to the RAE for arresting proofing prior to deck landing trials, and I could only but hope that they would do better in this than had the Sabre-engined version. I had pulled the entire hook installation out of that aircraft on 3 October 1944 when making a programmed 25 ft (7,62 m) off-centre landing into the arrester wires with a 55 knot (102 km/h) entry speed.

The Sabre-engined Firebrand had, in fact, left me singularly unimpressed, if one discounts the rather startling impression of sheer bulk that it conveyed, the first example that I had flown having been the fourth production Firebrand Mk I (DK366). Much was made of the fact that this aircraft had proven capable of out-diving a Spitfire in mock dogfights and it was to be admitted that this initial Sabre-engined model was quite fast for an aircraft of its size, but manoeuv-

(Above) The third prototype after reconstruction as the first Firebrand Mk II (NV636), and (immediately below) Firebrand TF Mk II (DK375) assigned to the Firebrand Tactical Trials Unit

(Immediately above) Firebrand TF Mk II (DK367) photographed during armament trials at Boscombe Down in the summer of 1943, and (below) TF Mk II (DK383) of No 708 Squadron mounting a torpedo and flying in the vicinity of the Solent in 1945

(Below) Four of the Firebrand TF Mk IIs (DK383 in the foreground) of No 708 Squadron, the Firebrand Tactical Trials Unit, at RNAS Lee-on-Solent. This unit received seven of the 12 Mk IIs built, but trials were plagued by unserviceability and constant modification

(Above) The second prototype Firebrand Mk III (DK373). This was a conversion of an airframe originally laid down as the 11th production Mk I. This aircraft was taken on charge on 8 May 1944. (Below left) The first Mk III prototype (DK372), originally the 10th production Mk I airframe

(Below) Firebrand TF Mk III (DK386), the first production example of this variant which was first flown in November 1944. This aircraft was retained by the manufacturer for development purposes

rability was very disappointing and particularly so with regard to rate of roll. The application of flap resulted in very large trim changes and there was a lot of unpleasant engine vibration. A half-dozen of the Sabre-engined Firebrand Mk IIs (DK380-385) were delivered to No 708 Squadron at Lee-on-Solent in September and October 1944, a shore-based trials unit which flew a number of combat practice sorties with these aircraft which were destined to be the only Firebrands actually taken on charge by a naval squadron prior to the end of hostilities in Europe.

Before flying the Firebrand Mk III (DK389) from Farn-borough to Henstridge airfield, which had a set of arrester wires and rather more runway length available, I had the opportunity to perform a few handling flights with the aircraft the first of these taking place on 12 March 1945. These flights left me with somewhat mixed feelings about this new Fire-brand, with its powerful Centaurus radial engine and 13 ft 6 in (4,11 m) diameter four-bladed Rotol propeller, spring-loaded tabs on all control surfaces and more rudder. In the first place, view from the cockpit, which had been very poor with the Sabre-engined models, had deteriorated even further, and both speed and range had suffered markedly as a result of the transformation, but the worst feature was its

inadequate directional control on take-off with full flap necessary on a carrier deck. To set against these shortcomings were a general improvement in manoeuvrability and a better rate of climb.

One feature of this aircraft which, prompted by the poor pilot view for deck landing. I found intriguing was an external low-speed sector airspeed indicator outside the cockpit, ahead of the port windscreen quarter light, to enable the pilot's eyes to remain uninterruptedly looking ahead during the vital final stages of the approach to the carrier deck at 80 knots (148 km/h) — a sort of embryonic head-up display!

At Henstridge, the Firebrand Mk III immediately revealed a weakness in arrested landings. At 20 ft (6,0 m) off centre the port elevator came off its hinge and, later, the hook pulled out. My old friend Peter G Lawrence, whom I had served with in the Service Trials Unit in 1943, had left the Royal Navy in 1944 to join Blackburn as a test pilot, and so I soon began to see a lot of him once again as his presence at Farnborough was frequently demanded to discuss the problems that we were encountering with the Firebrand. One such problem was the unpleasant tendency of the aircraft to drop a wing at the stall, this occurring at the critical stage just before touch-down unless engine power was held on right down to the deck.

The Firebrand Mk III possessed many faults and presented many problems, but it had at least earned full marks in its rocket-assisted take-off trials, which had included asymmetric firings, so its record was not entirely black. It was a long way from ready for issue to service units, however, and inevitably a Mk IV version of the Firebrand made its début, embodying, so it was said, cures for all the Mk III's ills. Despite the protracted development of the Firebrand and the innumerable problems that its various test programmes had posed, neither Blackburn nor the Admiralty ever admitted defeat and a contract for a further 102 aircraft had been placed, these being of the improved Mk IV variant. The first production example (EK601) was airborne for the first time on 17 May 1945 with a 2,520 hp Centaurus IX, vibration dampers being incorporated in the engine mounting and this version of the Bristol engine having supplanted the 2,400 hp Centaurus VII in the last 17 Mk IIIs commencing with DK396.

Major changes from the Mk III embodied by the Firebrand Mk IV included a horn-balanced rudder of substantially larger area to improve control during carrier landings and a commensurately larger vertical fin which was offset three degrees to port to compensate for the very considerable torque of the Rotol propeller. A greater diversity of external ordnance was catered for and a 500-lb (226,8-kg) bomb or three 60-lb (27-kg) rocket projectiles could be carried beneath each wing, the Mk XV or XVII torpedo being replaceable with a 2,000-lb (907-kg) bomb. For extended range operations, a 45 Imp gal (204 l) drop tank could be carried beneath each wing and it was also possible to fit a 100 Imp gal (455 l) overload tank in the torpedo crutches. The torpedo crutches were, incidentally, pin-jointed forward to provide two torpedo angles. With the undercarriage extended, the torpedo adopted a 6 deg nose-down attitude to provide adequate ground clearance, but as the undercarriage retracted, the nose of the torpedo was automatically raised until it rested at an angle one degree nose up for minimum drag in flight.

The arrested landing proving trials with the Firebrand Mk IV progressed well and the catapulting trials equally so, with all sorts of stores hung from the aircraft up to an all-up weight of 16,700 lb (7 574 kg). The RAE's second job was to evaluate the dive brakes which were of the transverse bar type extending above and below the mainplane leading edges and spanning the centre third of each wing. These brakes were hydraulically actuated and as originally tested, were very slow in operation, demanding 5·3 seconds to open at 300 knots (556 km/h) and 2·2 seconds to close at 260 knots (482

km/h). This tardiness of operation resulted in a sharp nose down trim change on opening and a relatively innocuous nose up trim change on closing, and throughout the actual movement of the brakes there was considerable buffeting and skin panting on the wings aft of the brakes and inboard to the wing root.

Fortunately, the solution proved to be a simple mechanical one and not a complex aerodynamic one. The RAE simply removed the restrictor valve in the hydraulic pipelines on the pressure side of the pump and this not only accelerated the rate of operation to something like half the time taken previously, it reduced the trim change effect on opening until it was apparent only above 250 knots (463 km/h) and completely eliminated the buffeting and skin panting. The dive brakes gave a drag effect equivalent to a 60 knot (111 km/h) reduction in level flight speed, the dive angle to reach terminal velocity being some 50 deg. The Firebrand IV could be held easily in a dive entered from trimmed cruising flight without retrimming, and if trimmed in the dive, the pull-out force required was 5 lb (2,27 kg) per *g* practically constant throughout the speed range, this being actually lighter than in an unbraked dive over the same speed range. On nearing the high-speed stall buffeting set in and acted as a most useful warning.

The Firebrand IV was by now shaping up into a strike aircraft with a useful performance, and light and effective controls, but without further major redesign little could be done about the very poor view offered the pilot on the run in to target, and it really needed an automatic supercharger gear change control in the dive. It was still officially referred to as a torpedo-*fighter* and while the first half of this classification was open to question, the latter half should most definitely have been abandoned, for, as a fighter the Firebrand could not be taken seriously, being short on performance, sadly lacking in manoeuvrability, especially in rate of roll, and presenting a large target for the opposition.

In order to rectify at least one of these faults, a series of

Blackburn Firebrand TF Mk IV Specification

Power Plant: One Bristol Centaurus IX 18-cylinder two-row radial air-cooled engine rated at 2,520 hp at 2,700 rpm for take-off, 2,225 hp at 2,700 rpm at 11,000 ft (3 355 m) for 5 min and a max continuous output of 1,975 hp at 2,400 rpm at 12,750 ft (3 890 m) driving a 13 ft 3 in (4,04 m) diam Rotol four-bladed constant-speed wooden propeller. Fuel capacity: 168 Imp gal (764 l) in main tank and provision for 71 Imp gal (323 l) in auxiliary tank.
Performance: Max speed (at 15,671 lb/7 108 kg), 320 mph (515 km/h) at sea level, 350 mph (563 km/h) at 13,000 ft (3 960 m), with torpedo, 342 mph (550 km/h) at 13,000 ft (3 960 m); cruising speed (75 per cent max econ power), 256 mph (412 km/h) at 10,000 ft (3 050 m), (max econ power), 289 mph (465 km/h); range (max internal fuel at 75 per cent max econ power), 745 mls (1 199 km); initial climb (clean), 2,600 ft/min (13,2 m/sec), (with torpedo), 2,200 ft/min (11,16 m/sec).
Weights: Empty equipped, 11,457 lb (5 197 kg); loaded (clean), 15,761 lb (7 108 kg); max take-off (full internal fuel and Mk XVII torpedo), 16,700 lb (7 575 kg).
Dimensions: Span, 51 ft 3½ in (15,63 m); span folded, 16 ft 1 in (4,90 m); length, 38 ft 9 in (11,81 m); height, 13 ft 3 in (4,04 m); wing area, 383 sq ft (35,58 m²); dihedral (outer panels only), 5 deg; undercarriage track, 11 ft 0½ in (3,36 m).
Armament: Four 20-mm Hispano cannon with 200 rpg and one 1,850-lb (839-kg) Mk XV or XVII torpedo.

Two Firebrand TF Mk 4s from the second production batch, EK660 (below) seen being flown by P. G. Lawrence and EK668 (above right) with wings folded. The Firebrand TF Mk 4 entered service with No 813 Squadron at RNAS Ford at the beginning of September 1945, this unit becoming the first Royal Navy squadron to fly single-seat torpedo-carrying aircraft for more than a score of years

trials were to be undertaken at Farnborough with a Firebrand Mk 5 (EK769) fitted with power-assisted ailerons. The ailerons on this aircraft had no spring tabs and only aerodynamic nose balance, and the power-assister gave a 25 per cent feed-back to the pilot. This system improved the rate of roll slightly, but there was a steep build-up in operating force with speed. This build-up was such that a push of 50 lb (22,7 kg) was required at 350 knots (649 km/h) to give full aileron and the rate of roll was then only 43 deg/sec. The Focke-Wulf Fw 190 had a rate of roll of some 180 deg/sec, so the Firebrand was way out of its class in mixing it with more specialised fighters.

Development of the Firebrand had, by this time, virtually spanned the entire period of World War II and although many of its more dramatic shortcomings had been eradicated with the passage of time, some of its faults were innate and impervious to the apparently interminable modification process. Nevertheless, if perhaps demanding a higher overall standard of airmanship than most of its contemporaries, the Firebrand, while still far removed from the proverbial pilot's aeroplane, at least now offered quite acceptable characteristics and, in September 1945, No 813 Squadron at Ford re-formed with 15 Firebrand Mk IVs to become the first Royal Navy squadron operating single-seat torpedo aircraft since the retirement of the Blackburn Dart a dozen years earlier. A couple more years were to pass before, late in

1947, this squadron took Firebrands aboard a carrier for the first time when it embarked in *Illustrious*. By this time, its Firebrand Mk IVs had given place to Mk 5s which had followed on the Brough assembly line with the completion in 1945 of the 102 examples of the earlier model. One hundred and twenty Firebrand Mk 5s had originally been ordered, although, in the event, the last 50 of these were to be cancelled, and deliveries began early in 1946, these being supplemented by about 40 Mk IVs which were brought up to the Mk 5 standard.

Featuring detail improvements, such as longer-span aileron tabs and horn-balanced elevators, the Firebrand Mk 5 was still not the definitive development, however. This was to be the Mk 5A introducing the hydraulically-boosted ailerons on which we had done so much work at Farnborough. As a *shore*-based strike fighter, the Firebrand Mk 5/5A was a competent enough aeroplane, but to the end it was a disaster as a deck-landing aircraft. Its Centaurus IX was a great engine which usually started smoothly on firing the Coffman

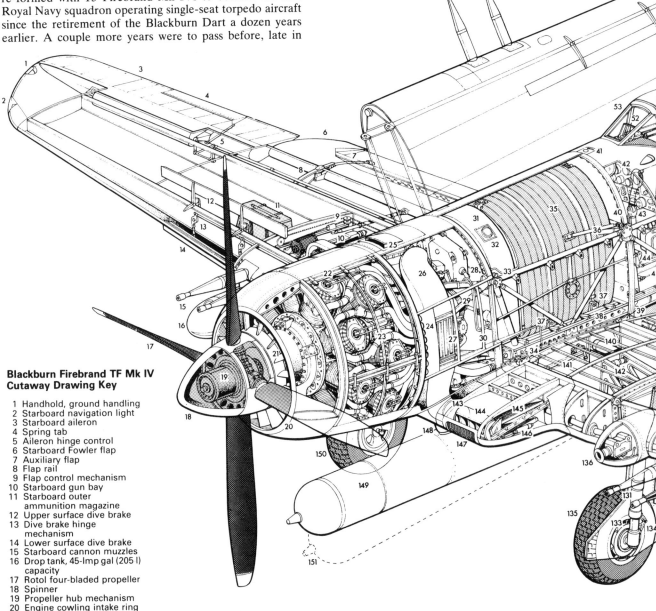

**Blackburn Firebrand TF Mk IV
Cutaway Drawing Key**

1 Handhold, ground handling
2 Starboard navigation light
3 Starboard aileron
4 Spring tab
5 Aileron hinge control
6 Starboard Fowler flap
7 Auxiliary flap
8 Flap rail
9 Flap control mechanism
10 Starboard gun bay
11 Starboard outer
   ammunition magazine
12 Upper surface dive brake
13 Dive brake hinge
   mechanism
14 Lower surface dive brake
15 Starboard cannon muzzles
16 Drop tank, 45-Imp gal (205 l)
   capacity
17 Rotol four-bladed propeller
18 Spinner
19 Propeller hub mechanism
20 Engine cowling intake ring
21 Cooling air fan

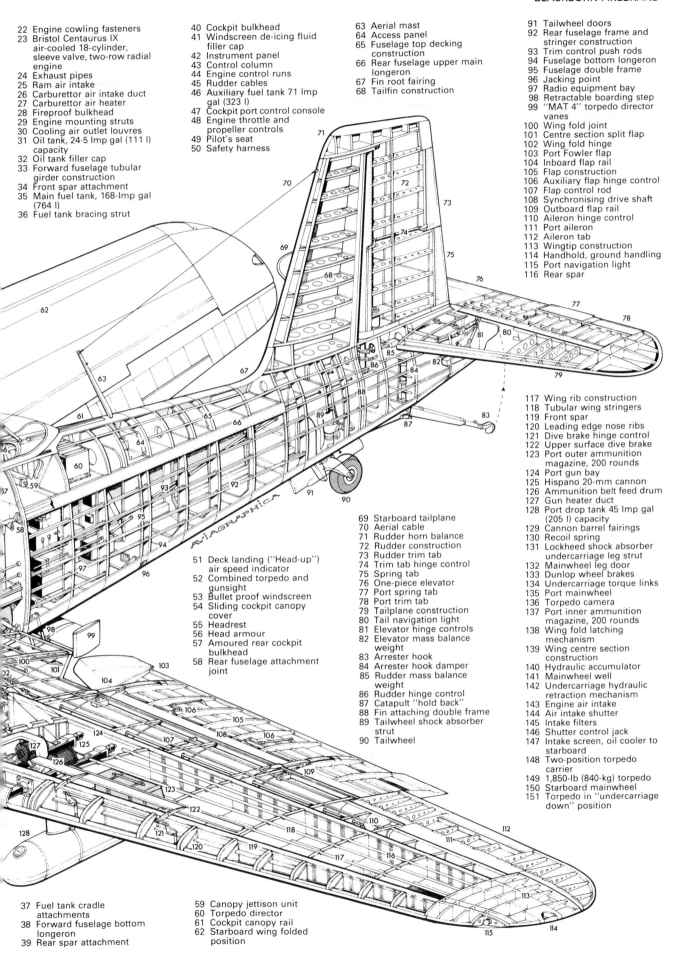

22 Engine cowling fasteners
23 Bristol Centaurus IX air-cooled 18-cylinder, sleeve valve, two-row radial engine
24 Exhaust pipes
25 Ram air intake
26 Carburettor air intake duct
27 Carburettor air heater
28 Fireproof bulkhead
29 Engine mounting struts
30 Cooling air outlet louvres
31 Oil tank, 24·5 Imp gal (111 l) capacity
32 Oil tank filler cap
33 Forward fuselage tubular girder construction
34 Front spar attachment
35 Main fuel tank, 168-Imp gal (764 l)
36 Fuel tank bracing strut

40 Cockpit bulkhead
41 Windscreen de-icing fluid filler cap
42 Instrument panel
43 Control column
44 Engine control runs
45 Rudder cables
46 Auxiliary fuel tank 71 Imp gal (323 l)
47 Cockpit port control console
48 Engine throttle and propeller controls
49 Pilot's seat
50 Safety harness

51 Deck landing ("Head-up") air speed indicator
52 Combined torpedo and gunsight
53 Bullet proof windscreen
54 Sliding cockpit canopy cover
55 Headrest
56 Head armour
57 Amoured rear cockpit bulkhead
58 Rear fuselage attachment joint

63 Aerial mast
64 Access panel
65 Fuselage top decking construction
66 Rear fuselage upper main longeron
67 Fin root fairing
68 Tailfin construction

69 Starboard tailplane
70 Aerial cable
71 Rudder horn balance
72 Rudder construction
73 Rudder trim tab
74 Trim tab hinge control
75 Spring tab
76 One-piece elevator
77 Port spring tab
78 Port trim tab
79 Tailplane construction
80 Tail navigation light
81 Elevator hinge controls
82 Elevator mass balance weight
83 Arrester hook
84 Arrester hook damper
85 Rudder mass balance weight
86 Rudder hinge control
87 Catapult "hold back"
88 Fin attaching double frame
89 Tailwheel shock absorber strut
90 Tailwheel

91 Tailwheel doors
92 Rear fuselage frame and stringer construction
93 Trim control push rods
94 Fuselage bottom longeron
95 Fuselage double frame
96 Jacking point
97 Radio equipment bay
98 Retractable boarding step
99 "MAT 4" torpedo director vanes
100 Wing fold joint
101 Centre section split flap
102 Wing fold hinge
103 Port Fowler flap
104 Inboard flap rail
105 Flap construction
106 Auxiliary flap hinge control
107 Flap control rod
108 Synchronising drive shaft
109 Outboard flap rail
110 Aileron hinge control
111 Port aileron
112 Aileron tab
113 Wingtip construction
114 Handhold, ground handling
115 Port navigation light
116 Rear spar

117 Wing rib construction
118 Tubular wing stringers
119 Front spar
120 Leading edge nose ribs
121 Dive brake hinge control
122 Upper surface dive brake
123 Port outer ammunition magazine, 200 rounds
124 Port gun bay
125 Hispano 20-mm cannon
126 Ammunition belt feed drum
127 Gun heater duct
128 Port drop tank 45 Imp gal (205 l) capacity
129 Cannon barrel fairings
130 Recoil spring
131 Lockheed shock absorber undercarriage leg strut
132 Mainwheel leg door
133 Dunlop wheel brakes
134 Undercarriage torque links
135 Port mainwheel
136 Torpedo camera
137 Port inner ammunition magazine, 200 rounds
138 Wing fold latching mechanism
139 Wing centre section construction
140 Hydraulic accumulator
141 Mainwheel well
142 Undercarriage hydraulic retraction mechanism
143 Engine air intake
144 Air intake shutter
145 Intake filters
146 Shutter control jack
147 Intake screen, oil cooler to starboard
148 Two-position torpedo carrier
149 1,850-lb (840-kg) torpedo
150 Starboard mainwheel
151 Torpedo in "undercarriage down" position

37 Fuel tank cradle attachments
38 Forward fuselage bottom longeron
39 Rear spar attachment

59 Canopy jettison unit
60 Torpedo director
61 Cockpit canopy rail
62 Starboard wing folded position

AVIAGRAPHICA

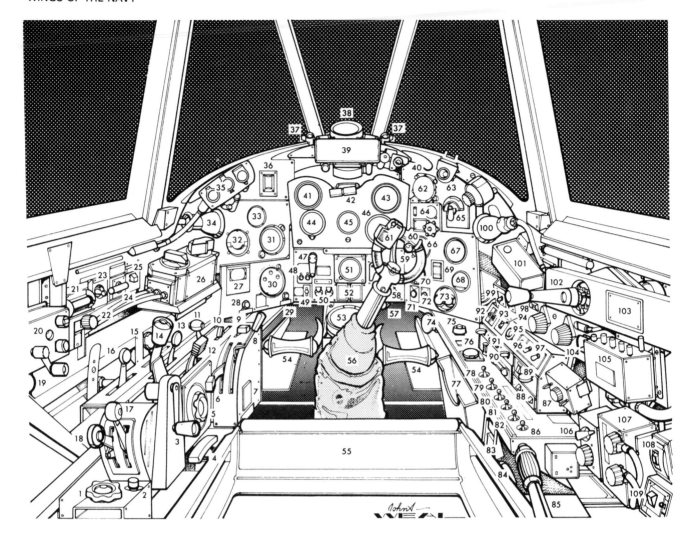

Blackburn Firebrand TF Mk 5 Cockpit Instrumentation Key

1 Rudder trimmer control
2 Deck arrester hook indicator light
3 Elevator trimmer control
4 Engine priming pump
5 Throttle and RPM control levers damper
6 Undercarriage control lever
7 Undercarriage safety lock acces patch
8 Flap control lever
9 Supercharger control
10 Air-intake filter control
11 Fuel cut-off control lever
12 RPM control lever
13 Engine cooling shutters control lever
14 Throttle control lever
15 Master engine fuel cock
16 Air-intake heat control lever
17 Tailwheel strut centralising control lever
18 Deck arrester hook control lever
19 Safety harness stowage
20 ZBX control unit
21 RP/bombs master selector 3-way switch
22 Auxiliary light switch
23 RP pairs/salvo switch
24 RATOG master switch
25 Torpedo director switch
26 Torpedo director control unit
27 Rudder and elevator trimmers indicator
28 Supercharger warning light

29 Undercarriage warning light
30 Undercarriage position indicator
31 Altimeter
32 Altitude limit switch
33 Torpedo depth indicator
34 Cockpit light
35 Altitude warning lights
36 Torpedo depth setting 3-way switch
37 Gunsight skid indicator lights (2)
38 Gunsight
39 Gunsight padded mounting
40 Windscreen de-icing handpump and regulator
41 Airspeed indicator
42 Hood jettison release handle
43 Artificial horizon
44 Rate of climb and descent indicator
45 Direction indicator
46 Turn and bank indicator
47 Dive brakes control lever
48 Ignition switches
49 Fuel booster pump switch
50 Oil dilution (left)/engine starter and booster-coil (right) pushbuttons
51 RI compass indicator
52 Correction card holders
53 Magnetic compass
54 Rudder pedals
55 Pilot's seat
56 Control column
57 Compass light switch
58 Cockpit and windscreen

heating control finger plates (obscured by control grip)
59 Wheel brakes lever
60 Radio "press-to-talk" switch
61 Combined guns/bombs/ RP/torpedo/cine camera "wobble" switch
62 Pneumatic supply and brakes pressure gauge
63 ASV warning light
64 Oxygen supply/regulator control panel
65 Fuel transfer cock
66 Boost gauge (partially obscured by control grip)
67 RPM indicator
68 Engine temperature gauge
69 Oil pressure gauge
70 Oil temperature gauge (partially obscured by control grip)
71 Fuel pressure warning light
72 Fire warning light
73 Fuel contents gauge
74 Cartridge starter re-indexing control
75 Fuel transfer warning light
76 Wing drop tanks/SCI jettison switch
77 Map case
78 Bomb fuzing (nose) switch
79 Bomb fuzing (tail) switch
80 Bomb (port) selector switch
81 Bomb (centre/or torpedo) selector switch
82 Bomb (starboard) selector switch

83 Signal pistol stowage clip
84 Seat-raising handle
85 Hydraulic handpump
86 Bomb distributor switch
87 IFF auxiliary control unit
88 Recognition lights control panel
89 Identification/resin lights control panel
90 Navigation lights control panel
91 Formation lights control panel
92 Camera "sunny/cloudy" selector switch
93 Camera ON/OFF master switch
94 Torpedo camera/camera gun selector switch
95 Power failure warning light
96 RI compass switch
97 Pressure head heater switch
98 Emergency lighting master switch
99 RP salvo switches
100 Cockpit light
101 RP auto selector
102 Cockpit canopy operating handle
103 Data plate
104 IFF demolition switches
105 Radio control unit
106 IFF control unit
107 IFF supply socket
108 Ground/flight switch
109 ARI.5748 DC and AC control switches

cartridge and purred beautifully — the reliability of this power plant was something for which Firebrand pilots were eternally thankful, for without engine their aircraft became a flying brick!

The tendency of the Firebrand Mk 5 to swing to starboard during take-off was easily controlled by its immense rudder and full power and full flap could be used. The tail came up at about 30 knots (55 km/h) IAS and at 90 knots (167 km/h) relatively little pull was called for to get the aircraft airborne. A noticeable nose-up trim change occurred with the selection of undercarriage up and the speed for maximum climb rate was 145 knots (269 km/h) from sea level up to 12,000 ft (3 660 m), but for ease of control a more comfortable climbing speed was 160-170 knots (296-315 km/h) up to operating altitude. During the climb and at low cruise the Firebrand Mk 5 was longitudinally unstable, although this was much improved when a torpedo was carried and at all other times stability was satisfactory enough. The critical stability condition with a fully-loaded aircraft was with the CG on the aft limit.

The ailerons were heavy, except at low speeds when they became rather ineffective, but both the elevator and rudder were light and powerful, care having to be exercised with the former to avoid inducing large accelerations in steep turns and when pulling out of dives. The rudder became increasingly sensitive with speed and any violent use induced strong changes in lateral and longitudinal trim. Careful use of the rudder trim tab was necessary to counter the marked changes in directional trim with variations of speed and power. Extension of the flaps produced a strong nose-up trim change, but use of the air brakes produced only a slight nose-down trim change with extension and a commensurate nose-up change with retraction. Trimmed in a dive, the heaviness of the ailerons became increasingly noticeable, although the other controls remained relatively light and effective, and care had to be exercised in use of the rudder as sudden movement of this surface produced violent yaw and skid.

In aerobatics, recommended speeds included 180-200 knots (333-370 km/h) for a roll, 280-300 knots (520-556 km/h) for a loop and 300-320 knots (556-593 km/h) for a roll from a loop, but care was necessary during aerobatics to avoid stalling owing to the possibility of spinning. With engine off, undercarriage and flaps up, the clean aircraft stalled at 95 knots (176 km/h), the aircraft pitching gently and the nose and either wing falling through 10-15 degrees. It was possible to hold the aircraft level, but the pitching con-

tinued and the aircraft lost height in a heavily stalled glide. Recovery was straightforward and easy, however. With engine off and undercarriage and flaps down, the aricraft stalled at 77 knots (143 km/h) with virtually no warning and when carrying a torpedo a pronounced nose drop characterised the stall, this condition being aggravated by any further backward movement of the stick. In a steep turn, a reduction in elevator control force warned of the onset of a stall and backward movement of the stick caused the aircraft to flick out of the turn.

With a clean aircraft and flaps down, the initial approach speed was 100-105 knots (185-195 km/h), reducing to 90 knots (167 km/h) on finals and at this point two of the most adverse characteristics of the Firebrand — the aft-positioned cockpit and the long nose — really made themselves felt, view ahead being very poor indeed and a flapless landing rendered a curved approach essential . For a deck landing, the final approach speed was 80 knots (148 km/h) at which aileron response was very sluggish indeed, and the constant indication of the approach speed close to the eye provided by the external low-speed sector ASI was a *very* necessary adjunct to a deck landing. The undercarriage of the Firebrand was firm and rode well, and there was no swing after touching down, but the landing run seemed to last for ever.

The Firebrand, as flown from *Illustrious, Implacable* and *Eagle* by No 813 Squadron between 1947 and 1953, and by No 827 Squadron between 1950 and 1953, was a very different aeroplane from that envisaged when "Jim" Petty and his team first began work on their answer to N.11/40 so many years earlier. The original concept was wrong, but this was more the fault of the Naval Staff than the contractor's design staff, and the end product arrived at by an unintended process of incremental design had little to commend it. At least the Firebrand was soundly built which meant that, if it didn't inspire the affection of the pilots that flew it, they at least

The seventh (EK747) and eighth (EK 748) production Firebrand TF Mk 5s below and above right respectively, the former eventually going to No 827 Squadron and the latter to No 813 Squadron. This version of the Firebrand was delivered between the end of January 1946 and late February 1947, serving aboard the carriers Illustrious, Implacable and Eagle

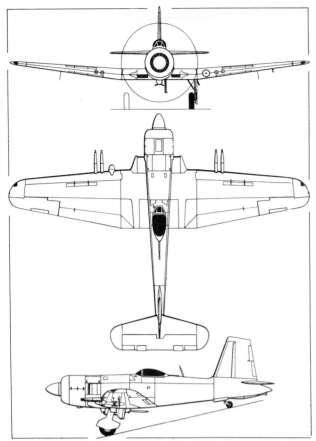

The general arrangement drawing (head of column) depicts the Fire-brand TF Mk 4. Illustrated by the photographs above is the first prototype B-48 'Firecrest' (RT651), the second prototype (VF172) being depicted below

knew that it offered them a better chance than most of walking away from the scene in the event of an accident.

The Firebrand saga did not, in the event, end with the completion of the manufacturer's contract in February 1947, for the Naval Staff had compounded the problem that they had created with N.11/40 and its offspring by dreaming up Specification S.28/43 for what could be loosely termed a Firebrand with a redesigned wing and improved pilot's view. Powered by a 2,475 hp Centaurus 59 and possessing a similar basic structure to that of the Firebrand, this aircraft, the Blackburn B-48, known unofficially for a time by its manufacturers as the "Firecrest", eventually flew for the first time on 1 April 1947, a date which may well have been an omen.

The second of the prototypes to be flown, VF172, finally arrived at Farnborough in February 1949, by which time the results of any testing that we undertook were of purely academic interest. This second aircraft differed from the first prototype, RT651, in having power-boosted ailerons, their introduction having necessitated a reduction in the dihedral on the outer wing panels from 9 deg to 3 deg, although the anhedralled centre section remained unchanged and thus the inverted gull effect of the original wing had not been entirely lost. This anhedral on the centre section allowed the use of a short, sturdy undercarriage which could absorb a vertical velocity of 12 ft/sec (3,66 m/sec). The wing itself, which was perhaps the most interesting feature of the aircraft, was of relatively thin laminar-flow section and, folding hydraulically in two places for economy of carrier stowage, featured four Fowler high-life flaps with auxiliary flaps on the outer pair.

I was to fly the "Firecrest" for the first time on 11 February 1949. It was certainly smaller than the Firebrand and the view from the cockpit was improved, but then this was one area in which any change could only have been an improvement. It had dive brakes like the later Firebrands and electrically-operated trim tabs on all the control surfaces. Upon clambering into the cockpit I received the impression of being seated higher than in the Firebrand, although this effect was in part due to the location of the cockpit so much further forward. The Centaurus installation was as neat and as compact as ever, and now had electrically-operated cowl gills and a multi-blade fan immediately behind the five-bladed constant-speed Rotol propeller, endowing the aircraft with a very pugnacious appearance.

On taxying the improved view immediately became obvious, as it did also during the take-off in which the rudder control was more positive than with the the Firebrand. The take-off run was short, being measured as 430 ft (130 m) in a 25 knot (46 km/h) wind. Climb was barely noticeably better than that of the Firebrand Mk IV, but in level flight the maximum speed was some 35 knots (65 km/h) higher with 330 knots (611 km/h) at 19,000 ft (5 790 m). However, the crucial test was, in my view, in its manoeuvrability and, sadly, the "Firecrest" proved to be, if anything, even less manoeuvrable than the Firebrand Mk 5A. The hydraulically-powered ailerons had zero feedback and artificial spring feel was provided, but this gave anything but satisfactory results. Pilot feel varied between lumpiness and overbalance, so that the aircraft tended to fly with a continuous lateral lurching motion, this being accentuated in turbulent air and quite unacceptable for instrument flying. In fact, for landing it was more comfortable to revert the aileron control system to manual and accept the heavier control loads in the interests of improved lateral stability.

Perhaps this fault could have been ironed out in time, but it must have been obvious from its first flight that the "Firecrest" did not offer performance gains sufficient to justify its further development and this time the Naval Staff did *not* attempt to make the best of a bad job. The Firebrand had been a loser and its intended successor just could not throw off the family weaknesses which were its inheritance.□

Grumman Hellcat

THE ANNALS OF WARPLANE DESIGN demonstrate time and time again that success in combat is by no means necessarily commensurate with time expended on the drawing board. To suggest that operational effectiveness depends as much on chance as design effort is, of course, an overstatement of the case, but few are the aircraft designers with successes to their credit who would place hand on heart and deny the part played by Dame Fortune; who would repudiate the proposal that her smile was in part responsible for the emergence of their progeny at perhaps the most propitious moment in time, when circumstances were at peak receptivity. In my view, no more outstanding example of skill and luck joining forces to produce just the right aeroplane is to be found than that provided by the Grumman Hellcat, unquestionably the most important Allied shipboard fighter of World War II.

Until comparatively recently, it was always considered axiomatic that when a new combat aircraft was added to the inventory, its design team would already have initiated the passage across the drawing boards of its potential successor. Perhaps on this premise the Grumman team, headed by Leroy R Grumman and William T Schwendler, might be viewed as having shown tardiness in waiting until mid-1941 to launch design of a successor to the Wildcat, which had begun to enter US Navy service in the previous year. But if Grumman had been tardy, this company was to more than make up any leeway by demonstrating quite astonishing rapidity in translating its eventual design for a Wildcat replacement into a prototype and then bringing it to production status, all without major problem and within 18 months. If such an unparallelled feat was possible *without* a very generous infusion of luck, then all other aircraft design teams should have thrown in the towel!

If the Hellcat was hurriedly conceived, engineered and manufactured, it certainly displayed no evidence of haste, yet no fighter of its era had briefer gestation and none progressed from prototype testing to squadron service within a shorter

timespan. It was assuredly the product of a most prodigious effort on the part of its creators and was to prove itself a phenomenal combat aircraft possessing outstanding lethality; an aircraft that, more than any other, was to turn the tide in the air war over the Pacific.

The Hellcat was born at a time when the state of flux that had permeated fighter development while the lessons of the first 18 months of WW II were being digested had finally

These contrasting photographs show (above) the first Hellcat prototype, the XF6F-1 and (below) the second prototype, the XF6F-3. (Head of page) One of the first Hellcat Mk Is (FN323) to reach the UK

An early production F6F-3 Hellcat of VF-9, the first US Navy squadron assigned to fly the Grumman fighter, this unit receiving its first aircraft in January 1943 and joining combat late in the following August

(Above) The XF6F-2 (BuNo 66244) was powered by a turbo-supercharged R-2600-15 engine and flew in January 1944, eventually being rebuilt as an F6F-5. (Below) The original XF6F-1 (BuNo 02981) after being reworked to F6F-3 standards

begun to solidify. Since formulation of the requirements that had resulted in such fighters as the Wildcat, the US Navy's knowledge of the tactics and weapons of aerial warfare had expanded apace on the basis of the experience of the European combatants. The conflict in Europe was, of course, primarily a land war, but the general lessons could, in many cases, be read across to carrier-based fighters, and the US Navy's observers would have been singularly obtuse had they not found Europe a fruitful field for investigation.

They had learned that speed, climb rate, adequate firepower and armour protection, pilot visibility and manoeuvrability were primary requirements in *that* order. In the case of the shipboard fighter, these desirable qualities had to be augmented by ample fuel and ammunition capacity, and the structural sturdiness that was a prerequisite in any aeroplane intended for the naval environment. Obviously, some of these characteristics could be obtained in full measure only at the expense of others; over-emphasis of any entailed unjustified risks and the equation was further complicated by the need for low-speed docility and good ditching qualities. It was the task of evolving an acceptable compromise between all these factors in the briefest space of time that faced Grumman, when, in mid-1941, it belatedly dawned on the US Navy that lack of a fall-back shipboard fighter programme as insurance against inordinate delays in or even the

complete failure of the F4U-1 Corsair programme could be extremely hazardous.

Accelerated development was implicit in the contract for two prototypes of what was assigned the designation XF6F-1, the US Navy Bureau of Aeronautics proposing a "minimum modification" of the F4F Wildcat to allow installation of the Wright Cyclone 14 engine affording 1,600 hp at 2,400 rpm both for take-off and as a military rating. There was also a proposal that a turbo-supercharged version of the same engine might later be applied to the fighter as the XF6F-2. Understandably, the Grumman team had already formulated its own ideas on the primary requirements in a Wildcat successor, these having been arrived at by consensus; the opinions of US Navy pilots had been canvassed and the results equated with analyses of European combat reports.

Inexorably, the design departed from the more powerful derivative of the Wildcat forseen by the US Navy; commonality diminished to a mere similarity in overall configuration. The requirements of the appreciably more powerful engine compounded by new range and endurance demands inevitably dictated a substantial increase in fuel capacity, and this, together with a commensurate increase in ammunition capacity, was largely to account for a 60 per cent increase in gross weight over that of the earlier fighter soon being estimated. This, in turn, dictated a very substantial increase in wing area to keep loadings within reasonable bounds — this was to result in the largest wing applied to any US wartime production single-seat fighter. The wing was mounted at the minimum angle of incidence to reduce level flight drag and a negative thrust line being adopted for the engine in order to attain the comparatively large angle of attack required for take-off, the disadvantage of such an installation in view for deck landing owing to the need to hold the nose high being consciously accepted as one of several basic compromises. This thrust line was to produce a pronounced tail-down attitude in normal cruising flight, but considerable attention was paid to the provision of the best possible view from the cockpit which was located at the highest point amidships — over the fuel tanks — and to result in a characteristic humped profile in side elevation.

Aesthetically, the result lacked any pretentions to elegance, but aestheticism had never been a strong suit in Grumman designs which made up for what they lacked in grace with a comforting practicality of appearance suggestive of immensely sturdy structures. In the case of the Hellcat, certainly, appearance was not to prove deceptive, but as weight escalated with design progress, the Grumman team began to have misgivings as to the ability of the XF6F-1 to meet the

US Navy's speed and climb requirements with the specified engine. Detail design and prototype construction proceeded at a prodigious pace and, meanwhile, US Navy sanction was obtained for the installation in the second airframe of Pratt & Whitney's magnificent 18-cylinder R-2800 Double Wasp in place of the Wright Cyclone 14. The Double Wasp two-stage two-speed supercharged air-cooled radial was perhaps the best large reciprocating engine ever to be built and its mating with the Grumman airframe was to produce an outstanding combination, whereas retention of the Cyclone 14 would have resulted in a fighter offering no more than a marginal improvement over that it was intended to succeed.

On 26 June 1942, test pilot Robert L Hall flew the XF6F-1 on its initial 25-minute test flight — three weeks after the decisive Battle of Midway and but four days short of the anniversary of the award of the prototype contract — and five weeks later, on 30 July, the second prototype flew with the Double Wasp engine as the XF6F-3*, again with Bob Hall at the controls, its initial flight test lasting 11 minutes. Although the XF6F-3 was to be lost as a result of a dead-stick landing after the failure of the Double Wasp engine in flight on 17 August, sufficient had been gleaned from initial flight trials to reassure the Bureau of Aeronautics as to the correctness of its decision to order the F6F-3 into production with a first batch of 184 aeroplanes on 23 May, more than a month before the début of the XF6F-1. Preliminary trials with the Hellcat prototypes had produced extraordinarily few major criticisms, the most serious of which were excessive longitudinal stability and an inordinate change of trim between "flaps up" and "flaps down". There was also a minor flutter problem which necessitated imposition of a limit of 456 knots (845 km/h) in diving.

Of the few changes introduced on the production F6F-3, the principal were the replacement of the Curtiss Electric propeller by a Hamilton Standard unit, the discarding of the propeller spinner and some redesign of the mainwheel fairings, and on 3 October, the first production F6F-3 Hellcat was flown by Selden A Converse. Thus, barely more than three months had elapsed between the first flight of the first prototype and the first flight of the first production aeroplane! A dozen F6F-3s had been built by the end of 1942,

For some inexplicable reason, Grumman records indicate that there was only one test airframe and that the original XF6F-1 was re-engined as the XF6F-3, but the logbook of Robert L Hall, the test pilot most directly concerned with the initial trials of the Hellcat prototypes, refutes this, clearly indicating two separate airframes. Furthermore, Bob Hall flew both the XF6F-1 and -3 within one week, providing proof positive that two different aircraft were involved.

and preliminary acceptance trials had been passed without revealing any serious shortcomings other than some elevator buffeting, although during arrested landing trials in November, an arrester hook was pulled out of the fuselage and during December a structural failure had been experienced. Some minor beefing up of part of the fuselage was speedily undertaken, no further difficulties arose and production began to accelerate rapidly, a dozen F6F-3s being delivered during January 1943, 35 in February, 81 in March and 130 in April.

The first US Navy squadron assigned to fly the F6F-3 Hellcat, VF-9, which had previously flown Wildcats from the USS *Ranger* in support of the invasion of North Africa, received its first three aircraft at Ream Field, near Norfolk, Virginia, on 16 January 1943, these having been ferried from the Grumman factory at Bethpage by the squadron's CO and two of its most experienced pilots. Deck landing qualification trials were performed aboard the escort carrier USS *Long Island,* some of the pilots making their first Hellcat deck landings after only a dozen landings in the type on airfields. VF-9 was not to join combat in the Hellcat until the end of August and then was to lose the distinction of being first to take the new Grumman fighter into action to VF-5. Both VF-9 aboard the USS *Essex* and VF-5 aboard the USS *Yorktown* participated in strikes against Marcus Island on 31 August, but the latter carrier launched its aircraft first.

Some weeks prior to this combat initiation in US Navy service, however, F6F-3 Hellcats had begun to arrive in the UK for use by the Fleet Air Arm under Lend-Lease arrangements, having first entered service on 1 July with No 800 Squadron which had re-equipped from Sea Hurricanes.

(Above right) F6F-3 (BuNo 08829) of VF-16 being manhandled into position for launching from the USS Lexington, and (below) F6F-5Ns warming up their engines prior to launching from the light carrier USS Independence in October 1944. These aircraft belonged to Air Group 41, the US Navy's first dedicated shipboard nocturnal air group

Grumman F6F-5 Hellcat Cutaway Drawing Key

The fact that Grumman, within nine months of flying the first production F6F-3 Hellcat and while catering for the high priority demands of the US Navy — which service was to have 15 squadrons equipped with the new aircraft and in combat before the year's end — could supply this warplane to the FAA at so early a date in its production life spoke volumes for the truly incredible acceleration of production tempo achieved by Grumman's new Plant No 3, the structure of which owed much to steel acquired as scrap from New York's old Second Avenue elevated railway. Indeed, barely

1 Radio mast
2 Rudder balance
3 Rudder upper hinge
4 Aluminium alloy fin ribs
5 Rudder post
6 Rudder structure
7 Rudder trim tab
8 Rudder middle hinge
9 Diagonal stiffeners
10 Aluminium alloy elevator trim tab
11 Fabric-covered (and taped) elevator surfaces
12 Elevator balance
13 Flush riveted leading-edge strip
14 Arrester hook (extended)
15 Tailplane ribs
16 Tail navigation (running) light
17 Rudder lower hinge
18 Arrester hook (stowed)
19 Fin main spar lower cut-out
20 Tailplane end rib
21 Fin forward spar
22 Fuselage/fin root fairing
23 Port elevator
24 Aluminium alloy-skinned tailplane
25 Section light
26 Fuselage aft frame
27 Control access
28 Bulkhead
29 Tailwheel hydraulic shock-absorber
30 Tailwheel centering mechanism
31 Tailwheel steel mounting arm

32 Rearward retracting tailwheel (hard rubber tyre)
33 Fairing
34 Steel plate door fairing
35 Tricing sling support tube
36 Hydraulic actuating cylinder
37 Flanged ring fuselage frames
38 Control cable runs
39 Fuselage longerons
40 Relay box
41 Dorsal rod antenna
42 Dorsal recognition light
43 Radio aerial
44 Radio mast
45 Aerial lead-in
46 Dorsal frame stiffeners
47 Junction box
48 Radio equipment (upper rack)
49 Radio shelf
50 Control cable runs
51 Transverse brace
52 Remote radio compass
53 Ventral recognition lights (3)
54 Ventral rod antenna
55 Destructor device
56 Accumulator
57 Radio equipment (lower rack)
58 Entry hand/footholds
59 Engine water injection tank
60 Canopy track
61 Water filler neck
62 Rear-view window
63 Rearward-sliding cockpit canopy (open)
64 Headrest
65 Pilot's head/shoulder armour
66 Canopy sill (reinforced)
67 Fire-estinguisher
68 Oxygen bottle (port fuselage wall)
69 Water tank mounting
70 Underfloor self-sealing fuel tank (60 US gal/227 l)
71 Armoured bulkhead
72 Starboard console

73 Pilot's seat
74 Hydraulic handpump
75 Fuel filler cap and neck
76 Rudder pedals
77 Centre console
78 Control column
79 Chart board (horizontal stowage)
80 Instrument panel
81 Panel coaming
82 Reflector gunsight
83 Rear-view mirror

84 Armoured glass windshield
85 Deflection plate (pilot forward protection)
86 Main bulkhead armour-plated upper section with hoisting sling attachments port and starboard)
87 Aluminium alloy aileron trim tab
88 Fabric covered (and taped) aileron surfaces
89 Flush riveted outer wing skin
90 Aluminium alloy sheet wing tip (riveted to wing outer rib)

91 Port navigation (running) light
92 Formed leading-edge (approach/landing light and camera gun inboard)
93 Fixed cowling panel
94 Armour plate (oil tank forward protection)
95 Oil tank (19 US gal/72 l)
96 Welded engine mount fittings
97 Fuselage forward bulkhead
98 Aileron control linkage
99 Engine accessories bay
100 Engine mounting frame (hydraulic fluid reservoir attached to port frames)
101 Controllable cooling gills

102 Cowling ring (removable servicing/access panels)
103 Pratt & Whitney R-2800-10W twin row radial air-cooled engine
104 Nose ring profile
105 Reduction gear housing
106 Three-blade Hamilton Standard Hydromatic controllable pitch propeller
107 Propeller hub
108 Engine oil cooler (centre) and supercharger intercooler (outer sections) intakes
109 Oil cooler deflection plate under-protection
110 Oil cooler duct

111 Intercooler intake duct
112 Mainwheel fairing
113 Port mainwheel
114 Cooler outlet and fairing
115 Auxiliary tank support/attachment arms
116 Exhaust cluster
117 Supercharger housing

118 Exhaust outlet scoop
119 Wing front spar web
120 Wing front spar/fuselage attachment bolts
121 Undercarriage mounting/pivot point on front spar
122 Inter-spar self-sealing fuel tanks (port and starboard: 87·5 US gal/331 l each)
123 Wing rear spar/fuselage attachment bolts
124 Structural end rib

18 months on, the 10,000th Hellcat was to be delivered!

The Hellcat made its impressive appearance at the Service Trials Unit at Crail in Scotland virtually as soon as the first batch reached the UK, and I was thus to be numbered among the first FAA pilots to fly what, to me, was always to be the big brother of the Wildcat for which I had earlier developed an abiding affection. In reality, one should have sought a *filial* resemblance between Wildcat and Hellcat, for the former had predated the latter by several years, but genealogical fact apart, it was difficult to view the portly little Wildcat in paternal relationship to this welterweight of a fighter. At Crail we were awe-struck by the sheer size of the Hellcat, but if this and its predecessor were disparate in very essence, at least they appeared to possess certain common attributes, apart from rotundity and large, angularly ugly wing and tail surfaces, the most important of which was robustness. In fact, few fighters imparted such an impression of hardiness and vigour at first sight as did this new "Cat".

The dominating feature of the whole design was its immense wing, which, when the Hellcat was perched on its rugged-looking undercarriage, towered way above my head. This wing was of three-spar structure, the two main spars running laterally and the third canted forward from the root to carry the flaps and the ailerons. It comprised five principal assemblies, with an abbreviated centre section passing through the fuselage and housing side-by-side self-sealing fuel tanks between the main spars, two stub sections providing bays for the main undercarriage members, the attachment points for which were at their outboard extremities and which rotated through 90 deg to lie flush when retracted, and detachable outer panels swivelled at the forward spar for manual folding aft along the fuselage sides. The movable control surfaces were metal framed, the ailerons being fabric covered, and the hydraulically-operated flaps were composed of four sections, two on the outer panels and two on the stub wings.

125 Slotted wing flap profile
126 Wing flap centre-section
127 Wing fold line
128 Starboard wheel well (doubler-plate reinforced edges)
129 Gunbay
130 Removable diagonal brace strut

131 Three 0·5-in (12,7-mm) Colt Browning machine guns
132, Esxiliary tank aft support
133 Blast tubes
134 Folding wing joint (upper surface)
135 Machine-gun barrels
136 Fairing
137 Undercarriage actuating strut

145 Underwing 5-in (12,7 cm) air-to-ground RPs
146 Mark V zero-length rocket launcher installation
147 Canted wing front spar
148 Inter-spar ammunition box bay (lower surface access)
149 Wing rear spar (normal to plane of wing)
150 Rear sub spar

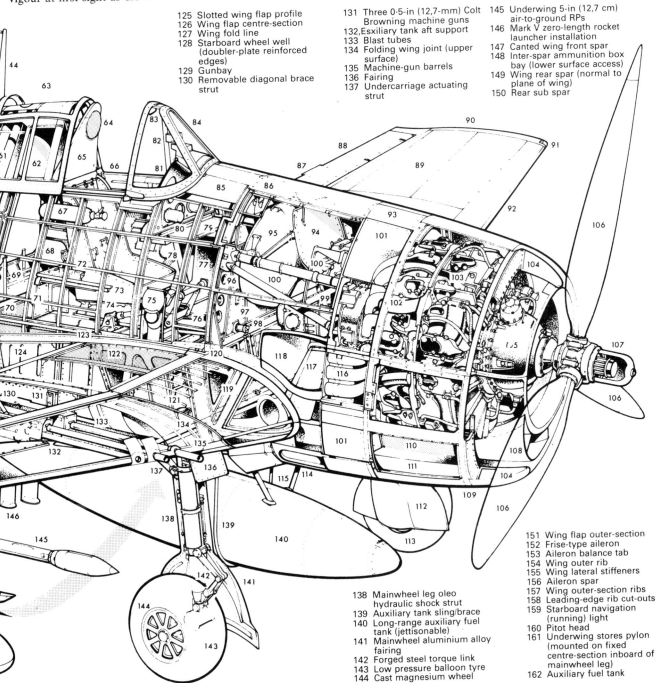

138 Mainwheel leg oleo hydraulic shock strut
139 Auxiliary tank sling/brace
140 Long-range auxiliary fuel tank (jettisonable)
141 Mainwheel aluminium alloy fairing
142 Forged steel torque link
143 Low pressure balloon tyre
144 Cast magnesium wheel

151 Wing flap outer-section
152 Frise-type aileron
153 Aileron balance tab
154 Wing outer rib
155 Wing lateral stiffeners
156 Aileron spar
157 Wing outer-section ribs
158 Leading-edge rib cut-outs
159 Starboard navigation (running) light
160 Pitot head
161 Underwing stores pylon (mounted on fixed centre-section inboard of mainwheel leg)
162 Auxiliary fuel tank

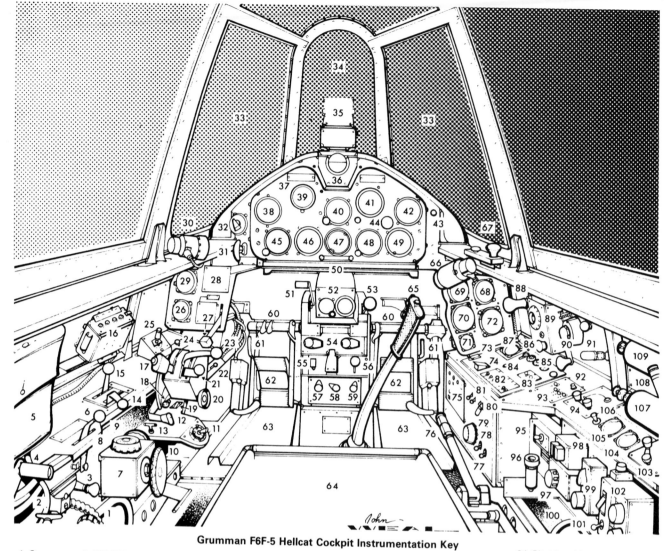

Grumman F6F-5 Hellcat Cockpit Instrumentation Key

1 Oxygen supply ON/OFF cock and supply tube
2 Arrester hook emergency control
3 Flap selector lever
4 Cockpit light (port)
5 Map/document holder
6 Tailwheel locking control
7 Trimming tab control box
8 Rudder trimming tab handwheel (box upper face)
9 Aileron trimming tab handwheel (box forward face)
10 Elevator trimming tab handwheel (box inner face)
11 Fuel cock control
12 Propeller speed control lever
13 Fuel tank pressurising control
14 Oil cooler and intercooler shutter control lever
15 Cowling gill control lever
16 Radio push-button controller
17 Throttle lever (with "Press to transmit" button)
18 Reserve fuel tank warning light
19 Drop tank jettison switch
20 Throttle lever friction device
21 Mixture control lever
22 Fuel booster pump switch
23 Supercharger control lever
24 Oil dilution switch
25 Flap control switch
26 Undercarriage and flap position indicator
27 Undercarriage selector lever

28 Check-off visual list plate
29 Clock
30 Fluorescent light (port)
31 Carburettor air intake control
32 Ignition switch
33 Fixed quarterlights
34 Armoured glass windshield
35 Reflector gunsight
36 Gunsight mounting
37 Spare lamp holder
38 Directional gyro
39 Directional gyro setting
40 Magnetic compass
41 Attitude gyro
42 Tachometer
43 IFF warning light
44 Attitude gyro caging control
45 Altimeter
46 Airspeed indicator
47 Turn and bank indicator
48 Rate of climb indicator
49 Manifold pressure gauge
50 Chart board (horizontal stowage)
51 Undercarriage emergency control lever
52 Oxygen pressure/contents gauges and regulator
53 Wing fold safety locking control
54 Gun charging handles
55 Windshield de-icing control
56 Cockpit ventilator control
57 Port fluorescent light switch
58 Cockpit heating switch
59 Starboard fluorescent light switch

60 Rudder/brake pedal mounting bar
61 Rudder pedal adjustment levers
62 Rudder pedals
63 Heelboards
64 Pilot's seat
65 Control column (with machine gun trigger switch and bomb release push-button)
66 Fluorescent light (starboard)
67 Morsing transmit key (TR 1196 or SCR 522A)
68 Oil pressure gauge
69 Fuel pressure gauge
70 Fuel tank contents gauge
71 Oil temperature gauge
72 Cylinder temperature gauge
73 Engine priming switch
74 Cartridge starter switch
75 Circuit breaker panel
76 Hydraulic handpump
77 Camera gun switch
78 Gunsight switch
79 Gunsight dimming rheostat
80 Gun master switch
81 Gun selector switches
82 Lighting switches (from front: landing light; section light ON/OFF/FLASH; section light dim/bright; wing navigation (running) lights; tail navigation (running) light; formation light ON/OFF/FLASH; formation light dim/bright)
83 Arrester hook switch and indicator light

84 Pitot head heater switch
85 Cockpit lighting rheostats (3)
86 Battery switch
87 Volt/ammeter and push-button
88 Canopy handle
89 Homing control unit
90 Remote control wave tuner (R 1147)
91 Cockpit light (starboard)
92 Recognition lights morsing key switch (visual identification)
93 Recognition light switches (from front: white; red) green (steady); amber (off)
94 Hydraulic handpump selector valve control
95 Radio beacon switch
96 Micro-/telephone socket
97 Volume control (R 1147)
98 ABK detonator switches
99 ABK wave-band selector switch
100 Target-towing release control (optional)
101 ABK controller ON/OFF switch
102 ABK controller emergency switch
103 Wing locking pin control
104 Undercarriage emergency air cylinder pressure gauge
105 Hydraulic accumulator pressure gauge
106 IFF key
107 Fire-extinguisher
108 Micro-/telephone socket (ABK ground-test)
109 Incendiary bomb

The fuselage was an all-metal monocoque with two vertical keels located on either side of the centreline. Pressed flange aluminium alloy frames were riveted to these keel members, extruded aluminium alloy stringers completing the basic structure, with aluminium alloy skinning being applied in lateral strips and flush-riveted. The mighty R-2800-10 Double Wasp engine, which offered an impressive 2,000 hp at 2,700 rpm for take-off, turned a commensurately large Hamilton Standard three-bladed propeller, and was protected by a substantial deflection plate built into the underside of the cowling. The oil cooler and oil tank were protected, and all internal fuel tanks were self-sealing, the side-by-side main tanks between the forward spars in the centre section each being of 87·5 US gal (331 l) capacity, with a contoured 74·5 US gal (282 l) reserve tank immediately aft and beneath the pilot's seat. The armament consisted of a sextet of 0·5-in Colt-Browning machine guns mounted in banks of three in each outer wing panel, just outboard of the joint, the ammunition trays outboard of the guns having a maximum capacity of 2,400 rounds.

The empty weight of the Hellcat, at 9,042 lb (4 101 kg), was some 15 per cent more than the *fully laden* weight of a Sea Hurricane Mk IIC, while with a 150 US gal (568 l) drop tank on the fuselage centreline, the gross weight of 13,221 lb (5 997 kg) approached that of a Blenheim Mk IV bomber. The Hellcat was certainly a lot of aeroplane! Clambering up the wing and getting a leg over the cockpit sill was akin to mountaineering, and the cockpit was the usual capacious American office apparently built for an all-American half-back. In fact, so spacious was the cockpit that when I first lowered myself into the seat, I thought that I would have to stand up if I was to see through the windscreen for take-off! However, the seat was adjustable over a wide range in height, and the pedals, which were rather widely spaced, adjusted fore and aft by a considerable amount. There was a great deal of engine ahead, but in spite of the bulk of the Double Wasp, the view was not unreasonable, thanks to the Hellcat's slightly humped-back profile, with the pilot perched at the highest point, and the downward curve of the nose cowling.

Engine starting was by an electrically-fired cartridge, and except for the first start of the day on a cold morning, one cartridge was usually enough to set the Double Wasp into a silky purr, the propeller having been turned through a few revolutions by hand. Prior to starting, the fuel cock was set to RIGHT MAIN, the mixture control to idle cut-off, the throttle opened one-quarter, the propeller control depressed fully, the cowling gills and oil cooler and intercooler shutters

opened, and the carburettor air intake control pushed fully in. The fuel booster pump was then switched to ON and the priming switch given a few one-second flicks. The ignition switch was set to BOTH and the starter cartridge fired. Once the engine fired, the mixture control was moved slowly to AUTO-RICH, with the firing switch depressed until the Double Wasp was running smoothly. The engine was warmed up at 1,000 rpm, and after reaching at least 40°C oil temperature and 120°C cylinder temperature, the magnetos were tested and then the engine opened up to 1,400 rpm at which the two-speed supercharger was exercised.

Taxying was quite easy with the wide undercarriage, but the tailwheel had to be locked in a crosswind or the Hellcat tended to weathercock, and as this fighter was nose-heavy with little clearance between propeller and ground, so it was advisable always to keep the control column held well back and essential to do so if the CG was at the forward end of its

(Above right) Hellcat Mk I (FN323) during pre-service trials at the A & AEE in June 1943, and (below) another Hellcat Mk I (FN322) of the initial batch of F6F-3s supplied to the Royal Navy under Lend-Lease, these eventually being assigned to No 800 Squadron

(Above) An F6F-3 Hellcat of VF-9 from the USS Yorktown, and (below left) an early production F6F-3 of VF-4 seen over the California countryside near NAS Alameda in May 1943

range (ie, with the reserve tank empty) or when taxying over soft ground. The take-off was straightforward, with a tendency to swing to port requiring gentle application of rudder, and acceleration was very satisfying, although the noise with the canopy open was quite something. For short take-offs, 20 deg of flap was normally applied, and even full flap could be used if a very short run was desired, but this meant that the elevator trim tab had to be set nose up to reduce the pull force for unstick, whereas once airborne the Hellcat displayed a tail heavy trim change and some lateral instability was evident. It was most important not to raise the tail too high, only a slight forward pressure on the stick being necessary to get the tail off the ground and a touch of back pressure flying the Hellcat off at 70-75 knots (130-140 km/h). Take-off power was developed at 54 in Hg boost and 2,700 rpm.

The wheels came up rapidly, locking with a hefty thump, flaps being retracted at about 100 knots (185 km/h) and maximum climb being established at 130 knots (241 km/h) IAS with 44 in Hg boost and 2,550 rpm, this producing a highly satisfying 3,000 ft/min (15,24 m/sec) plus and remaining good up to 20,000 ft (6 100 m), the 15,000 ft (4 570 m) mark being passed in around six minutes. Above 20,000 ft (6 100 m) climb rate began to moderate, reducing by two knots (3,7 km/h) per 1,000 ft (305 m) and 25,000 ft (7 620 m) being attained in a fairly lightly loaded Hellcat in about 11·5 minutes. The change to auxiliary LOW gear was made when the boost dropped to 6 in Hg and from LOW to HIGH gear when the boost dropped a further 3½ in Hg. The supercharger gave the Hellcat a service ceiling of 37,800 ft (11 530 m), but the aircraft was distinctly sluggish above 32,000 ft (9 760 m).

Although this big fighter was stable about all axes, there were marked changes of lateral and directional trim with changes of speed and power, and selecting undercarriage down, flaps down or gills open naturally pitched the aircraft nose down. Normal cruise power settings were very flexible, ranging from as low as 1,300 up to 2,050 rpm at 34 in Hg, and

at the higher settings cruise was about 190 knots (352 km/h) IAS with fuel consumption of the order of 60 US gal (227 l) per hour. The controls heavied up at high speeds and particularly the ailerons — although the introduction of spring tabs on the later F6F-5 model was to render these surfaces light and effective throughout the speed range — and with the aircraft "clean", the stall occurred with little warning and either wing could drop, but recovery was straightforward and easy. This meant that although aerobatics were easy to perform, careless application of g could result in a flick out of the manoeuvre without much warning other than a buffeting of the tail surfaces. Stalling speeds varied from as low as 58 knots (107 km/h) IAS at 11,500 lb (5 220 kg) with flaps and undercarriage down to 85 knots (157 km/h) at 14,600 lb (6 628 kg) when carrying bombs with flaps and undercarriage up. Buffeting of the tail surfaces heralding a stall was particularly pronounced in a steep turn, continued back pressure on the control column then causing the aircraft to flick out of the turn but recovery being immediate when this pressure was relaxed.

In a dive it was necessary to decrease rpm to 2,100 or less in order to reduce vibration to acceptable levels. The Hellcat had to be trimmed into the dive and became tail heavy as speed built up, some left rudder being necessary to counter yaw. With bombs under the wings speed built up very rapidly indeed and there was considerable snatching of the elevator and rudder. In manoeuvres involving the application of high g the degree of acceleration had to be reduced immediately undue vibration was encountered. The recommended speeds (IAS) for aerobatics included 240-260 knots (445-480 km/h) for loops, 180-200 knots (335-370 km/h) for a roll, 300 knots (555 km/h) and more for an upward roll and 280 knots (520 km/h) for a half-roll off a loop.

The Double Wasp engine was prone to auxiliary supercharger surging in HIGH gear and at weak cruise settings, the symptoms being rough running accompanied by an alarming rumbling noise, but the condition could be quickly and simply eliminated by either changing to LOW gear, or opening the throttle and reducing rpm, or selecting the alternate position of the carburettor air intake control.

The deck landing pattern was entered at 110 knots (204 km/h), when the arrester hook was lowered electrically and the undercarriage hydraulically. The tailwheel was locked, the mixture control set to AUTO RICH, the supercharger to NEUTRAL and the propeller selected in fully fine pitch. The booster pump was then switched on, the flaps lowered fully and the engine cowl gills closed. Final approach to the deck was at 80 knots (148 km/h) and the Hellcat was as steady as a rock, with precise attitude and speed control. Speeds as low

(Above) An F6F-3 of VF-5 operating from the USS San Jacinto in July 1944. This particular aircraft was named "Little Joe". (Below right) A Hellcat FR Mk II (JV270). equivalent to the F6F-5P with camera in lower aft fuselage is seen here with a rocket launching rail test installation

as 75 knots (139 km/h) were permissible but not very comfortable as the nose-up attitude increased and view forward became quite seriously impaired. In any case, I always used a curved approach to get a better view of the deck and left the throttle cut as late as possible to prevent the heavy nose dropping and allowing the main wheels to contact the deck first, thus risking a bounce, although the Hellcat's immensely sturdy undercarriage possessed very good shock absorbing characteristics.

The FAA was not to take the Hellcat into action until late in 1943, when No 800 Squadron flew anti-shipping strikes off the Norwegian coast with its Hellcats from the light escort carrier HMS *Emperor*, and by that time, the big "Cat" had become the most important carrier-based fighter in the Pacific and had already seen considerable air-to-air combat with what was to be its principal opponent, the A6M Zero-Sen. The Hellcat's first Zero-Sen "kills" had come, according to the records, on 5 October, when Ensign Robert W Duncan of VF-5 from the USS *Yorktown* claimed two in quick succession during a mission to reduce Japanese strength on Wake Island, these being the first of many encounters in the months

(Above and below) Hellcat NF Mk II (JX965), equivalent to the F6F-5N, with AN/APS-6 radar housed in a pod on the starboard wing. Two Royal Navy squadrons operated the Hellcat NF Mk II until 1946. The general arrangement drawing on the following page depicts the Hellcat Mk I alias F6F-3

that were to follow between the big and heavy Grumman and the nimble featherweight of the Imperial Japanese Navy.

The two fighters were, of course, products of totally different design philosophies. The Hellcat was the faster of the two in level flight at all altitudes, and above 10,000 ft (3 050 m) could almost match the climb rate of the Japanese fighter, while its altitude capabilities were markedly superior. The Hellcat had twice the power of the Zero-Sen, but it also carried twice the weight, which, affording an advantage in a dive — no Zero-Sen could escape its Grumman opponent in a prolonged dive — placed it at a definite disadvantage in close-in, tight-manoeuvring combat. The Japanese fighter was supremely agile and its turning radius was fabled. At airspeeds below 200 knots (370 km/h), the Zero-Sen's lightly loaded wing enabled it to outmanoeuvre the Hellcat with comparative ease, even though the airframe of the latter allowed more *g* to be pulled, and if a Hellcat pilot was sufficiently inexperienced to attempt following his opponent in a tight turn at comparatively low speed he would inevitably be forced to roll out to avoid a stall. At higher speeds the controls of the Japanese fighter stiffened up and the turn rate disparity was dramatically reduced.

The Hellcat could not follow the Zero-Sen in a tight loop and the US Navy Hellcat pilots soon learned to avoid any attempt to dog-fight with the Japanese fighter and turn the superior speed, dive and altitude characteristics of the American fighter to advantage. These characteristics usually enabled the Hellcat to acquire an advantageous position permitting the use of tactics whereby the Zero-Sen could be destroyed without tight-manoeuvring combat. A manoeuvre frequently adopted by the Japanese fighter pilots to evade Hellcats on their tails was a snap split-S to port at low altitude, pulling through over the water at a safe margin. However, once on the tail of a Zero-Sen, the Hellcat pilot could usually turn through 70-80 deg of a turn with his opponent, which was long enough to get in a burst, and when the position was reversed, the Hellcat could normally elude its pursuer by diving and twisting with the ailerons. In level flight, the Hellcat could almost invariably pull away from the Japanese fighter and its rugged structure stood up well to the fire of the Zero-Sen, whereas the latter was woefully vulnerable to the Grumman fighter's sextet of 'fifty calibre guns and burned readily.

From January 1944, 60 per cent of all production F6F-3s were equipped with the R-2800-10W engine in which water injection boosted emergency power to 2,200 hp, and from the beginning of April of that year, all new Hellcats were so equipped. From 21 April 1944, production of the F6F-3 model of the Hellcat ended with the 4,403rd machine in favour of the improved F6F-5 which was to be known in the FAA as the Hellcat Mk II. One of the noteworthy aspects of the production of almost four-and-a-half thousand Hellcats of the initial production model had been the insignificance of the modifications introduced over so large a number of aircraft. Early shipboard service had produced some criticisms concerning excessive tyre wear and reduced vision resulting from the ease with which the curved plexiglas windscreen scratched and dust collected between this and the inner armoured glass screen, but virtually every change on the production line had come within the category of minor refinement, such as the omission of the lower cowl flap from the 1,265th and subsequent aircraft, the relocation of the radio mast from the 2,561st aircraft, and so on.

The F6F-5 that succeeded the -3 did not introduce any dramatic changes and retained the R-2800-10W engine, the principal modifications being the introduction of aileron servo tabs, as previously mentioned; provision for two of the 'fifties in each wing to be replaced by a 20-mm cannon; a redesigned closer-fitting engine cowling to reduce drag; an increase of 242 lb (110 kg) in the total weight of protection carried; the elimination of the laminated plate glass windscreen and the incorporation of the flat, bullet-resistant

---

Grumman F6F-3 Hellcat Specification

Power Plant: One Pratt & Whitney R-2800-10 Double Wasp 18-cylinder two-row radial air-cooled engine with two-stage two-speed supercharger rated at 2,000 hp at 2,700 rpm for take-off and (maximum military) from sea level to 1,700 ft (520 m), with military ratings of 1,755 hp at 2,700 rpm at 5,400 ft (1 645 m) and 1,800 hp at 2,700 rpm at 15,700 ft (4 785 m), and normal ratings of 1,675 hp at 2,550 rpm from sea level to 5,500 ft (1 675 m) and 1,530 hp at 2,550 rpm at 18,200 ft (5 545 m). Three-bladed Hamilton Standard constant-speed propeller of 13 ft 1 in (3,99 m). Internal fuel capacity, 250 US gal (946 l) divided between two 87·5 US gal (331 l) maintanks and one 74·5 US gal (282 l) reserve tank. Provision for one 150 US gal (568 l) drop tank on fuselage centreline.
Performance: (At 11,381 lb/5 162 kg with fuel in main tanks only at military power) Max speed, 324 mph (521 km/h) at sea level, 376 mph 605 km/h) at 22,800 ft (6 950 m); initial climb, 3,650 ft/min (18,5 m/sec); time to 15,000 ft (4 570 m), 6·0 min, to 25,000 ft (7 620 m), 11·3 min; service ceiling, 35,500 ft (10 820 m); (at normal power) max speed, 304 mph (489 km/h) at sea level, 374 mph (602 km/h) at 23,700 ft (7 225 m); time to 15,000 ft (4 570 m), 6·9 min to 25,000 ft (7 620 m), 12·5 min; max range, 820 mls (1 320 km) at 177 mph (285 km/h) at 5,000 ft (1 525 m), (with full reserve tank), 1,085 mls (1 746 km) at 179 mph (288 km/h) at 5,000 ft (1 525 m), (plus 150 US gal/568 l drop tank), 1,620 mls (2 607 km) at 177 mph (285 km/h) at 5,000 ft (1 525 m); take-off distance (at 11,381 lb/5 162 kg) in calm, 193 yds (176 m), into 15 knot/17 km/h wind, 127 yds (116 m), into 25 knot/46 km/h wind, 90 yds (82 m).
Weights: Empty, 9,042 lb (4 101 kg); loaded (max internal fuel), 12,186 lb (5 528 kg); max take-off, 13,221 lb (5 997 kg).
Dimensions: Span, 42 ft 10 in (13,08 m); span folded, 16 ft 2 in (4,93 m); length, 33 ft 4 in (10,17 m); height (propeller vertical, tail down), 14 ft 5 in (4,40 m); wing area, 334 sq ft (31,03 m²).
Armament: Six 0·5-in (12,7-mm) Colt-Browning machine gun in wings with 400 rpg.

---

panel as an integral part of the windscreen; standardisation on red instrument panel lighting and built-in provision for underwing loads of bombs or rockets. The external loads toted by the F6F-5 could comprise a trio of 1,000-lb (454-kg) bombs, one on each of the stub wings close in to the fuselage and one on the centre-line in lieu of a drop tank, and six 5-in (12,7-cm) rockets, three under each outer wing panel.

The FAA was to receive a total of 252 F6F-3s (alias Hellcat Mk Is) and no fewer than 930 F6F-5s as Hellcat Mk IIs, plus 80 F6F-5N night fighters with AN/APS-6 radar. No 800 Squadron had, as already related, taken the credit of being the first to commission on the Hellcat, but had, in fact, worked up at RNAS Eglinton, Derry, alongside No 804 Squadron which was similarly equipped. The FAA, however, made most operation use of the Hellcat in the Far East theatre and, by August 1945, 10 squadrons were operational on the Grumman fighter, these serving for the most part aboard escort carriers (including *Ruler*, *Empress*, *Ameer*, *Ocean*, *Attacker*, *Pursuer*, *Khedive*, *Begum* and *Shah*), among the larger carriers, HMS *Indomitable* alone carried Hellcats, these being flown by Nos 1839 and 1844 squadrons which participated in the FAA's first major action against Japanese targets — the attack on oil refineries in Sumatra in January 1945.

The Hellcat had not been the fastest shipboard fighter of WW II, nor the most manoeuvrable, but it was certainly the most efficacious, and one of its virtues was its versatility. Conceived primarily as an air superiority weapon with the range to seek out the enemy so that he could be brought to battle, as emphasis switched to offensive capability, the Hellcat competently offered the strike potential that the US Navy needed to offset the reduced number of bombers aboard the service's fleet carriers. The Hellcat was certainly the most important Allied shipboard aircraft in the Pacific in 1943-44, for it turned the tide of the conflict, and although Japanese fighters of superior performance made their appearance, they were too late to wrest the aerial ascendancy that had been established largely by this one aircraft type.

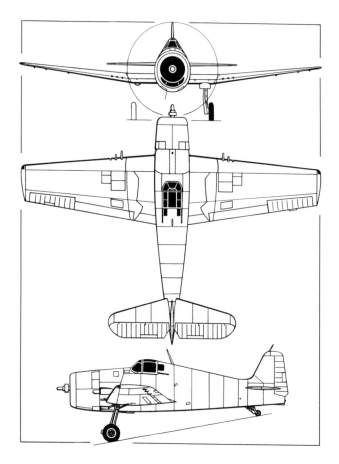